LAST BATTLES

BOOK FOUR
JACO JACINTO AGE OF SAIL SERIES

MARC LIEBMAN

Last Battles © 2024 Marc Liebman

All Rights Reserved in accordance with the U.S. Copyright Act of 1976, the scanning, uploading, and electronic sharing of any part of this book without the permission of the publisher or author constitute unlawful piracy and theft of the author's intellectual property. If you would like to use material from this book (other than for review purposes), prior written permission must be obtained by contacting the publisher. Go to the author's website, https://www.marcliebman.com, click on the 'Contact Marc tab' (https://marcliebman.com/contact/) and use the form to send Marc an email. Thank you for your support of authors' rights.

FBI Anti-Piracy Warning: The unauthorized reproduction or distribution of a copyrighted work is illegal. Criminal copyright infringement, including infringement without monetary gain, is investigated by the FBI and is punishable by up to five years in federal prison along with a fine of $250,000.

Any reference to names, characters, places, and incidents either are the product of the author's imagination or are used fictitiously, and any resemblance to actual persons, living or dead, business establishments, events, or locales is entirely coincidental.

Publisher:

Rotorhead Media, LLC
Savannah, TX

Proofreader: Cheryl Carathers
Book Cover, and interior design by – Deena Rae; E-BookBuilders, adaptation for ebook

BISAC Subject Headings:
    FIC – 014000 – FICTION/Historical
    FIC - 032000 – FICTION/War & Military
    FIC – 047000 – FICTION/Sea Stories

File version: 202403005.011

CONTENTS

Other Books .... e
Dedication .... g
Historical Backdrop i
Gaff Rigged Schooner .... j
Chapter 1 – Edmund's Wake Up Call 1
Chapter 2 – Committed For The Defense 11
Chapter 3 – Lessons In Law 25
Chapter 4 – Into The Mouth Of The Lion 35
Chapter 5 – What Will The Future Bring? 49
Chapter 6 – Justice Served 57
Chapter 7 – Not Buying The Farm 67
Chapter 8 – Libelous Words 87
Chapter 9 – Swordfight 93
Chapter 10 - Lifetime Friendship At First Sight 101
Chapter 11 – New And Unlikely Partners 117
Chapter 12 – Reducing The Bloodshed, One Step At A Time 137
Chapter 13 – Fleet Action 153
Chapter 14 – Mutiny By Another Navy 167
Chapter 15 – Beginning Of One And The End Of Two Marriages 175
Chapter 16 – Rum Is The Weapon Of Choice 189
Chapter 17 – Tightening The Noose 205
Chapter 18 - New Perceptions 221
Chapter 19 - Peace In Their Time 233
Chapter 20 – Planning For The End 253
Chapter 21 – Family Feud 267
Chapter 22 – Freedom, At Last 283
Chapter 23 – Coming To America 293
Chapter 24 – A New Man In Her Life 309
Chapter 25 – Helping An Old Friend In Need 325
Chapter 26 – Wedding Bells In The Future 337
About The Author 349

OTHER BOOKS

JOSH HAMAN SERIES
Cherubs 2
Big Mother 40
Render Harmless
Forgotten
Inner Look
Moscow Airlift
The Simushir Island Incident

AGE OF SAIL SERIES
Raider of the Scottish Coast
Carronade
Death of A Lady

DEREK ALMER SERIES
Flight of the Pawnee
Failure to Fire
Insidious Dragon

STAND ALONE
The Red Star of Death

DEDICATION

Most dedications don't start with math, but this dedication does to make a point and to help identify those to whom *Last Battles* is dedicated.

When the American Revolution began, the population of the Thirteen Colonies was about 2,500,000. Of these, roughly 20% or 500,000 were Loyalists who wanted the Thirteen Colonies to remain subjects of King George III.

Another 460,000 of the 2.5 million were African Americans; 90% were enslaved, and 46,000 were "freemen." According to the American Battlefield Trust, about 5,000 African Americans served with distinction in the Continental Army and Navy.

Between April 19th, 1775, when the Minutemen fired their first shots at the British Army, and the signing of the Treaty of Paris on September 3rd, 1783, approximately 6,500 Patriots — Americans fighting for independence from Great Britain — died on the battlefield or from the wounds they suffered. Roughly 20,000 Continental Army soldiers and sailors were taken prisoner and of those, approximately 17,000 died in captivity.[1]

Another 130,000 citizens - ~104,000 Patriots and 26,000 Loyalists – living in the cities, towns, and villages of the Thirteen Colonies died from disease. Smallpox and yellow fever were the major killers, particularly in South Carolina and Georgia. Neither diseases discriminated between Loyalists and Patriots.

The point is that between those who died fighting and those who died

---

1   American Revolution Facts, American Battlefield Trust, https://www.battlefields.org/learn/articles/american-revolution-faqs#:~:text=Throughout%20the%20course%20of%20the%20war%2C%20an%20estimated%206%2C800%20Americans,died%20while%20prisoners%20of%20war

in captivity or from disease, a combined estimate of 127,500 Patriots died for independence. That's a staggering 6.4% of the Patriot population of the Thirteen Colonies. Put another way, roughly one out of every 16 Patriots in the Thirteen Colonies died during the American Revolution.

To help put this percentage in perspective, during the American Civil War, the costliest war in American history, 618,222 Americans on both sides died from all causes. According to the U.S. Census Bureau in 1860, the population of the U.S. was 31,443,321. So, 618,222 represented 2.0% of the U.S. population.

More soldiers died in the American Civil War than were killed in all other wars in which the U.S. fought. That includes World War I, World War II, Korea, Vietnam, Desert Storm, Iraq, and Afghanistan combined.

Last Battles is dedicated to those who sacrificed their lives during the American Revolution for the freedoms we enjoy today. Their last battle paid for our independence, and we should all be grateful for their sacrifice.

Marc Liebman
April 2024

HISTORICAL BACKDROP

By August 1781, the American Revolution had been raging for six years and four months. The British still occupied Charleston, Savannah, and New York, but not much else. The strategy of British Army General Sir Henry Clinton's plan to split the rebellious northern colonies off from their southern brethren had come up snake-eyes during the Battle of Saratoga.

Cornwallis' surrender at Yorktown in October 1781 led to the fall of Prime Minister Lord North's government in March 1782. His successor, Lord Rockingham, began negotiations with the Americans, French, and Spanish to end the war.

Yet in the 25 months between Cornwallis' surrender and when the Treaty of Paris was signed on September 3rd, 1783, the war continued as the rebels fought to free South Carolina and Georgia from the British Army. In London during this time, four British governments rose and fell.

What started as a rebellion against British rule turned into a civil war between Loyalists and those who wanted freedom from England. Overseas, it had become a global war with France and Spain fighting the British in the Caribbean, South America, and India, and the French and Spanish were in the third year of their siege trying to force the British garrison in Gibraltar to surrender.

This is the historical backdrop of *Last Battles*. Enjoy the sailing.
Marc Liebman
August 2021

GAFF RIGGED SCHOONER

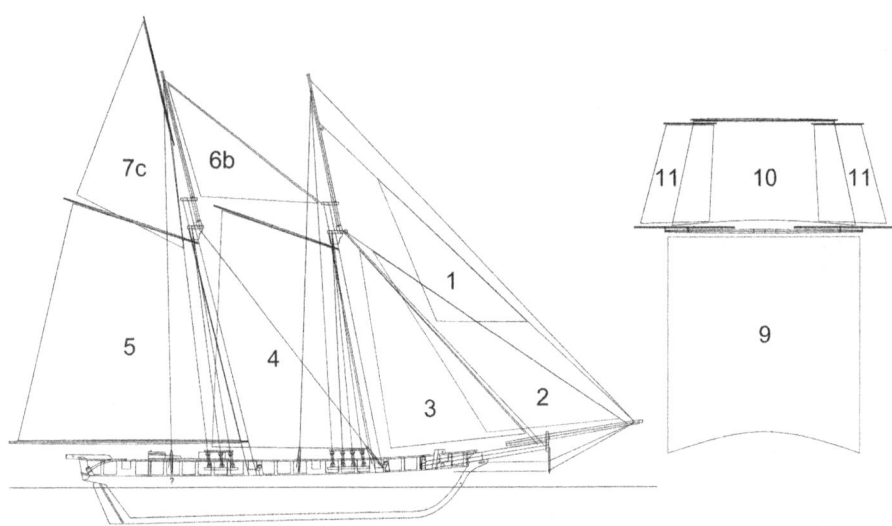

This is a sail plan for a "typical" two masted topsail schooner with one topsail on the fore mast and no topsails on the main mast. Schooners with three or more masts normally repeated the sails and rigging shown here on the main mast and may have, as in the ships in this novel gaff top sails on all three masts. The sails in this drawing are:

1. Flying jib
2. Jib
3. Fore staysail
4. Fore gaff sail or fore sail
5. Main gaff sail or main sail
6b. Main topmast staysail
7c. Mizzen fore course also sometimes called the mizzen gaff topsail

Not shown is the mainmast gaff topsail also called the main fore course.

Source: Phillip Hays, Model Ship World – Topsail Schooner Sail Plans and Rigging - https://modelshipworld.com/topic/25679-topsail-schooner-sail-plans-and-rigging/

LAST BATTLES

CHAPTER 1

– EDMUND'S WAKE UP CALL

CASABLANCA, THIRD WEEK OF MAY 1778

The pleasant aromas of cinnamon, cumin, and sesame mingled with the more pungent paprika and turmeric spelled opportunity to trader Jorge Fonseca. All the herbs present in barrels and burlap bags could be sold at a healthy profit in any of the Thirteen Colonies.

Jorge Fonseca was in Morocco, now that the country offered favorable trading terms through a treaty signed by the Continental Congress's Committee for Foreign Affairs and Morocco's ruler, Sultan Mohammed ben Abdallah (Mohammed III). The North African country was the first to recognize what the Continental Congress called the United States of America.

Fonseca first learned of the Moroccan agreement via a letter from his friend Javier Jacinto, one of South Carolina's delegates to the Continental Congress. In it, Javier offered to partner in a venture that would bring Moroccan spices to North America and share equally in the costs and profits.

With the formal arrangement completed between Jacinto's South Carolina Import and Exports and Fonseca's El Astro, Fonseca set sail for Morocco in *Aeolus*, one of his firm's nine merchant ships built to British East India Company specifications. Each was named after the Greek god for wind and air.

Aeolus sailed east along latitude 25^0 north to stay south of the Horse Latitudes with its lookouts first sighting the African coast near Safi. There, the ship headed north, staying within a few miles of the coast toward Casablanca, Morocco's capital.

The legend on how the Horse Latitudes got their name that made the most sense to Jorge was that while Spaniards had been transporting horses to the New World, their ships were often becalmed or delayed. With not enough food for the horses, as they died, the carcasses were tossed over the side.

After an uneventful voyage, which meant they didn't encounter any prowling Royal Navy frigates, *Aeolus'* anchored in Casablanca flying a large Continental flag. Five cannons boomed one after another. At first, Jorge thought that the Moroccans were firing at *Aeolus*, but when he didn't hear cannonballs scream overhead, he smiled at the formal welcome.

Two Moroccan Army officers, after they climbed on deck, welcomed Jorge and *Aeolus* in precise but halting English. The Sultan, he was told, would be delighted to meet with the captain or the ship's owner as soon as possible.

A letter from the Committee on Foreign Affairs referencing the commercial treaty was his license to come to Morocco to trade. He carried the precious document in a leather pouch with three brass buckles. On the way to Morocco, the letter was protected from moisture in an oilskin folder tied with string and kept in the ship captain's lockbox.

Jorge followed the two officers through the narrow winding streets of the medina. Above, he could occasionally see the palace. Fonseca couldn't resist a stall offering a flatbread with spices and olive oil. Prepared, he traded a Spanish 2 real provincial coin for a flatbread, took a bite, and smiled. The bread was sprinkled with ground cumin, rosemary, and garlic, which complimented the fruity taste of the olive oil. He offered a chunk to his escorts, who readily accepted, and then the threesome continued toward the palace.

Thick oak doors were pulled open by two soldiers as Jorge approached, and he was directed to a large room. At the far end, Mohammed III sat on cushions on a platform raised above the floor. Six men dressed in long sleeve, cream-colored *djellabas* stood waiting for his commands. At the entrance to the throne room, a servant took Jorge's letter, written in both Arabic and English.

Mohammed III asked if Jorge spoke Arabic. He shook his head. "No, Your Highness, I do not." He did not deem it relevant to tell the Sultan that he spoke Spanish, English, Portuguese, and Dutch fluently.

Mohammed held up the document written in Arabic. "Then who wrote this?"

"My wife. Her family is from the *mellah* in Marrakech and came to Savannah in 1750."

Both men knew *mellah* was the term for the Jewish communities in Morocco protected by the Sultan. Mohammed III relied on the country's Jewish community, its metal workers, tanners, coopers, and doctors, for trading with other countries. Each Jewish family paid a modest tax for living unmolested in Morocco.

Mohammed ben Abdallah smiled benevolently. "So, our culture has spread to your new country. This is good. What have you come to trade?"

"Your Highness, I have come here to buy Moroccan spices. In return, I brought a cargo of rice." *I won't mention that three of my nine ships are being used to smuggle munitions into the Thirteen Colonies. That is a personal project, not a line of business, as I only charge the Continental Congress for the cost of provisions and labor. Nevertheless, if we can find casks of gunpowder for sale, I'll buy them.*

Mohammed III nodded his satisfaction and waved his hand, "These men will help you fill your ship with the best spices we can offer at very attractive spices."

Jorge bowed his head slightly. "I am honored, and my country is honored."

"Anything your country can do to harm the British is welcomed by me. I do not like them, nor the Spanish nor the French. They all want to take over my country."

Jorge nodded in assent. *I, too, hate the Spanish because of the Inquisition and Alhambra laws. If I set foot on Spanish soil, I could be arrested. For the moment, the Spanish are our allies in our rebellion against the British. But once independence is won, what then?*

"Your war, how is it going?"

"We are fighting the most powerful nation in the world but are prepared to fight for however long we need to win our independence. We can always use more gunpowder and shot."

Mohammed III understood the sentiment. In 1774 he had tried to take the city of Melilla. However, the munitions sent by the British had been seized enroute by the Spanish Navy, and ultimately his effort had failed.

"I wish you and your country well. When you return to your country, please pass on my respects to the two Isaacs." The two Isaacs were Isaac de Pinto and Isaac Cordozo Nuñes, who had negotiated the trade agreement through their relatives living in Morocco.

Within two weeks of arriving in Casablanca, *Aeolus'* hold was packed with barrels of *karfa* (cinnamon), *skinibir* (ginger), *tguekoum* (turmeric), *kamoon* (cumin), *jinjelan* (sesame seeds) and *felfla hlouwa* (paprika) — and 10 barrels of gun powder that were a gift from the Sultan. With the fragrance of the spices wafting up from the hold, *Aeolus* smelled as wonderful as the profits its cargo would bring.

BOSTON, THIRD WEEK OF AUGUST 1779

Twenty-six-year-old Edmund Radcliffe sat at the writing table in his room on the third floor of his parent's house. He was the youngest son of one of the most successful lawyers in Boston and rather than choose law as a profession or work in one of the businesses in which his father had an interest, Edmund went to sea at 16.

Through the open window, he could see the small village of Cambridge across the Charles River. With a sailor's eye, he watched the dozen small boats that carried people and cargo back and forth across the river.

None of this mattered when a sharp, eye-watering stab of pain in what was left of his left arm stopped Radcliffe's writing. As he waited for the pain to subside, he told himself the stabs were getting farther apart. Each was a reminder of his duel with Jaco Jacinto. While he had managed to slice open Jaco's side, the captain of the frigate *Scorpion* had severed his left hand at the wrist. Damn that Jew Jacinto.

The same doctor whom Edmund had paid to attend the duel had directed him to dip the stub of his left arm, which ended about five inches below the elbow, into saltwater as hot as he could stand twice a day. This treatment and the fresh poultices the doctor applied between the soakings had helped the end of his arm heal.

Edmund had just turned 23 when his father had arranged a commission in the Continental Navy. He had been assigned the position of second lieutenant on the frigate *Scorpion* commanded by Jaco Jacinto. Clearly, Edmund thought, he himself should have been the captain, or at least the first lieutenant. After all, he'd had five years of experience as an officer on merchant vessels, and believed he was older and much more mature than that dark-skinned upstart who was what, 17 when he took command? Then, after *Scorpion* captured *H.M.S. Madras* with £1.1 million in gold bars in her hold, in Edmund's mind, Jacinto's raids at Aberdeen and Stornoway had put the ship, the gold, and his share of the prize money at risk.

Radcliffe had recruited a small cadre of Bostonians on board *Scorpion,* men who knew the influence his family could have on their lives and careers and had made plans to take command away from the obviously unfit Jacinto. When his plan had been discovered, Radcliffe had been humiliated: relieved of duty and put in irons until the frigate's return to Philadelphia.

Edmund scowled at the memory. No doubt the whelp had expected the board of inquiry appointed by the Continental Congress to hold a court martial. But most of the Massachusetts delegation were friends of his father. They had used parliamentary maneuvers to delay payment of the crew's prize money and deny Jacinto's continuation as *Scorpion's* captain as leverage. Edmund Radcliffe never faced trial, but he had been cashiered out of the Continental Navy, with the charges held in abeyance. Back home in Massachusetts, the governor had agreed not to prosecute. However, if Radcliffe moved to another colony, a local governor could try him for mutiny.

His father, Malcom Radcliffe, a successful lawyer and called the Boston's most powerful families – the Adams, Cabots, Hopkins and Lodges - amongst his friends and clients. Malcom was a founding partner in one of Boston's largest and most successful law firms entered without knocking. "Edmund, may I have a word with you?"

The son did his best to keep his annoyance at being interrupted out of his voice. "Of course, Father."

Their relationship had deteriorated. Malcom had voiced his disapproval of his son's actions on *Scorpion* and his son's ongoing boorish behavior. Edmund's mother had died suddenly in 1774, a year before the war began, so she wasn't there to mediate the simmering dispute. The relationship had flared into open hostility when the senior Radcliffe had questioned his son's judgment about challenging another man to a public duel. The elder Radcliffe's attitude toward his youngest son had mellowed with his concern about his son's health in the weeks following the loss of his left hand.

"Edmund, what do you plan to do now?" The unspoken, real question was, *"When are you going to stop spending time in taverns and do something productive?"*

"I am writing letters to the two consortiums here in Boston who own privateers and have openings. It is likely they could use a competent officer."

Malcom saw the letters as a step in the right direction; maybe his son had learned his lessons. "Are you sure they are looking for officers, not just seamen?"

"Aye, that I am. Yesterday I spoke to the captain of *Scythe*. He said to write to Josiah Baldwin, the head of the Patriot Consortium, and state my case."

The elder Radcliffe masked his reaction, just as he did when he was surprised in court by a ruling or testimony detrimental to his client. He was an investor in the consortium that owned both *Scythe* and *Sceptre*, and Baldwin knew the truth about Edmund Radcliffe.

"Do you think Mr. Baldwin and his investors will offer you a commission?"

"I do. I have proven myself in battle. That cannot be denied."

"Edmund, may I offer a suggestion?"

"Of course, Father." His tone was cautious, but not defensive, annoyed, or defiant.

"Given your past, you may want to look at other options. You may want to resume taking classes at Harvard. Or, if that is not to your liking, contact one of the five newspapers here in Boston to see if they need a reporter or an editor. You are an excellent writer. I could, if you so wish, put in a word at the *Continental Journal* or the *Independent Chronicle*. Both are clients."

"Father, are you suggesting I am wasting my time writing to Mr. Baldwin?"

"Suggesting, no. You are free to pursue whatever career you wish. However, my thought is that journalism is an avenue where you might find more immediate success."

"Your words suggest you think my past will haunt me, and the Patriot Consortium will turn me down."

Malcom Radcliffe stood still, not wanting to say a word lest it be misinterpreted.

The younger Radcliffe put his right hand over the end of his left arm. Since the amputation, the movement had become an inadvertent gesture. Edmund nodded his head. His father's comments implied that his days as a naval officer were over. "Father, please do not take this as an apology for my past behavior, but it may be time for me to follow your advice and see where it leads. On my own, I seem to have only found trouble." *Maybe I should heed my father's advice. There are certain advantages to staying in Boston. Frigates are not known for their comfort.*

Malcom Radcliffe felt relief flow through his body and allowed himself a wry smile. "If you wish, I will make enquiries."

"Father, please do." Edmund balled up the letter and put the cork stopper in his ink bottle.

SAVANNAH, THIRD WEEK OF NOVEMBER 1781

The clumping of heavy boots on the wood floor caused David Fonseca to look up from the bill of exchange he was reading. Voices raised in protest from the front of his law office caught his attention just as a British Army officer and three armed soldiers barged into his private office.

The major, resplendent in his red woolen coat and white breeches, came to attention at the front of his desk. "Mr. David Fonseca, in the name of King George III and the Royal Governor of the Colony of Georgia, you are under arrest. Please come with me."

"What are the charges? Where is the arrest warrant?"

The major placed a rolled sheet of paper with a red wax seal on his desk as if the document were diseased.

The 23-year-old graduate of the Honourable Society of Grays Inn popped off the wax seal and started to read. He was only partway down the page when the British Army major pulled the arrest warrant from his hands. "You will have plenty of time to read this later."

David Fonseca glared at the rude British Army major who hadn't had the courtesy to introduce himself, and then at the soldiers who had leveled their muskets with their bayonets affixed at him. Besides being the attorney for his father's El Astro firm, David Fonseca ran a thriving law practice of his own, with two other young lawyers and a law clerk to support his clients in Georgia. "This is an outrage! You cannot march into my office and arrest me. This is not a proper warrant."

The major placed his fingertips on David's desk. As he leaned forward, he checked to make sure he was out of the line of fire from the three men behind him. "Fonseca, whether the warrants are properly written matters not. You can either walk out of here under arrest, or we'll carry your bleeding body out."

As David came around the desk, the major started gathering the papers from his desk. David put a hand on the major's shoulder to pull him back. "You can't touch those. They are considered privileged and therefore protected."

"Not if you are a bloody treasonous rebel sympathizer."

David pulled his hand back when he felt the sharp tips of two bayonets pressing into his clothing. Outside his law office, passersby stopped to watch as David was shoved into the back of a jailer's wagon, where he joined his father, whose hands and feet were already manacled.

BETWEEN EBENEZER OLD AND NEW TOWNS, GEORGIA, THIRD WEEK OF NOVEMBER 1781

The 4th Carolina Dragoons were now officially part of what General Washington and the Continental Congress referred to as the Southern Department. The 200+ man unit was formed from men of the 2nd Carolina Infantry Regiment who had refused to surrender when Charleston fell to the British in May 1780. Led by Amos Laredo, the 4th Carolina's mission was to harass British Army and Loyalist reinforcements and supply trains while avoiding set-piece battles.

They were hidden in a wooded area near where the road from Savannah joined a road from Charleston, and their lookouts were posted where they could see anyone on the road. So far, they had not seen any sign of the British Army nor their Loyalist allies.

Amos wondered if the British in Georgia had pulled in their horns and were staying in their garrisons, as General Rawdon had done in South Carolina after Yorktown. But Amos had noticed many Union Jacks being flown on plantations; indicating that 30 miles north of Savannah, many of the locals supported the British. The 4th Carolina Dragoons were unlikely to receive support, shelter, or aid. They might even have to evade local militia.

Looking at his map made and printed in 1775 by British surveyors Robert Sayer and John Bennett, Amos moved the 4th Carolina north to a road junction where The Old Trading Road joined the Augusta – Savannah Road. Again, no British Army or Loyalist supply convoys or troops were seen.

Their current position was on Hidalgo Bluff, where they could see the bridge that crossed the Savannah River. After waiting two days, Amos decided to lead them back to their base in the woods north of Dorchester, South Carolina.

Corporal Billy Thornton, alone at the end of the column, lagged behind. Like the rest of the unit, he was tired from the stress of the week-long patrol, and hungry because this morning, they ate the last of their rations.

In the back of his mind, Thornton imagined what he could do with the £100 reward offered by the British Army for information on the location of the 4th Carolina's camp. It was much more than the £2/month Amos Laredo was paying the unit, which he could not spend, thanks to the 4th Carolina's operational tempo.

At a curve in the road, Thornton led his horse into the trees and dismounted. Once the 4th Carolina was out of sight, he remounted and headed directly to Charleston, the town where he was born and grew up.

CHAPTER 2

– COMMITTED FOR THE DEFENSE

CHARLESTON, FIRST WEEK OF DECEMBER 1781

The Burrows & Soriano library had a distinctive smell Shoshana Jacinto believed was a combination of leather from the bindings, glue that held the books together, ink and paper. It wasn't unpleasant and in fact, she thought was a reminder of the learnings contained on the pages.

Shoshana often used law library as a place to work because she could spread out documents to organize them as she prepared a filing or for an appearance in court. Other than the occasional intrusion by a law clerk wanting to find a specific book, she considered the law library her second office since the space she was given used to be a small sitting room on the third floor. It had room for her writing desk and chair and two other chairs against the wall, a very small bookcase and not much else.

Besides the privacy from being at the end of the hall, her corner office had windows on two sides. She had an unobstructed view of the Cooper River and Broad Street from her chair, which was the primary reason she didn't want another, larger office.

After Bayard Templeton was killed, Burrows & Soriano purchased his law practice from his estate and assumed the rent on his office for future expansion. This transaction gave the firm possession of all his legal work, his law library, which had books Burrows & Soriano didn't have, and the opportunity to offer their firm's services to Templeton's former clients. Shoshana was pleasantly surprised when all but two said yes.

The acquisition also gave Shoshana a reason to search Templeton's offices for the list of property he wanted to seize once the British had put down the rebellion. After removing all the drawers from Templeton's desk, she searched his desk for hidden compartments. Finding none, she tapped on the walls hoping to find a hollow section. Again nothing.

Frustrated, Shoshana stood in the middle of Templeton's office. She carefully studied each wall, trying to read the dead lawyer's mind as to where he would hide papers. Exacerbated, Shoshana pulled Templeton's desk away from the wall and noticed uneven floorboards. She stepped on one end, and it came up easily.

Underneath, wrapped in two layers of oilcloth, she found copy number 2 of what she called "Templeton's list." An accompanying note said copy number 1 was given to Curtis Armstrong, the senior clerk in the Royal Governor's office. Since the last Royal Governor fled in 1776, Armstrong promoted himself to First Secretary and claimed to have the authority of the Royal Governor. No one in Charleston believed him, and the officious and often pompous Armstrong was generally ignored.

Copy number 3 was sent to General Sir Henry Clinton's legal officer with the properties numbered in the order Templeton thought they should be seized. She did not know if Lord Cornwallis knew about the list when he was captured at Yorktown.

Cornelius Vickers, a wealthy rice broker in Charleston and a staunch Loyalist now living in Amelia Island in the British Colony of East Florida, had copy number 4. Vickers and most of Amelia Island's residents refused to join the rebellion. Despite their political differences, Shoshana's father, Javier Jacinto and owner of South Carolina Imports and Exports, found European customers for Vickers' rice that was transported to Europe on either a ship owned by Laredo Shipping or El Astro.

The fact that Templeton's list existed at all was disturbing enough. The additional notes Templeton made on his copy showed that Miriam Bildesheim's assets were his number one target. Number two were those owned by her parents and third were the Laredos. After them, Templeton listed other wealthy South Carolinians who supported independence.

When Shoshana told Miriam about Templeton's list, the elderly and very successful woman asked for a plan, so she was prepared in case the British decided to take legal action against her property. Shoshana had been working on the possible options for almost three days when Rafael Soriano and Edgar Burrows entered the law library.

Rafael was the first to speak. "Miss Jacinto, how close to finishing your work for Mrs. Bildesheim?"

Shoshana put the quill pen down and blotted the ink. The action gave her time to think. "This afternoon. I will send her a note telling her it is ready for her review. Miss Bildesheim's response will tell me when I should ride to Dorchester to review it with her or if she is coming to Charleston."

"Excellent." Rafael looked at his partner and put a letter down on the table. "Please read this."

Shoshana looked at the letter and then at the two men who helped her become a member of the bar. "What is going on? Am I in trouble?"

Rafael somber tone ordered. "Oh no. Please read." He didn't want to say that the contents would represent the kind of legal challenge Shoshana reveled in.

As she read, the expression on Shoshana's face changed. Her mouth opened, but nothing came out. When she finished reading, Shoshana dropped the letter on the table as if the paper was on fire. "The Fonseca's want me to defend David?"

"Yes."

The David was David Fonseca, son of one of Savannah's wealthiest ship owners and traders. He was also the nephew of Emory Fonseca, who was married to Leah Bildesheim. Their 10-year-old son was killed in cold blood by Bayard Templeton when he wouldn't give the Green Dragoons the steer he'd raised from when it was a calf.

Earlier in the year, Shoshana helped David, a graduate of Grays Inn, prepare the documents to create a Swedish company that would own El Astro's vessels. This made them off limits to the Royal Navy because they now belonged to a company based in a neutral country. "I'm not a member of the Georgia bar. I can't present arguments on his behalf in the court."

"David knows that, and the attorneys in his law firm know that. The court will allow you to represent him because the prosecution is bringing in a lawyer from New York who is also not a member of the Georgia bar."

"Rafael, you know Savannah is a hornet's nest of Loyalists."

"Aye, Miss Jacinto, 'tis just that, and the British bastards want to make an example out of El Astro."

Shoshana leaned back in her chair. "Sir, I can see that. There's no such charge in English law as illegal trading or overcharging. Is David or his father accused of fraud? Do they have evidence that either of them committed any treasonable offense?"

"Miss Jacinto, all we know is in that letter which came with a safe conduct pass from the British garrison commander, Lieutenant Colonel Campbell, and the Royal Governor, James Wright. By the way, the governor is a graduate of Grays and practiced here in Charleston before moving to Savannah."

"So, he knows both of you?"

"Aye. We were just becoming established in 1760 when Wright became Georgia's Royal Governor. At the time, he had property here in South Carolina. Most of it has been sold. Wright has done much to keep Georgia loyal to the king."

Shoshana looked at the letter again. She'd seen David three times since the first meeting. She had agreed to correspond with him to officially begin a courtship. Now, he was in trouble. "I'll go. We have a few weeks to prepare."

Rafael sounded relieved. "We thought you would. If you need help convincing your mother to give you permission, I will help."

"Mama won't be happy, but she will consent because she knows this is important for our rebellion and for me. Inform the court that I will bring my brother Saul as my assistant and another person as a chaperone. Also, let David's family know I am coming so they can find a suitable place for me to stay. I'll use David's office and need access to Georgia court rulings and case law in Savannah."

"May I ask why Saul?"

"Because he has a mind like a bear trap. He can quickly read and devour the most complex subjects, find the important points, and then explain what he read logically in an easy-to-understand manner. And I trust his judgment."

LONDON, SECOND WEEK OF DECEMBER 1781

Charles Oswald wrapped his heavy woolen cloak around him as his carriage rumbled over the cobblestones toward the Tower of London. The noise of the iron-rimmed wheels was partially drowned out by the cold rain that pummeled the canvass top making the 45^0 Fahrenheit temperature feel colder than it was.

Despite the warmth of the cloak, Oswald shivered in the raw dampness despite the news that the rebels were willing to exchange Lord Cornwallis for Henry Laurens. When Laurens was taken on a merchant ship in the fall of 1780, the South Carolinian was on his way to Amsterdam to continue as the Continental Congress' Consul to The Netherlands. The British claimed that since the Thirteen Colonies were not an independent country, they didn't enjoy diplomatic privileges. Laurens was being held in a two-room apartment in the Tower of London rather than a dank, cold stone cell in the old castle.

Laurens was both Oswald's friend and former business partner. Together, they ran a slave trading business that made both wealthy. With the blessing of Lords Rockingham and Shelburne, who led the "loyal opposition" to Lord North, Britain's current prime minister, Oswald frequently visited Laurens.

Once the news arrived about Cornwallis' surrender, Lord Shelburne asked Oswald and Laurens to create a framework for a peace treaty. Officially, formal peace talks could not begin until the North government fell and the new prime minister received permission from King George. When that would be, Oswald could not predict. While Shelburne waited to win a vote of no confidence that would cause Lord North to resign as prime minister, Laurens was moved to Oswald's house in London to begin negotiations to end the war.

CHARLESTON, THIRD WEEK OF DECEMBER 1781

Major General Alexander Leslie waited until Captain Isaiah Vickers from the 1st Regiment of the Camden District militia and Corporal Billy Thornton of the 4th Carolina were ushered out of his office. Left behind at the table was Lord Islay, now the deputy commander of the British Army in South Carolina. General Leslie had taken over from the seriously ill Rawdon, who left for England in July 1781.

The British general's manservant poured a glass of Madeira wine and handed it to Lord Islay before pouring one for General Leslie who thanked him and said politely, "That will be all," It was a way to ask the manservant to leave him alone with Lord Islay.

Leslie held up the glass, "The king."

After Islay replied with the same phrase, Leslie took a large sip. "What do you make of the young Captain Vickers' report and Corporal Thornton's map?

Islay, who had just turned 50, was a professional soldier. His family managed to survive the confiscations of property and trials after the 1745 Jacobite rebellion. Islay, along with many other Scotsmen were encouraged to join the British Army. "Sir, what the lads said was clear and concise and, I suspect, quite accurate."

"My Lord, what do you think about either of those men?"

Lord Islay put the glass down on the table to give himself time to think. His graying hair, tied in a neat ponytail was a compliment to his white wig. Besides being the commander of the 11th Regiment (Highland) of Foot and a member of the nobility, Lord Islay was a respected general and a veteran of many campaigns during the Seven Years War. "Vickers seems straight enough. From what I hear, he did well for himself at the battles at Eutaw Springs and Kings Mountain. His father is from Charleston and he is from the Camden area, so he knows South Carolina far better than we. Thornton, I don't know. I always suspect the motives of deserters or traitors."

"Do you think Thornton was really a member of the 4th Carolina? If so, he would be the first."

"General Leslie, are you implying that Thornton may be a plant trying to draw us into a trap?"

"Aye, Lord Islay, that is exactly what I am thinking."

"General, if your orders from General Clinton give you the latitude to seize this base, we should consider doing so. If not ..." Islay let his voice trail off. He had lost half his regiment on an attack on Dorchester a little over a year earlier. Since then, three British relief convoys were decimated while attempting to re-supply British forts along the Congaree River.

Already, the Star Fort in the Ninety-Six District of South Carolina had surrendered, and the rebels had taken Fort Watson. Leslie had beleaguered 800-man garrisons at Fort Granby and Fort Motte to keep supplied. Doing so was costing the British Army men it could ill afford to lose, along with supplies that benefitted the rebels.

Before Vickers and Thornton were ushered into his office, the two men discussed the best way to bring the soldiers at Granby and Motte back to Charleston. One option was asking General Greene to agree to a truce so they could bring the men to Charleston. Leslie referred to the city where he was by the name listed on the Crown's records for South Carolina as Charles Town. Only the locals, he noted, referred to the city as Charleston.

Both officers rejected the truce idea because neither man believed Greene would accept it. Leslie tapped his finger on the map where the 4th Carolina's base was marked, "My Lord, I believe a raid by a small force is doomed to fail. The 4th Carolina will cut them to pieces in an ambush. Therefore, I would like you to take the 11th, along with the Hesse-Kassel Regiment and the 33rd Regiment of Foot and have a look for this rebel base. Take this Corporal Thornton with you, but make sure that Captain Vickers does not let him out of his sight."

Leslie nodded and then looked Lord Islay in the eye. "If you find the 4th Carolina, take your revenge for Dorchester, and destroy them. If not, continue north to Fort Motte. There, gather up the troops and supplies and come south after burning the fort and anything you cannot carry. Do the same at Fort Granby on your return to Charles Town."

Lord Islay held up his glass, "Aye, sir. I will come back in a few days with a plan we can execute in the New Year."

The two men chatted for a few minutes about what additional units could be assigned to the force if Lod Islay formally requested them. As Lord Islay walked out of the room, his stomach churned. He was sure that Lieutenant Colonel Rafer Muir, the man who was back in the 11th Infantry (Highland) of Foot as his chief of staff and on whom he relied on for operational and logistics planning, would not like planning another re-supply mission.

CHARLESTON, THE SAME DAY, 4:44 P.M.

As Shayna Enterprises' attorney, Shoshana Jacinto was also their "agent." During the month, she would collect the bills from the Dockside and Charleston Inns and those for food and supplies sold to the British Army and Royal Navy from the Charleston General Store and present them for payment. She watched the British Army paymaster count out the pound notes when she saw Billy Thornton walk by with another man in a British Army uniform, she did not recognize.

Shoshana kept her head down, finished her business, scrawled her name on the receipt acknowledging payment, and hurried out of the man's office. Thornton, Reyna, Jaco, Melody, Shoshana, and most of the other young adults her age had all gone to the same school. She hurried up Front

Street to the large warehouse where South Carolina Imports and Exports stored cargo waiting to either be loaded on ships or about to be distributed.

She found Isaac, her older brother, sitting at her desk. Without a greeting, Shoshana said, "I need a pen and paper. Then, you need to send a rider to Mrs. Bildesheim in Dorchester with my letter."

Isaac stopped what he was doing and looked at his sister, "Well, good afternoon to you, my tall sister Shoshana. What brings you here all fired up?"

Ignoring the teasing that came from having two brothers who were at least a head shorter than she, Shoshana said as she positioned an inkwell and blotter near the paper. "This has to get to Amos as soon as possible."

"I have some wagons leaving for Dorchester at dawn tomorrow and should be there around noon. They can carry whatever you are writing, and it will be safer and less dramatic than a rider galloping along the road."

Shoshana nodded to acknowledge her brother's wise words and kept writing. The loudest sound was the scratching of the quill pen on the paper, which only stopped when Shoshana dipped it in the ink well. Finished, she used the blotter, folded the sheet, and sealed it with wax.

Handing the letter to her brother, Shoshana said, "I saw Billy Thornton in British Army headquarters this afternoon, and he wasn't a prisoner."

"Billy Thornton, as in the ironmaker's middle son?"

"The one and the same."

Isaac, not prone to hyperbole, gasped, "Oh my!!!"

"Oh, my indeed!" The two chatted for a few minutes, and then Shoshana left for the Shayna Enterprise's General Store to deliver the cash she was carrying in her satchel that was one part purse, one part briefcase and one part carry-all.

PORTSMOUTH, FOURTH WEEK OF DECEMBER 1781

The past two weeks had not gone as Darren expected. First, the convoy sailing date had been postponed until after the first of the year. Second, the barracks ships only had enough sailors to bring *Pompeii's* crew to 200, 20 men short of its full complement.

While he and his officers could deal with the shortfall, what happened yesterday was the most vexing. He was about to hold his first court martial.

Given the holiday and that a third of his crew died from yellow fever last fall, Darren allowed 24 men to go ashore every evening. *Pompeii's* long boats ferried them to the naval base's landing at five p.m. and brought them back at midnight.

When he announced the plan two days before *Pompeii* arrived in Portsmouth, Darren emphasized to the crew gathered around him on the main deck that if they did not return on time, they would be treated as deserters under the Articles of War and shore leave for all would stop immediately. Darren wanted his sailors to police themselves.

Any sailor who missed the boat would also forfeit his prize money. To emphasize his point, he read aloud Articles 15 and 33 so the crew knew that if found guilty, they could be flogged or hung.

Darren sent his First Lieutenant Christopher Abbott along with Bosun Poteet ashore to buy hams and the ingredients to make plum pudding and gingerbread. He wanted to give his crew a break from the standard Royal Navy menu with a nice Christmas day dinner. The funds for the food came from his own pocket.

No sailor missed the boat until December 27th, when four did not return on time. The quartermaster commanding the two boats, sent one back to *Pompeii* and dispatched two men to find the missing sailors.

When the sailors returned empty-handed, the quartermaster ordered the boats to row back to *Pompeii*. Darren, who was spending the night aboard, was immediately awakened and entered the missing men's names in the log.

At dawn, Midshipman Culver who had the watch, spotted Seaman Sean Mackinaw waving from the landing. He ordered Bosun Poteet to take six men ashore to see if they could find the other three missing sailors.

While he waited for the boat, Mackinaw, still tipsy, was steadied by several of his shipmates who had rowed ashore, cast up his account. The arrival of his vomit on the harbor water sent fish thrashing for the new food.

When a Royal Navy officer came calling at the East Anglia orphanage looking for ship's boys and powder monkeys, Poteet was 11 years old. Bigger than most, he saw the Royal Navy as a way out of the hell where the children were underfed, under-clothed, and where the larger boys bullied the younger, smaller ones. Resistance often led to a brutal beating.

Poteet worked his way up the ranks and had been appointed as the bosun on a brig and then on a sixth-rate frigate before being assigned to *Pompeii*, 38 guns. The 39-year-old Poteet knew where sailors hung out in Portsmouth and most of the places where they might be sleeping off a drunk.

By noon, he'd found the three disheveled men reeking of beer, horse dung, urine, and smoke in the doorway to a stable. Poteet and the sober sailors pushed and prodded the hungover men to the pier.

Once on board, all four were clapped in irons. Before they were taken below to the orlop deck, Poteet, knowing his captain's preference for cleanliness, had the men sprayed down with seawater and washed with soap.

One bleated as he stood soaking wet and shivering in the 40-degree air, "You'll cause us to catch our death."

Poteet was unsympathetic. "Aye, that may be a blessing because your mates may draw and quarter you for stopping their shore leave. Or your captain may flog or hang you for desertion."

"We didn't desert. We had too much to drink and fell asleep."

"Tell it to your court martial."

Since *Pompeii* was in Portsmouth, Darren could hold the court martial on board his frigate with his officers and men sitting in judgment from his crew. Or he could ask officers from other ships to be members of the court.

After Darren discussed his options with his officers, *Pompeii*'s First Lieutenant Christopher Abbott; the ship's Captain of Marines, Eldon Palin; and Quartermaster Hiram Spivey, agreed to be members of the court along with two leading seamen, Reginald Castner and Elijah Westfield. The two sailors were picked by Bosun Poteet and Quartermaster Spivey who thought the two men were well respected by their shipmates and would not be intimidated by an officer if they differed in their view of guilt or innocence.

The mix of officers and seamen Darren hoped would make an objective assessment of the testimony and a fair recommendation to him as the captain. Even though it was within his lawful power to do so, Darren agreed not to overturn the results of the five-man board or what punishment the board recommended if the men were found guilty.

As he waited for the other members of the court-martial to come to his cabin, Darren fidgeted as he read and re-read Poteet's report dictated to Judah Barton, *Pompeii*'s third lieutenant. He referred to his copy of the Articles of War that were initially written in the 1650s, revised by Parliament in 1740, and again in 1757.

Other than being required to read the Articles of War to their crews every month, captains of Royal Navy ships had considerable discretion on when and how they fulfilled this requirement. Darren preferred to gather the crew on Sunday mornings and read nine of the 35 articles. After he was finished, he would answer questions so that every member not only knew the words but the implications of the words and how he intended to enforce the articles.

After explaining to the court martial members that he wanted them to ask any questions they felt needed to determine guilt or innocence, Darren poured a glass of port for each man and held up his. "The king and to your judgment, may it be fair and just."

The men acknowledged the salutation and filed out of his cabin. Castner, the junior man, led and Darren, the senior member of the court-martial, was last.

Waiting on the berthing deck, the crew sat on their sea chests in rows. Those who wanted to stand lined the bulwarks. At the aft end of the berthing deck, the table from Darren's cabin was positioned athwartships so each member of the court-martial faced the crew.

Poteet's voice boomed out as soon as he saw the white breeches of Christopher Abbott appear on the companionway below the gun deck. "Attention on deck."

The ship's crew stood. Darren took his position behind the center chair, thinking a court-martial is as much theater as it is a court. Castner and Westfield sat on Darren's right to signal to the crew that they were equal members of the court-martial. Spivey, Abbott, and Palin sat on Darren's left.

Darren hoped his voice would not crack as he ordered in a loud, clear voice, "Seats."

Except for Darren, the panel sat, as did the crew. Second Lieutenant Shamus O'Steen and Third Lieutenant Judah Burton remained standing on the starboard side of the deck with their backs to the bulwark. Burton had the charges and the report in his hand. Dyer Culver, *Pompeii's* only midshipman, stood next to Burton.

After clearing his throat, Darren spoke slowly, carefully enunciating each word to ensure the crew would understand what he said. "Crew of *Pompeii*, this court-martial is about to sit in judgment of four of your shipmates, Sean Mackinaw, Antonio Drago, Jared Thornborough, and Mark Simpson. All are charged with missing muster and being absent without permission. During this trial, we will also determine if the charge of desertion will be added. I am convening this panel under the authority given to me by the Royal Navy's regulations and the Articles of War. Mr. O'Steen, please bring the prisoners into our presence."

The loudest sound was the clanking of the chains linking the manacles around the accused men's ankles and wrists. The four prisoners were followed by six Marines with empty muskets but fixed bayonets. When Drago, Mackinaw, Simpson, and Thornborough stood before the panel, Darren ordered the restraints removed.

Still standing, *Pompeii*'s captain solemnly repeated what he said before the prisoners were brought up to the berthing deck. He finished with a "Do you understand what is…. "Darren hesitated for the right word. He wanted to use transpiring but instead said, "…. happening and the seriousness of this proceeding?"

After hearing ayes from the four men, he turned to Judah Burton, "Lieutenant Burton will now read the charges, which are the same for each man. After he is finished, each of you will have a chance to respond. Members of the panel will then ask questions. Mr. Burton, proceed."

Darren sat down as if to say to the crew that his lieutenant now has the floor. Judah Burton took three measured paces forward so that he was two steps from the accused's right shoulders and between the table and the four men. He read slowly and clearly. When finished, he nodded to his captain and the panel before returning to his position along the starboard bulkhead.

As the president of the courts-martial, Darren wanted the others to ask their questions and allow the men to defend themselves. He told the others that he would ask the first question. "Is the report accurate?"

The four men looked back and forth at each other. Sean Mackinaw decided he needed to speak. "Sir, I was drunk as Davy's sow, and it's a bloody miracle that somehow I managed to make my way back to the landing. By then, the boat was already gone. That's where I passed out huggin' a bollard for dear life to keep from fallin' into the harbor. When I awoke, I knew I was in the shite."

Mark Simpson waited for his shipmate to finish. "Aye, sir, the report is accurate. What is missing is what happened after we went into the Iron Anchor Tavern."

Sensing that this would be part of their defense, Darren responded quickly. "Enlighten us, then."

"Sir, I can't speak for Mackinaw, but me, Drago, and Thornborough are ashamed of what happened. All three of us were really mauled. We didn't intend to get so drunk that when we left the tavern, we thought we were heading for the landing, but honestly, we didn't know where we were going. I don't think any of us remember much. When we stumbled into the barn to sit a spell, we passed out."

"Why didn't you come to the fleet landing straight away when you woke up?"

Simpson again answered. "I heard what I thought was a ship going through the water, but something in my brain told me I was not back on *Pompeii*. The sound that woke me was a horse pissing. We didn't know where we were, and we were still tipsy. I just lay on the hay with my stomach a-churning and my head a-pounding. Drago and Thornborough flayed the fox all over the hay. The stink from their puke was so bad that the horses moved away. I tried to get up and then fell back, landing in a pile of horse shite."

He used a closed fist with only his thumb out and pointed at Drago. "My mate Drago couldn't stand, and while we were laying there, wondering what to do next, Bosun Poteet found us."

Lieutenant Abbott, like the other members of the court-martial, forced himself not to laugh. He rested his wrists on the edge of the table and leaned forward. "So, your defense is that the four of you got so mauled that you couldn't find your way to the fleet landing. Mackinaw, all by himself, staggered around and stumbled to the fleet landing. Simpson, Drago, and Thornborough passed out in a barn in the middle of Portsmouth. When you three awoke, you had no idea where you were?"

The four men nodded. Sean Mackinaw spoke again, "Aye, that's the ruddy truth. And I'm ashamed of meself because me and my mates here have cost all my shipmates their shore leave."

Having grown up across the harbor, Darren had seen his share of drunken sailors. They would laugh at what they just heard if he were at home or in his cabin talking to his officers. As testimony in a court-martial, what was said could be the difference between lashes of the cat-o-nine tails or being hung. "What were you drinking?"

Drago spoke. "Ale mostly, but I think I had a glass or two of whiskey that went right to me head."

Once the charges had been handed him before the court-martial was convened, Darren quizzed both Spivey and Poteet about the men wanting to know if they were troublemakers. Mackinaw and Thornborough were respected gun captains. Simpson was a leading topman on the mainmast and one of the better lookouts. Drago was just promoted to quartermaster mate.

Darren had a dilemma on his hands. He had no choice but to punish them and keep his word that if any sailors missed muster, shore leave for all would end. He could have them all flogged, but that seemed extreme to him.

When the questions petered out, Darren called for a vote. There were four guilty votes, and his made the decision unanimous. Darren stood up and looked at each man in turn. "So, the question facing this court-martial is what punishment should I award. The easy one is to have each of you flogged."

Darren waited as his mind processed what he was about to say. "Unfortunately, I must keep my word. All shore leave is henceforth canceled. You four will have to live with your shipmates, knowing that you are the reason no one from *Pompeii* other than the officers will leave the ship except for work details. In addition, beginning today, if Bosun Poteet needs men for special work details, you four are on them. When we go to sea, for the first month, you will alternate watches so you will be four on, then four off. Maybe thirty days with little sleep will teach you a lesson. If this doesn't work, there is always the cat."

Darren looked around, debating what he just said as he walked behind the four prisoners to address the crew. "While many of you may wish to take out your frustration on Drago, Mackinaw, Simpson, and Thornborough for costing you shore leave, I suggest you do not. Your disdain for their actions should be enough while they try to work their way back into your good graces by doing extra work that could be assigned to any of you. Dismissed."

CHAPTER 3
– LESSONS IN LAW

SAVANNAH, FIRST WEEK OF JANUARY 1782

The small, two-masted schooner the Fonsecas sent to bring Shoshana, her brother, and Emory Fonseca – David's cousin – to Savannah was designed for cargo, not speed. Built in 1770, *Choctaw's* shallow draft allowed it to carry manufactured goods up rivers and inlets to plantations and return with barrels of rice and sugar along with crates of dried indigo.

Choctaw's wide beam made it slow, and the ship needed 28 hours to make the 90-mile journey down the coast. As the only woman on board, Shoshana was given the small captain's cabin as a place to sleep. To enter the cabin, she had to bend noticeably at the waist to avoid banging her head on the crossbeam. It was a nice gesture, but the bed was made for someone half a foot shorter than the 6'2" tall Shoshana. By curling up and with her feet up against the end of the bed, she fell asleep.

Before she left Charleston, Perla Jacinto cut her daughter's lush sandy brown hair that had reached her waist. Now, the braid ended just below her shoulders.

Shoshana came on deck well before dawn to watch the sunrise. Jaco often talked about how beautiful sunrises and sunsets were at sea, and she wanted to see one for herself. Overhead, stars twinkled in the black sky, and other than the creaking of the ship's rigging, the loudest sound was the water rushing past the hull. It was, she thought, so very peaceful.

Other than visits to Miriam Bildesheim's farms north of Charleston, this was the first time Shoshana had been this far from home. Traveling and seeing new places was exciting, and she decided that after the war, she would travel more.

The smell of bacon and grits being cooked wafted up from the ship's stove as the sun rose. *Choctaw's* captain, a stocky man whose last name was Jones, handed Shoshana a steaming cup of coffee, and Emory Fonseca handed her one of the two bowls of grits he was carrying and two slices of bacon.

When *Choctaw* bumped against a pier in Savannah just before lunch, Shoshana could see clouds to the west. Their dark gray color meant rain was coming soon.

The wagon carrying their baggage stopped in front of the three-story house on Julian Street where Nora Fonseca, David's mother, greeted Shoshana on the porch. After Shoshana assured Nora that the trip on board the *Choctaw* was both pleasant and uneventful, the lawyer in Shoshana took over.

"Nora, where is David being held?"

"On a ship out in the harbor. I believe Jorge is with him, but the damned British won't tell me."

"On which ship?"

"The British will not tell us that either."

"Do you know if David and Jorge are alive?"

"No. We haven't seen either David or my husband since they were arrested."

"Was David in his law office when he was arrested?"

"Yes."

"Did the British take any papers from his office?"

"His law clerks said the British major took several contracts and bills of exchange he was reviewing. They made a list but are sure it is incomplete."

A rumble of thunder said the rain was getting closer. It wasn't the only storm brewing.

"Has either of them been formerly charged?"

Nora shook her head and then looked at the sky. "The Goddamned British are trying to make an example of my Jorge and David. Last year, they imprisoned Abigail Minis because she wouldn't kowtow to British demands that her farms provide food to the British Army at ridiculously low prices. Then they arrested Mordecai Sheftall because his ships were suspected of smuggling arms to the Continental Army. At the time, his ships were taken, they were carrying cargoes from Naples and Morocco. The British knew Mordecai kept kosher, so while he was confined on the British ship, they smeared his plates with bacon grease and fed him only pork. Mordecai refused to eat and after two days, they allowed food to be brought to him, so they didn't face the embarrassment of him dying from hunger."

Shoshana was trying to be gentle, but alarm bells were ringing in her head. Even the British Army follows British and Colonial law and need evidence on which to base a warrant so they can make an arrest. "Nora, how far is the judge and the court where the trial is being held from here?"

"Three blocks."

"Does the judge office there?"

"Yes."

Shoshana stopped Emory Fonseca as he was carrying a chest of clothes inside. "Emory, please finish unloading while Saul and I go to the courthouse." She turned to her host, "Nora, you can come with me or stay here. I have no idea how long this will take."

The courthouse was a three-story brick building in the heart of Savannah. Shoshana strode up the 10 steps using her long legs to take them two at a time. Halfway up, Shoshana stopped and turned around to wait for Saul, who was taking one step at a time with Nora at his side. Shoshana turned and softened, "Saul, I am so sorry."

Saul was grinning when he said, "Shoshana, this will be like a tiger devouring a lamb. Watching you reminds me of the line William Congreve's play, *The Mourning Bride*, in which one of the characters says hell hath no greater fury than woman scorned!"

Inside, a clerk, full of importance, strode up to Shoshana. His air of superiority irritated Shoshana, who towered over the paunchy, middle-aged clerk who spoke condescendingly. "Excuse me, miss. Are you sure you are in the right place?"

Shoshana took his tone and words to mean women don't belong in this building which is a man's place. "Where is Judge St. James' office?"

"I am sorry, he is a very busy man, young lady. Maybe you should come back another time."

Shoshana bent at the waist to get her green eyes even with the clerk's. "First, don't trifle with me, sir. Second, I am a member of the South Carolina bar invited by Judge St. James and the Royal Governor James Wright to defend a client here in Savannah. Now, where is Judge St. James?"

"In his office."

"Excellent, then I suggest you take me to him, right now!"

Shoshana didn't wait for the clerk to exit Judge St. James' office. She pushed the door open to find Wendell St. James hurrying to put his wig on. The surprised clerk started to say something but didn't when Saul limped in.

After placing Judge St. James' letter inviting her to appear in his court as David Fonseca's defense counsel attorney on his desk, Shoshana said politely but firmly. "Your honor, we'll dispense with the social formalities. I am Shoshana Jacinto, representing David Fonseca and his father, Jorge Fonseca. My assistant, Saul Jacinto, and Mrs. Fonseca are in the anteroom."

"We were not sure if you were going to come. Welcome to Savannah."

That is the first lie. I will not challenge you because it may have been one of your clerks who answered my letter and sent the passes. "Thank you, sir. I would like to meet with my clients immediately. Where are they?"

"That would be, ahhhhh, difficult, Ms. Jacinto...."

"Because they are on one of your awful prison ships. Bring them both to Savannah where they can be released on reasonable bail. Neither he nor his father Jorge are prisoners of war nor, to my knowledge, have they been officially charged."

"You know, Ms. Jacinto, you cannot barge into my office and start making demands. There is another side to this discussion. He is called a prosecutor."

"Excellent. Get him. I'll wait."

"Getting the Fonsecas to Savannah may take a few hours."

Shoshana looked at the clock sitting on the bookcase behind the judge. "Assuming your clock is accurate, the time is now one in the afternoon. I'll be back at four expecting to see David and Jorge Fonseca sitting in this office."

"Ms. Jacinto, your aggressive behavior may not sit well with me or a jury of Georgians, most of whom are loyal to the king. We do things differently than you do in Charleston."

"Your Honor, an accused man has certain rights guaranteed to him by English law. Insisting the court and its officers obey the law is not being aggressive. It is my duty. Already your actions are grounds for appeal. All I am doing is asking the court to follow both English and Georgian law."

St. James pursed his lips. "Well then, do you have any other demands for today, or may I go about my work." The sarcasm of his tone was not lost on Shoshana.

"I do. I'd like to see the arrest warrant, assuming there is one, along with the evidence the prosecutor collected to support its issuance and any statements from witnesses that were used as the basis of the arrest warrant. I am sure they have been filed with the court, and you saw them before you signed the warrant for David and Jorge Fonseca's arrest. By before, I mean before they were arrested and taken to a ship in Savannah harbor and held incommunicado without bail."

The judge coughed. His nostrils flared, and he glared at the tall woman in front of him.

Shoshana's tone softened, and she gave him a conciliatory smile. "If you don't have the papers then I am sure the prosecutor has copies for me to study. They are necessary for me to prepare a defense and to determine what witnesses the defense will call."

"I don't need a tutorial in the law."

Shoshana's smile broadened, and she batted her eyelids. "Sir, I wouldn't even think of doing that. I am just asking for what my clients and I are entitled to review."

St. James mashed down a ringer on a bell. A different clerk appeared in the doorway. "Go bring Mr. Fredrick Blaze here immediately with his file on the Fonsecas."

Shoshana was led to a small conference room where she was allowed to pore over the requested documents, which included two contracts and bills of exchange. Both were taken from El Astro's offices. While there, St. James' clerk informed her that both Jorge and David Fonseca would be at the courthouse at five or shortly after.

VIDEAU'S BRIDGE ON THE WANDO RIVER, THE FIRST WEEK OF JANUARY 1782

The 4th Carolina Dragoons gathered at Amos Laredo's farm he called Peaceville. It was a few miles North of Dorchester and was where his men assembled to replenish their supplies and let their horses rest.

Amos was writing in his diary, which was also where he kept the notes for his formal reports, when four riders came galloping up the road. They stayed calmly on their horses while the guard detail questioned them. When the sergeant held up his dispatch bag, he was led to the room where Amos was sitting.

"So, what unit are you?"

"Sir, 9th Carolina State Dragoons and assigned to General Marion's headquarters. I have urgent orders for the 4th Carolina." The sergeant fished in the dispatch pouch and handed Amos a folded sheet of paper held closed with a blob of blue wax.

> *Major Laredo,*
>
> *Our intelligence suggests General Leslie is sending patrols up the Wando River to attack our outposts near Cainhoy. You are to immediately send a detachment of 50 or more men to report to Colonel Richard Richardson of the Berkeley County Regiment and his deputy, Major Samuel Cooper of the 9th Regiment of State Dragoons. They will assist Colonel Richardson in defending our flank near Videau's Bridge to help keep the British penned in Charleston.*
>
> *Once that mission is completed, you are to resume searching for British and Loyalist foraging parties and attacking their supply trains.*
>
> *Francis Marion*
> *General*
> *Continental Army*

Amos stood up. "Captain Giffords, have Lieutenant Pruett gather twenty-four pairs to leave within the hour for Cainhoy with four day's provisions. I will lead, and you, sir, will remain here with the rest of the 4th Carolina."

"Sir, would it be better to send me?"

"Captain, under most circumstances, I would agree. However, Colonel Richardson and Major Cooper's men lead inexperienced units and are expecting me. If anyone is going to take on a fool's errand, it shall be me."

He sent the couriers back with a note saying he would lead 50 men to Videau's Bridge.

On the second day of their ride, Amos and the 4th Carolina heard gunfire. Amos held up his hand, stopping his column. Up ahead, he could see two of his scouts riding toward him at full gallop.

"There's Redcoat cavalry up head who have just charged our men. Our boys are having a bad time of it, sir."

"Where are our men, and where are the Redcoats?"

"Videau's Bridge. The Redcoats have a small unit of our cavalry trapped on this side and we have infantry on the other side of the Wando River."

"Lieutenant Pruett, let's move forward until I can see the enemy."

The pop and cracks of musket fire grew louder, and Amos held up his right hand just before the road exited the trees. Through his spyglass, Amos could see the Redcoats of the British Army. Off to their right, gathering to make a charge, he estimated 100 or more men in a green coated cavalry unit. Opposite them, he could see the flag of the 9th Carolina Dragoon Regiment. One of its soldiers had stuck it in the ground as the unit's rally point. Through his glass, he could see the unit was backed up against the river, which suggested to Amos that they were about to make their last stand.

Pointing at the waving sawgrass, "Pruett, take ten dismounted men into that high grass there. On my command, pick off the British officers and force the British cavalry to pay attention to us. If they charge us, I will have the rest ready."

Pruett nodded and led 10 men who ran hunched through the chest-high grass carrying a rifled musket in each hand while five others walked their horses back into the trees. Once Pruett waved, Amos led the remaining 25 members of the 4th Carolina out into the open so they could be seen by the British cavalry.

Amos cupped his hands around his mouth and yelled, "Pruett, tell them we are here."

All 10 muskets fired almost as one. Three British officers and a sergeant toppled from their horses while others in the ranks fell dead or dying. A captain pointed to the puffs of smoke rising from the grass and at the 25 men on horseback.

The 4th Carolina was much closer to the larger British force than the 9th Carolina. If the British charged, Amos' unit would be overwhelmed, and there weren't enough men in the 9th Carolina to turn the tide even if they could join the fight in time. The words of General Greene – do not engage the British Army in a set piece battle on ground not of your choosing – ran through his head.

Pruett's men fired the second volley, and at least a dozen more British soldiers fell, including the captain. The last surviving British officer must have thought he would catch the 4th Carolina's sharpshooters reloading and ordered half his force to wheel and charge the 4th Carolina.

The British hadn't gone 50 feet when a ragged second volley rang out from the men on horseback. They weren't as accurate as those on the ground, but their firing was joined by Pruett's men who had reloaded.

When the gray-white smoke cleared enough so Amos could see a third of the British saddles out in front of the 4th Carolina were empty. Their occupants having been hit by .50 caliber lead balls in the chest were on the ground dead or dying. The charge was over.

Off to his left, Amos saw red coated British infantry marching toward the bridge now abandoned by the Continentals. The 9th Carolina Dragoons were retreating across the river, leaving Amos and the 50 men of the 4th Carolina as the only Continental Army troops on the battlefield.

Amos yelled, "4th Carolina pull back!!! Pull back, lads."

Now mounted, the men who had not yet fired remained along the trees while those who did reloaded their muskets and mounted their horses. Through his spyglass Amos spotted a British officer looking at him through his spyglass. He collapsed the brass tube and slid it into the canvas pouch just in front of the pistol by his left thigh. Wheeling his horse, Amos ordered, "Lieutenant Pruett, lead the column. I will stay behind to watch the Redcoats. When we are clear of the enemy, I will take my position at the front."

Two hours later, the men of the 4th Carolina crossed the Wando River four miles upriver from Videau's Bridge. They were heading south toward the bridge when they met a disorganized group from the Berkeley County Regiment. Its commander was at the tail end of his ragged column urging his men to move faster away from the British.

Amos rode to Colonel Richardson and introduced himself. The colonel looked up at the 6' 2", 200-pound Amos Laredo. On his Percheron, he towered over Colonel Richardson whose head barely reached his horse's chest.

The commander of the Berkeley County Regiment gave Amos' and his gray trousers, white shirt, and floppy hat a disdainful look. Amos wore no insignia of rank.

Richardson's tone combined annoyance and impatience. "Who, pray tell, are you?"

Touching his index finger to the brim of his hat, Amos responded pleasantly. "Major Amos Laredo, commander of the 4th Carolina Dragoons."

"Where have you been, sir? The British got around both flanks and pushed us right off the bridge."

"How many Redcoats?"

"At least three regiments, one of them was mounted. Why?"

"How far behind you are the British?"

"I don't know. Major Laredo, why are you being so impertinent?"

Amos didn't want to say what was on his mind, which was why are you running from the British who are not chasing you, but he didn't. "Sir, we paralleled the Wando before we crossed and saw no Redcoats on the road behind you."

Richardson started to say something but didn't. The pause gave Amos time to suggest a course of action. "Sir, we will work our way back to the bridge and see what the British are up to. My guess is that this may have been a foraging expedition since there are two plantations nearby that may have cattle and stored grain."

Richardson didn't like Amos' assessment. "Laredo, who sent you, and what are your orders?"

He took the orders from his map case and handed them to Richardson. "General Marion, sir. To my way of thinking, I did what I was tasked with. Now, I am free to do what General Greene has ordered: stop British Army foraging parties."

"You cannot do that without my permission, Major. Your men are assigned to me. If you go off on your own, I will have you court-martialed."

"Colonel, I think not. If it were not for my men, the remnants of the 9th Carolina Dragoons would not have been able to escape across the Wando River. Now, sir, I suggest you gather up your men, give them time to rest, and have another go at the British. Meanwhile, the 4th Carolina will do what General Greene intended, and that is keep the British Army bleeding and hungry."

Amos wheeled his Percheron and motioned at Pruett to follow him. Behind him, he could hear Colonel Richardson yelling that he would bring him up on charges of insubordination when he meets with General Marion.

A half a mile down the road, the survivors of the 9th Carolina Dragoons galloped up, and the 4th Carolina halted. Its commander rode up to Amos.

"Sir, I am Major Samuel Cooper, commander of the 9th Carolina." He touched the brim of his hat, as did Amos, who said nothing.

"Major Laredo, thank you for your action at the bridge. If the British had charged us, we would have been overwhelmed."

Amos nodded but said nothing to let Major Cooper continue. "Sir, if you'll have us, I'll place the 9th Carolina under your command. My only request is that you allow me to lead them into battle. Colonel Richardson would not let us scout and find the British, who surprised us by coming from two directions. We charged into the leading element of the British cavalry. We gave a good account of ourselves by forcing them to back off. But they outnumbered us four to one and had to retreat."

Amos looked over the group of men off to the side of the 4th Carolina. "How many men do you have?"

"Twenty-six plus me."

"Are they all fit?"

"Aye and itching to give the British a bloody nose."

Amos smiled. "Major, do me the honor of riding with me at the head of the column." Amos turned to Lieutenant Pruett. "Lieutenant Pruett!"

"Sir?"

"Introduce our men to Major Cooper's. As you do, check on their ammunition supply and weapons. Once that is done, have the 9th Carolina Dragoons form up as a unit at the end of our column."

Pruett rode off leaving Major Cooper alone with Amos. "Major, how much do you know about the 4th Carolina?"

"The unit has an excellent reputation and is feared by the British Army and their German friends. To them, you are ghosts that keep killing their soldiers. I suspect there is a price on your head."

"Aye, there is. It is up to £250 pounds. I want the British to keep raising it. Now, this is the way we fight."

Amos described the 4th Carolina's tactics and how they avoided fights like the one at Videau's Bridge. He also noted that his men all carry two rifled muskets, two pistols, and a sword. He deliberately didn't tell Cooper about von Korbach and the Germans guarding Dorchester or their stash of rifled muskets, powder and shot at Peaceville, and their hideout in the marshy land off Goose Creek. He wanted Cooper and his men to prove themselves before he told them everything.

CHAPTER 4

- INTO THE MOUTH OF THE LION

SHEERNESS, FIRST WEEK OF JANUARY 1782

Even though the sun peeked out between the puffy clouds that dotted the sky, it was still cold and damp. Afterall, this was English weather in the winter – damp, cold, and when it rained, raw. Today, it was just chilly with the thermometer on the binnacle saying it was a balmy 42^0 F.

As he pulled on his woolen coat in his cabin, Jaco couldn't help but wonder if he was sailing *Zephyr* into a well-planned trap. The three-masted schooner was built for speed and designed to carry passengers, their baggage, and some cargo. Its scantlings and bulwarks while sturdy, were not designed to take hits from cannon balls. Before sea trials, Jaco had the 6-pounders and their ammunition removed to reduce the vessel's weight by 8,000 pounds.

During trials, the brand-new ship easily cruised at 14 knots. Jaco believed that *Zephyr's* speed and his skill as a sailor was the schooner's best defense, not firepower.

The schooner's first mission was to carry John Jay, a member of the Continental Congress' Committee of Foreign Affairs and his secretary from Philadelphia to Brest as fast as possible. With that mission accomplished, his next task was to "collect" Henry Laurens from where he was being held in London and take him to Amsterdam.

His sailing orders and the chart showing the dock's location in Sheerness sat on the table in his cabin. They'd been given to him by John Jay in Brest after *Zephyr* crossed the Atlantic in less than a month.

Jay, Jaco suspected, was carrying instructions for Franklin now that negotiations with England were about to begin. Even though the war for independence continued, Jaco hoped peace might be on the horizon.

As Jaco buttoned his coat, he looked at the orders again, just to make sure that the wording hadn't changed. If needed, he could recite them from memory.

Captain Jacinto,

Now that you are underway from Brest, you are to sail directly to Sheerness which is part way up the Thames River. There, you will dock at the summer home of Charles Oswald. A chart showing the location of the summer home in Sheerness has been enclosed with this letter. By the time you arrive, Mr. Oswald will have instructed his household staff to support your requests for housing, horses, a carriage, provisions, clothing, etc. Mr. Oswald's staff will provide a guide to take you to Oswald House in the most expeditious manner.

The address of Mr. Oswald's house in London is 1 Lyndhurst Place in Hampstead. Those in Congress who have been to London tell me it is north of the Thames. A map to his house in London accompanies these orders, along with a chart showing the location of Sheerness and a pass granted by the British Foreign Ministry that gives Zephyr and its crew diplomatic privileges. We do not, unfortunately, know the veracity of any of these documents.

At Oswald House, you will gather Mr. Henry Laurens and his baggage, bring him to Sheerness and then transport him on Zephyr to Amsterdam as expeditiously as possible so he can assume his duties as our ambassador to the Dutch court. Your father assures us that you have met Mr. Laurens several times, and he will remember you. I feel it is necessary to remind you that before the war, Mr. Laurens was Mr. Oswald's business partner.

Mr. Laurens has been held prisoner in the Tower of London since his ship was taken by the Royal Navy in 1780. We have been assured by His Majesty that Mr. Laurens is in good health. Your mission came about when the Continental Congress agreed to exchange Lord Cornwallis for Mr. Laurens.

However, we do not trust Parliament, King George III, or many of his ministers, so the utmost discretion should be exercised when you collect Mr. Laurens and deliver him safely to Amsterdam.

Once you have taken Mr. Laurens to Amsterdam, return to Brest to collect any dispatches that must be brought back to Congress.

Good luck and Godspeed.
   Stephen Hopkins
   Co-Chairman
   Marine Committee

With John Adams already in France, Stephen Hopkins and Jaco's father were the co-chairmen of the Marine Committee. At the bottom of the page, he'd recognized his father's handwriting.

Jaco, please do not burn London down while gathering Mr. Laurens! J.J.

Jaco folded the hand-drawn diagram showing the dock's location at Oswald's summer house along the creases before walking onto the deck carrying the paper and his Dollond spyglass. The sun was starting to light the horizon, and a light but cold wind greeted Jaco who hated being cold.

Seeing Hedley Garrison on the quarterdeck and land over several miles away, "Mr. Garrison, are we close enough to put the boat in the water."

"Sir, I'd like to sail for another bell or so before we do. The men will get chilled to the bone in a long boat under sail."

Jaco looked around and, seeing all was ready, used one of his favorite words. "Perfecto."

"Any Royal Navy ships about?"

"No, sir. I find it strange because there is a Royal Navy base on the south side of the River Medway. Where we're going is just north of the river's mouth."

Jaco said nothing and looked at the whitecaps trying to gauge the wind direction and strength. As *Zephyr's* bow sliced through the choppy water, it sent cold spray that coated the deck and soaked those on the schooner's small quarterdeck – the quartermaster and his assistant, the bosun mate on watch, and Hedley Garrison. With Jaco on the platform as the fifth person, it made it crowded.

Jaco rested his elbow on the bulwark and studied the land between two and three points off the port bow, hoping to see the dock.

"Deck there. River mouth two points off the port bow. Ships are anchored on the south side. By their crosstrees, they are frigates."

Garrison looked up, "Deck, aye."

To Jaco, spotting the naval base meant their navigation was spot on. Now, they had to find the dammed dock just north of the river mouth. Jaco could see the tops of the masts of the Royal Navy frigates, which increased the knot in his stomach. Every foot *Zephyr* sailed on this course took it and his crew farther into the lion's den. When he sets out to collect Laurens in London, he will spend at least a day maybe two in the lion's mouth. Where he did not want to go was its stomach!

"Deck there. The dock is one point off the port bow at about two miles."

Jaco couldn't see it from the deck, but he trusted Landry sitting on the gaff boom of the main sail 40 feet above where he stood. His perch was a good 10 feet above the lookout platform.

"Mr. Garrison, I have the deck." Jaco waited for an acknowledgment before ordering. "Mr. Preston, launch the long boat. Then make sure all the three dagger boards are up and secured."

The bosun waved his acceptance of the two orders. The boat was held even with the top of the bulwark on the port or lee side of the ship. The last to board was Abner Jeffords, *Zephyr's* quartermaster. "Mr. Jeffords, once you get the mast up, we'll alter course to so' west by so' and head right toward the pier."

"Aye, cap'n. We'll get you good soundings and a good slate of the depths around the pier."

"Do that." Jaco waved, and the long boat started down toward the water as soon as Jeffords had both feet in the boat. The hand-drawn chart showed the water by the structure to be two fathoms or 12 feet at low tide. Jaco wanted to approach the dock from the south so that when they left, *Zephyr* could fall off the wind and sail away. By now, every man on the crew was on deck, ready to handle sails.

Earlier in this trip, once *Zephyr* was steady on a course due west away from the French coast, Jaco gathered the crew in the berthing area to outline why the ship changed course and what they were about to do.

When Lieutenant Geiger and Quartermaster Jeffords were recruiting a crew, they had many more volunteers from *Scorpion* than billets, even though there was no hope of prize money. All Jaco could offer was a chance to help their cause for freedom, adventure, and danger from the Royal Navy and the sea.

"Mr. Preston, loosen the jibs and all the mainsails to slow us to just faster than a crawl."

The bosun touched the back of his hand to his forehead. "Aye, captain. Dagger boards are secured, sir."

Zephyr slowed noticeably as the sheets to the three mainsails and the jib were let out. The masts and rigging groaned in protest as if to say, "We don't want to go slow." The long boat, with Jeffords in the stern, two men in the middle, and one in the bow, shot out in front of the schooner.

Jaco couldn't help but study the ships anchored in the River Medway. All had tightly furled sails; from what he could see, each ship had at least two anchors out with enough distance to allow them to swing as the tides went in and out.

Still, they could come out…

As *Zephyr* neared the coast, the water shallowed and turned from gray blue to brownish. Between studying the enemy frigates, Jaco watched the long boat as it maneuvered off the end of a small pier that jutted out into what really was the mouth of the River Thames. He was studying what he was sure was a large frigate with two gundecks when his first lieutenant, Morton Geiger called out. "The longboat is headed our way."

Jaco had the crew luff the sails to make getting the long boat aboard easier. Calm water on the leeward side let the crew quickly attach the cast iron shackles and hoist the longboat out of the water.

A smiling Jeffords strode up to his captain. "Cap'n, there's plenty of water around the pier. From where we are now, we can steer just to the south, luff her sails, and coast in. When we dock, we should have 12 – 15 feet under her keel."

Jaco nodded. "Quarterdeck, Mr. Jeffords is going to guide us in."

Zephyr and its crew were about to begin what was, in Jaco's mind, the most dangerous part of the mission. Once tied to the dock, the schooner could not use its speed to disappear in the vastness of the Atlantic.

Under Jeffords' expert guidance, the schooner ran out of speed just as the bow passed the middle of the T-shaped down. A man in a servant's uniform was hurrying down the wooden dock as members of *Zephyr's* crew tied lines to the bollards on the pier. On the deck, Bosun Preston had half the men securing the sails while the other stood behind the bulwarks with loaded rifled muskets primed but out of sight.

The servant stood with his hands clasped behind his back as Jaco waited for a gangway to be tied in place. He strode toward the servant, who was now joined by a black man and a woman from what he assumed was the household staff.

Clearing his throat, the servant said, "This is a private dock that can only be used by permission from the owner, Mr. Charles Oswald, I am Jared Cuthwaite, head of the household. Who may you be?"

"I am Jaco Jacinto, captain of the schooner *Zephyr*…"

By plan, no flags were flying from anywhere on the schooner.

"Are you the …"

Jaco smiled and interrupted as the man struggled for the right words. "… the rebels who are here to collect Mr. Oswald."

"Yes, those people. Welcome to Medway House."

"Aye, thank you. I have been told that someone in the household will guide us to Mr. Oswald's house in London. And, Sheerness will provide horses, a carriage and a wagon for Mr. Laurens's baggage."

"Yes, I will have the stable get them ready. How soon do you want to leave?"

"As soon as possible. I think it best if we don't dally around here any longer than is necessary."

"Yes, sir. I agree."

Cuthwaite nodded to the black man standing next to him. "Josiah Sims is Mr. Oswald's stable master and will accompany you. He knows the way to Oswald House better than any man, along with all the alternate routes. Do you want others from the household staff to accompany you?"

"I do. Can you provide a driver and coachmen for the carriage, a driver for the wagon and horses for myself and four of my sailors. One of my men will ride on the wagon."

"Aye, we have what you need. We need an hour to ready them, and I will have the staff put food for the horses and the men in the wagon."

"Will you be armed?"

"Yes, with pistols which will be holstered, and cutlasses in scabbards."

Cuthwaite cleared his throat. "Captain, sir, arms should not be needed. We have not seen any highwaymen in these parts for years. We are about five miles from the main road between London and Chatham which is in good shape and well-traveled. From there, it is about thirty-five miles to Oswald House. Plan on four hours from here to Westminster Bridge which is the shortest route. Once in London, it is a ruddy crawl through the crowded streets to Lyndhurst Place. You will, however, need money for tolls."

Jaco nodded. In the strongbox in his cabin, he had a purse full of English coins.

THE SAME DAY, 10:07 A.M.

While they waited for Cuthwaite to have the horses hitched and saddled, Jaco gathered Lieutenants Geiger and Garrison, Bosun Preston, and Quartermaster Jeffords in his cabin. He suspected those being left behind were unhappy. Still, they understood they had to keep *Zephyr* ready for sea and out of the Royal Navy's hands. If that meant going back to sea without the ship's captain and those ashore, then so be it.

Jaco concluded by saying, "We should be gone for no more than three days. After that time, unless someone brings word of a delay, assume we have been taken by the British, and you are to return to Brest. You are not, repeat not, to attempt our rescue."

"Do we know who is at the house?"

"No, but I suspect Mr. Oswald may have some staff."

"Do they know we are coming?"

"Supposedly, but not who or when."

Hedley Garrison tapped the table with his forefinger for emphasis. "Sir, you know that this could be a fool's errand and an attempt to capture a Continental Navy captain who has given the Royal Navy many a black eye."

"Aye, Mr. Garrison, I share your concern. If I read the tea leaves correctly, based on what Mr. Jay has told me, Lord North's government is in trouble. If or when it falls, official peace talks will start straightaway. Jay believes Laurens and Oswald have already agreed to most of the terms, so a treaty may be quickly concluded."

Morton Geiger looked at the other officers and then at Jaco. "Captain, I don't trust the British."

"Neither do I. But if we do not take the first steps to end this war, the killing will just continue. Mr. Geiger, I think the British are ready to quit."

Jaco placed five glasses from a rack in his cabin on the table. As he filled each glass with port, he handed one to each man who held his up. "Gentlemen, this is cause for a drink. I am unsure if we are celebrating a step that may bring peace or that the Royal Navy has created an elaborate ruse to get its tar-covered hands on Jaco Jacinto."

Geiger touched his glass to Jaco's. "To the first, not to the latter."

Jaco estimated that Josiah Sims was a head taller and a good 70 pounds heavier than he was. The man mounted his horse easily and waited for Jaco to bring his horse alongside at the head of the convoy.

The cold January sun didn't provide much warmth as Sims and Jaco rode on horses in the front and were followed by the carriage, then the wagon with Brandon Grantham next to the driver, Colin Landry, and four sailors on horseback.

Sims was not talkative other than to provide a commentary as they approached each bend in the road and the toll booths. He did learn by direct questions that Sims was brought to England by Oswald, taught math, and how to read and write. Sims had a notarized paper saying that when Oswald died, he, along with his wife and children who were servants at Medway House, would be free and British citizens.

To Jaco, there was no rhyme or reason to the amount charged at the toll booths on the road. Supposedly the rates were based on the number of people or wagons. At the second booth, he handed a two-pound note to the man expecting change.

When he received none in turn, Jaco was about to say something when he felt a hand on his arm. Sims shook his head slightly and nodded in the direction of the road. Once they were out of earshot, Sims turned to the American and said, "For this convoy, the tolls should have been one pound, five shillings. But I suspect the man either didn't have change or know how to make it. So, he didn't know what to do. By the cut of your coat, I suspect you or your rebel government can afford the extra cost."

Jaco didn't know what to say, so he said nothing. Just before they entered the city of London proper, another toll booth charged him £2, 10 shillings. The toll taker handed Jaco one gold, £1 coins, two five-shilling coins known as crowns as the change to his two-pound notes.

They had been on the road for three hours when Sims led them to a wide spot in the road to let the horses take a break. There were troughs for the horses to drink, and the Americans gathered around their leader and Sims.

"London is very crowded, and the streets are very narrow. Keep together, and we should be fine. We will cross the Thames at Westminster

Bridge and then pass the Parliament Building and the Admiralty on the fastest way to Oswald House."

LONDON, THE SAME DAY, 3:07 P.M.

Rear Admiral Stacey Davidson was hurrying to an appointment with his tailor when he stopped to let a column of the King's Household Cavalry pass. He looked down the road to see if more traffic was coming, and a rider on horseback caught his eye. The dark-haired man wearing a blue woolen coat looked familiar. Davidson stared, sure he had seen the face before, but struggled to place it.

Then Davidson realized he was seeing the devil himself. His head exploded as if it was hit by a canister ball. Jaco Jacinto!!! In London!!!

Sims had stopped the convoy to let the King's Household Cavalry pass. The delay allowed Davidson to step in front of the man on horseback he believed was Jaco Jacinto.

Davidson held up his hand. "Captain Jacinto, pray tell, sir, what mischief are you planning for London?"

Jaco rested his hands on the pommel of his horse and leaned forward. "Forgive me, admiral, I don't believe we've met. Who are you?"

"Rear Admiral Stacey Davidson. We met at the business end of our cannons when I was the captain of His Majesty's Ship *Puritan*, and Darren Smythe was my First Lieutenant."

Jaco's eyes flashed recognition. Through letters back and forth with his fiancée, Reyna Laredo, he'd learned that Darren was now captain of the *Pompeii*. "Sir, on what are you basing your assumption?"

"Off the island of Islay in January 1778, you were the captain of the rebel frigate named *Scorpion* that gave my little squadron a lesson in seamanship and gunnery. Darren pointed you out, and through my spyglass, I saw your face quite clearly."

"Is Darren well?" By asking the question, Jaco admitted his identity.

"As far as I know, he is and is now a captain of a fifth rater. Again, why, sir, are you in London and out of uniform? I could have you arrested as a spy."

"Admiral, I think not. If you did, the arrest would create an awful smelly mess that would embarrass you."

"Enlighten me."

"In one of my saddle bags, I have documents giving my men and me safe passage to travel to London to collect a fellow citizen being exchanged for your Lord Cornwallis. My mission here is diplomatic and will, I believe end this dammed war. I didn't think riding around London in a Continental Navy uniform would be helpful."

Davidson forced himself not to chuckle. "You're bluffing."

Jaco sighed and said, "I can show you my pass signed by an assistant secretary in the Foreign Ministry. It is in my saddlebag."

"May I ask where you are going?"

"Sir, you may ask, but I am not obligated to tell you. Now, do you want to see my pass or not. If not, we'd like to be on our way."

Davidson patted the neck of the horse as he edged closer to Jaco. He motioned for Jaco to bend down so he could speak softly. "Captain, after this dammed war is over, I wish to break bread with you and have Darren join us. We have much to discuss and should be friends, not enemies."

Jaco smiled. *Admiral, I wonder if you know that Darren is madly in love with a woman from Charleston whom I've known since childhood and is one of my fiancé's closest friends. And she passes on every tidbit of intelligence she can glean from Darren's letters.* "Admiral Davidson, sir, that is a capital idea. And, with a bit of luck, it may happen before we are old and gray."

Davidson stepped back. "I'll drink to that. Now, be on your way, and please do not burn my city down."

Jaco laughed. Davidson was the second person who said that to him. *Maybe they know me all too well.*

LONDON, THE SAME DAY, 3:57 P.M.

The sun was setting when Jaco knocked on the door of Oswald House. When no one answered his hard raps on the oak door, Sims led the wagon, Landry, and the other sailors around to the back of the house.

A liveried butler opened the door, clearly not expecting anyone to call after tea. His annoyance showed in his demeanor and tone of voice as he looked Jaco up and down, ready to dismiss him as an unwanted peddler. "Who are you?"

"Captain Jaco Jacinto, Continental Navy. I am here to take Mr. Henry Laurens of Charleston, South Carolina, to Amsterdam so he may resume his mission as the United States Consul to The Netherlands. Mr. Laurens should recognize me, although I was a few years younger the last time we met. I also have a letter of introduction from Mr. John Jay."

The butler started to close the door, but Jaco put his foot in the door jamb to prevent it from being closed. "I'll wait inside, even if you mind."

"That is highly irregular, Captain J…. "The butler struggled with his last name."

"Sir, my last name is pronounced hay-cento. And we live in very unusual times. Once you bring me to Mr. Laurens, I suggest you assign your staff to help Mr. Josiah Sims and my men load Mr. Laurens' baggage."

The butler recoiled. "You are planning to leave immediately?"

"We, that is Mr. Laurens and the men who came with me, need to leave as soon as we can."

Pointing to the anteroom just inside the door, the butler said, "Wait there," and walked off, shaking his head and muttering.

Jaco was looking at the paintings on the wall when he heard a booming voice. "My God, Jaco, it is good to see you. I heard you were doing well in the Navy. A captain now, well done lad! How is your father?"

"Sir, he is well."

"Good, good. I don't have much in the way of baggage. It should all fit into three chests in my room. The British seized the ship, and my baggage was, I believe, sold off. I only have what I have collected since I have been here, and my servant can pack them quickly. How soon do you want to leave?"

"As soon as we can."

"Excellent. I should be ready to go within half an hour. I'll instruct the staff to feed your men so we can travel on a full stomach. Where is your ship?"

"I will tell you later. We won't get there until late tonight."

Laurens nodded. "I need to write my friend Charles Oswald a thank you note for his hospitality and efforts on my behalf, and then we shall be off."

ON THE ROAD BACK TO SHEERNESS, 11:29 P.M.

Sims suggested that since Mr. Laurens' baggage would fit in the boot of the carriage, they leave the wagon in London, and the men who manned the wagon could ride on horseback, and Mr. Laurens' servant would ride next to the coachman.

Instead, Jaco turned to Landry and Grantham. "You two ride inside the carriage with Mr. Laurens. Do not allow anyone to capture him."

With that, they slid the weapons the two men carried into the carriage, and the group set off on streets emptier than when they arrived. At the last toll booth, Sims had to wake the toll taker. Jaco flipped him four Crown coins and two, five-shilling pieces this time. The man nodded, and the group was off with less than 10 miles to go.

The convoy was about a mile from the road to Medway House when their path was blocked by two logs across the highway. Sims started to dismount when two men appeared out of the trees. Both carried short muskets with the end of the barrel flared noticeably which, even in the dark identified them as blunderbusses. Both men pointed the weapons at Jaco. "Don't get down. Just drop your purses on the ground and instruct the men in the carriage to do the same. If you do, no harm will come to you. If you don't, me and my mates will do you in."

Jaco eased his horse forward, causing one of the highwaymen to back up. The speaker waved his weapon back and forth. "What are you doing?"

"Coming closer so I can hand you my purse with just a few gold sovereigns left. The rest went to toll takers."

One man with the blunderbuss laughed. "Them's the real highwaymen. They take everyone's money."

Jaco waved the purse to make the coins jingle and focus the attention of the man with the gun. A loud gasp caused the highwayman by his horse to turn toward his mate, only to see Landry pulling his cutlass out of the man's midsection. It was the last thing the man saw as Jaco buried the small blade of his tomahawk in the second man's head.

Sims asked Landry as he got down from his horse. "Did you see any more?"

"No, sir. They were bluffing because if they had more, they would have stuck their muskets in our faces."

Jaco asked Oswald's stable master. "Do you know these men?"

"No. There have been rumors that a pair were in the area, but no one has seen them for a week or so. I'll move the logs and send someone from the staff to arrange a proper burial in the morning. There's a pauper's cemetery in Chatham, and no one will miss them or ask questions once it is known that they were out to rob one of Mr. Oswald's guests."

The middle watch had just begun when Jaco stood at the dock end of the gangplank that was ready to be hauled aboard. He held out his hand. "Mr. Sims, thank you for a job well done, and thank Mr. Cuthwaite for his help. There is no need to wake him."

Minutes later, *Zephyr* was under full sail on a beam reach headed nor' nor' est. Destination – Amsterdam.

CHAPTER 5

– WHAT WILL THE FUTURE BRING?

CHARLESTON, SECOND WEEK OF JANUARY 1782

Lieutenant Colonel Rafer Muir stared at the map held down on the table by lead weights made from canister balls, heated, and then flattened on one side. On the copy of the same 1775 Sayer/Bennett chart Amos Laredo used, Rawdon's staff had placed red-coated toy soldiers where British Army and German units were. A solitary soldier in a light blue coat was positioned north of Dorchester, where Corporal Thornton said the 4th Carolina was bivouacked.

Muir was in what used to be the dining room of the three-story home that was now the headquarters of Lord Islay and the two Scottish infantry regiments in Charleston – the 11th and 42nd. The Loyalist owners of the home had moved into what used to be the servant's quarters next to the small stable at the back of the house.

In recognition of the sunlight, Muir blew out the candle in the lantern he was using to cast light over the map. Nothing in his mind had changed since his initial analysis. This effort, like each one before, would turn into a bloody affair.

With its victory at Yorktown, Muir was convinced the Continental Army was emboldened and spoiling for a fight in which they would inflict another defeat on the British Army. No longer was British Army experience, training, and firepower enough to carry the day. The rebels, as his generals called them, were now every bit as good as the British Army.

The events leading to being ordered to plan another re-supply effort were as predictable as the sun coming up. There was now enough sunlight so that the toy soldiers, each representing a regiment of British or German troops, were casting shadows on the map.

Lord Islay had bought the molded lead soldiers from a toymaker in London who had painted their faces and given some red coats and white breeches for the British Army and dark blue for the German regiments. The soldiers representing the Highlanders wore dark blue-green kilts.

Each cannon on the map represented a battery of artillery, and each horseman, a troop of dragoons. Off in the corner of the table, there was a grouping of figures painted light blue. They were supposed to represent the enemy, but Muir had taken all but one off because the British Army did not have accurate intelligence of where General Greene and the Continental Army were or its strength.

By only putting one light blue soldier on the map, Muir gently reminded Lord Islay what little they knew about the enemy. Today, he was supposed to discuss his plan to march 80 miles through rebel-held territory to Fort Granby. Once the fort was burned, the garrison would join Islay's column, move south to Fort Motte, and repeat the process. General Leslie's objective was to bring every British Army and Loyalist unit in South Carolina to the place he called Charles Town.

Muir responded to a sharp knock on the door. "Come in."

A young lieutenant on Lord Islay's staff opened the door holding a tray. "Sir, I thought you'd like a breakfast of bacon and eggs and some tea."

"What's in the bowl?"

"Something the locals call hominy that I know you like with a pat of butter on the top."

"Thank you, Lieutenant MacRae. Please put it down on the side table."

MacRae did as he was told and then turned to his superior officer. "Lord Islay will be served breakfast in a few minutes."

This was MacRae's way of saying Muir had time to eat.

The young lieutenant who grew up near Aberdeen, had a Scotch brogue as thick as the hominy grits. He'd arrived along with almost a thousand other replacements after Cornwallis surrendered. MacRae glanced at the map. "Sir, are we going after the rebels in the interior?"

Muir almost said, "I am not sure if the rebels are going after the British Army, or the British Army is going after the rebels." But he didn't. Instead, he said, "Aye, MacRae, we're going to bring our soldiers back from the forts up north."

Satisfied, MacRae left Muir alone with his breakfast, thoughts, and the map.

After breakfast, Muir needed less than 20 minutes to explain his plan to Lord Islay. The British Army's options were dictated by the two roads.

When he was finished, Lord Islay understood Muir's plan's geographic and operational constraints. He confided that what was holding Leslie back was the arrival of promised reinforcements. A thousand more men should arrive sometime in early February. "So, Muir, what say you about the chances of finding the 4th Carolina and destroying its base?"

"Sir, I have little doubt we will find the 4th Carolina. But, my lord, I think they and their musket balls will find more of us than ours will find them."

Lord Islay wanted the private meeting to get Muir's candid opinion without it being filtered and heard by his staff.

"Colonel, something is eating at you about this operation, tell me."

"Sir, we owe it to our men to attempt to negotiate a deal with the rebels to let our men march back to Charleston without fear of being attacked. We could agree not to conduct offensive operations if they agree not to attack us. We could even promise to leave."

"You think the rebel General Greene would agree?"

"Sir, I do. It is a bloodless victory for him. For us, we get stronger because we have all our men here in Charleston." Muir wanted to add to be evacuated but didn't dare.

"And if General Greene doesn't agree to this parlay you propose, then what?"

"We follow my plan, or another General Leslie may prefer. If we want to rescue our men, we need more than two regiments of foot and a squadron of dragoons to succeed. Mark my words, my Lord, without an agreement, this will be a bloody affair."

Lord Islay nodded his head. The battle in which the 11th (Highland) Regiment of Foot, augmented by a battery of artillery and the 200-plus Loyalists in the Green Dragoons, attacked Dorchester was still fresh in his mind. That day, the 4th Carolina decimated the Green Dragoons, and the 11th lost over 200 men.

"Your plan is a good one, and I agree, we should convince General Leslie to try to work out a temporary truce with General Greene."

Later in the morning, General Leslie was adamant. He would not, under any circumstance, attempt to negotiate a truce with General Greene. He believed such an agreement was tantamount to surrender. He added two more infantry regiments, one Hessian and one British, to augment the force and approved Muir's plan.

As the two officers left Leslie's headquarters, Lord Islay pointed to a rampart overlooking the Ashley River on Charleston's west side. Seeing the two senior officers, the British soldiers manning the battery moved out of the way to give the two senior officers privacy.

Islay faced the river so none of their words would carry to those wanting to overhear what was said. "Muir, we've been together for over a decade. Out with it, man! What is on your mind?"

"My lord, may I speak very candidly?"

"Aye, that is why we are here."

"My lord, nothing I am about to say is meant to sound disloyal, but continuing this war is utter madness. The rebels don't want us around and will fight us for as long as it takes to win. The whole war reminds me of when our Scottish forbears under William Wallace fought Edward I for our independence. We lost, and many died on both sides. Frankly, sir, I think we should leave and let the rebels have a go at governing themselves. If they cock it up, then we can offer to help and even bring them back into the Empire. Continuing to fight these rebels is foolish, no, I take that back. It is the height of stupidity. Many of our lads will be maimed or killed. Again, for what? The rebels will win in the end because they are willing to die for the same freedoms we enjoy."

"You know, Muir, one could take your comments as defeatist."

"Sir, I think I am a realist. If you want, you can cashier me out of the Army and cost me my pension."

"I could, but I won't. This war has gotten to you. Some might say you've gone native. You like Charleston, don't you."

"I do, sir. After many of the shite holes you and I have been to in the British Army, Charleston is quite nice. And, sir, I serve at your pleasure, so if you want me to go on half pay, I will do so immediately."

"No, Rafer, I do not want you to retire. I need you, and the British Army needs you. However, like you, I question why we are here, and I suspect this will be our last campaign in South Carolina. Peace, I believe, may be coming. In the meantime, I need you to do your duty."

Muir nodded gently. "That, my lord, I will do to the best of my ability."

Lord Islay turned to face his subordinate. "That is all England, and I can ask."

SO' WEST OF THE CANARY ISLANDS, THIRD WEEK OF JANUARY 1782

Sensing that the weather had changed from the dreary cold of the Celtic Sea and the waters off western France, Emily Smythe Burdette forwent one of the woolen sweaters she'd worn since *Star of India* left London. Instead, she pulled on a light blue busk over her linen top and slipped out of their midship cabin just below the main deck.

Her husband Francis was still asleep when she gently closed the sliding oak door. Francis had been seasick for the first week after the East Indiaman left the Thames estuary. Now, toward the end of the second week of their voyage, he'd been able to keep food down. Last night, Francis and the other male passengers were invited to drink with the captain, and Emily suspected that Francis had more than he should.

Emily didn't care if Francis was indisposed and hung over. She was drunk on the excitement of the trip. For the first time in her life, she was outside of England. Emily wanted to visit France to practice the French she studied hard to learn in school but hadn't. The family tradition was that the wives kept the Smythe & Sons books which is why she was allowed to attend school. Education made her different than other women she knew whose responsibilities were to have and raise children and, if wealthy, run the household.

A light breeze greeted Emily as she emerged from the shelter of the companionway and stepped onto the main deck. It was cool enough to give her goosebumps. The wind was from the so' west and had the *Star of India* heeled to starboard.

The merchant ship was one of 20 surrounded by Royal Navy ships in a convoy led by *Lenox, a* 74-gun three-decker. Emily knew the names of the other three-decker *Warspite* and the two, two 64s, *Dilletante* and *Stirling Cross*, only because her brother gave her a list of all the escorts. The three-deckers defined the front two corners of the box in which the merchant ships sailed and set the pace while the 64s were at the aft corners.

Darren Smythe's *Pompeii* was assigned to scout for French and Spanish squadrons that might want to capture the convoy's ships carrying supplies, reinforcements for the British Army, and goods to sell in North America. He told her that once the convoy passed Bermuda, some vessels would head north to New York, some would sail so' west to British-held islands in the Caribbean, while the majority would head for Charleston and Savannah.

She did not know if *Pompeii* would be one of the escorts that would accompany *Star of India* to Charleston. As much as she loved her brother and wanted to see more of him, Emily's mission given to her by her mother was to evaluate Melody Winters. Without Darren hovering about, Emily was confident that she could take the measure of the woman Darren loved.

In a locked jewelry box in one of her trunks, she had a letter of introduction to Melody written and sealed by her brother. Darren would not tell his sister what was in the letter, but when they met for the first time, she was supposed to give the letter to Melody.

Her father wanted Emily's husband, Francis Burdette to finalize a licensing agreement with Dr. Reyna Laredo that would give Smythe & Sons license to manufacture her designs. The contract, Lester hoped, would give Dr. Laredo the option of becoming the Smythe & Sons distributor for the new country that the elder Smythe was sure would soon be independent.

Every morning, weather permitting, Emily set out in long, purposeful strides up and down the main deck between the aft end, which was the entrance to the captain's cabin, and the beak of the ship, which was the bow. *Star of India* was, according to its captain, an 1,150-ton, 150-foot-long merchant ship. By her count, 120 feet or roughly 48 paces between his cabin and the forecastle were available for her morning exercise.

Emily walked vigorously for at least an hour beginning at six bells on the Morning Watch, which was, as her brother taught her, 7:30 a.m. When eight bells rang – four pairs of two rings of the ship's bell – the watch changed, and she continued until a single bell rang, telling her that the first 30 minutes of the Forenoon Watch had passed, at which time she'd been walking for an hour, and it was 8:30 a.m.

After her morning walk, Emily liked to read. Even though she had not requested one, the crew provided a chair from an empty cabin that let her sit on the lee (downwind) side of the deck and read.

In her chest, she had a copy of Voltaire's *Candide* in French printed in 1759. She brought a French-to-English dictionary to help, thinking this was an excellent way to improve her French. Next to it in the chest was Henry Fielding's *Tom Jones*, printed in 1753, four years after the book was initially published. Emily found a 1778 edition of Francis Burney's *Evalina* in a London bookshop the day before she and her husband boarded *Star of India*, and it, too was in her chest.

Her most prized possession from the visit to the bookstore was a collection of books containing much of Eliza Haywood's work. One was titled *Giving Way to Passion*, a bound collection of novellas written between 1720 and 1723. She also bought the three volumes of Haywood's writing called *The Works* printed in 1724, and *Secret Histories, Novels, Etc.*, published in 1727.

Haywood was a prolific writer of over 70 romance novels, and Emily Burdette was an ardent fan. In addition to her popular novels, when Haywood died in 1753, she left a rich collection of articles on the importance of education to women and gaining acceptance in the workplace. Haywood's ideas resonated with Emily and her mother, who disliked the arbitrary constraints imposed on women by British society.

Darren told her she would meet three fascinating women in Charleston. Shoshana Jacinto, an attorney, and a member of the South Carolina bar. Dr. Reyna Laredo, as in medical doctor, was the fiancée of a Continental Navy Captain, Jaco Jacinto. And then there was the love of his life, Melody Winters, who spoke seven languages. When the war ended, she would be a professor of languages at the College of Charleston. Emily Smythe Burdette wanted to meet these women. She admitted to herself that she was jealous that women in the rebellious colonies had opportunities not available to women in England.

Finished with her morning walk, Emily ignored the leather-bound copy of Jonathan Swift's *Gulliver's Travels* printed in 1726 that she had wedged into a small space between the main mast and a rack of belaying pins and looked at the sea. She scanned from horizon to horizon, admiring the ships escorting her on this grand adventure to Charleston and wondering what the future would bring.

CHAPTER 6

– JUSTICE SERVED

SAVANNAH, THIRD WEEK OF JANUARY 1782

Shoshana sat quietly at the table set aside for the defense, looking at but not focusing on the empty bench where Judge St. James would sit. Her mind was rehearsing the points she would make in her opening argument.

Next to her was Saul, who had carefully arranged the papers in the sequence that Shoshana wanted. David Fonseca sat beside Saul and his father Jorge at the table's far end.

Behind the defendant's table, the Fonsecas did their part which was to pack as many friends and family members into the courtroom as there were seats. Theoretically, they had no role in the trial other than those Shoshana intended to call as witnesses. Their reactions to the points she makes in her client's defense might be noticed by the jury of 12 men.

Five paces to the right side of the defendant's table, Ebenezer Lozenge, a Colony of New York prosecutor, and a staunch Loyalist, sat with his hands clasped, forearms resting on the table's edge. When he entered, the New Yorker smiled at Shoshana as if to say, "Young lady, you do not have a chance against the great Frederick Lozenge and you are about to be schooled in the law."

Fredrick Blaze noticed none of this as he emptied a leather pouch of its documents and placed them on the table. Then, Lozenge re-arranged them three times until he was satisfied.

Lozenge was a round man in his fifties whose contemptuous attitude toward Shoshana was that of a schoolmaster about to administer a painful lesson to one of his students. Each time he addressed Shoshana in their pre-trial meeting with St. James, Lozenge never stood because at 5' 5", if they were both standing, Shoshana would tower over him.

For her part, Shoshana played to Lozenge's ego as if she was a law intern gobbling up wisdom from a legal legend. The broad smile and feigned impression that Lozenge was dispensing valuable knowledge hid Shoshana's determination to win a not-guilty verdict for her client.

While waiting for Judge St. James to enter, David leaned across in front of Saul and touched her arm to get her attention. "Shoshana, did I ever tell you that you are the most beautiful woman in the world."

Shoshana blushed as she tried to stay focused on the moment. The large clock in the corner of the room bonged and the bailiff's command "All rise" brought her back to reality.

Wendell St. James looked far different than when Shoshana first met him in his office. Now, he was wearing his white judicial wig that flowed down to his shoulders and his black robe and wide white collar tied around the neck. He sat in the chair behind the elevated desk, looked around the courtroom, and banged the gavel. "Let the case of His Majesty King George III and England's Royal Province of Georgia versus Jorge and David Fonseca begin. Counselors, are you ready?"

The judge looked at the prosecutor from New York, who had a hooked nose that resembled a vulture's beak. Lozenge was wearing a white powdered wig with hair down to his shoulders. Each time Shoshana looked at Ebenezer Lozenge, she had to force herself to keep from laughing.

As was her option, Shoshana eschewed the wig since it reminded her of the country preventing independence. As a precaution, she did ask Judge St. James what he preferred women attorneys to wear. He thought momentarily before saying, "I have never had a woman argue from either side in my court. Wear something presentable." When she left the office, she wondered what presentable meant but didn't ask the man for a definition.

Lozenge stood up. "Aye, your honor. We are ready to proceed and promise not to waste the court's time."

Really? Shoshana stood and nodded emphatically in the direction of the jury before speaking, "The defense is ready. We will provide facts to support our arguments so the jury can make an informed decision."

Before St. James could speak, Lozenge stood, faced the jury and then the judge before addressing Judge St. James. "Before I begin my opening argument, I feel it my duty to make both the court and the jury aware that it is most unusual for a woman to defend a man in a court of law. As …."

The word "objection" came out of Shoshana's mouth as she stood. "Your honor, my sex has nothing to do with my legal skills, which I have demonstrated to you in our discussions over motions. I think the jury would find it helpful to know that on my motions, you sided with my legal arguments rather than those put forward by Mr. Lozenge and Mr. Blaze. That is point one. Point two is we all know that men are anatomically different from women, but in the eyes of the court, we should be equal. So, while I will agree with Mr. Lozenge that women are not equal to men in many physical respects, such as strength. Nonetheless, men are not equal to women because they cannot have babies. So, the man versus woman has no merit. However, if my esteemed colleague Mr. Lozenge insists on demonstrating the superiority of men, I propose to put this matter to rest via a simple test of manly skills."

Judge St. James, while not expecting Shoshana's statement, was not surprised, and smiled, thinking that this would be interesting. "Counselor, what do you propose?"

"A duel in which neither of us is hurt, except maybe our egos."

There were chuckles from the jury and the spectators. Shoshana looked at Lozenge but was addressing Judge St. James. "In addition to Mr. Lozenge's skills as a prosecutor, he is also the victor of several pistol duels, so I am sure he would consider pistols at twenty-five yards fired at targets a fair test of his shooting skills. He should easily be able to defeat a mere woman such as I."

Judge St. James tilted his head toward Lozenge. "Mr. Lozenge, are you game?"

"Of course! I will be a gentleman and allow my opponent to choose her own weapons as I have mine."

"Then it is agreed, pistols aimed at twelve-inch targets twenty-five yards. I am adding a requirement of five balls to eliminate any luck. On the north side of this building, there is an embankment by the river so that any misses will either hit the soil or fly into the river. We will reconvene there in two hours to give time to the duelists ample opportunity to retrieve their weapons and the bailiff to put up the targets."

Wendell St. James pounded the gavel.

SAVANNAH, THE SAME DAY, 1:16 P.M.

While Shoshana was pouring powder down one of the two rifled pistols her father had given her for self-defense, David stood holding the .40 caliber balls. "Shoshana, are you sure you want to do this? He may be an expert shot."

"David, the point is not who wins the duel but the fact that I can compete with men. Anyway, if Baba Miriam learns I lost to a man using one of the pistols her shop made, I will hear about it for the rest of her life. So, the pressure is not from Lozenge or the court but from within me. I know I am a pioneer, so I must prove myself every step of the way."

She pushed the lead ball wrapped in waxed paper into the mouth of the barrel and used the loading rod to push the ball hard against the powder. With the ball seated, she primed the pan and closed the cover as she again checked the flint to ensure there was enough stone to create a spark. Each pistol was placed back in the wooden case with the powder flask, bullet mold, spare flints, and a dozen one-ounce lead balls.

The bailiff had placed two boards on the grass in front of each to mark where the shooters should stand. In front of the embankment, 25 paces in front of the shooter's marks, he placed two rough cut planks on which he had drawn the required circle with a white three-inch diameter circle filled with white chalk.

Shoshana put the felt-lined case, built from red oak by a Charleston craftsman, with the two pistols on the table. She noticed Ebenezer Lozenge had done the same.

Judge St. James strode in front of the two contestants. "Again, the rules. One shoots, then the other. Five balls and the one with the most hits closest to the circle's center is the winner."

The judge used the palm of his hand to point toward the firing line. Lozenge spoke in his usual snide, condescending tone. "I'll repeat what I said earlier that as a gentleman, I'll allow the young lady to shoot first."

"My pleasure." Shoshana took one of her pistols from the box and checked the powder in the pan. Keeping the barrel pointed at the ground, she strode to the firing line before she pulled the hammer back to full-cock, just as her father taught her. With the sights aligned, Shoshana pulled back on the heavy trigger. The frizzen snapped down, sending sparks into the pan, and milliseconds later, the pistol fired. A tongue of red flame shot out of the barrel, along with a cloud of white smoke.

The three scorekeepers ran out, looked at the plank, and then stepped back to their position well to the side of the targets. One yelled, "Hit well inside the circle." A piece of charcoal was used to make an X over the hole.

Shoshana was smiling as she turned to Ebenezer Lozenge. "Your turn."

Lozenge stood sideways in the traditional dueling position and pointed the pistol at the target. His pistol barked.

Hit on the line of the circle was the report yelled back to the shooters.

Shoshana's tone was conciliatory. "Mr. Lozenge, bad luck. The wind is a bit gusty."

There was little wind, and at 25 yards, the light breeze would not have much, if any, effect on the flight of the ball. Her second ball also hit well inside the chalk circle. Lozenge's ball made a hole just outside the chalk circle, and he said nothing as he reloaded both his pistols.

David handed Shoshana a ball from the case after she poured in the powder. "These don't have any mold marks. Why?"

"Because my father taught me to file them off so each shot flies true."

David's eyes opened in surprise. He said nothing as Shoshana finished reloading both pistols. Her third and fourth shots all caused chalk from the bullseye to fly. All four were in a group about six inches in diameter close to the center. Lozenge's third missed the board as it flew low and wide, kicking a puff of dirt.

"Judge St. James, I concede. Ms. Jacinto has four in the circle, and I only have two. There is no way I can win, so there is no need to fire a fifth ball."

The judge looked at Shoshana, who had fire in her eyes that softened as she spoke. "One, the match calls for five balls each, so I say we fire all five and then compute the score by adding the distance from the center of the target. I believe we can measure how wide of the mark Mr. Lozenge's third shot went."

Wendell St. James nodded his head noticeably. "Five balls it is, and the measurement. Please reload."

Lozenge's fifth ball was high and wide and barely clipped the wood. Shoshana's last shot was in the center of the other four.

SAVANNAH, THE SAME DAY, 3:33 P.M.

Back in the courtroom, Judge St. James announced the score. All five of Shoshana's balls hit within three inches of the center of the target. Only three fired by Lozenge were inside the circle, and none were as close as Shoshana's. Once he finished, Judge St. James pointed to Ebenezer Lozenge, saying, "Mr. Lozenge, please present your opening statement."

Lozenge's long-winded opening argument was one part lecture on the value of loyalty to the king and one part a summary of the government's case. He contended that since the Fonsecas supported the rebel cause, they were, by definition, traitors. As Jews, they were experts at fleecing the good citizens of Georgia to help finance a revolution. Satisfied, he sat down and looked at Shoshana as if to say, top that.

Shoshana wore a dark blue busk that came down to her ankles over a white linen blouse. The navy-blue color was chosen to honor her brother. Around her neck, she wore a simple necklace a Cherokee Indian gave her as a 16th birthday present. Today, her sandy brown hair was in a loose ponytail that flared at her shoulders. She was, the men in the jury box noticed, as did those in the audience, more than "presentable." Shoshana was beautiful.

Slowly walking toward the open area between the jury, the judge's raised bench, and the terraced jury box, Shoshana could feel the 12 pairs of eyes on her. Some of the jurors had quizzical looks on their faces. In a flash, she decided to play on that to open their minds.

"My name is Shoshana Jacinto, and I was born and raised in Charleston, just 90 miles up the coast." She paused to let the contrast sink in that she was a neighbor, not some stranger from 1,000 miles away in New York. "My family has been in South Carolina for over seventy years. We have friends in Savannah, and my clients are competitors to my family's business. I am honored by the Fonseca's faith in my skill as an attorney, which is why I am standing before you."

Shoshana nodded slightly as she spoke. "This morning, you all witnessed a test of manly skills. I was shooting to prove that my arguments would be right on target while my opponent's, like his pistol balls, would be far to the right and low or high and wide. As this trial progresses, I will provide you with facts that prove my clients, David and Jorge Fonseca are not guilty of anything other than being astute businessmen who, for generations, have been valued members of the Savannah community."

She took several steps toward the jury box. "The prosecutor brings up our religion; yes, I am a Jewess. One's religion – Catholic, Lutheran,

Anglican, Jewish, or Muslim – is not an indicator of wrongdoing. We all believe in God, just not in the same way."

The faces of the men in the jury box told her that her reasoning was being evaluated, maybe even accepted. Confident, Shoshana spoke slowly, measuring each word and looking at each jury member as she spoke. "For the record, I am a very eligible woman, and so far, no man has captured my heart, and I will not agree to an arranged marriage."

Shoshana saw the smiles on the men with daughters and wanted the best for them. "I'm also the first woman to be allowed to appear in court in South Carolina. I did so without going to one of the law schools in England, which don't allow women. Instead, I started as an apprentice, and I learned the law and how it is applied with the help of two men. This is important since what I am about to share with you are neither high and wide nor low and off-center accusations but simple facts of law."

She turned toward her table, and Saul held up two pieces of paper. "First, the accusation and charge that my clients were conducting illegal trade and fleecing the citizens of Savannah have no basis in either English law or that adapted by the Royal Colony of Georgia. When David Fonseca was arrested, he was reviewing a contract and bill of exchange bringing a shipment of cinnamon, turmeric, cumin, and other spices from Morocco to Savannah on a Swedish-registered ship. That is not illegal."

Shoshana exuded confidence when she handed the documents to Judge St. James, who had already seen them. "Judge St. James, may I pass them on to the jury?" He nodded his assent, and Shoshana waited until each juror looked at the papers before the jury foreman handed them back to her.

Saul handed Shoshana three more sheets. "Let us dispense with the accusation the Fonsecas were overcharging the citizens of Savannah first. This is just one of many invoices of those spices sold by the Fonsecas to a store here in Savannah." She held up a second sheet. "This is an invoice from the duly chartered British East India Company for those same spices in the same quantities billed to a different business here in Savannah. This shipment arrived less than a week before my clients were arrested."

Shoshana looked at the judge, who held out his hand. He glanced at them and handed them back. "May I share them with the jury?"

"You may."

She handed both sheets to the foreman of the jury. "You'll notice the prices from the British East India Company are almost three times that which the Fonsecas charged."

"Objection.... The amount charged by one company versus another is irrelevant. Two invoices by themselves are not a trend."

"Really, Mr. Lozenge. How else do you determine who is overcharging and who is not, except by comparing two invoices from different companies for the same goods sold at the same time?" Shoshana turned to Saul, who handed her a stack of papers. "Your honor, these are eight different invoices that show the difference in prices charged by my client versus other importers. In each case, Fonseca's prices were the lowest. The defense believes the jury should see these invoices."

"Objection."

"Overruled. Please continue, Miss Jacinto, and give the jury the invoices."

Lozenge wasn't finished. "I demand to know the origin of those invoices and how they were obtained. For all we know, they could have been purloined, forged, or both."

Judge St. James looked down at Shoshana. "Mr. Lozenge brings up a fair point. How did you obtain them?"

"I asked the purchasers to provide them. They have nothing to hide. While they are not happy that the Fonsecas can sell spices from Morocco at better prices than the British East India Company offers, they have no recourse. They have contracts that require them to buy from an English company. Other than, of course, to encourage the Royal Governor to use the courts to put the Fonseca's out of business. On the other hand, the Fonsecas have no such contractual obligation and are free to buy from whomever they choose."

"Objection, that is a baseless accusation."

"I am aware of the contract terms of the British East India Company. Ms. Jacinto, please explain your theory before I rule on Mr. Lozenge's second objection?"

"With pleasure, sir. Mohammed III, the Sultan of Morocco, granted traders in the Thirteen Colonies favorable concessions. Unfortunately, the Sultan is not a fan of the British or the East India Company, and, therefore, does not enjoy the same pricing and terms given to traders in the Thirteen Colonies, such as the Fonsecas. So, if I were a competitor of the Fonsecas in these trying times, I would explore every avenue to take away any advantage they have. Putting one's competitor in jail is one option. Killing is another. So, it is logical to ask the prosecutor if any of Mr. Fonseca's competitors encouraged him to file charges."

Lozenge jumped to his feet. "Objection, the prosecutor and the Royal Colony of Georgia are not on trial. The Fonseca's are."

"It is, however, a fair question. Overruled. Mr. Blaze, please answer the question. Do I have to put you under oath, or will you answer it truthfully?"

Fredrick Blaze looked first at the jury and then turned toward the spectators when Judge St. James spoke in a commanding, almost harsh tone. "Mr. Blaze, the answer is not in the jury box or the gallery. It is in your head. So, sir, what is your answer? Before you answer, may I remind you that in the Royal Colony of Georgia, we take a dim view of perjury by officers of the court and an even harsher view of prosecutors who manufacture evidence."

The prosecutor took a deep breath. "Yes, I was contacted by several businessmen here in Savannah who gave me the information on which I based the charges."

"Did you investigate the veracity of the information before filing charges?"

"I did not. To use the defense counsel's words, the men who approached me confidentially are respected members of the Savannah business community."

"So, Mr. Blaze, you are confirming what Ms. Jacinto has alleged, which is that the information on which the charges were based is, at best inaccurate. Am I correct?"

"I believe that is a possibility."

"Thank you."

Before Judge St. James could speak, Shoshana stood up. "Judge, I think I can solve the court's dilemma about whether or not the trial should continue based on, well, the baselessness of the second charge, which is trading illegally with Morocco. In fact, the Sultan of Morocco, Sultan Mohammed III opened his ports to U.S. merchants in December 1777. Furthermore, I have searched the law library here in Savannah and in Charleston and found no law on the books prohibiting anyone in Georgia or any of the other colonies from trading with Morocco. So, logic tells me that if there is no law, no law can be broken, and therefore, one cannot be charged."

Judge St. James leaned forward. "Ms. Jacinto, will you take me through that again?"

Shoshana held out several sheets of paper that Saul had given her. "Judge St. James, I went through every act of Parliament beginning in 1620 to see if there were any that prohibited British citizens or those who live in a British colony or territory from trading in Morocco. There are none."

She stopped to let what she said sink in. "Then, I searched the Royal Governor's law library here in Savannah and the two I have access to in Charleston, searching for any law or court case that would provide precedence to prohibit one from buying or selling goods in Morocco. Again, there were none."

She turned to place the papers on the table and Saul handed her a letter with a seal which she held up.

"Still not satisfied, on my last visit to Savannah, I made an appointment with the Royal Governor's secretary who, by the way, was familiar with this case and asked him if there were any Royal Colony of Georgia laws that would prohibit one from doing business in Morocco. Again, there are none, and this is the Royal Governor's Secretary's letter attesting to this fact."

"Now I follow you. Go on."

Shoshana faced the jury as she spoke. "Therefore, if no law exists, one cannot break a non-existent law nor can charges be filed. It is simple as that."

"So, Ms. Jacinto, what you are telling the court is that the charges are not based on any law?"

"Correct." Shoshana could see the understanding on the faces of the jurors. She almost added they are bogus but didn't.

Judge St. James rummaged through the papers on his bench. Then he looked directly at Fredrick Blaze. "Mr. Blaze, can you cite the specific law you based your illegal foreign trading charges on?"

Blaze stared back at Judge St. James, who was becoming angrier by the minute. "I'm waiting. I am sure you had a clerk find one." He held up the warrant. "Now that I have re-read the warrant, no specific law is listed."

Blaze sat frozen in his chair.

"I thought so." Flushed with anger, Judge St. James used an even tone as he ruled. "I am dismissing all the charges against Jorge and David Fonseca. In addition, for the Royal Colony of Georgia, I apologize. This court will happily entertain a liable suit against the Royal Governor's office for damages. In addition, I am ordering the Royal Governor to pay all Fonseca's legal expenses that, include any money spent by Ms. Jacinto and her assistants to travel to and from Savannah. Last, Mr. Blaze, I am filing a complaint with the Royal Governor recommending at the very least, you be suspended pending a decision to revoke your privileges to appear in court. Case dismissed."

Shoshana walked over to Eugene Lozenge and stood close enough so that he was forced to look up at her. Her white teeth flashed, and her eyes sparkled as she looked down at the New York-based attorney. "Not bad for a young lady who's a Jewess and can shoot better than a man, ay?"

She didn't wait for an answer and left Lozenge to digest what she just said.

CHAPTER 7

– NOT BUYING THE FARM

BREST, FOURTH WEEK OF JANUARY 1782

Now that *Zephyr* had delivered Charles Laurens to Amsterdam, the schooner rode easily at anchor in the French harbor about a half mile from the piers. The schooner would be anchored in Brest for at least 10 days while they waited for a courier to make the five-day, 390-mile ride to Paris, wait for an answer and then ride back. Bosun Preston would have the crew perform whatever maintenance was needed to keep *Zephyr* ready to sail.

On prior visits, *Zephyr* was tied to a pier until the French Port Captain, with whom Jaco had met many times, beginning when he was the captain of the schooner *Cutlass*, had increased the daily fee. If *Zephyr* anchored in the roadstead, there was no charge.

Anchored in Brest also meant the crew would have to endure temperatures in the 30s and 40s. The steady wind coming off the North Atlantic brought a chilling dampness; no matter what one wore, one felt cold. The best word to describe January weather in Brest was raw.

From where the schooner was anchored, *Zephyr's* lookouts had a clear view of the entrance. When Royal Navy frigates came close to the harbor entrance, their lookouts could peek into the estuary, their top and topgallants were visible.

Twice a day, one of *Zephyr's* officers and four sailors sailed the longboat to shore to purchase food. In the morning, they bought milk, eggs, bread, and bacon for breakfast and smoked or aged salamis and cheese for lunch.

On the afternoon noon trip, the officer would stop by Samuel Gardner's office to see if any dispatches arrived before going to the market for meat and vegetables for dinner and bags of coal or bundles of wood for the stove used for cooking and heating *Zephyr's* berthing compartment.

The captain's and the passenger cabins were warmed by 6-pound cannon balls heated in the ship's stove until they glowed and then gingerly transferred to iron pots that were hung from the overhead beams. Heat radiating from the cook's stove warmed the crew's berthing compartment.

Zephyr's designers had left an open area between the crew's berthing compartment and the passenger cabins. It had two tables that came 10 feet inboard from the port side between benches bolted to the deck. Along the cross-ship bulkheads, the shipbuilders installed floor-to-ceiling bookcases on the aft cross-ship bulkhead and small writing desks on the forward one.

The open area became the crew's mess. While the entire crew of 50 could not squeeze into the space at the same time, it became the center of life on board the schooner. Every day, crew members speculated if peace was coming and, if so, how soon. While Jaco and the other officers who dined with John Jay on the way to Brest and then with Henry Laurens on the uneventful voyage to Amsterdam were optimistic, none believed a treaty would be signed soon.

Jaco went ashore on the morning boat without expecting any change in the routine. A stiff wind and a choppy harbor sprayed all on board the 20-foot-long boat with cold seawater. By the time he climbed onto the pier, Jaco was shivering and soaking wet.

To Jaco, Brest smelled old. The streets stank of the residue from centuries of sewage, garbage and horse dung that lay on its cobblestone streets, only to be washed away by heavy rains. Then, it smelled clean for a few hours and then the stench returned, only to be reinforced by a new layer of sewage, garbage, and horse dung.

Samuel Gardner, who knew when *Zephyr's* boat would arrive, waited for Jaco on the pier holding a leather pouch. "Captain, the courier arrived late last night with these messages from Franklin and Jay. How soon can *Zephyr* get underway?"

"We need to top off our stock of beer and provisions. Assuming we get them by lunch, we will leave just before dark."

"Captain, Mr. Jay sent me a personal note asking me to urge *Zephyr* to make its best possible speed to Philadelphia. There is exciting news in these dispatches."

"Understood. We shall do our best. We can be in Philadelphia in four weeks with luck and decent weather."

"Let us hope the Royal Navy does not interfere."

"Amen to that." Jaco turned to Abner Jeffords. "Mr. Jeffords, sail back to *Zephyr* and tell Mr. Geiger we sail just before dark this evening. Then, bring back the other two boats with a list of all the necessary provisions."

The sun was setting, and the moderate wind from the nor' west had not abated. Once the provisions and the boats were on board, Jaco ordered the anchors weighed. He wanted to be in the Celtic Sea by dark, so finishing stowing the provisions could come once they were underway.

Standing on the quarterdeck, as soon as the port anchor left the rocky bottom, he could feel *Zephyr* straining against the starboard anchor's hawser. "Sheet home the jib and weigh the starboard anchor. Lads let's get the anchor off the bottom so we can bring in the mainsails on all three masts. Time's a wasting!!!"

Eight men pushed on the oak bars in the slots of the capstan. Six more stood lined up on the deck, ready to pull the starboard anchor hawser onto the deck. Colin Landry's loud voice could be heard over the wind through the rigging and was in tune.

> <u>Landry</u> – Way hay, we'll haul away!!! Way hay, we'll haul away!!!
> An' I sailed the seas for many a year not knowin' what I was missin', Then I sets me sails afore the gales an' started in a-kissin'.

> <u>The sailors</u> – Way hay, we'll haul away!!! Way hay, we'll haul away!!!

> <u>Landry</u> – Now first I got a Spanish gal an' she was fat an' lazy,
> An' then I got a Scottish tart-she nearly drove me crazy.

Zephyr weathercocked so her bow was into the wind as the men sang. This forced the men at the capstan to pull the ship forward to get the hull over the anchor and off the bottom. It was hard work, and once the anchor came free, sailors not on the capstan or handling the hawser had to pull in the sheets to the jib and the three main sails to keep *Zephyr* from being blown onto the rocks less than half a mile away.

> <u>The sailors</u> – Way hay, we'll haul away!!! Way hay, we'll haul away!!!

Landry – Oi found meself an English gal an' sure she wasn't civil, So I stuck a plaster on her back an' sent her to the Devil.

The sailors – Way hay, we'll haul away!!! Way hay, we'll haul away!!!

Landry – Then I got meself an Irish gal an' her name wuz Flannigan,

The sailors – Way hay, we'll haul away!!! Way hay, we'll haul away!!!

Landry – She stole me boots, she stole me clothes, she pinched me plate an' pannikin.

The sailors – Way hay, we'll haul away!!! Way hay, we'll haul away!!!

Landry – I courted then a Frenchie gal, she took things free an' easy, but now I've got a Yankee gal an' sure she is a daisy.

The sailors – Way hay, we'll haul away!!! Way hay, we'll haul away!!!

Landry – So list while I sing to you about me darlin' Nancy, she's copper-bottomed, schooner-built, she's just me style an' fancy.

The sailors – Way hay, we'll haul away!!! Way hay, we'll haul away!!!

Landry – Ye may talk about yer Yankee gals an' round-the-corner-Sallies, but they couldn't make the grade, me boys, with the gals from down our alley.

The sailors – Way hay, we'll haul away!!! Way hay, we'll haul away!!!

Zephyr lurched noticeably when the anchor came free. Suddenly the capstan moved easily, and the men handling the hawser pulled the four-inch-thick rope onto the deck and the anchor up where it could be secured.

The wind pushed *Zephyr* toward the lee shore, Jaco yelled from the quarterdeck, "Sheet home the jib and all three main sails. Do it smartly lads, or we'll go swimming."

Three teams of eight men pulled on the sheets to each masts' main sail while three more sheeted home the jib. *Zephyr* started moving forward, gathering speed.

"Bosun Preston, send men below to lower the keels." They had been kept up until the anchors were on board to eliminate any chance an anchor line would inadvertently wrap around one of the keels and damage it.

Getting an acknowledgement from the bosun on his desire to minimize leeway, Jaco turned to his two quartermasters, Abner Jeffords, and Cato Cooper, standing at the wheel. "Steer straight for the mouth of the channel. There's no one but us sailors on *Zephyr*, so on this reach, we will put her rail down to give us maximum speed."

Satisfied that his quartermaster knew where to head the schooner, Jaco stepped to the forward railing of the quarterdeck. "Mr. Geiger, once the anchors are stowed, give the capstan crew a ration of grog and ask Mr. Landry, if he is up to taking a glass up to the gaff topsail and tell me how many of our Royal Navy friends are waiting for us."

The schooner was entering the open ocean, free of the spits of land that made up the entrance to Brest. Dusk was fast approaching, and Jaco estimated there was about an hour before darkness set in.

Landry called out. "Deck there, there are two Royal Navy frigates, one point on either side of dead on the bow. Both are bending on full sail headed toward us. Distance less than five miles."

"Mr. Landry, what tack are they on?"

"The southern one on our port side is running with the wind straight at us. The one to starboard is running on a starboard tack and is heeled well over."

The fastest and most direct route to Philadelphia was a base course of west so' west. At this time of the year, once the schooner was in the Atlantic, the wind was from the so' west meant that after *Zephyr* passed west of Lisbon, it could sail straight to the entrance to Delaware Bay.

Zephyr's deck tilted as Bosun Preston adjusted the trim of the sails. Both the flying jib and the jib were out, and the tips of the main sail booms for all three masts were less than 10^0 degrees off the centerline. The inclinometer on the binnacle said the schooner was heeled 11^0 degrees. The bow went up three feet and then down as *Zephyr* sliced through the four-foot swells at an angle. The ride was not uncomfortable, but the corkscrew motion required a good pair of sea legs to stay on one's feet.

Heeled over like this, the stove could not be used for either heat or cooking. Meals would be salami, cheese, and hardtack for as long as needed.

Jaco could not see the hull of either Royal Navy frigate from the quarterdeck either with his naked eye or through a spyglass. He cupped his hands and yelled toward the lookout on the mainmast. "Mr. Landry, how far away is the southern Royal Navy frigate?"

"Three miles at most."

"Is she on a constant bearing?"

"Aye."

Damn!!! If Zephyr *continues this course, the Royal Navy frigate will be in range to fire warning shots or worse, engage.* "Mr. Landry, what about the frigate to our north?"

"She's eased her course a bit to the west. Looks as if she is sailing as close to the wind as possible."

"Distance?"

"Four miles at most."

"Let us know if either ship changes course."

A cold spray splashed by the bow, coated Jaco's face. As he wiped his face clean and tasted the salty water, a plan began to form in his mind. *To the west, the sun was just on the horizon. The Royal Navy captains and I are all in a hurry. I want to be past them by nightfall, and they want a prize before dark.*

"Mr. Geiger, show our friends in the Royal Navy who we are."

"Aye, sir. Mr. Garrison is happy to report that all the provisions have been stowed, and we have a wonderful selection of French cheeses, jams, wines, hams, and smoked meats to enjoy for the first week or so. Even some butter that should last for a day or two and a pot of mustard."

"Good to know! Before we can enjoy the bounty of Brest's markets, we must slip past these frigates."

Jaco could see both frigate's mainsails, top gallants, and royals. Once their hull was visible from the deck, they would be within three miles. If they had 12-pounders, at a mile *Zephyr* would be in gun range. He waited until the four-foot by six-foot Continental Navy ensign was streaming from the stay a few feet over his head.

Thinking it should be easily seen by the Royal Navy lookouts, Jaco ordered. "Mr. Jeffords, ease off to starboard to west by so'. Mr. Preston take in our sails to maximize the push of the wind. I intend to pass within two miles of the northern frigate that, if its captain wants to chase us, must tack through the wind. That will cost him time and distance, and I would wager a hundred pounds Sterling that he doesn't have the speed to catch *Zephyr*. Our move increases the distance the southern ship must cover, which should let us run away into the coming darkness."

Jaco waited until the sail trimming was done. "Mr. Preston, raise the gaff topsails and get them sheeted home. It should give us more speed and cock-up the geometry of our foe's carefully planned intercept."

The extra sails filled the gap between each mainsail's gaff boom and the mast's top. *Zephyr's* masts groaned as they absorbed the additional pressure, and the stays holding the masts were taut as bowstrings as they absorbed the strain.

Zephyr heeled over to 12^0, and its bow plunged into each wave, sending spray that wet the deck before disappearing into the scuppers. Those on the quarterdeck were soaked, and those who sought dryness went below. A hearty few stayed on deck to watch *Zephyr* show her heels to a pair of Royal Navy frigates.

This was, Jaco believed, the moment of truth. By now, the Royal Navy lookouts had reported that the schooner added sail, which suggested to their captains that the schooner was running. *Zephyr's* sail locker was now empty. Either the schooner slipped past the Royal Navy frigates, or it would be captured.

A dull boom reached the schooner. Jaco saw the smoke from the southern frigate but did not see the spout showing where the ball landed. Three more - a second from the southern frigate and two from the northern one - followed in rapid succession.

None of the balls landed within a half-mile of the schooner. Abner Jeffords stood next to Jaco and leaned toward him. "Cap'n, we're flying!!! I just logged our speed. *Zephyr's* making fifteen and a half knots."

"Good, I hope we can keep this up and not bring down a mast."

"We'll be fine. *Zephyr* is built well and sails even better."

Jaco nodded at the backhanded compliment to the shipbuilder. The northern frigate was tacking toward the west and assumed the Royal Navy captain intended to fire a broadside or two at maximum range, hoping for a lucky hit.

Before he gave his next order, Jaco looked at the southern frigate wearing to port to bring its broadside to bear. Apparently, *Zephyr's* change in speed had foiled his intercept geometry. Jaco looked up, "Mr. Landry, how far to each Royal Navy frigate?"

"Inside a mile at most after they finish their turns."

A mile is roughly 2,000 yards. Even 1,500 yards is a long way for a 12-pounder.

"Mr. Landry, you and the other lookout come down. I don't need you up there to get hit by an errant cannonball."

The broadsides started from both Royal Navy frigates. At this distance, they weren't deafening, just distant thunder hurling 12-pound cast iron balls in their direction. Jaco thought it was strange that he had no gun crews to order to fire back. His only weapons were *Zephyr's* speed, sound construction, his crew's skill, and his wits.

The waterspouts made by the cannon balls erupted as if they were a fence. Not one came near the schooner as darkness fell.

NORTH OF DORCHESTER, SC, FIRST WEEK OF FEBRUARY 1782

The 24 men behind Amos Laredo and Lieutenant Gabriel Pruett were in 12 rows of two. One long rifled musket, primed but not cocked, rested easily across their thighs. A second unloaded rifled musket was in a holster behind the rider's legs. On either side, just in front of the pommel, the men had loaded pistols, primed but not cocked.

In this part of South Carolina, 23 miles north of Charleston, the members of the 4th Carolina were not expecting a fight. While they were not complacent, rarely did the British Army venture this far north in less than regimental strength.

Amos Laredo went on these patrols to scout to ensure the British weren't attempting to reinforce their remaining forts farther north along the Congaree River. The patrols allowed him to visit the plantations and talk to his fellow citizens, almost all of whom supported the rebellion.

Now, the 200+ members of the 4th Carolina were using the farm that Amos had purchased. Its old base in the swamps along the Cooper River was still stocked with powder and shot and was now used as a backup in case they were being chased and needed to shed their pursuers.

Lieutenant Gabriel Pruett, one of the 4th Carolina's platoon leaders, held up his hand. The column bunched up as Pruett climbed down from his horse and squatted by the horse prints. He looked up at his commanding officer.

"Sir, these are recent and looking at the ground, I'd guess they were made after the rain stopped by a patrol of at least thirty or more men. That was less than two hours ago. I think they gave the horses a break before heading in the direction from whence we just came."

The hair on the back of Amos' neck stood up. Pruett had just told him that they may have passed a British Army unit that may have set up an ambush. Softly, Amos ordered. "Everyone down. Make sure your rifles are still primed."

He looked at the grassy field to the east. "We're going out into that field to see if anyone is coming at us. The longer the range, the better for us. We'll walk inside the horses, and let's move out."

They'd moved about a hundred yards into the field when the man at the tail end of the column yelled. "Dragoons!!!"

Amos stepped out of the column and turned to see about 50 mounted British cavalrymen charging with their sabers drawn. "Everybody, pick a target and fire."

He checked the pan on his musket and selected a target as he pulled the hammer back to full cock. At less than 50 yards, the man was hard to miss. The pan flashed, smoke shot out of the side, and the rifled musket bucked back into his shoulder. He didn't have to wait for the smoke to clear to see if the man was down. He dropped the musket and pulled a pistol from one of the holsters. A dragoon was almost on top of him, his saber raised, ready to slash. Without time to check to see if the pan was still full, he pulled the hammer back, aimed, and fired. At less than 10 feet, the .60 caliber lead ball knocked the British dragoon from his saddle.

Holding onto the reins of his terrified Percheron, Amos yanked his sword from its scabbard. It wasn't a traditional cavalryman's weapon but an edged sword that his father had ordered from Germany. It had a sharp point and edge, which made it perfect for slashing or stabbing.

Amos stuck a foot in a stirrup and swung up onto his horse, knowing that it made him a better target, but he wanted a better view of the close action. Three of his troopers were lying on the ground with at least twice as many British Dragoons in their green coats, dead or dying in the grass around the South Carolinians.

The British dragoon's rush had carried them 100 yards farther into the field. They paused to reorganize before deciding if they would charge again. The delay gave the men of the 4th Carolina time to reload their muskets. Amos checked the pan of his second musket. It was empty. He poured powder into the pan and brought it to half cock before checking his unfired pistol, which he reprimed before reloading his fired rifled musket and the pistol he'd just fired.

Out in the field, the British dragoons spread out in a single line, their short-barreled carbines resting on their thighs as they readied their second charge. He rested his musket on the back of his horse, selected a target, and fired. The other men in his unit did the same just as the British dragoons started to move forward, less the 11 men wounded or dead that fell from their horses.

Suddenly the officer in charge yelled and pointed toward the south. The remaining British dragoons galloped off, leaving the 22 survivors of the 4th Carolina patrol alone in the field and very surprised.

They loaded the dozen dead British dragoons and the three dead South Carolinians on their horses before bringing them to the farm the 4th Carolina used as a base. While the men were being buried, Amos had others pack their belongings and get ready to move out. They were going back to their base in the woods. The extra horses were let out into the fenced fields, and their extra stocks of weapons, powder, and shot they could not carry were buried in prepared cellars in the woods.

On the way to their base along the Cooper River, Amos sent Lieutenant Pruett and eight men into Dorchester to ask his grandmother if she would send a family to live in the house for the next month or so and promised he would compensate them for their time.

16 MILES NORTH OF DORCHESTER, SECOND WEEK OF FEBRUARY 1782

The 250 men of the British Army's 17th Light Dragoons dismounted and led their horses into the trees far enough so they could not be seen from the road. While the men patted and comforted their horses, Major Jude Arundel crept through the trees to where the land was cleared. He steadied his spyglass against a tree trunk to study the farmhouse, barn, and surrounding buildings. A dozen horses were gathered in a corral while a small herd of cows grazed in a fenced field. A dozen pigs were snorting and guzzling food from a trough in a pen beside the barn. Two wagons, with their tongues resting on the ground, were next to the pig pen.

What interested Arundel was not what he saw but what he did not see. He looked for slaves or people working in the field and saw none. Then he looked for the owners. His brief said that many farms in this area and farther north were farmed by communal business with an odd name he couldn't remember. This, he thought, might be one of them.

Arundel spotted a man, and a boy walk from the house to the barn. So, there were people here! He turned to a young man wearing the cream-colored uniform of the 1st Camden Loyalist Volunteers who led him to this farm. "Mr. Thornton, are you sure this farm is the 4th Carolina's base?"

"Aye, sir, I am. I have been here several times. Major Laredo had his grandmother buy the property about two years ago from a Loyalist family my parents know who moved to St. Augustine to start over."

"Where are the weapons, Corporal Thornton?"

"When I was here, Major, the rifles and pistols were on the second floor of the barn and the barrels of powder were on a raised platform in the back of the barn. But, sir, I must warn you. Major Laredo is a cagey man. Just because they were there when I was here last, does not mean they are in the same place."

"Then, Corporal, we need to find the arms and ammunition wherever it 'tis. If this is their base, then we need to destroy it."

Arundel went back to his two captains and explained his plan. He, along with Captain Vickers, the commander of the 1st Camden, who would be accompanied by an unarmed Thornton, would lead half the men up the access road to the house. Under Captain Cadell Myrick, the other half would spread out and approach through the field with the cows ready to fight.

What neither Arundel nor Vickers nor Myrick saw was the small detachment of 16 members of the 4th Carolina watching from the far side of the farm, near where the weapons coated lightly with pig grease before being wrapped in cloth were stored in cellars and whose entrances were carefully camouflaged. Also in the cellars were barrels of powder and boxes of lead balls for their rifled muskets and pistols.

Another detachment of the 4th Carolina saw the 17th Light Dragoons, identified by the flag carried by a soldier riding just behind its commander, move into the trees. Once the British cavalrymen started down the access road, two of its men rode off, headed toward the 4th Carolina's base along the Cooper River, leaving 14 to watch the entrance.

Malcolm Drummond saw the British Dragoons from the second-floor window long before they reached the open area under the large oak trees in front of the house. He volunteered to bring his wife and six children - four boys and two girls aged from a 16-year-old boy to his youngest girl who was just four - out to Amos's farm. He wasn't doing this for money but because he believed in the cause of freedom. If he weren't here, Malcolm would be a sergeant leading a 16-man section in the 4th Carolina.

When Arundel rode up, the 36-year-old Drummond stood on the porch with his arm around his 10-year-old daughter. His oldest – a

16-year-old boy - warily looked at the British from the end of the porch as 17th Light Dragoons fanned out around the house with their pistols drawn. Malcolm Drummond stared at the British major looking down at him from his horse.

"I am Major Arundel of the 17th Light Dragoons. Who are you?"

"Malcolm Drummond."

"Are you the owner of this farm?"

"No." Amos encouraged him to say as little as possible should the British come calling.

"Well, you won't mind if we search the house and the farm."

"I do object. Do you have a warrant?"

"No." Arundel bristled. "Nor do I need one."

Drummond decided to antagonize Arundel. "So, the British Army doesn't follow British law in a British Colony."

Arundel glared back at him. His look was intended to intimidate, and he gave Drummond the answer he expected, "No, it doesn't when we are at war with traitors."

Drummond calmly asked, "What are you looking for?"

"Muskets, pistols, powder, shot."

"You won't find any here other than my two muskets, some powder, and shot for hunting."

Arundel waved, and eight men entered the house with their pistols drawn. Another section of eight went into the barn. Eight more started toward the old slave quarters that the 4th Carolina made much more habitable.

"Where are the slaves?"

"There aren't any. There were some several years back, but no more. The owner now just raises cows, pigs, and chickens."

Drummond spotted Billy Thornton and turned away before they made eye contact. Now he knows where the deserter went. *Will Thornton identify me as a member of the 4th Carolina?*

One dragoon carried two rifled muskets out of the house and leaned them against the house. He was followed by three men who pushed Molly Drummond and the remaining four children ahead of them.

Seeing the woman, Arundel doffed his hat. "Well, I see we have the whole Drummond family. Excellent. We're going to stay for a few days and make a thorough search of the property. While we are here, all of you will be confined to the upstairs of the house except to prepare and eat your meals."

Arundel turned to his officers and directed them to set up outposts with a minimum of four men rather than just sentries. He wanted them to find what they could to build a defensive perimeter around the buildings. Once that was done, since they had ridden all night in a failed attempt to surprise the 4th Carolina, half of those not on duty could go inside the barn and house and sleep.

Arundel's orders from General Leslie gave him broad discretion on what to do. He could wait for the 4th Carolina to return or return to Charleston immediately. And, if he suspected the farm was used by the 4th Carolina, he was instructed to burn all its buildings to the ground and seize all its livestock. He dismounted and walked up the two steps to the porch brushing the road dust off his green coat. He stopped in front of Molly Drummond. "Mrs. Drummond, has the 4th Carolina been here?"

She shook her head. "No."

Arundel looked back and forth between the two adults. His voice was cold. "For your children's sake, I hope we do not find any weapons. If I do, I will hang both of you for treason in front of your children from the oak tree behind me."

Convinced he had made his point, Arundel walked around the complex of houses and the barn. The smokehouse was full of meat, too much, he believed, for a family to eat. Missing were wagons to carry the meat to either Dorchester or Charleston. Arundel was no farmer, but a few cows, chickens, and horses do not a farm make. It was time to have another chat with Mr. and Mrs. Drummond.

The remaining 200 odd "effectives" of the 4th Carolina were moving north toward Amos' farm in four companies of 50, each led by a lieutenant. And, while they were not within sight of each other, they were within hearing distance. The disbursement enabled them to search for additional British or Loyalist units along their route.

Pruett's company would arrive first, late in the afternoon, to contact men watching from the forest. The other three would reach the outskirts of the property after dark.

At dawn of the day after the 17th Light Dragoons rode onto the plantation grounds, Arundel ordered one of his lieutenants to check on the outpost by the main road a half mile from the house. The young officer, Giles de Mornay, the 7th Earl of Thanet, rode with three other dragoons into the thicket of oak and pine trees more than 100 years old, expecting to find the 20 men at their post watching the road. If attacked, the men in the post were supposed to fire a volley and withdraw immediately to the farmhouse.

When the 7th Earl of Thanet arrived at where the outpost was stationed, Amos Laredo stepped out from behind an oak tree that was, chest high, two feet in diameter. His pistol was pointed at the Earl's chest. Other members of the 4th Carolina had their muskets aimed at his three soldiers.

"Sir, please dismount. If you do, no harm will come to you."

De Mornay looked around for his fellow dragoons. Seeing none, he asked indignantly, "Where are the other members of my unit."

"Safe and sound. Soon you will join them. Please, lieutenant, get down now, or I will drag you off your horse."

Amos Laredo knew he could be physically intimidating. He was broad-shouldered, 6' 2", and a lean, muscular 200 pounds. The young Light Dragoon officer complied. Even though he was shorter and at least 60 pounds lighter than the rebel pointing a pistol at his chest, Giles de Mornay was defiant. "Who in the bloody hell are you?"

"Major Amos Laredo, commander of the 4th Carolina. And you?"

The Englishman stood as tall as he proudly could. "Giles de Mornay, the 7th Earl of Thanet, Captain, 17th Dragoons."

"Excellent. Now that we know each other, have any of the Drummonds been harmed in any way?"

De Mornay shook his head. "They spent the night in a room on the second floor. I must say, they have not been very cooperative."

"Why should they when their home has been occupied. What are your commander's orders?"

"Seize any contraband we find and if we do find munitions, burn all the buildings, seize the farm animals, and hang any adults as traitors."

"And pray tell, what kind of contraband did you hope to find?"

"Arms and ammunition."

"Have you found any?"

"No. Only Mr. Drummond's two muskets which I must say, are fine-looking firearms, a pistol, and some powder and shot. He said they were for hunting. Major Arundel believes there are more weapons at the farm and intends to find them."

Amos nodded his head and turned to Lieutenant Pruett. "Tie his hands, gag him, and attach the rope to the string of other prisoners. It is time to have a chat with this Major Arundel. But first, we need to send him a message."

Amos rode slowly out of the woods on his Percheron and headed towards his house. He was followed by four of his troopers; next to him was his second-in-command, Captain Luke Giffords.

When he was in clear sight, 200 yards from the house, Amos stopped, sure he was well out of effective range of the British Dragoons' carbines and their short, 20-inch barrels. British sentries, seeing the six men turned to face them. Others stepped out from behind trees, exposing themselves to the sharpshooters of Captain Ethan Ravenel's company. Two men ran into the house to find Major Arundel.

Amos put two fingers into his mouth and blew a loud whistle. Seconds later, muskets began to fire, not in a volley, but individually aimed shots. The two Light Dragoon sentries on the second-floor deck above the portico toppled, and one thudded to the ground and didn't move.

Four other Light Dragoons fell dead or wounded. Amos wasn't counting the shots but thought enough were fired to send a message. Major Arundel came running out of the house when the first shots rang out yelling to his men to man their prepared defensive positions.

Clouds of gray-white smoke gave away the positions of the marksman lying on their sides, reloading the musket they had just fired. Others, were still hidden in the field, waiting for a target.

At 100 yards, the 4th Carolina's standard was that nine times out of ten, the shooter's lead balls would hit a man between the crotch and the neck. From 200 yards, the company's standard was eight out of 10 balls must hit the desired area.

Amos waited and watched. Each time a British soldier peeked out to aim his carbine, he was greeted by a musket ball from a 4th Carolina shooter. Two men, hiding in the windows of the house's second story, fired at Amos. He heard the musket balls sing as they zipped past. Neither was close.

Satisfied that more than a dozen Light Dragoons were either dead or wounded, Amos turned and asked one of the troopers behind him to have Captain Pruett lead the prisoners into the open. The glint of a spyglass from a third-story window told Amos that someone was trying to get a closer look at the prisoners. Since de Mornay was the first prisoner on the string, he was confident that whoever was looking recognized the British captain.

Amos reached into the saddle bag behind him and pulled out a white cloth that he tied to the end of his 54-inch long, rifled musket. With the butt resting on his left thigh urged his Percheron forward.

One hundred yards from the house, Amos stopped. He would not go any closer.

Three saddled horses were led to the front of the house, where a stocky man tightened the chin strap of his hat before he mounted. As he rode forward with two other men, his gold buttons sparkled in the sunlight, and the yellow front of his uniform was clearly visible. The officer reined in his horse 50 feet from Amos.

Amos believed he had the initiative and began speaking loud enough so the British officer could hear him easily. "I am Major Amos Laredo, commander of the 4th Carolina. Who are you?"

"Major Jude Arundel, commander of the 17th Light Dragoons. What have you done with my men?"

"Other than capture and tie them up, nothing." Amos waited while his Percheron shifted its front feet. "Where is the Drummond family?"

"Safe."

"Not good enough, major. Where are they?"

"I said safe. That is all you need to know, rebel."

"Major, the 17th Dragoons are surrounded. Please release the Drummonds and leave my land now so those of your men still alive can return to England."

"So, this is your farm?"

"Aye, it 'tis that and if you burn it, I promise you that you will die on my land, and I and my descendants will walk on your grave every day."

"You're bloody arrogant to think you can defeat half a regiment of Kings Light Dragoons in a pitched battle."

Amos ignored the man's bluster. "Major, if you don't leave within the hour, we will continue to pick off your men, one by one, until you surrender. If you leave within the hour without your weapons, I can assure you that all of you who have not been shot will make it back to Charleston, embarrassed maybe, but alive. You can take the wagons to carry your wounded."

"You can go to hell." Arundel turned in his saddle and yelled, "Bring them out."

Four British soldiers pulled Molly and Malcom Drummond out onto the porch. One held their arms while another held a pistol to their heads. "See, they are safe."

Amos controlled his rising anger and spoke forcefully. "Release them, now!!!"

"Bloody hell, I will. Give me back the men you are holding."

"Not a chance, major. They are soldiers who were captured. The Drummonds are civilians, not part of this fight."

"They're bloody rebel sympathizers. Traitors to England and King George!"

Amos put his hand to his mouth and whistled. Four shots rang out. Dull sounds like the sucking sound a rock makes when dropped in soft mud were not heard by Amos Laredo or Jude Arundel, but the two saw the effect.

The man aiming a pistol at Molly Drummond buckled at the waist from the impact of the .45 caliber lead ball. His pistol thudded to the wooden deck as he held his midsection, screaming in pain. The three other Light Dragoons collapsed to the porch's planking, either dead or dying from musket balls that destroyed their hearts or ripped their guts apart.

Amos leaned forward over the pommel of his Percheron, which was a foot taller than the Light Dragoon major's animal. His voice was firm and forceful. "Major Arundel, if you do not surrender within the hour, we will kill every one of you, starting with the officers. If you harm any of the Drummonds or destroy any portion of my property, I promise you that no member of the 17th Light Dragoons will leave this farm alive. Whether or not more English boys die today is now up to you. If you leave now, we will bury your dead with full military honors in the British Cemetery in Dorchester." Amos looked at his Swiss-made Breguet pocket watch. "It is almost ten. You have until eleven to march out without your firearms. Good day, sir."

A tug of the rein cued his Percheron to take several steps back. Before Amos turned to go back to his men, Major Arundel galloped back to the house.

Captain Vickers was waiting for him along with his two other captains. Already, the bodies of the dead dragoons were pulled into a row in the shaded area between the two barns.

Arundel looked around at his Dragoons. Their worried faces reflected what they had seen. They knew they were targets and that the marksmen of the 4th Carolina would pick them off every time they showed their faces.

He toyed with mounting 50 men and charging into the field to flush out the riflemen. He guessed they may kill a few from the 4th Carolina, but more of his men would die in a futile charge. Now that he'd seen the effects of the 4th Carolina's marksmanship, he could attest that the reports were true.

Then Arundel had a better idea, "Where's this man Thornton?"

Billy Thornton stepped around from where he was standing behind Captain Vickers. He'd been in Lieutenant Butterworth's troop before he was killed. Now, that unit was commanded by Lieutenant Meysonnier whom he suspected was embarrassed by his desertion. Thornton was sure that Drummond had recognized him as he did Drummond. If he identified Drummond as a member of the 4th Carolina, and Arundel killed him, he was sure that his former commander would kill the British major and every man who rode with him. Before they arrived, Thornton had decided he was not going to say anything.

Arundel leaned over the right as he patted the neck of his horse. "Thornton, you know his man Amos Laredo, how good is he in battle?"

The British officer had read reports and talked to his fellow officers. Many believed that Laredo was lucky at Dorchester because Islay waited a day after arriving to attack, letting the 4th Carolina prepare. The consensus was that Laredo was good at ambushes and raiding but untested in a set-piece fight."

"Sir, Major Laredo does not like the killing, but I would not trifle with him in a fight." Thornton was sure that as soon as one of the members of the 4th Carolina recognized him, he would become a prime target.

"Is he a man of his word?"

"Aye sir, that he is. Trust me, if he says he will kill every man in the 17th Light Dragoons, he will and not think twice about it."

Arundel pulled the reins around to the left to face the road to the plantation. From where he sat on his horse, Arundel could see Laredo on his Percheron with a dozen other members of the 4th Carolina on their horses. His captured dragoons were sitting in a row in the field under the bright sun. If there was a battle, they were going to watch the slaughter.

Amos was not surprised when he saw the members of the 17th Light Dragoons mount up. Through his spyglass, he watched them stack their carbines and then toss their pistols and cartridge-boxes into four large piles.

The Light Dragoons approached in an orderly column of fours past where Amos sat on his horse. He ordered the prisoners released, and they formed up behind the wagons carrying the wounded. When the Arundel passed with the unit's flag bearers right behind, Amos rendered a sharp salute which Arundel returned and ordered his men to dip his unit's flags.

100 MILES, SE OF BERMUDA, SECOND WEEK OF FEBRUARY 1782

The heavy weather that slowed the convoy down for the past two days had passed. The winds that forced the convoy to plow through eight-foot waves and reef its sails as heavy rain pounded the deck had been replaced by warm sun, a bright blue sky dotted by a few puffy clouds.

With the two transport ships that fell out of formation now escorted back into what Darren referred to as "the box," the convoy was again whole. As Darren could see through his spyglass, *Star of India* was in its assigned position, number three in the port column.

Midshipman Dyer Culver took two steps from where he was standing next to the quartermaster at the wheel towards his captain, who was, for the umpteenth time this morning, studying *Star of India* to see if it was damaged in any way. Besides a torn topsail that was being replaced, it appeared to have weathered the storm in good order. "Sir, the flagship is signaling."

"Us?"

"Aye, and six other ships."

"Well then, what does the admiral have to say?"

Throughout the voyage, the admiral commanding the convoy hoisted signals several times daily from his three-decker. Most were addressed to the merchant ships and transports, admonishing them about their station keeping. As the storm approached, *Pompeii* was ordered to take station two miles behind the convoy and assist any ships that suffered damage or fell behind. That mission accomplished, Darren ordered the jib and fore staysail set along with the top gallants, tops, and mainsails set so it could pass in front of the convoy and resume its role as the convoy's scout.

Darren studied the string of flags running up the flagship's signal halyard through his spyglass. Without looking at the signal book, there was no way he could decipher what they meant. Midshipman Dyer Culver wrote the sequence of flags on a slate and rushed below to check the signal book kept in a cabinet just forward of Darren's cabin. From there, he would try to make sense of the string of flags. If it was, as it appeared, a long message, then the process may take him some time.

When he finished deciphering the message and returned to the quarterdeck, Culver saw his captain staring out at the water, probably wondering what the signal meant for *Pompeii*. "Begging the Captain's pardon, here's the admiral's message." The 15-year-old midshipman and recent graduate of the Royal Naval Academy held out a sheet of paper on which he had written both the flag sequence and his translation.

> *Stirling Cross, Pompeii, and Jason to escort transports Richmond, Sussex, Queen Anne, and Cardiff to New York. Rejoin flagship in Charleston soonest.*

"Very well, Mr. Culver. We should anticipate signals from *Sterling Cross* momentarily. Until then, we will do nothing."

Darren turned back to watching the sea and the ships thinking damn, it will be another two weeks before he gets to see Melody. By then, Emily and Melody will be either good friends or mortal enemies.

CHAPTER 8

– LIBELOUS WORDS

PHILADELPHIA, THIRD WEEK OF FEBRUARY 1782

Zephyr slipped into Philadelphia just before dark. Jaco was sure the schooner was spotted coming up the Delaware River because two members of the Foreign Affairs Committee of the Continental Congress – Thomas Johnson and Benjamin Harrison – along with his father were waiting at the pier braving the stiff wind and biting cold.

Once on board, Jaco nodded to his father, who was led to the crew's berthing compartment, the warmest place on *Zephyr* while his son finished his official business in his cabin. The first question once the two committeemen entered came from Johnson, a Marylander and well-known jurist before becoming a member of the Continental Congress. "Did you deliver Mr. Laurens to Amsterdam?"

"Aye, sir, we did." Jaco was not going to mention meeting Rear Admiral Stacey Davidson. The encounter with the highwaymen was in his log and official report, but he didn't think it was relevant.

"How long ago did you leave Brest?"

"Sixteen days ago. We made very good time."

"I'll say you did. Any close calls with the Royal Navy?"

"No, once we got past the two frigates watching Brest, it was clear sailing with no storms and moderate winds."

"Do you have any news?"

Jaco took the cast iron key from around his neck and unlocked the dispatch box in his cabin. "When Mr. Gardener handed me the pouch, he said, please get this to Philadelphia as fast as you can."

"Does *Zephyr* need any repairs?"

"No, sir. Once we reprovision, we will be ready to go anywhere you wish."

Jaco escorted the two men to the gangway. Once they left, he went forward to see his father, who had the victualling list prepared by Hedley Garrison in his hand. He addressed his son, "Captain, I've given Mr. Geiger a purse with the crew's pay plus a 15% bonus for the fast trip. However, you must come to my house. We have a matter of importance to discuss."

"Is it personal?"

"Yes, but it doesn't involve Reyna who sent you several letters."

"Father, what is it about, then?"

"Edmund Radcliffe. He is now a reporter and columnist for the *Continental Journal*."

Overhearing Radcliffe's name caused several members of *Zephyr's* crew who were on *Scorpion* to turn around and stop what they were doing. Bosun Preston blurted out what was on his, and probably everyone else's mind when they heard the name Edmund Radcliffe. "You should have hung that mutinous bastard when you had the chance."

Lieutenant Geiger added, "You should have run him through when the bastard tried to kill you during the duel."

Jaco moved his hand horizontally in a sweep that suggested his crew calm down. "What exactly did Radcliffe write?"

"Rather than me tell you, I would prefer if you read the articles yourself. By now, probably every member of the Congress has seen them."

"Father, by them, do you mean there is more than one."

"Yes, there are four that I know about. Jack Shelton sent a note to the publisher of the paper asking him to send copies of all of Radcliffe's work via *Alacrity*. I suspect they should arrive any day now."

Jaco sat at the table with a lantern resting on the end with the four editions of the *Continental Journal* with Radcliffe's articles in a neat row. One headline read, "Continental Navy Captain Decisions Put £1.1 Million in Prize Money in Danger."

In the article, Radcliffe focused on Jaco's decision to conduct two raids in Scotland, one at Aberdeen and the other in Stornoway, after *Scorpion's* crew transferred the gold from the hold of *H.M.S. Madras*, a British East Indiaman, to the frigate. Radcliffe was clever in not mentioning either his or the ship's name or his captain's sailing orders that directed him to use *Scorpion* to "disrupt British commerce." Instead, in his critique, Radcliffe used the words "the young, inexperienced" and the "aggressive, young captain" and referred to *Scorpion* as "the new, small, but well-armed frigate."

Radcliffe referenced sources who confidentially told him that one of the ship's senior officers strongly suggested *Scorpion* take the more direct route from Amsterdam down through the English Channel as a faster way back to Philadelphia. In his analysis, Radcliffe did not mention that he was the ship's Second Lieutenant or that all the other officers believed sailing into the wind through the narrow English Channel past the Royal Navy's main fleet base at Portsmouth, might take longer and was much riskier than sailing north around Scotland and into the Atlantic.

A second piece with the headline "Arrogant Continental Navy Captain Attacks Three Royal Navy Frigates Unnecessarily." Radcliffe questioned Jaco's tactics during a battle in which *Scorpion* under Jaco's command heavily damaged two Royal Navy frigates – *Hussar* and *Griffin*. The third was damaged and forced out of position so it could not engage and pursue the faster *Scorpion*. The fight occurred off the north of the Isle of Lewis in January 1778 after *Scorpion* raided the town of Stornoway.

After the chance encounter with Rear Admiral Davidson in London, Jaco now knew the unknown ship was *H.M.S. Puritan*, 38 guns.

Radcliffe's analysis concluded that the fight against a superior force would not have been necessary if the captain sailed through the English Channel. He also did not mention that he was in chains in *Scorpion's* hold because he was planning a mutiny. Radcliffe's plan was that during a battle, his fellow planners would kill *Scorpion's* captain – Jaco – and the first lieutenant – Jack Shelton – so he could take over the ship.

Again, Radcliffe noted his information came from someone "on board the "well-armed Continental Navy frigate."

What Radcliffe did not mention was that *Scorpion* mounted 20 long 12-pounders, which were more accurate, fired balls at higher muzzle velocities which meant they hit harder and out-ranged the Royal Navy's 9- and 12-pounders. Nor did Radcliffe discuss *Scorpion's* hull, which had a layer of pine sandwiched between two layers of tough oak and protected the gun crews by absorbing the energy of Royal Navy 9- and 12-pound balls or the fact that the frigate was two to three knots faster than anything of comparable size in the Royal Navy.

Scorpion's speed, hull and its more effective cannon gave it significant tactical advantages in a fight. While Jaco was grateful that Radcliffe did not divulge details of *Scorpion's* unique design which enabled him to take risks that would not have been prudent in any other vessel. Radcliffe also did not mention that in every fight with the Royal Navy, Jaco and *Scorpion* emerged victorious because Jaco used *Scorpion's* advantages to quickly defeat Royal Navy ships that were larger and more powerful than the Continental Navy frigate.

Jaco suspected that Radcliffe did not mention any of *Scorpion's* secrets because they might have led to charges of treason. And, given that the charges of mutiny were held in abeyance, sharing information on the ship could lead to charges of treason.

When he read the article titled "Patronage Used to Give Inexperienced Officer Frigate Captaincy," Jaco laughed. Radcliffe claimed his sources were within the Marine Committee and wrote, "Jaco Jacinto was selected to be *Scorpion's* because his father was on the Marine Committee and other, more qualified men were passed over."

The truth was that Stephen Hopkins and John Adams initially opposed giving Jaco *Scorpion's* captaincy. They only relented when John Paul Jones, who was, at the time, captain of the *Ranger*, wrote a letter strongly recommending Jaco deserved an opportunity to show what he could do with a bigger ship than the fast schooner *Cutlass* with which he'd captured a bigger, more heavily armed Royal navy sloop-of-war.

Had Stephen Hopkins of Boston had his way, Jaco would not have been the captain of *Scorpion*, and its commander would have been one of his Bostonian's friends. Only Joseph Hewes insistence that demonstrated performance was the primary selection criteria over who on the Marine Committee one knew carried the day.

The article that made Jaco the angriest baited the reader by stating "Continental Navy Captain Picks Port Based on Love Not Common Sense." Radcliffe again questioned Jaco's judgment in this thinly veiled personal attack. After *Scorpion* defeated the bigger, more heavily armed Royal Navy frigate *Coburg*, Jaco decided to bring the prisoners to Charleston rather than Hampton, Virginia. Radcliffe opined that he chose Charleston, only 90 miles from British-held Savannah, because "the captain's hussy lived in Charleston."

After reading the last article, Jaco clasped his hands and rested his forearms on the table's edge. Freedom of the press was one of the liberties that he and every man in the room believed was necessary. Yet, there had to be limits on what someone could write without fear of retribution.

His anger and indignation that Radcliffe had slurred his fiancée name and honor grew. Rather than lash out at the five other men in the room – his father; his good friend Jack Shelton who was his first lieutenant on *Scorpion*; Hedley Garrison was a midshipman on *Scorpion* on that first cruise; and Morton Geiger who was his second at the duel in which Radcliffe attempted to kill Jaco through treachery and wound up losing his hand – Jaco had questions.

"Does the publisher of the *Continental Journal* know who Edmund's source is?"

Morton Geiger quick to answer. "I doubt it. My father says none of the privateer consortiums will take Radcliffe on as a seaman, much less as an officer. Most didn't know the details, but everyone on the waterfront knew Radcliffe was cashiered from the Navy for disciplinary reasons."

"Was Radcliffe given a copy of my report or the statements by his co-conspirators?"

Javier Jacinto answered. "No, not to my knowledge. The documents are kept locked away by the Marine Committee. They would only be released if a state requested them to prosecute Radcliffe for mutiny. Several attorneys working for the Marine Committee had reviewed them and prepared formal charges. Still, the agreement reached with the Massachusetts delegation was that Radcliffe would leave the Navy and never be eligible to serve in either the Army or the Navy. Why are you asking?"

"Because there are details in these articles that were only in my log and official report that I am sure Radcliffe would not have seen. So, it is possible someone let Radcliffe read them?"

Jaco's father's tone showed his concern. "It is possible, yes. Are you suggesting that a member of the Marine Committee or the Continental Congress gave him the report that was considered secret because of the details on the effectiveness of the long-12s, your initial tests of the guns, and the construction of *Scorpion's* hull."

"Yes. The question is who? Mr. Hewes passed away suddenly. If you remember, he admonished me for not hanging Radcliffe while we were at sea."

Javier shook his head. "I don't believe it was Adams. He became a champion of yours. I know where the records are being kept and am sure no copies were made. Nonetheless, I will make enquiries tomorrow."

Jaco looked around the room. "Edmund Radcliffe, as much as I despise the man, is entitled to his opinion. However, he is not entitled to misrepresent the facts. Jack, Hedley, and I know, Radcliffe left out key details that would have blown his arguments out of the water. So, can we sue the bastard for libel?"

Leaning forward, Morton Geiger said, "Radcliffe's father is a partner in one of Boston's oldest and largest law firms, and his two brothers also work in the same law firm. However, if asked, my father could recommend an outstanding lawyer in Boston who would love to take the Radcliffe's down a peg or two."

Jaco nodded emphatically. "Morton, ask your father and tell him why."

Hedley Garrison leaned back and placed his empty glass of beer on the table with a noticeable thunk. "There may be a better way to get back at Mr. Radcliffe without suing him. So, I've not thought through all the details, but here's my line of thinking. If Morton's father knows the publishers of the other papers in town, we may be able to discredit Mr. Radcliffe. If we do not get him fired, we can force the publisher to muzzle him or publish embarrassing corrections. Then, Jaco, if you want to go after Radcliffe for libel once we have kicked the British out, you will have the means."

Jaco leaned forward on the table to look at an officer he'd known since he was a midshipman. "Hedley, how? I'm all ears."

Garrison outlined his idea, and Jaco looked at Morton, who said his father would likely be willing to do his part. Others in Boston dislike the Radcliffes and would love to see them suffer.

Two days later, letters were posted, and *Zephyr* was en route to France.

CHAPTER 9

- SWORDFIGHT

VICINITY OF 33°NORTH, 73°WEST, THIRD WEEK OF FEBRUARY 1782

The thudding of feet on the deck above the Burdette's compartment woke Emily and her husband Francis. The shouted commands and the creaking of spars being hauled around were muted but still very noticeable.

Emily asked her husband, "What could be going on?"

"I don't know. It is probably a change in course or the wind. Go back to sleep."

Emily shook her head as her husband pulled the light cloth cover over his head and turned on his left side. She took a light blue busk from a peg on the cabin wall and slipped on a pair of wooden clogs before she slid open the door to the gun deck.

The Burdette's cabin and the other seven for passengers were at the forward end of the gun deck. Besides the twelve 12-pounders, the open area was where they took their meals and spent time when not in their cabins or on the main deck.

Emily climbed the forward companionway to the main deck. Avoiding a row of men hauling on a brace to finish trimming the topgallant sail on the mizzen mast, Emily stood with her hands gripping the top of the bulwark on the starboard side.

Flags were being run up and down Lenox's halyards as the ship peeled off from leading the convoy's starboard column followed by the other 74-

gun three-decker, *Warspite* and *Dilletante*, 64 guns. One of the frigates, Emily believed was *Diomede* was joining the three larger ships.

Looking around, Emily could see all the merchant ships in the convoy had raised their royals and staysails. She saw *Star of India's* captain lean over the railing and give orders to his first officer. Emily waited until he finished before asking, "Captain Horner, what is going on?"

"*Cleopatra* spotted a squadron of Frenchies, and our esteemed admiral will head them off with *Warspite, Lenox, Dillettante,* and *Diomede*, a 44-gun heavy frigate. We, along with *Alarm, Cleopatra, Minerva,* and *Pearl* will continue on our way to Charleston."

From the sheet she compiled with Darren's help, Emily learned that *Minerva* was a 36-gun frigate. *Alarm, Cleopatra,* and *Pearl* mounted thirty-two 12-pounders. Emily glanced to the north, the direction the larger ships were headed, "How far away are the French ships, and how many of them are there?"

"Our lookouts say they are less than five miles from *Star of India*. We don't know the composition of the French squadron. I guess the French will try to occupy the three-deckers while they send their frigates and smaller ships around to pick off a few in the convoy. Should be an interesting day."

Horner moved aft on the quarterdeck and picked up a spyglass leaving Emily standing alone. He returned a few moments later and leaned over the railing. "Mrs. Burdette, it might be a bloody affair if the Frenchies get amongst the convoy. *Star of India* will be one of the first ships they will try to seize due to its size and value in a prize court. I will not give up my ship without a fight. And, if it comes to that, your husband will be expected to join a gun crew. What you do, Mrs. Burdette …."

A series of booms rolled over the ship, which caused both Emily and Horner to look in the direction of the sound. The number continued to grow, and Emily thought she could hear the difference in the size of the cannon by the loudness of the boom.

"If you'll excuse me Mrs. Burdette, the fun has begun."

Emily gripped the railing on the top of the bulwark tighter as fear gripped her stomach and excitement filled her brain. At last, she could understand what her brother felt at the beginning of an action. Hopefully, the fighting will not come to *Star of India*, but she was determined to do her part.

She went below and found Francis standing next to a cannon, as one of the gunners explained each task required to load and fire a 12-pounder. *Star of India* had six cannons on each side. For most of the voyage from

England, they were covered by canvas and tied down under a wood table. The table was now gone. Where it was stowed, Emily did not know.

Standing next to the first gun on the starboard side, Emily asked, "What can I do?"

The gun captain, a man with a scraggly beard, looked at Emily. "Nothing, you're a bloody woman."

Emily responded in an annoyed tone, "And you're a man, so what. Now, what can I do to help fire your cannon?"

She spent the next 15 minutes learning how to use a rammer and a sponge. When the gunner, who introduced himself as Mortimer, was satisfied she knew how to load and ram home a powder charge and cannonball, he showed her how to prime the breech.

A ripple of cannon fire that seemed closer brought Emily and the gun captain on deck. To the north, they could see the masts of ships engulfed in gray-white gun smoke.

Closer to *Star of India*, each Royal Navy frigate left to escort the convoy was engaged with one or two smaller French Navy ships. A ship with two masts Emily recognized as a brig flying the French ensign was coming alongside the *Star of India*.

Captain Horner yelled, "Open the gun ports and run out."

Holding her busk so it was calf high, Emily ran down the companionway behind Mortimer to the #1 gun on the starboard side. It would be the last to fire. *Star of India's* first officer strode up and down the deck. "Depress the gun and aim at the hull. Range about one hundred yards."

She joined the men on the ropes as they pulled the 3,300-pound gun into battery. Emily picked up the wooden staff with the sponge on one end and the cloth-covered rammer at the other. To be ready, she'd dipped it in the bucket, and it dripped water as she stood waiting to use it.

Inside, Emily fought the paralyzing fear that she would be maimed or killed and concentrated on running the steps of what she would do once the gun was fired.

The first officer bellowed. "Fire as your gun bears."

The aft three guns fired, and the noise inside the ship was deafening. Through the open gunport, Emily could see the bowsprit of the French brig and then the bow. Mortimer looked down the barrel from the breech end of the 12-pounder and turned the jack screw to depress the barrel before touching the powder in the touch hole.

Emily remembered seeing the flash of powder but was momentarily stunned by the concussion and the deafening noise. The acrid smoke caused her eyes to tear making it difficult to see the end of the gun. Even with her sight blurred by tears, Emily rammed the sponge down the cast iron barrel twice. From the other side of the cannon, a sailor shoved the powder charge into the muzzle, and Emily used the rammer end of the staff to push against the powder charge.

She ignored the blasts from the other guns as she shoved the rammer against the cannonball that was slid into the barrel. Again, Emily stepped aside and looked out the gun port. The French brig was only about 50 yards away as the gun boomed.

The starboard #1-gun crew fired two more balls when Emily heard and felt a loud thump. The first officer ordered, "Close the gunports and stand by to repel boarders."

He was too late. A grapnel flew through the gun port, and the thought of a Frenchman on *Star of India* made her intensely angry. She looked around for something to cut the rope, but when she saw a hand grasp the inside of the gunport and then a face, she shoved the rammer as hard as she could into the man's face. Where he went, Emily did not know.

She tried to close the gunport, but the rope connected to the grapnel kept it open. Frantically, she looked around for something to cut the rope when Mortimer showed up with three pistols, two cutlasses, and an axe.

Emily took the axe and waited until another hand appeared. She amputated it with one expert stroke, cut the rope, and lashed the gunport closed. Elsewhere on the gun deck, French sailors were in hand-to-hand combat with the passengers and *Star of India's* crew.

A French marine gave her a lewd look and rushed at her with his sword in one hand and knife in another. Emily stood feigning fear until he was within 15 feet and then fired the pistol. The ball went where it was aimed, his chest, and the man went down.

Emily bent down to pick up the French Marine's sword when another French sailor grabbed her from the side and tried to spin her around. She uppercut him with a blow as hard as she could to the chin with the sword's hilt. The man's eyes rolled back into his head as he went down, out like a light.

She whirled as she stood. It had been years since Emily practiced with a sword, but her father insisted that she know how to handle one if she ever had to defend her children. The sword she picked up was a rapier, and while not as well balanced as the ones Smythe & Sons made for those who wanted a custom-made weapon, it was acceptably balanced.

What Emily didn't know was that the French brig *Francoise* was packed with French sailors and Marines. Their tactic was to approach *Star of India* from the rear, close enough so its guns could not depress to fire into its hull. Once alongside, men hurled grappling hooks attached to lines to bind the ships together. As the grapnels were thrown, the quartermaster would try to hold *Francoise* next to the targeted ship to let the French Marines and sailors board and overwhelm the merchant ship's crew. If successful, they would capture the merchant ship and its cargo intact. A bonus would be if they captured wealthy passengers who could be held for ransom.

Captain Horner knew what the French would try to do, so he kept altering *Star of India's* course slightly, trying to keep *Francoise* far enough away so his 12-pounders could do their work. He could see flying wood and bodies each time one of his 12-pounders scored a hit on the much smaller French ship.

When the French brig finally banged into *Star of India's* side, no one on the merchant ship knew that two 12-pounder balls went through the forward companionway and punched holes in its bottom. Knowing their ship was doomed, motivated the French sailors and Marines to take *Star of India*.

The swirling mass of men fighting with whatever they could pick up to defend themselves surrounded Emily. She had no choice but to fight. Adrenalin filled her veins as she made short work of a bearded French sailor whose handling of his cutlass was clumsy. Or maybe, it was that he thought he could easily kill a woman. A parry and a thrust to the man's midsection sent him writhing in pain to the deck with blood flowing out of the large cut made when Emily flicked her wrist up as she yanked the sword out of his belly.

Her next opponent also carried a rapier and was smaller, almost her size. He had thick, bright red hair that cascaded down to his shoulders. His locks flew around as the two parried each other's attacks. But he was no match for Emily, who was fueled by anger. How dare these Frenchmen attack *Star of India*! How dare they try to hurt ME!

The red-haired sailor came in low to cut her calf or thigh but only succeeded in slicing open Emily's busk below her knees which freed her legs from its confines. His crouched position made him vulnerable and was all Emily needed. Her downward slash gashed the man's forearm above the hand holding his rapier, which clattered to the deck unheard above the shouting and grunts of men exerting themselves or the cries of pain from the wounded and dying.

In one smooth motion, Emily stepped to the side as she raised her rapier and swung the blade horizontally, hoping to cut the Frenchman's side open. He ducked, and the blade glanced off the top of the redhead's shoulder and stopped in his neck, against his spine. Blood spewed from the severed arteries, and Emily spun to find another opponent.

Opposite her, a young French officer smiled as he stepped back and brought the hilt of his sword to his face before saying in accented English, "Mademoiselle knows how to handle a sword just like Joan d'Arc. *En garde!*"

They were in their own world as Emily and the Frenchman waved their swords, gauging their enemy. She had never been in a real sword fight before today. As a teenager and young woman, it was always drills. Now, if she made a mistake, she could die. Fear made Emily's arm feel heavy, but the smug, confident face of the French officer fueled her.

The Frenchman, probably feeling the pressure of time, and thinking he could overwhelm Emily, attacked. Muscle memory and watching his hand and arm, not the tip of the blade, enabled Emily to easily parry the Frenchman's moves.

Emily wanted to avoid getting close where her opponent could overpower her. She sidestepped his next thrust, spun, and slashed the Frenchman's side with the tip of her rapier as he charged past to get out into the middle of the deck giving him room to move and Emily with her back against the bulwark.

He was about to charge again when a man said in poorly accented French, *"Lâche ton épée ou je te fais sauter la tête…"* Drop your sword, or I will blow your head off."

Emily recognized her husband's voice, who spoke again, "Tell your men to surrender."

Before the Frenchman could respond, there were shouts of *"Miséricorde, miséricorde!!!"* Mercy, mercy!!! Mixed with *"Arrêt! Arrêt!"* Stop! Stop!

Abruptly, the clanging of swords stopped. Emily could see a dozen French sailors and Marines standing with their hands above their heads at the forward end of the gun deck. Between where Emily stood with her sword in one hand, there were at least a dozen dead and dying men spilling their blood on the wooden deck. Sand, spread by the crew before the fight, made it less slippery.

A cheer from the main deck was easily heard on the gun deck. Captain Horner came halfway down the aft companionway to tell them to come up on the main deck. The French have surrendered.

Curious, Emily went on deck, where she could see a mass of French sailors and Marines lined up against the bulkhead. Looking aft, she could see *Francoise* settling in the water and those on board boarding the ship's boats not destroyed by cannon balls.

Looking down, she saw blood splatters on her busk and feet and retched into one of the buckets used to wet the sponges for the cannon. At first, nothing came out, but after two dry heaves, her stomach emptied itself, leaving a metallic, unpleasant bilious taste in her mouth.

Gently, Francis Burdette peeled Emily's fingers from the hilt of the rapier and stood it against the bulkhead before pulling her close. As he did, Emily sobbed softly.

ON BOARD *STAR OF INDIA*, THE NEXT DAY, 1:43 A.M. LOCAL TIME

That night, Emily tossed and turned in her bed, unable to get what she had experienced earlier in the day out of her mind. The men's facial expressions when they realized their wound was mortal were more vivid now that she was resting in the relative comfort of a bed.

She didn't feel haunted or guilty since if she didn't kill them, they would have killed her. What she felt was sadness, not guilt, that she took another human life. Eventually, she hoped, the faces would fade from memory.

Unable to sleep, Emily went up on deck. The bright moon let her see the other ships in the convoy. *Lenox*, *Warspite*, and *Dilletante* all rejoined the convoy, battered but still sailing. Work repairing their damaged hulls, masts, and rigging continued even after sunset. Only *Diomede* was missing, and she wondered what happened to the British frigate.

On the one hand, the experience gave Emily more confidence as a person. On the other, the nightmare was that by dying, she'd leave her three boys motherless. Deep in her soul, she was afraid that Francis could or would not care for them. Emily often thought Francis had a wife and children primarily to advance his career, not for the joys and trials of being a father.

She was proud of Francis, who acquitted himself well in the battle. He killed two Frenchman with pistol shots and then, by his count, three more with the blade. Francis was an excellent swordsman who practiced frequently and carried a cane with a rapier blade concealed in the shaft.

After dinner, Francis was a bit blasé about the experience, brushing off killing another man in hand-to-hand combat as if it was just another contract he negotiated. But then again, Francis was not one to readily share his emotions.

Emily felt a splinter under her hand and a lump of cold metal. Looking down, she could barely make out a pistol ball lodged in the railing above the bulwark. She was trying to pry it out when she heard a voice behind her.

"Mrs. Burdette…" It was Captain Horner. "Lovely evening, isn't it?"

"Aye, Captain. It is so peaceful. Quite a contrast to yesterday." By the five bells in two rings of two and then one on the Middle Watch, Emily knew it was around 1:30 a.m.

"Hopefully, the Frenchies won't bother us again before we reach Charleston. Are you alright? It was very close work and a near thing."

The waxing Gibbous phase of the moon shed enough light so that Emily could see the concern on Horner's face. She took his meaning to be that the French almost took his ship.

"Aye, I think so. It will take me some time to put this experience to bed."

"Mrs. Burdette, please do not think me impertinent, but it helps if you chat candidly with someone you trust about the fight. It will help you put it in perspective and allow you to sleep."

"Captain, I am not at all offended. Your suggestion is most appreciated."

Horner nodded. "Mrs. Burdette, there are several members of the gun crews who say that you saved the day!"

"I don't think so."

"That is not what Mortimer and others believe. I put their statements in my ship's log and recommended that the company give you an award of some sort."

"Captain Horner, that is not necessary or warranted."

"Yes, it is, Mrs. Burdette. You are an extraordinary woman. Mr. Burdette is fortunate to have you as his wife."

"Thank you, sir, you are most kind." Neither said anything for a few minutes. Then Emily asked, "Do you know what happened to *Diomede?*"

Captain Horner's tone was flat and emotionless. "No. I suspect we will find out in due course."

He then left Emily wondering about the fate of the frigate *Diomede*. It could have been her brother's ship *Pompeii*. Knowing he was, hopefully safe, let her mind wander back to trying to determine what she did that was so special. Those thoughts led to her replaying every movement she made from the moment she walked onto the gundeck.

CHAPTER 10

- LIFETIME FRIENDSHIP AT FIRST SIGHT

CHARLESTON, FOURTH WEEK OF FEBRUARY 1782

One by one, the merchant ships in the convoy made their way up the harbor to the piers on the Cooper River. When the military transports anchored in the Ashley River they were greeted by a small flotilla of lighters to carry their cargo ashore.

Emily Burdette was the first of *Star of India*'s passengers to set foot in Charleston. She enjoyed the bright sun and the 63^0 F temperature as she studied the small town from the pier while her husband negotiated with a wagon driver to take their baggage to the Dockside Inn.

Charleston smelled different than Gosport and Portsmouth Harbor. She always thought one could smell the age in Portsmouth and that the water in the harbor was dank and old. In Charleston, everything seemed fresh.

Spring was already in the air. Emily liked Charleston immediately, thinking that if she was back in Gosport, she'd be wearing a heavy woolen sweater instead being comfortable in a dress made from linen. The shawl around her shoulders was more for style than warmth.

The entrance to the Dockside Inn didn't do justice to the simple, functional, and very nice furnishings. The wood paneling, chairs padded with dark blue cloth, and the quality appearance of the tables with their shell motifs all spoke quality. She stood back from her husband as he addressed the tall woman, she guessed was her mother's age in a formal, almost imperious tone. "Good afternoon. My name is Francis Burdette. You should have been notified that my wife and I will be staying here for some time." He handed her a letter from the Dockside Inn.

Yael Bildesheim Baez looked at the letter for a few seconds. Before she could say anything, Burdette offered, "Miss, if you need, I can read the letter to you."

The woman, whose hair had streaks of gray, eyes hardened, but her tone was soft and pleasant. "Mr. Burdette, I read and speak English, German, and Spanish quite well. The hotel is full of British officers, and I was debating which suite would give you and your wife the most privacy."

Emily looked at the floor, smiling. The woman put Francis, who could be pompous at times, in his place gently but firmly.

Francis Burdette, again trying to be helpful, offered, "Maybe, if you asked the hotel owner, he could help."

Yael looked Francis, and her eyes went from soft to a cold, hard stare. "Sir, I am the owner of the Dockside Inn. My husband Ricardo helps with the upkeep of the building, prepares the meals for our guests, and runs the tavern. Now, if you'll excuse me for a few minutes while I have some things moved so you can have a small suite with a bedroom and sitting room with a view of the harbor."

Francis turned around to his wife, his face red with embarrassment. Emily forced herself to keep from laughing in his face.

Yael returned, followed by a young woman who was, Emily guessed, a teenager. "Mr. and Mrs. Burdette, my daughter Ester will show you to your room. Your baggage will be brought up in a few minutes. Meals are taken in the large room to the left of where you are standing. We serve breakfast from seven to eight, the midday meal from twelve to one, and supper, as you English call it, from six to eight. The food is simple and tasty. We vary the menu depending on what we can buy in the local food markets. Good day and I hope you enjoy your stay in Charleston."

Later in the afternoon, as Francis and Emily walked around Charleston, she wondered where *Pompeii* was since none of the warships that escorted the convoy had come into the harbor. She remembered seeing *Pompeii* leave the convoy and wondered if his ship would be ordered to rejoin the squadron in Charleston.

When they returned to the Dockside Inn, Francis went into the tavern for a drink. Seeing several British officers at the table, he struck up a conversation.

Emily didn't like taverns, nor did she want to be an ornament to which the others would pay attention to her out of courtesy which would keep the conversation from what Francis wanted to discuss. She stood for a moment while she decided what she would do next when Yael came out from the office behind the front desk and asked her new guest, "Mrs. Burdette, did you enjoy your walk?"

"Aye, I did, and I think my husband did as well."

"Where did you go?"

"Just up and down the waterfront."

"If you walk farther into the city, you'll see many shops and nice homes. Right now, Charleston is crowded with British soldiers."

"I noticed." Emily lowered her head and decided to trust this woman. "My husband is here to negotiate a contract for my father's business. While he is working, I was hoping to meet a friend of my brother."

"Do you have the address?"

"I do, and I have a letter of introduction."

"May I ask the name of the family?"

"Winters."

Yael nodded emphatically. "The Winters live on King Street, just north of Broad."

"How far is that from here?"

"If you know the way, it is a pleasant ten-minute walk. Or, if you prefer, I can arrange for a carriage."

"No, I think I would like the walk. Is it safe?"

Yael laughed. "Before the British came, if one was not near the houses of civil union along the waterfront, a woman could walk anywhere in this town without fear. Now, I don't know. The city is full of British soldiers who want to take a woman. Before the war and even now, the custom in Charleston is that women do not walk alone. So, I think it would be safer if you were escorted."

Emily smiled at Yael calling the two brothels they passed as houses of civil union. "I don't know anyone in Charleston. My husband would be bored with the conversation, and I could be there for some time."

"I see. If you wish, either my daughter Ester or I could write a note asking the individual to come here where you can sit and talk in the great room for as long as you wish. Either Ester or I can make you tea or coffee. We always have leftovers from the meals."

"Ms. Baez, I can read and write."

"Mrs. Burdette, I meant no disrespect."

"None taken. Women in England are not welcomed in schools. My parents insisted that I be educated, and I assist my mother with the Smythe & Sons books, so I do sums as well."

Yael laughed. "Good for you." She pointed to a table in what she called the great room. "Please. I will bring you a pen and paper. When you are finished, I will ask one of my children to deliver the letter. They know the Winters. Their daughter Melody teaches in their school."

Emily scratched out a note with the quill pen in what some experts would say was a "fine hand."

Ms. Winters,

Accompanying this note is a letter of introduction from my brother Darren. He urged me to meet with you now that I am in Charleston. Yael Baez of the Dockside Inn has offered a table in the inn's great room where we can meet for the first time.

I am excited to finally meet you after hearing Darren speak so highly and lovingly about "his Melody." Please let whoever drops off this note know when you will come to the Dockside Inn or if I should come to your home.

Emily Smythe Burdette

She took the note to Yael who dripped sealing wax on the fold and then pressed the inn's imprint into the hardening wax. "I'll bring down the note of introduction."

CHARLESTON, THE SAME DAY, 6:49 P.M.

Rafer Muir was delighted when Francis and Emily entered the Great Room for dinner. Muir walked over to Francis and invited the couple to dine with one of his fellow officers, Colonel Stuart Mac Ewen. As newcomers and a source of new stories, Muir hoped they would bring news and information from England.

Introductions were made while Muir held out the chair for Emily. Francis Burdette, sensing someone new to talk to besides his wife, picked the seat next to Mac Ewen, a full colonel in 41st Regiment (Highland) of Foot.

The seating arrangement put Rafer Muir opposite Emily, whom he thought was beautiful. She was dressed simply but elegantly. What stood out were her green eyes that took in everything around her. She had a lovely face with crow's feet just starting to appear at the corners of her eyes. Muir could tell from holding out her chair Emily didn't need a corset drawn tightly to have an attractive figure.

The conversation continued for a few minutes, and Rafer noticed that Emily hadn't said anything. Rafer wanted to see if she had a voice by posing a question requiring a thoughtful answer. "Mrs. Burdette, besides accompanying your husband on what must be an important business trip, why did you come to Charleston?"

Her smile, at least to Rafer Muir, who, by profession and choice, was still a bachelor, lit up the table. "Curiosity mostly. I wanted to see someplace other than England or, God forbid, France. Everyone in Gosport and Portsmouth talks about New York, Boston, and Philadelphia. From what I understand, the rebels fought to hold Charleston and failed to take the town back from the British Army. So, it must have some value. I want to know why?"

Muir's regular dinner partner, Colonel Stuart Mac Ewen's eyes lit up while Francis Burdette looked at the two officers. "I'm here on business that involves her family's firm, and Emily was gracious enough to accompany me."

One of the joys of having a degree from the University of Edinburgh was that Rafer learned a few things about a business from his studies within its limited curriculum. When Muir glanced at Emily, her eyes flickered as she acknowledged his interest. He wasn't sure if they were hardening or softening. "Mrs. Burdette, value is an interesting choice of words. Would you care to explain?"

Eager to participate and not sit at the table as if she was a flower in a pot, Emily spoke evenly. "I chose the word deliberately because both sides value Charleston. We and the rebels expend treasure in terms of money and supplies as well as men to hold the town. So, besides having a lovely climate in the middle of winter, I am again asking you, gentlemen, what is Charleston's value to the British Army and England? It is a simple question."

Stuart Mac Ewen looked at Rafer as if to say, you invited the couple to sit at our table and asked the question, you answer. Rafer liked the direct, well-thought-out answer. Clearly, Emily Burdette was no dolt whose only value was her looks and ability to produce children and maybe cook a decent meal.

Rafer sensed Emily's husband was uncomfortable with her reasoned restatement of the question. Something in his mind told him that his wife was not afraid to speak her mind.

He explained the British Army seized Charleston as part of General Clinton's strategy to force Washington to divide his army to fight around New York and New England while protecting the southern cities of Savannah and Charleston at the same time. From what Muir had learned, Charleston exported indigo, rice, lumber, and some cotton to England before the war.

Emily listened intently with her eyes focused on Rafer. When he finished, she nodded to Stuart Mac Ewen as if to say, "Colonel, do you have anything to add?"

He didn't, so Emily asked, "Well, Lieutenant Colonel Muir, that strategy seems to be in tatters since Burgoyne surrendered back in '77 and Cornwallis surrendered another army in October '81. To someone like me who knows nothing about military strategy, all the British Army has left are enclaves around three cities and not much else. 'Twere I adding sums, there's more in the minus column than the plus, which tells me that the British Army has failed in its mission. Would you gentlemen not agree?"

Francis Burdette blurted out, "Colonel, you don't have to answer that question. My wife is being impertinent to the point of being impolite."

Rafer Muir shook his head. "I disagree, Mr. Burdette. Your wife is asking the same question we ask ourselves every day. However, sir, we are soldiers in the King's Army, so if we are told to stay in Charleston, that is what we do. We have no choice."

The waiter delivered the first course - a bowl of thick pea soup. Stuart Mac Ewen used the opportunity to change subjects. "You'll find that the fare at the Dockside is hearty, quite good, and plentiful. The menu doesn't vary much, but eating here is much better than British Army rations. The desserts, however, usually baked fruit pies, are superlative."

Francis Burdette eager to talk about something other than the war, bobbed his head. "That is good to know."

The lawyer used dinner to ask the two colonels about their service in the British Army. Emily listened politely and didn't say another word.

Being the quiet, dutiful, obedient wife was a role she hated almost as much as not being allowed to pursue her own career. She believed she had a good mind and should be allowed to use it.

Desert was made from candied berries, and the Burdette's were about halfway through when a man and a woman were guided to the table by Yael Baez. Seeing a woman, the three men at the table stood.

"Excuse us for interrupting, I am Theodore Winters, and this is my wife, Amelia. Melody is our daughter. Mr. Burdette, is there someplace we can speak in private?"

Francis Burdette looked around the room and spotted an unoccupied table in the corner. Pointing in the general direction, "I think that table will do." Then he nodded to Muir and the other officer. "Gentlemen, if you'll excuse us, please."

The British officers stood when Emily did, and the couple followed the Winters to an empty table. The walk gave Rafer Muir the time to admire Emily from behind.

Seeing his interest, Mac Ewen said, "That Mrs. Burdette is a handsome woman."

"Aye, my good friend. And apparently, a fine mind to go with her good looks. But, alas, she is married, so it is hands-off. But one cannot help but admire beauty when one sees it."

Before the Winters and Burdettes sat down, the two men shook hands and held out the chairs for their wives. Ted Winters began. "We apologize for not responding to your note, but we were not at home when it was delivered. We came thinking that by now, you would have finished dinner."

Putting her hand on Ted Winter's arm, Emily said, "That's perfectly fine, Mr. Winters."

Amelia offered. "Melody is in Dorchester where she teaches school Tuesday evenings, Wednesday, and Thursday mornings. She comes home Thursday nights."

Emily nodded. It confirmed what Darren told her. "Then she will be home tomorrow night."

"Yes, God willing."

"Is she in danger?"

Amelia spoke before her husband. "From us patriots, no. From the British, always. You never know what they will do."

Theodore put up his hand. "Amelia is exaggerating. The British Army controls who can enter or leave Charleston from the north. Sometimes they can be, shall we say, difficult."

Confused, Francis asked, "Why?"

"Well, they are afraid of spies and saboteurs. One of Melody's best friends is Dr. Reyna Laredo. Her brother Amos is the commander of an army unit that has given the British Army fits. Melody and Reyna have been searched several times when returning to Charleston. Now, they need a special pass signed by General Alexander Leslie to travel to Dorchester."

Francis muttered, "I see." The war was something that he read about in the newspapers. Now he was in the middle of the revolt in a city occupied by the British Army. He wondered if the Winters wanted to continue to be the subjects of King George.

Emily touched her husband's arm. "Dear, why don't you and Ted have a drink at the bar and let Amelia and I chat for a few moments."

Both men knew an order from a wife when they heard one. The women wanted some privacy, and Francis wanted to learn more about the business climate in Charleston.

Amelia looked at the woman a few years older than her daughter. "How much has Darren told you about his relationship with my Melody?"

Emily laughed. "He has confided his deepest thoughts, more so than what he has told our parents. Darren is madly in love with your daughter and wants to marry her in the worst possible way. He is willing to give up everything for Melody."

"Did he tell you that Melody will not move to England?"

Emily nodded.

"Let me tell you about the world around Charleston. My husband is a Loyalist. Asa, my oldest is serving with General Washington in the Continental Army. Ezekiel is my youngest son and wants to join the Royal Navy but thank God, he has not. My daughter's and my sympathies are with those we call patriots. The British call them rebels, traitors, and other derogatory terms."

"Do you oppose the marriage?"

"Good lord, no. Darren is a fine man, and they adore each other. Their love is quite genuine."

The two women were still talking about Darren and Melody when their husbands returned to the table. Theodore Burdette spoke first, "So, have you sorted out how we are going to get Melody and Mrs. Burdette together."

"Aye, we have."

"Excellent, then we shall be off. I have a busy day tomorrow." He turned to Francis, "If you need an office, please consider my firm to be yours."

The Burdettes walked the Winters to the inn's entrance and then went to their room.

THE NEXT DAY, 4:14 P.M.

Each boom of the thunder, louder than she'd ever heard, rattled the windows and lightning turned night into daylight. With each flash that lit up their hotel room for seconds, Emily could see all the ships anchored in the river.

Emily thought God must be angry at Charleston or maybe at her for coming to Charleston. Butterflies flew around her stomach as she wondered what Melody Winters would be like. And then there were Amelia Winters's comments the night before about the war that swirled around Charleston kept running through her mind.

This rebellion against King George III, the man who was her king, was much more than about the citizens of the Thirteen Colonies wanting to rule themselves. The fight was about personal freedom to choose what profession one would pursue; where one would live; what religion one could practice; and having a voice in what taxes were assessed and laws made and enforced.

On a more personal level, both Amelia and she had grown up in a world with few opportunities available for women outside the home. Amelia supported Melody's desire to have a professional career and fulfill the traditional role of a wife. Amelia's views went further than Emily's mother, whom she thought before she arrived in Charleston, was very progressive.

If it were not for her mother's insistence, Emily's education would have been limited. In England, accounting was a profession only available to men even if she, as a woman, could demonstrate her knowledge. Most professional accountants were members of law firms and were often attorneys. The Inns, a.k.a. law schools, would not accept women as students, thus making it almost impossible for women to pursue accounting as a profession.

Every year, Francis offered to introduce Lester Smythe or his sons to the accountants at his law firm. The pretext was the same, the firm had professional accountants and could, should the firm ever want to become a joint stock company that offered shares to the public, they would "need" professional accountants to assure investors and keep the books.

At each inquiry, Lester would ask the same question, why should I pay your firm to handle Smythe & Sons accounting? What Olivia and Emily do meets English stock company standards for accounting, and they do it for free?

Watching the rain pummel the cobblestones, Emily wondered if Melody and Reyna had made it back to Charleston before the rain started. She turned to light one of the candles to put in the lantern so she could continue reading Haywood's *The Fatal Fondness*. She finished putting the glass on the lantern before she responded to the soft knock on the door.

"Come in."

Ester Baez opened the door far enough to look inside. "Mrs. Burdette, Mrs. Amelia Winters, and her daughter Melody are downstairs. The Great Room is quite crowded, so you will find it difficult to find a place to speak privately."

Francis was one of the men in the Great Room having a drink or two or three. *In other words, do you want me to bring them up here? I'm in my nightgown but can change quickly.*

"Please bring them up, and if they are wet, some cloths to dry themselves."

Ester nodded her understanding and disappeared.

Figuring she had only two or three minutes, Emily wouldn't have time to get "properly" dressed, so she slipped into a rust-colored house coat with a cream-colored linen collar and tied the belt around her slim waist. She then closed the door to the bedroom adjacent to the small sitting room with a table, a small couch, and three chairs.

A quick look around the sitting room said nothing seemed amiss. When there was a soft tap on the door, Emily said, "Please come in."

The door opened and was filled with a woman with bright, ice-blue eyes and light brown hair who was neither petite nor tall and was wearing a simple dress. "Mrs. Burdette, I am Melody Winters." A nod to the woman next to her. "You have met my mother. May we come in?"

"Please, please. I am so happy to finally meet you." The young woman's beauty almost took Emily's breath away. No wonder Darren was attracted to her. She held out her hand and Melody's grasp was firm.

"I as well."

The two women's clothing was not as wet as Emily feared. "I asked the inn's staff to bring some dry cloth, thinking you must have gotten soaked in this dreadful rain."

Melody laughed softly. "Welcome to Charleston or Charles Town as the Englishmen here call our city. A carriage parked under a portico works wonders in keeping one dry. Our feet are wet, but not much else. Thank you for thinking of us."

Waving to the chairs with dark blue padded seats in which the backs had the traditional shell design made from white pine. The upholstered couch had the same shell made from mahogany in the center of the frame below the cushion, "Thank you for coming. Please, sit down."

Melody and her mother took the two padded chairs which she suspected were made by her father's shop, leaving Emily on the couch. "Do you know where Darren is?"

"Frankly, no."

"Is he well?"

"I believe so. I saw *Pompeii* leave our convoy with several other ships about a week out of Charleston. I suspect he will be back here shortly."

Melody nodded softly. "Did Darren tell you what was in his note to me?"

"No."

Emily suspected where Melody was going and stood up just as she heard a knock on the door. "Come in."

The door opened, revealing Ester holding several large sections of clean cloth, and her younger brother Ethan was holding a tray with a pitcher and three cups. "Mrs. Burdette, have you ever tried chocolate?"

"No. What is chocolate?"

Ester smiled as she spoke. "Ma'am, I think it is the nectar of the Gods. My grandfather was a chocolatier and learned his trade in Brazil before he came here in 1740. Now, we get the cocoa beans from Grenada or St. Vincent and grind them into a powder to make chocolate. Then, we add fresh milk, sugar, and some vanilla when we have it."

Emily sniffed the liquid in the cup she was handed. "Hmmmmm, smells wonderful."

The young girl continued with the history of chocolate as she knew it. "Ma'am, back in 1767, we were all drinking and eating chocolate as much as tea and coffee. Chocolatiers in the big cities in New York, Pennsylvania, Rhode Island, and Massachusetts were exporting better quality cocoa powder to England at a lower price than English chocolatiers could buy through their own sources. So, when Parliament passed the Townsend Act of 1767, they included a tax on chocolate imported to North America along with the big tariff on tea."

"Do you still pay the tax?"

"No. When we had a Royal Governor, he didn't enforce the tax because he liked his chocolate and didn't want to pay more."

"If I may ask, what happened to your Royal Governor?"

"He fled back in 1778, and we heard he died in England. King George III hasn't replaced him and when we're independent, we won't need one."

Emily was a bit taken aback by the 16-year-old's candor. She focused on the aroma coming from the cup.

"Ma'am, you can add sugar, if you wish. Most do."

After taking a tentative sip of the warm liquid, Emily took another longer drink, savoring the taste of chocolate for the first time. "Oh my, this is delicious. And yes, I will add a bit of sugar."

A half spoonful of white sugar went into Emily's cup. After stirring, she tasted it again. "This is quite good. Thank you."

"Mrs. Burdette, we don't serve chocolate to the British officers staying with us." Ester face lit up with a knowing smile. "My father makes a chocolate pie as a treat for our family on Saturday, our Sabbath. I'm sure he wouldn't mind me bringing you a portion."

Amelia leaned forward and put her hand on the British woman's arm. "Emily, do try it. The chocolate candy that Ricardo makes is sold in stores here in Charleston and is divine."

The other two women in the room sipped their cups, and Amelia didn't add any sugar while Melody added a spoonful. Satisfied that her mission was done, Ester left the three women alone.

Melody's eyes bored into Emily's face. She wasn't being hostile, but she wanted the truth. "Why did you come to Charleston?"

"Miss Winters, please allow me to bare my soul."

Before she could continue, Melody said, "Mrs. Burdette, if we are to be related by marriage, please use my first name."

Emily bobbed her head and began again with a speech she thought she had scripted out on the *Star of India*. "Melody, what started out as a simple request, I now realize, is much more complicated. My father genuinely believes there will be a strong market for Smythe & Sons products in what you hope will be a new country and he wants to license Dr. Laredo's designs. By encouraging me to come along, he hoped the two of us could meet…"

"Because your mother was afraid that her son fell for some dasher who would steal Darren's heart and then break it when she left him in the gutter, a broken man…."

Emily thought Melody's use of the word dasher, meaning a well-turned-out harlot who was also involved in some type of con, was appropriate. She nodded in agreement. "Yes, that sums it up nicely, but there is much more…."

The English woman refilled her cup with the warm chocolate drink and took another long swallow. She didn't mean to leave the two Winters women hanging, waiting for the rest of the story, but the pause gave her time to compose her thoughts. Emily slid off her chair, knelt before Melody, and held her hands.

"Melody, I did not come here to dissuade you from marrying Darren. Our mother is a very traditional woman who wants Darren to be happy. That is all."

She looked into Melody's eyes which had softened. "In some ways, my mother and I are trapped in the old ways and are jealous of women like you. You have opportunities I may never have…."

The door opened, and Francis Burdette entered. "Oh, I am so sorry. Mrs. Winters, my apologies." The attorney bowed slightly, "And you, young lady, must be Melody. Darren's description of your beauty did not go far enough. It is my pleasure to meet you."

Melody giggled, "Thank you, Mr. Burdette. You are most kind with your flattery."

The attorney looked around the room. "I think I interrupted an important conversation, so I shall return to the tavern for a few more drinks with some British Army bagpipes. But I am duty bound to remind you that I have to be up bright and early tomorrow, so I will be back shortly."

With that statement, Francis Burdette left the ladies. He would have another drink or two and return. In the morning, Francis Burdette was meeting Ms. Shoshana Jacinto at the law offices of Burrows & Soriano at 10.

By the time he returned, the rain had stopped, and the Winters had left. Emily had accepted an invitation to dine at the Winters' home tomorrow evening. Melody promised to introduce Emily to Reyna and Shoshana. In Emily's mind, a plan was forming, one unconnected tidbit at a time.

NEW YORK, FIRST WEEK OF MARCH 1782

With the supply ships safely escorted to New York, Darren was impatient to sail with *Stirling Cross* and *Jason* to escort a convoy filled with reinforcements and supplies for the British Army in Charleston. Charleston meant a few precious hours or days with Melody.

As the junior captain, *Pompeii* was the last ship of the three escorts to be re-provisioned. The loading and storing the casks of beer, water, rum, flour, peas, oatmeal, and the list went on was almost complete. He expected to be summoned to *Stirling Cross* to learn when they would sail. He was surprised when his third Lieutenant Judah Burton knocked on his door to tell him he was wanted at General Clinton's headquarters.

The boat ride to the tip of Manhattan was choppy due to the cold wind that made it downright chilly. Darren was wet and cold when he stepped ashore, a British Army colonel was waiting for him. "Captain Smythe?"

"Aye, I am Captain Smythe of His Majesty's Ship *Pompeii*."

"Good." The Colonel handed him a sealed letter. "These are your sailing orders. You are to take Brigadier Hutchins to Halifax as expeditiously as possible where you will pick up Captain Exeter of the Royal Navy and transport him safely to Bermuda. From there, you shall rejoin your squadron in Charleston. The Brigadier and two members of his staff will be here shortly with their baggage. General Clinton's Navy liaison officer has approved these orders."

The bosun's chair that lifted Brigadier Hutchins from the long boat over the main deck bulwark was swung smoothly over the spot between the two lines of six Royal Marines. When the general was on his feet, Bosun Louttit piped "All Call" and announced, "Brigadier Hutchins, arrrrrivvvving!!!"

The Marine with the snare drum rapped out a beat as the British Army general walked between the line of Royal Marines. As he did, the Marines snapped to port arms. Their muskets were all perfectly aligned and vertical, with the musket butts held mid-thigh.

At the end of the line of Royal Marines, Darren waited. When the general reached him, Darren held out his hand. "Welcome to *Pompeii*, sir."

"Quite a nice ceremony, that."

"Thank you, sir. Piping senior officers of either service or captains is one of our traditions. Now, if you come aft with me, I can show you to my cabin and introduce you to my officers, who will bring your aide and chief-of-staff with them."

Hutchins looked around Darren's cabin, particularly at the two shiny black-painted 9-pounder stern chasers. "I hope we don't have to use these between New York and Halifax."

Darren didn't want to tell him that if *Pompeii* fired its stern chasers, something terrible had happened in a fight. "Sir, unless we encounter an impertinent rebel privateer or a French frigate, these guns shall stay silent. I hope my cabin is satisfactory."

Hutchins looked around, "Where, then, are you going to sleep?"

"I'll sleep on the berthing deck with the crew. We should be at sea for only three nights, so I can manage. The officers take their midday meal and supper in my cabin, so I hope you and your officers can join us. We eat what the crew is served. The only difference is that we have a better bar."

"You don't have your own cook?"

"No, one of the ship's cooks prepares our meals. And, as a matter of course, I dine with the crew one day a week. My officers do the same."

"That is very plebian of you."

"Sir, we all share the same danger from the sea and from the enemy's fire. There is no place to hide on a man-of-war, so I think it best that the men take their measure of their officers to give them confidence in their abilities. And we must know our sailors as well. One more thing, sir. During the day, we use the table for our chart as we plot our progress. If you need some privacy, just let me know and we will do our best to accommodate you.

Hutchins nodded. "Well, then, this will have to do."

Darren didn't say anything because his cabin was all he had to offer.

CHAPTER 11

– NEW AND UNLIKELY PARTNERS

CHARLESTON, SECOND WEEK OF MARCH 1782

While Francis was at the courthouse researching contracts to make sure the terms in the agreement were compliant with both South Carolina and English law, Emily found a well-lit table in the corner of the Great Room to read. Since arriving in Charleston, Emily had become very fond of chocolate. Seeing her in the Great Room, Ester Baez brought her a cup of warm chocolate milk that she was sipping when the hollow clump of boots on the wooden floor changed the focus of attention from the novel to Rafer Muir.

When he saw her, Muir felt dragged to the woman as iron filings are to a magnet. His conscious brain kept warning him that he was playing with fire. An affair with a married woman would ruin his Army career, but his heart said keep walking.

Rafer took a pot of tea and two cups and saucers from a table against the wall and put them on tray and walked across the room. "Good afternoon, Mrs. Burdette, I hope I am not intruding."

He was tired of the monastic life of a soldier who, at a moment's notice, could be sent anywhere in the world to do and most likely die. So far, he had been lucky since many of his colleagues had succumbed to wounds and disease. Muir believed this new country he was fighting to prevent from becoming independent would let him be free to do what he wanted, and that was important to him. What role, if any, Mrs. Burdette would play in his future was unknown, but he did want to spend more time with her.

He held out the pot of tea. "Mrs. Burdette, would you like me to freshen your cup?"

"No, but thank you, Colonel."

There was an awkward silence for a few seconds before Emily pointed to the chair opposite her. "Please, sir, sit down. I need a break from reading."

Muir put the tray on another table, poured himself a cup of tea, dropped two lumps of light brown sugar into the liquid before doing as Emily suggested. "Pray tell, what are you reading?"

"A romance novel by Francis Burney called *Evalina*. It is a way to pass a few idle moments. Have you read it?"

Muir took a deep breath. Sunlight streaming through the windows highlighted loose strands of her sandy brown hair. "No, Mrs. Burdette, I can't say that I have. One of the disadvantages of not being a general on a campaign is that one is limited in what one can carry in a pack or saddlebags. If one is lucky, one is allowed a small chest. Books are heavy and take up space, so those few I own are back in Inverness."

"So, Colonel, you do read for pleasure?"

"I do. When I can. Unfortunately, I have not had much time to read since arriving in Charleston. We've been busy." He started to say being target practice for the rebels but didn't.

"Do you socialize with any of the residents of Charleston?"

Muir chuckled. "Unless they have a reason to speak with me or they are Loyalists, no. I have, however, met one rebel professionally."

"May I ask who?"

"Aye… 'Twas Reyna Laredo, who our regimental surgeon says is a first-rate doctor."

Emily closed the book. The name Reyna Laredo piqued her interest. "Were you wounded?"

"Aye, there was that. She redid my regimental surgeon's work which had become infected. Within a week of following her instructions, the infection was gone, and I still have a functioning left arm."

Emily's movement of her head suggested that he continue with the rest of the story.

"The British Army in Charleston had a smallpox epidemic and learned that Miss Laredo was familiar with variolation. Are you familiar with what this is?"

Emily nodded her head. "I am. Everyone in my family has had the procedure. What did she do?"

"Our regiment volunteered to test the process after we had a dozen cases. Miss Laredo knows how to produce the powder, and we paid her to variolate the entire regiment. Since then, the 11th hasn't had one case of smallpox while other regiments have had many."

To Emily, young Dr. Reyna Laredo became more interesting with every passing moment. This meant the agreement between Smythe & Sons had become even more critical, and she was now determined not to leave without one.

Lieutenant Colonel Muir stirred and then took a sip of the tea that he poured when he sat down and added another lump of sugar. "Have you met Miss Laredo?"

"No, but I would like to. She seems to be an interesting woman." *And so unlike those of us trapped in traditional English roles of wife and mother. Trapped is an excellent word to describe my situation, and how to escape the trap is my problem.*

Neither Francis nor she mentioned they were in Charleston to negotiate a contract with Reyna. Francis said he was here to conclude an important contract with a local firm at an earlier dinner. *And in my mind, it is getting more and more important by the minute.*

"Mrs. Burdette, if I may, I'd like to share my observation about the locals based on my experience here and in New York."

Emily wasn't sure what she would hear but kept an open mind. She liked the Scotsman and his strong brogue. "Please do."

"These colonials are a stubborn polyglot lot and very determined. They come from everywhere and have learned to get along with each other, survive and prosper. Then King George came along and said, we need you to pay for the Seven Years War that we – the French, Spanish, and English – forced upon you. And, also, you need to pay for the British Army's presence in the Colonies to protect you, henceforth, from our, not your, enemies. So, without asking the colonials what they thought, Parliament passes a series of laws designed raise money for England and restrict their trade and freedoms. The colonials say a pox on you, England go away. Henceforth, England has a rebellion on its hands that has been damned difficult to put down."

"Do you think the rebels will win in the end?"

Muir took a deep breath. "Aye, I do. Eventually, Lord North and his supporters will get it through their thick noble heads that it is smarter to make peace and trade with these rebels than to be at loggerheads."

Both were engrossed in the conversation, and neither heard Francis Burdette's footfalls. "Ahhhhh, Lieutenant Colonel Muir, what brings you to the Dockside in the middle of the day?"

"I was going to General Leslie's headquarters and stopped by the inn to change into a clean uniform. That's when I saw your lovely wife sitting here, reading. She asked me to share my experience with the locals."

Burdette was more than curious. "Rebels or Loyalists?"

"Both."

"Damned rebels…. They should end the rebellion and resume being good English citizens if they had any sense."

Muir stood up and didn't want to explain to him that many of the rebels didn't come from England, nor did they wish to continue to be British citizens. Instead, he thought a bit of history might enlighten the officious Burdette. "Sir, as a Scotsman, I fully understand the colonials' desire for independence. After all, in 1296, William Wallace rebelled against King Edward II, and we lost. Until Scotland joined England in 1707, the relationship was stormy, so we rebelled and lost again in 1745. England would do well to give the rebels their due. Good day, Mr. Burdette." He nodded to Emily, "And you, Mrs. Burdette, as well."

Francis Burdette remained standing as he watched Muir leave. "Interesting fellow, that Lieutenant Colonel Muir. Not afraid to speak his mind."

"Aye, so Solicitor Burdette, how was your day?"

Francis sat down and poured himself a cup of tea. "I believe I have finished a draft of the basic terms that will be acceptable to Miss Laredo and Smythe & Sons. So, it has been a good day."

Emily thought for a second. "Francis, I want to attend the meetings with Miss Laredo and her barrister, Shoshana Jacinto."

"Why? It will be boring business talk about legal terms." He almost added that you know little or nothing about but didn't.

She decided to try a bit of sugar in her answer. "I still would like to be there. If my family is to license and patent Dr. Laredo's designs, I'd like to tell my father I have taken her measure. And I know the firm's financials far better than thee."

"Aye, but I thought you wanted to spend more time with Miss Melody Winters so you could report back to your mother."

"I have already fulfilled that mission and posted my first letter today."

"I see." Burdette paused, trying not to show his annoyance at Emily's desire to insert herself into his world. In his view, he would present the contract to Ms. Jacinto and Ms. Laredo and possibly accept a few modifications around the periphery to give the appearance of concessions. But in the end, the agreement will be very favorable to Smythe & Sons.

"Emily, I don't see this meeting taking very long. An hour or two at most. We discuss the terms, and they will want to review it, and then in a day or so, we meet again. Miss Laredo either signs what we offer, or she doesn't. Very cut and dry."

"Nevertheless, Francis I still want to participate."

"Participate?" To Francis Burdette, Emily just said she wanted to do more than listen. She wanted a role in the negotiations.

"Yes, Francis, participate. As a shareholder of Smythe & Sons, I have a vested interest in the outcome of this trip and any other future meetings here in Charleston. I suspect there may be more here that will benefit Smythe & Sons and I intend to ferret it out. Therefore, it is best that I participate."

"Emily, my dear," Francis Burdette forced himself not to be condescending, "This is a simple royalty contract …" Burdette let his mouth speak before his brain censored his words. "… that we could have negotiated by mail instead of coming to this…"

Emily knew her husband of 12 years quite well and his favorite phrases. "God forsaken place?"

Flustered, Francis simply nodded his head.

"If this is as you say, then we will be finished quickly and be able to book our passage home. However, I still insist on coming."

"Insist?"

"Yes, insist, as in you do not have a choice. I will be the company's representative, that is, your client, who also happens to be your wife who also owns twenty percent of Smythe & Sons shares."

Weakly, Francis asked, "Emily, may I ask that you rethink this. The session will not be worth your time."

"My answer will not change. And, in the future, please allow me to judge what is worthwhile and what is not."

Francis did not respond because he knew arguing with his wife would be pointless. Emily found as she was speaking, there was a hardness in her tone she had not used before.

One of Emily's responsibilities at Smythe & Sons was invoicing customers. To ensure the bills were accurate, she had read every in-force contract held by Smythe & Sons and knew the financial and legal terms. The agreement with Reyna Laredo couldn't be that different.

Emily was now determined not to be just a wife and mother. *The swordfight on* Star of India *has given me the additional backbone and confidence.*

CHARLESTON, THE NEXT DAY, 10: 00 A.M.

When Shoshana walked into the small sitting area of Burrows & Soriano's office, she was surprised to see a man and a woman waiting. Both Emily and Francis stood when Shoshana entered the firm's front office. Before seeing this woman, Emily, thought she was tall. The young woman standing before her was almost a head taller than both she and her husband.

"Good morning, I am Shoshana Jacinto." She held her hand out to Emily first. "Thank you for coming all the way from England."

"I'm Emily Smythe Burdette." Emily emphasized her middle name as a subtle way of making the point that she is a member of the Smythe family.

"Francis Burdette, the firm's solicitor and a partner at Helmsley and Cole. We have offices in Portsmouth and London."

Shoshana took Burdette's use of the term solicitor to mean he did not spend much time in court defending clients. "Pleased to meet you, sir. Please, follow me. We will use our law library for our meeting because it has the most room. I have refreshments waiting."

When Emily saw Reyna Laredo, the young woman was not at all what she expected. Then again, she reminded herself that she didn't know what to expect. The petite woman who shook her hand had dark eyes that bored into Emily's eyes intently, not trying to intimidate but showing curiosity and interest. Reyna's skin was dark, somewhere between the color of brown sugar and olive oil and she had braided long jet-black hair that hung on one side.

"Mrs. Burdette, I am Dr. Reyna Laredo, and I am so happy you came to Charleston. I do hope my fellow Charlestonians are taking good care of you."

Emily took the lead. "Aye, the accommodations at the Dockside are most agreeable, and the staff has been extremely helpful."

"Good. Please sit, have some tea, coffee, or chocolate." Reyna pointed to the plate in the middle of the table that filled the room with the pleasant aroma of freshly baked bread, cinnamon, nutmeg, and sugar, a combination Emily had never had. "My mother made some sweet rolls, so please, enjoy. We have much to discuss."

Before Francis Burdette could open his briefcase and pull out his draft royalty agreement, Emily started asking Reyna questions. One followed another, starting with when she knew she wanted to be a doctor. The back and forth went on for about half an hour.

Emily, now feeling comfortable working with Reyna, turned to Shoshana, who had been sitting quietly. Emily asked about Shoshana and her journey to the South Carolina bar. Ever conscious about the billable hours, Francis cleared his throat, "Emily, I believe you are wasting Miss Jacinto's and Miss Laredo's valuable time and running up Miss Laredo's bill. Why don't we begin the formal discussions on the royalty agreement I've prepared. I have all the letters that went back and forth with me, and I think we can quickly conclude our business with Doctor Laredo."

Emily put her hand on her husband's forearm. "Those discussions can wait, Francis. I want to know more about Doctor Laredo, what she has found that works, and her plans. If there is a cost, so be it, and Smythe & Sons will pay it. My thinking is that maybe, there is more to this potential relationship. It would be a shame, after coming all this way, not to examine, if I may use that word, all the possibilities. Then, Francis, we can discuss an agreement."

The English lawyer buckled his black leather briefcase sitting vertically on his lap and placed it on the floor. He clasped his hands and rested them on the edge of the table, trying not to show his annoyance. Emily sensed her husband was frustrated but didn't care.

Emily was excited. "At Smythe & Sons, my mother and I handle all the accounting and finances." Emily looked at Reyna, "I think you have all met my brother Darren who has, from what I understand, unsuccessfully chased your fiancée Jaco around the Atlantic and Caribbean. Anyway, Smythe & Sons has been in business since the firm was founded in 1606 by my many times over grandfather. The firm now has an annual turnover of over £200,000 (~£37,790,301 or $47,993,682 in January 2024). We are, I believe the largest medical instrument manufacturer in England and are known not only for the quality of our instruments but for innovation. We also make swords, other cutting tools such as wood chisels and saws, and the firm frequently adds new products. About fifty years ago, we began to expand into pharmacology and now have a line of effective medicines which, Doctor Laredo, you may have prescribed."

"I have. With this damn war on, one may never receive one's order because the ship is seized en route."

Emily bobbed her head in agreement and squeezed her husband's arm as if to say, don't say anything. "Aye, that is unfortunate, but I do not think this war will continue much longer."

Shoshana smiled, as did Reyna, who said, "On that, Mrs. Burdette we are in agreement."

"Darren said in one of his letters to my father that you have been conducting medical research. Can you share what you have discovered?"

Reyna looked at her friend and her attorney. The look she got back said, tell her. Shoshana stood up, "Excuse me for a moment. I will get Reyna's research that she has licensed to the College of Philadelphia's medical school so she can show you. Some of this work is, along with some of her instruments, can be, I believe, patented."

Not used to keeping quiet at a meeting which was, in his mind, out of control, Francis blurted out, "If they are patentable, then one would want an English patent."

Shoshana stopped at the door. "Along with one here in our country, once we become independent. We can sort what is needed for patents in England and other European countries after we become independent."

When Shoshana returned with the book Reyna presented to the University of Pennsylvania's School of Medicine, Reyna looked across the table. "Mrs. Burdette, why don't you sit next to me, and I will explain some of what I have learned."

The clock on the mantel chimed 12 times, saying it was noon. One of Burrows & Soriano's law clerks opened the door. "Shoshana, if you want lunch at the Dockside, I suggest you go now. I asked Yael to set aside a large table in the corner to give you some privacy."

"Yes, yes." Emily was excited to learn more about Reyna's research. "Let's continue this discussion over a meal."

As the Charlestonians called their noon meal, lunch was a rice pilaf made with brown rice, and curried chicken served with a bread the Germans called *baurenbrot* – a dense peasant bread made from rye flour. To drink, glasses of Portuguese Madeira were provided. Ester, when she served the table, noted that the curry was imported from India.

Emily used the new setting to ask questions about Charleston and its history before the talk shifted back to business. After pausing for the dishes to be taken away, Emily wanted to know what type of business arrangement Reyna would consider. Reyna wanted something flexible that it could be expanded to include more products that could be manufactured in Charleston. To both Burdettes, it was clear that Reyna and Shoshana had spent much time discussing the terms and conditions of an agreement with Smythe & Sons.

While Shoshana emptied the second bottle of Madeira when she refilled their glasses, Reyna spotted Miriam Bildesheim at the door with Yael, who was pointing in the group's direction. Reyna excused herself to escort her grandmother to the table.

Francis Burdette stood and waited patiently for his introduction to another woman who was much taller than he. "Mr. Burdette, this is my grandmother Miriam Bildesheim whom I call Baba. And, this is Mr. Burdette's wife Emily, one of Smythe & Sons accountants and a shareholder in the firm interested in licensing my medical instrument designs. She is also Darren's sister."

Miriam bobbed her head. "It ist a pleasure to meet you and velcome to Charleston."

Reyna pointed to an empty chair at the next table which Francis Burdette, as the only male, took as a signal to bring to the head of the table. He stood behind it as Reyna offered. "Baba, please join us. When did you arrive in Charleston?"

"Yesterday, I heard you vere making a business deal, so I vanted to hear zee gut news." Once she sat down, Miriam looked at her granddaughter. "Und, how are zee negotiations going?"

"We just started. I was describing my research to the Burdettes."

Apparently not satisfied with the answer, Miriam turned to Emily. "Frau Burdette, tell me about your family's business?" The German-born Miriam used the term Frau or Fraulein or Herr as a term of respect.

Surprised, but happy to be put on the spot, Emily gave Miriam a precis of Smythe & Sons history telling how Joakim Schmeitz, the founder of Smythe & Sons, escaped from Germany. He never changed his name to Smythe so customers wouldn't think he owned the business. After he passed away, his sons changed their last names to match the door sign.

During the Seven Years' War, Lester and his father convinced the Royal Navy to allow his firm to provide a standard set of high-quality surgical instruments for every ship. The Royal Navy deal led to contracts with the British and Dutch East India companies.

She finished by saying her father was very interested in expanding into North America since many doctors were trained in English medical schools and were already familiar with their instruments and medicines. Emily said newly certified doctors graduating from English medical schools can buy a full set of Smythe & Sons medical instruments at a 50% discount.

"Zo, Frau Burdette, vere ist your factory?"

"In Gosport. We get the coal and iron ore to make the steel from mines in Wales."

"Zo, zer ist no factory in Canada or any of zee Thirteen Colonies?"

Emily bobbed her head. "That is correct, Mrs. Bildesheim."

"Vould you be interested in von in South Carolina or another colony?"

Emily didn't hesitate. "Yes, I believe my father would be."

"Gut, you agree to license a factory in South Carolina or another colony zat vill make Smythe & Sons tools to zell in Nord Amerika. Ze new company vill pay Smythe und Zons in Gosport a royalty zat is zee same as the zee royalty Reyna gets for her instruments zold outside Nord Amerika."

Emily liked the older woman's aggressiveness and acumen. "Mrs. Bildesheim, building a factory and training the staff will take time, but more importantly, money. I would need my father's approval for such an investment."

"Your vater doesn't have to spend a pfennig. Zee Laredos, Jacintos und I will make zee investment. Zo, Reyna, make zis deal. Shoshana vill write up a gut, but fair contract for both sides. Zee Jacintos vill use zere offices in New York, Hampton, and Philadelphia and zee Laredo offices in Boston and Philadelphia to zell zese products. Zis vay, zee business vill be successful from zee start. Und, I am sure zee College of Philadelphia's Medical School und zee Columbia medical school in New York und zee new Harvard school in Boston object vill like zis buying instruments made in our new country."

Reyna looked down at the table smiling and thinking, that's my Baba. Shoshana glanced at Emily, who was still processing Miriam's suggested offer. She couldn't find any holes and could easily convince her father in its wisdom.

Emily thought for a few seconds to let her brain process the commercial part of the relationship before saying, "I think the twenty percent royalty that Reyna wants is too low. Make it twenty-five which still leaves each factory a healthy profit margin assuming the North American factory can make our products at fifty percent of the cost. And, please add one more clause: a Smythe & Son executive must come to North America to help manage the new business."

Reyna promptly responded, "Agreed."

Emily held up her hand. "Wait, Dr. Laredo, we will require you to sit on the board of directors. We can decide who from my family will also be on the board and any individuals from Charleston you think are appropriate."

"My baba should be one, and my fiancée's father, Javier Jacinto, the other."

Emily looked at Doctor Laredo. "Reyna, what do you want to call the new business.

"American Medical and Industrial Products. This way, the title covers medical and anything else we want to make."

"Done." Emily looked at her husband and smiled broadly as she spoke, "Francis, don't you and Miss Jacinto have some legal work to do?"

Before the two attorneys left, they asked Ester Baez to bring another bottle of wine so they could toast the new business deal.

90 MILES SO' WEST OF BERMUDA, THIRD WEEK OF MARCH 1782

Zephyr sliced easily through the long swells of bright blue water. During the night, they could see a storm ahead, and fearing gusty and unpredictable winds, Jaco ordered the gaff topsails furled, the flying jib taken to the sail locker, and the main sails on each mast furled so that only half the sail area was pushing the schooner.

Now that dawn had broken, and they could see the back side of the squall line behind them, *Zephyr* was back under full sail with a light to moderate breeze pushing from the rear port quarter. As the quartermaster on watch, Cato Cooper waited until six bells - three-quarters of the way through the Morning Watch - before casting the log to see how fast the schooner was going. His assistant quartermaster was at the wheel the first time he tossed the triangular-shaped piece of wood over the stern and let the string play out.

According to the string, *Zephyr* was making 14.5 knots, and the quartermaster thought maybe he miscounted and cast the log again. His first measurement was correct.

After breakfast, Jaco came out on deck carrying his Dollond spyglass. The sea appeared empty, but he felt better when it was in the rack on the front of the binnacle.

"Deck, I see two longboats in the water, two points to port at about two miles!"

Jaco looked up and should have known it was the sharp eyes of Colin Landry on duty. "Are there men on board?"

"Aye, the boats appear to be loaded and low in the water."

Looking down at the binnacle, Jaco calculated the new course to approach the boats on *Zephyr's* leeward side."

"Mr. Cooper, alter course from nor' west by west to west nor' west." Jaco waited until Cooper acknowledged the change. "Mr. Preston, get all hands on deck. We're going to wear to port and then retrim the sails. Once the sails are trimmed, break out a dozen muskets, pistols, and cutlasses just in case these people decide to try to take our ship."

The burly Preston acknowledged by putting the back of his hand to his forehead and issued a stream of commands. When Hedley Garrison awakened by all the commotion, came on deck, Jaco gave him an important task. "Mr. Garrison, go into my cabin and figure out how far we are from Bermuda. The midnight sighting is in my log and should be on the chart. Mr. Cooper, tell Mr. Garrison how fast we are going...."

The former slave grinned, "Mr. Garrison, *Zephyr* is doing her name proud. We are making fourteen and a half knots."

He said the speed loudly enough so men on the deck could hear, and the information was cheered. Bosun Preston stood just forward of the small quarterdeck. "Sir, do you want to bring their boats on board?"

"Aye, if they are seaworthy. If they don't fit between the masts, see if we can lash them down athwartships."

Preston's departure let Jaco look at the now visible longboats. "Deck there, I can see men waving an oar with a bit of cloth on it. There are at least forty men in those boats."

No wonder they are low in the water. "Deck, aye." Jaco turned to his first lieutenant, "Mr. Geiger, I have the deck. I intend to luff up, so we are upwind of the long boats to find out who they are. As mariners, we are duty-bound to rescue them. Where we take them is, in my mind, yet to be decided. You will be responsible for the defense of *Zephyr*. I want twenty men armed and the rest ready to help the survivors on board."

"Sir, do you want to show them our colors?"

Jaco thought for a few seconds. "No, not yet. They'll find out soon enough."

The schooner luffed up parallel to the long boats less than 100 feet on the port side. A man stood up at the stern of one of the long boats. "What ship are you? Can you save us?"

"We are. Who are you?"

"Lieutenant Glastonbury of Her Majesty's Sloop-of-War *Gertrude*, 16 guns. And you?"

"Captain Jaco Jacinto, Continental Navy schooner *Zephyr*." The officer's shoulders slumped, but he remained standing. Jaco continued speaking, "Lieutenant, you have two choices, one we can leave you out here. According to my latest fix, Bermuda is ninety miles to the nor' east. The North Carolina coast is seven hundred miles to due west. Or, if you agree not to interfere with running my ship, we will welcome you aboard and bring you close enough to Bermuda so you can row into the harbor. I have no desire to hold you as prisoners."

Glastonbury looked around at the waterlogged men and nodded. "We'll come aboard."

"And I have your word that you will not attempt to interfere with running my ship? Any violations will be subject to harsh punishment under the Articles of War. We use the same ones you do."

"You have my word as a gentleman and a Royal Navy officer."

"Good then, my men will toss lines to you. We'll haul you alongside so your men can climb aboard. We plan to haul your boats out of the water."

The Royal Navy lieutenant nodded and gave a series of orders. The lead boat caught the line the first time it was tossed to it. It took two tries for the second boat to catch the monkey fist. The men on board *Zephyr* hauled the boats until they were alongside the schooner and used pikes to keep the longboats from banging into the schooner's sides. Gertrude's sailors clambered over *Zephyr's* gunwales and onto its deck.

Once the men were aboard, Bosun Preston and Quartermaster Jeffords mustered the Royal Navy sailors at the forward end of the ship. "Cap'n, I count 42, including Glastonbury and a midshipman."

"Send Mr. Glastonbury aft and do what you can to help dry these men out. Feed them if they are hungry. Once the boats are on board, Mr. Gaskins will inspect them and, if they are keepers, lash them down. If not, we break them up for firewood. And get us underway toward Bermuda at a speed that gets us off the mouth of the harbor before dawn tomorrow."

In his small cabin, Jaco handed Lieutenant Glastonbury a glass filled with two fingers of port. "I think you need this."

The young officer nodded and gladly took the glass. He wore nothing but a linen shirt and breeches that would be caked with salt when they dried. "I'd be happy to give you some dry clothing if you wish."

"Thank you, sir, but if we are only to be on board for the night, I do not want to impose."

Jaco nodded. "What happened?"

"We were sailing as fast as we could from Charleston to England when this terrible storm overtook us. Our captain waited too long to reef the main sails. Strong winds took down our foremast, and then the mainmast fell. Then, the sheets to the reefed mainsail on the mizzen snapped, and we lost all control. The ship went parallel to the wind, and we were freeing up the boats when the ship rolled over and went down. Those that were below went down with the ship, I'm afraid. All this happened very quickly. At first, there were about sixty of us in the water, clinging to what wreckage that floated about."

Glastonbury finished the glass of port that Jaco refilled. "Several of us got into the boats and started rowing around, collecting those we could find. Once the wind died and the sun came up, the sharks started attacking. They hit a few corpses first but also got several men still floating about. There were large pools of red with blood in the water. It was bloody awful."

The lieutenant wasn't finished. "I had the men toss a line between the boats so we could stay together. We were trying to make a sail out of our shirts when, thank God, you spotted us."

"We'll get your men fed, and they can rest up. Assuming your boats are still seaworthy, my plan is to leave you at the mouth of Bermuda's harbor so you can row your way in."

"Captain Jacinto, I have been to Bermuda many times. The surf and reefs have made a mockery of some very good seamen and navigators. I promise I will steer you clear of any danger."

"Let us see how things go in the morning. Hopefully, the winds and the weather will cooperate." Jaco waited a few seconds and pointed to the locked leather pouch on the table. "Do you have the key?"

Glastonbury shook his head. "No. I was the first lieutenant on Gertrude, and the captain had the key."

"Do you know what is in the pouch?"

"No. Whatever was in there must have been bloody important because our captain was hellbent on sailing to England from New York via the southern route."

"Why didn't you toss the bag over the side?"

"When we spotted you, I was much more interested in getting out of the ruddy longboat and forgot about the damn thing."

"Well, I am going to cut it open front of you with my officers present as witnesses to what we remove."

Morton Geiger rapped on the door before sticking his head into the cabin. "Captain, Mr. Gaskins says the boats are sound, and he'll make sure they'll have a full set of oars in the morning. They're lashed down, and we're headed toward the west side of Bermuda where the naval base is located."

"Very well. Please fetch Mr. Garrison and I need both of you to join us. Tell Mr. Jeffords that he has the deck until you return."

With the three officers standing around the table, Jaco stated that he was about to open the pouch and would remove any military or diplomatic correspondence. Personal letters would be left alone. With that statement and acknowledgment by the officers as witnesses, he used his hunting knife, which was his grandfather's, to slice open the water-softened leather.

Inside, there were two packages of letters wrapped in oilcloth and then tied in a bundle, but no lead or cast-iron chunks to make the pouch sink quickly. Jaco pulled the string on the bow and unfolded the cloth he thought was impregnated with tallow. Inside, the letters were all dry, and wax seals of the British Army and the Royal Navy were on several of the letters. There was one for Lord George Germain, the Secretary of State for the Colonies; three for John Montague, the Earl of Sandwich, and the First Lord of the Admiralty; one from General Sir Henry Clinton addressed to Lord North, the Prime Minister.

The other larger bundle contained personal letters and their stamps indicating they were sent via the Royal Mail. Jaco rolled them back up in the cloth, tied the knot, and handed them back to Lieutenant Glastonbury. He held up the official correspondence. "These, Lieutenant would be of interest to my government, so we will keep them. Now that our official business is concluded, would you and your midshipman join my officers and me for dinner. The fare is simple, but hearty."

He did not tell Gastonbury that the North government had fallen, and John Jay, John Adams, and Benjamin Franklin were negotiating an end to the war.

"Captain, 'twill be our honor."

The heeling of the hull and a groan from the mizzen mast just forward of the captain's cabin told all in the captain's cabin that *Zephyr* was again underway and making good speed.

BERMUDA, THE NEXT MORNING

Pompeii was due to get underway at the beginning of the Forenoon Watch. Destination, Charleston. Melody was, with decent winds and weather, less than four days away. By now, Darren assumed that either Melody and Emily were good friends or, if the worst happened, fighting like lions. He would bet on friendship because Melody and his sister could be, in many ways sisters.

Darren was watching the crew prepare to weigh anchor when someone yelled from the deck. He saw the man point at two longboats rowing toward the naval base. Darren looked toward the channel and saw a three-masted schooner raising its gaff sails as it fell off the wind and headed into the Atlantic.

He grabbed a spyglass from the rack in front of the binnacle. He cursed the standard issue device for the blurry image when he found the ship in the circular field of view. He could not read the ship's name, but streaming from the aft halyard, the Continental Navy flag was in clear view. Flying from the main mast, he could make out the yellow flag with a coiled snake he'd seen before on the *Scorpion*.

Irritated at the poor resolution, Darren snapped the spyglass shut. Based on their course, the boats would pass within 100 feet of the anchored *Pompeii*. "Bosun Poteet, would you fetch me a speaking trumpet."

One was handed to Darren, who went to the railing of the quarterdeck. As the first long boat approached, he yelled out. "What ship was that?"

The man in the stern stood up, "A bloody rebel schooner named *Zephyr*."

"What's the captain's name?"

"A chap who looks like a bloody Spanish pirate. Name's Haychento and seems to know what he's about."

"You mean Jacinto?"

"Yes."

"What ship are you from?"

"The sloop *H.M.S. Gertrude*, 16 guns. We were de-masted in a storm and capsized. All that is left of one hundred and twenty good men are in these boats."

Darren watched the long boats pass, wondering what happened to *Scorpion*, but glad Jaco was alive and well. Melody may know the story.

IN THE ATLANTIC BETWEEN BERMUDA AND PHILADELPHIA, FOURTH WEEK OF MARCH 1782

What Jaco laid out on the table in his cabin told him that the war was going to end. In the letters to the First Lord of the Admiralty, the British commanders in Savannah and Charleston estimated how many Loyalists, former slaves, and soldiers they thought would want to be evacuated, along with an estimate of the cargo to be carried away.

In his letter to the Secretary to the Colonies, Clinton said more troops would be needed to expand its influence beyond his New York enclave. His letter to Lord North stated that unless Parliament was willing to commit at least 30,000 more soldiers, he could not guarantee that he could defeat Washington's Continental Army augmented by several thousand French soldiers. He recommended that Lord North should consider opening peace negotiations with the rebels.

It was clear each writer believed Lord North's government was in political trouble due to its handling of the war and may lose its majority which would force Lord North to resign. Once the Committee on Foreign Affairs read these letters, Jaco was sure that *Zephyr* would be sent right back to Brest.

Excited, he put the folded letters back in his dispatch box. This cleared the table for him to write a letter to Reyna.

My dearest Reyna, a.k.a. Dr. Laredo,

He loved to start letters off this way because he was just as proud, if not prouder than she was, of earning the title of medical doctor. He knew, more than almost anyone, how hard she worked to achieve it.

I am, as you can imagine, again at sea. As I write, we are within a day of Philadelphia after another fast trip from Brest. We came across some survivors from a Royal Navy ship and delivered them to Bermuda, which added a day and a half to our transit. We routinely make the trip in either direction in less than three weeks.

So far, the fastest is in 15.5 days, and Zephyr has been making her builders proud by cruising at 14.5 knots. And I suspect that within a few days, we will be headed back to Brest. At this moment, I am even more optimistic than ever that we will win this war and our freedom. I have good reason to think peace is in the air and closer than most suspect.

Father keeps me informed of developments in and around Charleston and South Carolina. Amos and the 4th Carolina continue to make us all proud. My father says Shoshana's firm will make her a partner next year. I've always thought she was the smartest of all the Jacinto siblings, but if you tell her I said that I will rub pounds of mud in your hair just like I did when you were 10.

All my love, and I will see you soon, my lovely fiancée and doctor.

Jaco

Satisfied with what he wrote, Jaco went onto the deck and told his officers that he suspected *Zephyr* would spend at least two days in Philadelphia before returning to Brest. Neither Geiger nor Harrison was surprised.

CHARLESTON, FOURTH WEEK OF MARCH 1782

As *Pompeii* slowly worked its way up the Cooper River, Darren was surprised that there were no rated warships in the harbor. Only two brigs and a sloop-of-war were anchored in the brownish water. As his frigate was working its way past the Lower Middle Sandbar, a long boat under sail hailed *Pompeii*. The Royal Navy officer on board said he would lead the frigate to where the port captain wanted the ship to anchor. When the second anchor splashed into the water and was secured, the officer handed him a note from the senior Royal Navy officer in Charleston before offering to take Darren and one of his officers with the ship's provisioning list ashore in his boat.

Darren wanted to go into Charleston, but not to a meeting with another Royal Navy officer. However, duty called. Judah Burton, his Third

Lieutenant had *Pompeii*'s victualling order ready and was the first to climb down into the waiting boat followed by their visitor and then Darren.

The meeting in the port captain's office was short and in Darren's mind, disappointing and exciting. It also explained why there were no rated ships in the harbor.

Pompeii was ordered to depart Charleston as soon as it was re-supplied and head south to the island of Dominica to join Admiral Rodney's squadron. The former captain of a second rater wore a patch over his left eye and had a jagged scar on his left cheek. He said he received orders to send all rated ships to Rodney unless they were currently engaged in operations supporting Clinton's army. The captain said the French were trying to take back all the islands they lost during the Seven Years' War, and the First Lord of the Admiralty feared they were about to invade Jamaica.

Lieutenant Burton put a hand on his captain's arm when they were out of earshot from the building where they just met. "Sir, go see Melody. You've been moping around the ship for days. Don't worry, while we're envious, the officers will cover for you, and we'll stretch this re-provisioning out as long as we can. Just come back for a few hours each day to make decisions we need you to make."

Darren, somewhat taken aback, then smiled. "Splendid!!! I am most appreciative of your efforts on my mental well-being!"

Burton laughed. "Aye, sir. A good and beautiful woman will do that. Based on what we need, we can stretch out the loading for three days, but no more."

"Aye, thank you. I will return this afternoon and then go ashore for a few hours in the evening."

Burton nodded, and Darren headed into town. The Winters' residence was only a few minutes away, and the school where she taught was nearby.

When Darren stood in the doorway of the classroom, Melody stopped midsentence. The students noticed her distraction and giggled as she ran toward the Royal Navy officer. "Darren, go to the Dockside Inn and wait. That's where Emily and Francis are staying. I'll be along as soon as I can. There is much to tell."

"One question before I go, how are you and Emily getting on?"

"We're already best friends. She loves Charleston."

Darren couldn't walk to the Dockside Inn fast enough. Yael Bildesheim Baez looked at him from behind the reception desk with her disdain and dislike of the British well hidden. "Sir, how may the Dockside be of service. If you are looking for a room, we have none. If you are hungry, we start serving lunch at noon. If you are looking for a drink, our tavern is closed until this evening."

Darren wasn't at all put-off. He sensed the dislike simmering below the polite tolerance and words that suggested he leave. "I'm Captain Darren Smythe. I understand my sister Emily Burdette is staying here. What room is she in?"

Yael's demeanor changed instantly. "Room 11, I'll take you there, and I didn't mean any disrespect, but many a British officer comes in and wants to know when we are serving food and drink."

Darren nodded his acknowledgment of what was an apology and followed Yael to Room 11. If they were still children, he would have barged in, if nothing else, to bother and irritate his older sister. Instead, he rapped on the door. "Who is it?"

"Your brother." He said it in the way only Emily who'd heard him speak with a feigned annoyed tone would have instantly recognized. The door flew open, and Emily couldn't hug him fast enough.

Seeing Yael walking away, Emily pushed the door closed and pointed to a chair. "Sit, we have much to talk about." It was a command, not a request.

"I am all ears, and I have at most about two, maybe three days which will be interrupted by trips back to my ship. What do you think of Melody?"

"I think she is wonderful and have already written to mother to tell her so."

"Splendid!!!"

Hearing Darren's favorite word, Emily went into transmit mode. After she described what had transpired since she arrived, she said, "It will be hard for me to leave Charleston. I want, no I will come back, with or without Francis, and I now have the means to make it so."

Darren felt his jaw drop but said nothing wanting to hear more. He suspected Emily saw this new country as filled with opportunities.

CHAPTER 12

– REDUCING THE BLOODSHED, ONE STEP AT A TIME

PHILADELPHIA, FIRST WEEK OF APRIL 1782

Jack Shelton was surprised when Micah Chaffetz, the *Boston Gazette* reporter, introduced himself in the crowded rotunda of the Pennsylvania State House. He said that the building the Continental Congress was using to run the rebellion was the easiest place to find the naval officer acting as the chief of staff for the Marine Committee.

Chaffetz handed Jack two letters the naval officer tucked into his coat and said, "One is from my publisher, who is excited by the prospect of this important story and wants to, after the war, turn the articles into a book. The other is from Abraham Geiger, who has volunteered to finance a book about *Scorpion's* exploits."

Lest someone from the Massachusetts delegation recognize the *Boston Gazette* reporter, Jack Shelton wanted Chaffetz out of the building. "Your timing is impeccable. Where do you want to start? Several men you should interview are here in Philadelphia and, I suspect, are leaving within a day or two."

"Are they coming back?"

"Yes, but I know not when. Do you mind if we go someplace other than here to speak in private?"

"Not at all."

The men walked in silence along Fifth Street and headed north. With no one around the pair, Chaffetz answered Jack's question. "I would like to start by reading through the reports written by Captain Jacinto and his log. I understand that Congress has Radcliffe's diary and statements from other officers and the men he recruited. Also, I'd like to read any correspondence or notes on the construction of *Scorpion*, prize money payouts, and anything else you may have. What I am envisioning is a series of articles to set the record straight. How many there will be, I do not know until I begin my research. I will, of course, reference my sources so the newspaper's readers will know that what I am reporting is accurate."

Shelton gave Chaffetz an address and said, "Meet me there, and I will have material for you to read. I cannot leave you alone with the documents, but I will also not restrict your time to take notes. Each day, I will bring them to this flat where you can stay to save you the cost of accommodations."

"That is very generous, but the paper would prefer to pay its own way, so there is no commercial relationship."

Shelton nodded in agreement. "I understand. Then, you can pay the rent when it is due on the first of every month. You will be on your own for meals except if we or others dine with you."

"Agreed."

"One more thing. You cannot report how or who gave you access to these documents, only that you read them, took notes, and there were no restrictions."

"I understand."

Jack pointed to the building and handed Chaffetz a key. "Your rooms are on the second floor. Where's your baggage?"

"I left it at Mr. Javier Jacinto's house, as instructed."

"Good, go back and ask George to hire a wagon and a driver to bring your luggage to this flat. I will return around four with Radcliffe's diary, Captain Jacinto's log, the officer's statements, and the men who said they would join him. I must go back to the Congress."

Jack left Chaffetz and hurried back to the building where the delegates were trying to manage a revolution by a loose coalition of separate entities who wanted to remain independent from each other. Once the war was won, he was sure the colonies would have to create a more effective government that did not have a king of some sort as its head.

6 MILES NORTH CHARLESTON, FIRST WEEK OF APRIL 1782 – DAY 1 OF THE EXPEDITION

General Leslie had delayed sending the relief column to Forts Motte and Granby until the troops that had arrived in March had time to get ready. Based on Lieutenant Colonel Muir's recommendations, Leslie augmented the force with two regiments of British Army infantry and two of Hessian infantry. He also sent the 17th Light Dragoons to screen and scout for the column and the 200 men of the 1st Camden District Loyalist Volunteers to provide knowledge of the countryside.

The formation that marched out of Charleston with flags flying and drums beating numbered 3,350 men. Leslie intended to send a unit large enough to deter a rebel attack. The column, including the supply wagons, was a mile long.

A half mile in front, Major Arundel had one troop of 50 dragoons on the left of the road and another 50 on the right, with the main body of 100 fanned out 20 abreast across the road directly in front of the column. He was confident his men would flush out any rebels concealed in the high grass on either side. At Lord Islay's request, Arundel had a fourth detachment of 50 riders a quarter mile behind the column as a rear guard.

This was the first time Arundel had been outside Charleston since the aborted raid and his embarrassing ride back to Charleston. If the 4th Carolina or any rebel unit showed itself, he was confident his Light Dragoons would avenge their previous meeting.

Next in the line of march were the 200 men of the 1st Camden District Loyalist Volunteers who had Billy Thornton in the ranks. The 11th Regiment (Highland) of Foot now numbered 900 men thanks to recent reinforcements. The 11th was the first British Army infantry unit in the column, and Lord Islay, the expedition's commander, and his staff road rode at the head of the regiment. The Scottish lord felt that this position would enable him to quickly evaluate any action and make the necessary deployments of his force to defeat an ambush.

Neither Lord Islay nor Rafer Muir had any illusions about this foray into South Carolina and were prepared for a bloody affair. Given the 4th Carolina's preference to shoot officers first, both men wondered if they would return to Charleston alive.

General Leslie's orders to Islay were simple. Force his way to Fort Granby, the closest fort, and gather up the garrison and any Loyalists who wanted to take sanctuary in Charleston. Then he was to proceed to Fort

Motte and do the same. General Leslie gave Lord Islay the desired result and latitude in how his force would accomplish the mission.

Behind Lord Islay came the regiment's bagpipers. Next on the road were the 900 men in the 33rd Regiment of Foot. The British supply wagons came next followed in the line of march by the thousand men in the two Hessian regiments under Colonel Johann Mohn. Its supply wagons were in the middle of the German unit.

The 16 men of the 4th Carolina assigned to watch the main road from Charleston into the interior watched the British Army column pass from 50 yards inside the trees. The troop leader looked at each unit's flags through a spyglass and called them out to one of the cavalrymen who noted them on a slate with a piece of chalk. When the Light Dragoon rear guard passed. He turned to the man tallying the units. "I make this column to be about three thousand five hundred men. If I were a betting man, I'd say that the British Army is putting its money on the side that we won't attack such a large force that is probably a relief effort to their two remaining forts."

The men slid back into the trees and paralleled the British Army unit. Once their detachment was well ahead and out of sight of the Light Dragoons, two men galloped ahead to inform Major Laredo that the British were coming.

MID-MORNING, NORTH OF THE DRAYTON PLANTATION – DAY 2 OF THE EXPEDITION

Captain Pruett's 25 sharpshooters were 10 yards inside the tree line, which made them hard to see, thanks to the bright sun and the shadows. Each man had two muskets loaded, primed, and ready to fire. Pruett's mission was to fire on the light dragoons so Amos Laredo could watch the British Army's reaction.

A mile farther down the road, another group of the 4th Carolina under Captain Giffords would wait until the bagpipers passed before they opened fire from long range at the 11th Regiment (Highlanders) of Foot. Again, Amos wanted to see what the British would do.

The unit he referred to as the South Carolina Germans were already on their way north, headed toward a junction where the road passed through a gap between several small hills. They already had camouflaged positions readied and a battery of four captured 6-pounders as they rode north.

The plan Amos explained last night was that they would conduct harassing attacks on the British column until the gap. Once there, the Germans would fire canister at the trapped British Army units and force them to either attack their entrenched positions uphill or withdraw.

If the British did manage an organized assault, the Germans and the 4th Carolina would withdraw. His plan was within his orders from General Greene, but barely.

Pruett waited until the Light Dragoons were directly opposite where his men were hidden. None of the British cavalrymen heard his soft voice order his men to fire. The first sound the British dragoons heard was the crack of long barreled, rifled muskets and the hydraulic sucking sounds of musket balls ending their flight in a man's or horse's body. Eight men fell off their horses that ran from the firing.

The Dragoon lieutenant did what he was both trained and ordered to do - charge the source of the gunfire. Speed, he was told, would make him hard to hit.

The long-barreled muskets barked again, and more Light Dragoons dropped from their saddles. Others slumped over, wounded.

Behind him, Arundel directed the first troop to support the flanker's charge. At the same time, men in the left two columns of 1st Camden District Loyal Volunteers peeled from the main body and charged into the field spread out rather than forming up in a neat, shoulder-to-shoulder line. A hundred feet from the road, the men dropped to their knees and sought out targets for their muskets. Seeing what they thought was the enemy, a few fired. By the time the light dragoons reformed and reached the edge of the woods, Pruett's platoon was long gone.

LATE IN THE AFTERNOON, NEAR THE PRICE PLANTATION – DAY 2 OF THE EXPEDITION

The branches from the mix of pine and oak trees blocked anyone's view of Captain Francois Meysonnier's 25 men unless they moved 15 to 20 yards into the trees. The leaves and branches also helped dissipate any noise made by their horses as they waited for the light dragoons, then the skirmishers for the two British Army regiments and their supply wagons to pass almost 200 yards away. Silently, the sharpshooters moved into position, supporting the long barrels of their rifled muskets on tree limbs or against a trunk as they aimed at the Hessian troops marching four abreast.

Meysonnier's Huguenot forbears escaped from Catholic France and came to South Carolina after a brief stay in England. A dislike of kings, particularly those who supported one religion over another, was passed down from generation to generation. The son of a blacksmith, Francois was one of the first to join the 4th Carolina after Charleston fell and was promoted when his company commander Cuddy Butterworth fell in a skirmish that stopped a British cavalry charge. Several days before he was killed, Butterworth recommended that Meysonnier be promoted to lieutenant. Last week, Meysonnier had been promoted to captain.

The main body of the first Hessian regiment was about halfway past when Meysonnier gave the order to fire. From where he sat on his horse, just outside the tree line to have an unobstructed view of the German soldiers, he watched a half-dozen blue-coated men drop. The second volley of twelve shots was more accurate. He counted eight new German casualties.

Hearing the gunfire, Colonel Mohn ordered his men to keep marching as he wheeled his horse to the side being attacked and galloped down the column to where several soldiers were helping their wounded comrades. He quickly learned that of the 18 men shot, 10 were already dead, two were dying, and the other six may not live more than a few days. The colonel waited until the wounded were tended to by their regimental surgeon and the dead loaded into the last wagon in the column before resuming his position at the head of the regiment.

Mohn was determined not to panic and charge into the trees because it would play into the hands of the rebels. He believed that if they kept marching, all the rebels could do was sting his Hessians like a bee. It would be painful, but the unit would march on.

BRITISH CAMP, 16 MILES NORTH OF CHARLESTON, AFTER MIDNIGHT – DAY 3 OF THE EXPEDITION

Rather than pitch tents, Lord Islay ordered the men sleep in the open. The encampment was a large circle bounded by the wagons. In the center, a makeshift corral held all the column's horses. Sentries were posted 100 feet out from the wagons, and Lord Islay ordered them to be replaced every two hours.

According to their intelligence, the nearest large force of the Continental Army was near Augusta, Georgia, several hundred miles away. The 4th Carolina wasn't big enough to take on a 3,200-man force, but Lord Islay expected the rebel unit to continue its ambushes.

The 1st Camden District Loyalist Volunteers commander waited until Lord Islay finished his plan for the coming day before asking, "Sir, my men are itching to follow the 4th Carolina into the woods because we are tired of being targets waiting to be picked off. We know how they move and believe we can hunt them down. All we need are fifty horses which we can take from plantations as we pass."

Islay waited until the Loyalist Colin Gibbes finished. "Sir, I understand your desire to close with the enemy, but our mission is not a hunting expedition. We are here to reach our beleaguered soldiers at Fort Motte and Fort Granby and bring them back to Charleston. If you go off half-cocked and are ambushed a mile from this column, your rescue will slow us down, which is an outcome that is unacceptable."

"But sir, if we give the 4th Carolina a bloody nose, they will be weaker and less eager to attack us."

The Scotsman stood his ground. He had his orders and would not deviate from or delay their execution. General Leslie had told him privately that 600 to 800 men were at each fort and would starve if his army could not reach them.

"Colonel Gibbes, my decision is final. Unless something drastic changes, your men will resume their position in the column and will be the first to engage any unit that opposes us. Or, if you prefer, you can follow the Germans and their supply wagons."

Gibbes didn't answer.

The partial moon was all that was needed for Captain Pruett's shooters. They slithered through the tall grass until they could see their assigned sentry. Deployed in pairs, one would shoot at a sentry and then run toward the woods, while the other took aim at another target. They would then leapfrog back to the woods, stopping only to fire at any pursuers. Amos was confident the maneuver would discourage any pursuit.

Pruett lit the tip of the arrow that was soaked in rum and lit the match. The rag flared as he pulled back on the bow and sent the arrow into the sky as a signal.

The British sentries all looked up at the fire arrow at the same time Pruett's men fired. Six sentries crumpled to the ground dead. Four screamed in pain from their soon-to-be mortal wounds.

Awakened by the 12 shots, British and German soldiers grabbed their muskets and cartridge pouches and started forming up, ready to repel an attack. When Lord Islay arrived on the side where the arrow landed, it had started a small grass fire which was quickly stomped out.

18 MILES NORTH OF CHARLESTON, LATE MORNING – DAY 3 OF THE EXPEDITION

Thanks to the spring rains, Arundel was looking at a small river through his spyglass rather than a shallow creek. The roadway of the bridge was just inches above the flowing water. On the far side, he could see one wagon turned on its side blocking the road, and two were placed to protect the flanks.

As he studied the position, he knew that the Ashley River, less than a half mile to his left, was too deep and wide to cross. According to his map, there was a bridge to cross the Ashley west of Dorchester. Crossing the river there wouldn't help because there was no road for the column to follow directly to Fort Motte, two more days of marching away. Lord Islay had stated every evening that he wouldn't accept a detour or a delay that would add more days to reach Fort Granby.

The British column had no artillery that could make short work of the roadblock, and Arundel assumed that the 4th Carolina knew that. He was formulating a plan in his mind when Lord Islay and Lieutenant Colonel Muir rode up. The front of the column was less than 150 yards from where he sat on his horse.

'What have we here?"

"A roadblock that may be well-defended. I think sir, if you let my dragoons go around to our right, we can find a place to cross and come down on their rear while you keep them busy."

"And what do you propose if the 4th Carolina has anticipated your plan that is the only logical course of action other than a frontal assault?"

"We do both. Assuming what our intelligence says is true, this Laredo fellow has only two to three hundred men and can't hold off an attack from both directions for long. Sir, if you wait until we threaten his flank before attacking, we should carry the day."

Lord Islay looked up at the sky that was beginning to cloud over. He'd been in South Carolina long enough to know that when the rain started, it would be heavy. The Scotsman focused his spyglass on the wagons. "Have you seen any defenders behind those wagons?"

"No, my lord."

"So, there is a chance they are undefended and only put there to slow us down while the rebels plan something else."

"Aye, my lord, that is a possibility. This Laredo fellow is quite wily."

Islay studied the wagons and the bridge for a few moments before turning to Muir. "Send for Colonel Gibbes. I have a task for his South Carolina Loyalists."

The men in Captain Vickers' company spread out so there were at least two yards between the men in each of the four rows as they advanced on foot on the road and the grass on either side. Billy Thornton was in the middle of the second row and felt very exposed after his experience in the 4th Carolina. He was also sure that if spotted by his former comrades, he would become a target of not one but several sharpshooters.

Fifty of Arundel's light dragoons swung out to Lord Islay's right to find a place to cross and flank any defenders at the bridge. Vickers walked down the road in the center of his men and held up his arm. The South Carolina Loyalists stopped 75 yards from the wagons in a ragged row.

Vickers studied the wagons, looking for signs of defenders. Seeing none, he waved his men forward. He started to jog toward the five wagons expecting any moment to see a musket appear and belch fire and smoke and feel a musket ball enter his body.

At 25 yards, point-blank range for an expert shooter with a rifled musket, Vickers saw nothing. His heart pounded as he pointed his pistol at the wagons but found no targets.

He climbed onto a wagon and saw the road was blocked as far as he could see by felled trees. Lord Islay reined his horse in after galloping to the roadblock just as the troop of light dragoons cantered up. The men and their horses were splotched with mud. After the cavalry commander said that the fields were on either side were very marshy and the men would be up to their ankles in mud and the ground unsuitable for their heavily laden wagons, Lord Islay looked at the blocked road.

"Captain Vickers, have your men scout the trees on either side of the road to make sure our friends from the 4th Carolina have not taken up residence while I detail the 11th to start clearing the road."

Then he turned to his chief of staff. "Colonel, what trick do you think our friend Major Laredo has up his sleeve?"

Muir leaned forward to speak softly and still be heard by his commander, "My Lord, Major Laredo may not be playing tricks but is sending us messages. The first ambushes said we are going to make you bleed every day. Last night, he told us that we had our last good night's sleep until we returned to Charleston. Here is he telling us that he will delay our progress every place he can."

Islay nodded as he led his horse away from the soldiers who were now moving the wagon off the road. Outside hearing distance from the others, he asked, "Rafer, you like this Laredo chap, don't you?"

"My Lord, I would be lying if I said no. He is an excellent tactician and a very effective leader. Would I like to get to know him better? Aye, sir, I would."

"Well, Rafer, I think your analysis of Major Laredo's strategy is spot on. The question is how much British blood must we trade for time?"

"Aye, sir, that is a vexing problem which we can ponder on the sleepless nights ahead of us."

Lord Islay began to wheel his horse away, "Right you are, colonel."

Two hours before sunset, the column started moving again. It made camp in the same field where it prepared to attack Dorchester in November 1780. As he lay down, Rafer Muir felt very, very vulnerable, and afraid he would not see many more sunrises.

THREE MILES NORTH OF DORCHESTER, LATE AFTERNOON – DAY 4 OF THE EXPEDITION

Between the rain that pelted his troops and the two attacks during the night that killed 11 more men, Lord Islay could sense the fatigue starting to affect his command. They were tired, muddy, wet, and in constant danger. But, as the commander, he had no choice to but drive them forward.

The large Union Jack flying over the British Army cemetery outside Dorchester was visible from the road as the column marched past. Lord Islay wondered if this was another subtle message not just to every member of his column, i.e., you too could be lying here.

According to his excellent Robert Sayer and John Bennett map printed in London in 1775, they were near the place where the Ashley River on his left veered west away from the road.

On his right flank, a creek, heavy with water from the prior night's rain, protected his right flank. Combined, Lord Islay was confident his men would make good progress today. On his left, the plowed fields made setting an ambush difficult.

At a break, Lord Islay decided they would spend the night on the Saunders plantation just before the bridge over Cypress Creek. In the morning, the column would cross the Cypress and press on to Fort Motte, about 20 miles ahead. Lord Islay admitted to himself that Major Laredo would have a vote on whether he would keep his schedule.

The column had just started out when Lord Islay heard musket fire. Arundel led the main body of his men at full gallop. Some were drawing carbines as they spurred their horses forward. When Arundel arrived at the sight of the skirmish, all he found were 24 dead and seriously wounded men. The horses were gone, as were the enemy. The only one who probably would survive was sitting on the ground bleeding from a leg wound.

Arundel's light dragoons spread out in a circle to protect the wounded as the regimental surgeon rode up with one of his assistants. The meat wagons, as the medical wagons were known, would arrive later.

Lord Islay surveyed the scene. On either side of the road were small stands of trees. He couldn't believe that Arundel's men allowed themselves to be surprised, but this was not the time for recriminations. He waited until the wounded man was treated before he dismounted to kneel next to him.

"What happened here?"

"My Lord, they were upon us like a pack of wolves. There was a volley of fire from the trees, and most of my mates went down. Before I was hit and fell off my horse, I fired at one of the bastards."

"How many did you kill?"

"I don't know, sir, the ambush happened so fast. They hit us and were gone like ghosts. I don't know how many of us fired their carbines."

"Get well, young man." Lord Islay didn't know what else to say as he looked at the dark spots on the sandy, light brown soil made by British blood. He again wondered how much more would spill before the column returned to Charleston.

NEAR THE BRIDGE OVER CYPRESS CREEK, EARLY MORNING – DAY 5 OF THE EXPEDITION

Three times during the night, 4th Carolina riflemen picked off British sentries. By the time the dawn broke, the butcher's bill was 21 dead, three seriously wounded who would not survive the march, and two wounded who, with luck, would live.

The oatmeal served to Lord Islay was the same as that which was being eaten by his soldiers. The only difference was that his manservant stood in line at the officers' mess to collect his lord's bowl. Islay was eating with Rafer Muir when Major Arundel rode up. Last night, he was ordered to seize the next bridge before first light.

Arundel doffed his dragoon helmet before speaking, "My Lord, that bastard rebel Laredo is on this side of the bridge with overturned wagons and men behind them. He has a white flag tied to a musket, and I suspect he wants to parlay, not surrender."

"How many men does he have with him?"

"There are three total. Sir, I suspect his men are hiding on the other side of the creek. Do you want me to go around and teach the rebel bastards a lesson?"

"Major, no, and that is an order. I understand you want to avenge the losses of your men, but if you disobey, I will see you hang. Later, if nothing comes of this, we can sort out how we will cross the river."

"Aye, sir. My men do want their pound of flesh."

"I promise you that if the situation presents itself, you will get your chance to take a ton or two out of the rebels' hides. But right now, you are to remain in our camp."

Arundel walked away, disappointment showing on his face. Lord Islay said to his manservant. "Go find Lieutenant MacRae and ask him to join Lieutenant Colonel Muir and me when we ride out and meet Major Laredo together. This should be educational for the young man."

The 4th Carolina arrived at the bridge the night before and after the bundles of hay were removed, the wagons were turned on their side. The bundles were stacked to provide protection against musket balls and to provide a place to stand. The side of the wagons would provide a stable rest for their rifled muskets.

Off to either side of the road, the men of the 4th Carolina had selected shooting positions that were two or three feet inside the tree line which made them difficult to spot. The three-foot diameter oak trees were both concealment and protection.

Amos was chewing on a piece of jerky when he spotted the three British Army officers riding toward him. Without turning his head, he spoke to Captain Giffords who, with his section of 25 men, hidden behind the wagons, "I'll be within 100 yards. If they try anything stupid, you know what to do."

Lord Islay was the first to speak. "Good morning, Major Laredo, I gather you have something to say to me."

Amos smiled at the directness of the Scottish nobleman. "Good morning, Lord Islay and Lieutenant Colonel Muir. It is good to see you again. And who is this young gentleman?"

The young Scotsman answered for himself. "Lieutenant Lachlan MacRae, 11th Infantry (Highland) Regiment of Foot."

Amos nodded in the direction of the man on his right. "Colonel Muir, you know Captain Pruett. On the other side is Captain Meysonnier."

Once the nods acknowledging the introductions had been made, Amos began. "Lord Islay, allow me a brief soliloquy as to why I thought we should have a serious chat. Based on the wagon train, the number of soldiers in your command, and where you are headed, I believe you are there to gather up the British garrisons at Fort Motte and Fort Granby and bring them back to Charleston. You know, and I know Lord Cornwallis' surrender has changed everything. The British in Georgia have withdrawn to Savannah, and from what I hear, Clinton has done the same around New York. I won't insult you by asking you to confirm your orders, but that is my assessment."

Neither British officer said anything. Amos looked at Lord Islay and then at Rafer Muir before continuing. "My orders are to do what I can to make your mission as difficult as possible. By now, probably two hundred men in your command have been killed or wounded. I can continue to ambush your patrols, keep you awake at night, and put obstacles in your way to slow you down, and the number will keep rising."

Suspecting that the tall man on the huge Percheron wasn't finished, Lord Islay nodded as if to say continue.

"I am here to make you an offer to end the bloodshed and allow us both to accomplish our objectives. General Greene and I, along with General Washington, want all the British soldiers in South Carolina in Charleston. You and I both know why. I propose that my men escort you and no more than ten members of your staff to Motte and then Granby. At each fort, you can order the garrisons to leave, and they will march unharmed back to Charleston. No one will attack them. If they need food, we can supply it."

"You want me to go with you as my escort?"

"Aye, we will escort you to each fort under a flag of truce and wait outside. Your men can gather what they want but must leave their weapons, powder, and shot behind. Once you leave the forts, your men will be protected by the 4th Carolina, so no harm will come to them. You have my word."

"You will not take Lieutenant Colonel Muir or me as prisoners?"

"No, why would I do that? Frankly, sir, I want you in Charleston to make it easier for you to leave."

"Major, you are asking me to trust you."

"Aye, Lord Islay, that I am, but if you remember, after the battle at Dorchester, I promised you that your wounded would be treated well and that those who gave their lives would be buried with honor. I believe you saw the Union Jack that flies over the cemetery in Dorchester. We consider that hallowed ground, and even after you leave, it will remain so."

"If I don't agree?"

"Then, I will ratchet up the amount of British blood that will be spilled. We have just begun to make your lives miserable."

Lord Islay forced himself not to react. "How much time do I have to consider your offer?"

"How much time do you need?"

"Give me an hour."

Amos pulled out his pocket watch. "Sir, it is just after seven-thirty in the morning. How about you give me an answer by nine?"

"Done." Lord Islay wouldn't acknowledge that what Laredo proposed was more than reasonable. It was brilliant. He'd already made up his mind to accept and was sure that Muir would agree. It was now only a matter of telling the others what to do.

Lord Islay waited until his watch said it was just past eight-thirty when he and Lieutenant Colonel Muir mounted their horses. They let the animals canter toward the bridge where the Americans were waiting. This was going to be a wonderful day.

Reining in his horse, Lord Islay stopped just a few feet in front of Amos. "Major, we accept your offer. I, too, am tired of the bloodshed. My command will reform, and once they are on the road to Charleston under Lieutenant Colonel Muir's able leadership, I will join you with several officers."

He was just about to say something when he heard a man yelling. Lord Islay turned around to see a member of the 1st Camden Loyalist Volunteers on a horse charging at him with a pistol in each hand and the reins in his teeth. "What the bloody hell!!!"

Amos, whose sight was blocked by the Scottish officers, shifted his horse to the side and drew his pistol. Three musket shots rang out from the woods behind him. Blood sprayed from the attacker's body, and the impact of the one-ounce lead balls knocked him from his horse.

On the ground, the bleeding attacker managed to stagger to his feet, one arm limp at his side, his uniform wet with his blood. He was trying to aim a pistol at Amos when he was struck by the ball fired from Rafer Muir's pistol. The man grunted and screamed, "Amos Laredo, you bastard, I will see you in hell." His pistol went off, and the ball made a deep furrow along Amos Laredo's left forearm. A chunk of muscle hung loosely down as blood poured down his arm.

Two more musket balls knocked Vickers off his feet. Giffords was quick with a bandage as Amos looked down at the dead man.

Lord Islay had a horrified look on his face. "My god, I am so sorry! I can assure you that this man was acting on his own."

Rafer Muir looked at Amos. "Do you know him?"

The commander of the 4th Carolina winced as Giffords pulled the bandage tight. " His name is Isiah Vickers, and we grew up together in Charleston. We have known each other since we were six."

Lord Islay was concerned and offered, "I'll have my surgeon take a look at your arm."

"Not necessary. But thank you. My sister is in Dorchester, and I'll have her look at this. Meanwhile, Captain Giffords will escort you, and I will catch up when I can."

Amos was weak from losing blood when he was helped down from his horse by the two men who accompanied him to his grandmother's house. Seeing her wounded grandson, she directed one of the men to fetch Dr. Reyna Laredo, who came running, followed by the member of the 4th Carolina carrying her medical bag and a basket of clean bandages.

"Lay him out on the dining room table after I clean it."

As he was helped onto the cleaned, varnished oak and a pillow slipped under his head, Amos tried to make light of the situation, "Is this where you get back at me for when I made you mad and threw mudballs at you?"

"Amos, the thought has crossed my mind, but for me to enjoy it, I want to make sure you live! Now shut up and let me work." She placed a leather covered wooden dowel between his teeth.

When Reyna was done, Amos was sleeping on the table. She sat on a chair, planning to stay there until he awoke, when she would have to tell him that his left arm will never be fully functional again. And worse, if the wound festers, she will be forced to take much of it off.

CHAPTER 13

- FLEET ACTION

BREST, SECOND WEEK OF APRIL 1782

On this trip east from Philadelphia, from the twice daily plot of the winds, Jaco believed the prevailing westerlies were slowly moving northward. The area between the easterlies and westerlies known as the Horse Latitudes was also making their seasonal move north. The change would allow *Zephyr* to sail a more direct course to Brest with the wind at its back.

Confident in the schooner's ability to carry three gaff topsails, the main sails, and two jibs, Jaco ordered the ship's sails reefed only when they passed through squall lines. Today, with the sun out and a steady wind coming over the port side, the sails on the 100-foot-long schooner were out to the starboard side as the wind from the so' west pushed them across the Atlantic at an average of 12 knots. *Zephyr* needed only 15 days to make landfall off the Brittany peninsula.

The two British frigates patrolling outside Brest tried to intercept the fast-moving schooner when they spotted it at first light. By holding a course closer to the wind than the frigates could sail, neither got within three miles of the schooner.

Jaco kept *Zephyr* under full sail as it passed the Pointe du St. Mathieu until it was less than a mile from where they planned to tie up at a pier. Only then did he order the sails to be slackened.

When *Zephyr* moored to the pier, Samuel Gardener rushed on board. He took the pouch with the messages and handed Jaco one that was full.

"You need to get back to Philadelphia as fast as you can. Lord North's government fell on March 27th. Lord Rockingham was asked to form a government, and Lord Shelburne is supposed to be his Foreign Secretary. Official negotiations have begun in Paris."

"Perfecto!!! Maybe we'll have a peace treaty in a few months!"

"Aye, we can only hope. How soon can you sail for Philadelphia?"

"We need provisions. I will send my officers out into the markets to buy what we can. Once we have them on board, we'll leave. With luck, we can sail a more direct route."

Gardner walked away, and Jaco issued a series of orders. From their last trip, Hedley Garrison knew which merchants had the best smoked meats and cheeses, along with some fresh eggs and butter to go along with the wine and beer.

OFF DOMINICA, SECOND WEEK OF APRIL 1782

Once *Pompeii* entered the Atlantic on the 27th of March, Darren ordered the royals set along with the main, top, and top gallants along with the jib and the flying jib. With the winds from the west and *Pompeii* on a course of so' east, the frigate's masts and yards groaned when the slack came out of the rigging as the ship heeled to port and pitched down slightly. His orders said, "Sail as fast as possible to the islands of St. Lucia and Dominica and join Admiral Rodney's fleet."

If what he was told in Charleston was true, Lord North and Parliament would do whatever it took to keep Jamaica which was the biggest prize of all the British-held islands in the Caribbean. It had been in British hands since the days of Oliver Cromwell.

Pompeii made landfall on the Dutch island of St. Maarten, the northernmost of the Leeward Islands, on the 6th of April by averaging eight knots during the day and six, under reduced sail, at night. Every afternoon, he exercised his gun crews to ensure his men would be ready for what Darren assumed was an upcoming battle with the French fleet.

After supper and alone in his cabin, Darren thought about Melody and what life would be like when they were finally together. Their commitment to each other was stronger than ever and was now supported by his sister Emily.

Even though Emily wanted to be the family board member at American Medical and Industrial Products, there was the possibility that if he left the Royal Navy, he could sit on the board. That, he realized, was one of the issues that had to be worked out because his father had not yet approved the new venture. Given what Emily said, sometime late this month, Emily and Francis would probably leave Charleston for Gosport so a decision would be forthcoming, and he would not be present to make his case.

If he did, doing so would push Emily to the side, something he would not do. Darren admitted to himself that if he were to get involved in a business, it had to be something to do with the sea and ships, so who would be the family member on the board might be moot.

Darren planned to sail past St. Maarten's eastern shore and then, just before dark, turn south toward St. Kitts and Nevis to pass between those islands and reach Antigua, where Darren thought it logical for Admiral Rodney to gather his fleet. If Rodney wasn't between St. Kitts and Antigua, he planned to sail *Pompeii* west into the Caribbean to avoid the French-held island of Guadeloupe and then so' east to British-held Dominica.

Pompeii's lookouts had yet to see another ship since leaving Charleston. Now east of St. Nevis, all they had seen were small, single-mast, gaff-rigged boats favored by the local fishermen.

"Many sails, two points off the starboard bow, a good ten miles. English by their rigging."

Darren steadied his Dollond spyglass on the railing that ran around the quarterdeck. He could see small off-white smudges on the horizon. From where he stood, he couldn't tell if they were English, French, or Dutch. Although, in this part of the world, this many ships had to be either French or English.

Based on the time of day and their last sighting that put *Pompei*i west of Dominica, it made sense that the ships were English. Darren believed *Pompeii* had found Admiral Rodney and his fleet and hoped his frigate was not too late to help defeat the French.

If this is the French fleet, I will need to keep my wits about me to escape from their clutches.

"Mr. Culver, fly our largest Union Jack from the aft stay and get out your signal book. I suspect you will be very busy shortly."

At two miles, the lookouts began calling out signals. Midshipman Culver copied them down on a slate, then looked up each flag. First signal, "What ship?"

Response – *Pompeii*, 38 guns.

Signal – Fitness?
Response – Ready for action.
Signal – Take station leeward of flagship.
Response – Will comply.
Signal – When on station, captain repair on board flagship
Response – Will comply.

For a few seconds, Darren debated how best to approach the flagship. They were sailing to the so' west. He decided to pass down the flagship's starboard side, tack almost 180^0 to sail up the port and leeward side of the flagship. This approach will demonstrate his crew's skill at handling the 938-ton *Pompeii*.

"I have the deck, Mr. Abbott." Hearing his first lieutenant, who was the officer of the deck, acknowledge his statement, Darren announced, "Mr. Spivey, Mr. Poteet, and Mr. Abbott. The flagship is sailing nor' nor' west, so I intend to alter course to the south. When we have passed the flagship, we will tack *Pompeii* to starboard to a course parallel with the flagship on its lee side. We'll sheet home the sails to maintain a position alongside the flagship at which point, we will lower the long boat, and I shall sail over to meet Admiral Rodney. Mr. Abbott, please plan to accompany me."

After hearing acknowledgments from those he addressed, Darren felt compelled to add, "Gentlemen, I feel compelled to remind you that there will be many spyglasses trained on *Pompeii* behind which, there will be critical eyes looking for any mistake however large or minor it may be. So, let's not cock this up!"

A quarter mile past the formation, Darren yelled out, "Prepare to come about to starboard. New course, nor' nor' west."

He saw Bosun Poteet wave. On the main deck, on either side, beside each mast, there were three teams of sailors, one each for the main sail, top sail, and topgallant yards. The royals had been reefed and furled once Rodney's squadron had been spotted. Up forward, there were separate teams on the port and starboard sides for the jib and flying jib.

Before Darren gave the next order, he stepped toward his quartermaster and said in a normal tone, "Mr. Spivey, once we are parallel, we'll adjust our course to port to angle toward the flagship. I want our station to be two hundred yards to starboard so that the three-decker's sails do not blank ours."

"Mr. Poteet, Mr. Spivey, ready about to starboard, now. Let's get the two jibs through without fouling."

Pompeii must have sensed it was putting on a show for an admiral. The ship turned effortlessly, and the yards on all three masts came around stacked (perfectly aligned) and in sequence – mizzen, main, and fore.

Watching with the critical eye of an experienced seaman, Darren couldn't see any faults. "Nicely done, lads! While I'm visiting our flagship, Mr. Poteet will arrange for a ration of grog for all hands. Try not to run into another ship while Mr. Abbott and I are gone. It would be most embarrassing!"

Pompeii's quartermaster had already altered course slightly. At 200 yards, the starboard side of the 90-gun, three-decker towered over the frigate. The longboat was hoisted over the side with a mast in place and a furled sail on a boom. Once the 18-foot-long boat was in the water, it would be rigged as a single-masted sloop with a main sail and a jib.

Darren climbed down the blocks of wood that was the ladder on *Pompeii's* side after Lieutenant Abbott made the trip. Carefully, conscious of the eyes on him on the flagship, he stepped into the long boat. He was more worried about falling into the water and either being crushed between the longboat and his ship or drowning before he could doff his uniform coat, shirt, and shoes than making the descent gracefully. The helmsman eased the boat under the bosun's chair dangling from a davit on the main deck of the two-decker.

Darren held on for dear life as he was hauled 40 feet up and over the thick bulwark of the third-rate ship of the line. Abbott followed quickly, and once aboard, a bosun piped all call and announced, "*Pompeii* arriving."

Darren walked past the line of six Marines standing at attention with their muskets at port arms on either side of a red carpet. He saluted the Navy captain at the far end of the line. Before he could speak, the senior officer spoke, " I am Captain Thomas Symonds, commander of *H.M.S. Formidable*, 90 guns. You are?"

"Captain Darren Smythe, frigate *Pompeii*, 38 guns."

Symonds was cheerful and pointed aft. "Glad you can join us for this party!"

If my ship handling didn't pass muster, now would have been the time I would have heard about it. No comments are good news.

After introductions and glasses of port handed out all around, Admiral Rodney got right to the point. On the large table in his cabin one deck below the captain's quarters, Admiral Rodney had a large chart of the Leeward Islands.

"Captain Smythe, welcome to my squadron. When was the last time *Pompeii* was in the yard?"

It was another way of asking if the frigate's bottom was clean. "She's less than two years old and copper plated. We averaged eight knots on the way down here from Charleston."

"Aye, then I'll signal Captain Byron on *Andromache* that you will join his frigate squadron. They've been tracking de Grasse and his Spanish allies. In February, de Grasse captured St. Kitts and Nevis. Antiqua, Barbados, and St. Lucia are still ours. From what Byron and his frigates learned, de Grasse has designs on Jamaica. He has 15,000 French soldiers and equipment on 100 ships, along with thirty-five ships of the line and 10 frigates. We think the Spanish are here in the Caribbean with 12 – 15 ships of the line and are about to join de Grasse. As far as French admirals go, de Grasse is very competent."

Darren nodded and said nothing.

Rodney pointed at the map and the straight between the southern end of Guadeloupe and the northern tip of Dominica. The Saintes was a cluster of small islands between the two larger islands.

"Our job is simple. Stop de Grasse from invading Jamaica or any other British possession. With *Pompeii,* I now have thirty-seven ships, most of which are new. Included in the fleet are three ninety-eights – Rear Admiral Hood's flagship *Barfleur, Duke,* and *Prince George* - plus *Namur* and *Formidable* with ninety guns."

Darren listened intently to Rodney's plan. "When we do find de Grasse's fleet, assuming that the wind is from the east, I intend to take the French ships down the line's starboard side. If the action breaks up, find a Frenchman you can take."

"Aye, sir, we'll do that."

Rodney looked at the young captain he guessed was less than half his age. "Captain Smythe, have you fought the French before?"

"Aye sir. On board *Puritan,* Captain Martingdale was killed in the French frigate *Oiseau's* first broadside. As the first lieutenant, I managed to bring the action to a successful conclusion."

Darren didn't want to say that their casualties were heavier than they should have been because Martindale wanted to fight it out broadside to broadside rather than take advantage of *Puritan's* superior speed and maneuverability.

"Then, while captain of *Gladius,* we managed to capture the French frigate *Gracieuse* and two troop transports, *Daphne* and *Louise.*"

"Any other actions?"

"Yes, sir. I was Rear Admiral Davidson's number one on *Puritan* when we fought the rebel frigate *Scorpion* and a midshipman on *H.M.S. Deer* when we were handled roughly by the rebel privateer, *Duchess.*"

"So, you're the midshipman who sailed *Deer* back to Bermuda?"

"Aye, sir, that I am."

"Glad to have you. Admiral Davidson has an eye for talent." The admiral stuck out his hand. "Good luck in the coming action. I am confident that you will do well."

Sensing the meeting was over, Darren left, followed by Abbott. The longboat was underneath him when he was halfway down *Formidable's* side. He sat on a thwart just aft of the bow, thinking that in his eight years in the Royal Navy, this would be his first fleet action. The prospect was scary.

OFF THE NORTHERN TIP OF DOMINICA, THREE DAYS LATER

As Darren noted in his journal, the wind in the eastern end of the Caribbean could be as fickle as the weather. On the way south from Charleston, the wind had been steady from west-nor' west. Since arriving, it varied from calm to moderate, mostly from the west, but sometimes from the nor' west and even the east.

On the 10th of April, the crew of the *Pompeii* heard distant rumbles from cannon fire, but from where the frigate was at the end of the line, they could not see where the action was taking place to the north. Yesterday on the 11th, *Pompeii* and the rest of the fleet were becalmed; no ship was moving.

While *Pompeii* and its crew baked in the hot sun, and rocked in the gentle swells, it sailed nowhere. Sightings twice put them at the same place on the chart - 25 miles west of Dominica. There was nothing Darren could do.

Kedging – towing a ship by men rowing in four or six boats – was exhausting. If his ship was in danger, he would consider kedging. They were in deep water, and no order came from the flagship to do so.

On the 12th, the wind freshened as the sun came up. The stately procession sailed north toward the Guadeloupe Channel where the French fleet was located.

Darren sensed the tension rising amongst the crew. Chasing an enemy ship required tasks that built excitement for the forthcoming action. This was much different. There was nothing to do but wait until the fleet found the French and *Pompeii* found a ship to fight.

With the fleet moving again, albeit paced by the first-rate ships of the line, *Pompeii* easily maintained its station with the top gallants and royals furled as the frigate crept along at four knots behind the two- and three-deckers.

From the signals they monitored, Darren was confident that Admiral Rodney and his deputies, Rear Admirals Hood, and Drake, could see the French Fleet or knew where it was.

The slow pace and being confined to staying in line conflicted with the tactics Darren favored. Frigates scout, blockade, take privateers and prizes, escort convoys, and even carry dispatches and important people. Rarely do they take on first, second, and third-rated ships of the line.

He believed frigate captains should use their ship's superior speed and maneuverability to even the odds when forced into battle with a third-rater or higher. Asking a frigate to sail in a battle line and risk taking a broadside from a two- or three-decker was madness, sheer madness. Rodney wanted the frigates to support the bigger ships and rake the enemy from the bow and stern while his larger ships traded broadsides. This was, Darren believed, easier said than done and exposed the frigate to potentially crippling broadsides.

"Deck, there. The whole bloody French fleet in sight one point off the starboard bow at about 12 miles."

Several miles ahead of *Pompeii*, *H.M.S. Marlborough* was leading the British fleet, and Rodney and *Formidable* were in the middle of the Royal Navy formation. The sound of gunfire, distant in the beginning, was getting louder.

From the quarterdeck, Darren still couldn't see the French ships, but his lookouts kept him informed of where they were relative to *Pompeii*. The French fleet was in two lines; the one leeward were fourth-rated ships of the line and frigates.

Like the men on the gun deck, Darren was barefoot, wearing only a linen shirt and faded white breeches. Last night at dinner, he told his officers that he would not wear a uniform. The men knew who he was and his voice, so why make himself an easily identifiable target for the French Marines and infantrymen positioned in their ship's rigging.

With the French ships in sight, Darren went to his cabin and put on his sword belt. Once that was buckled, he made sure his two pistols were loaded and stuffed them into the belt with the box with two dozen cartridges.

"Sir, the wind is shifting from due east to from the so' east." The speaker was the ship's quartermaster, the willowy Hiram Spivey. Looking at him, you thought a gust of wind would blow him over, but the man had the grip of a vise.

"Captain, aye. Mr. Poteet, re-trim our sails to maintain our speed and position. Get the watch ready to go aloft in case the wind dies!"

Thinking that the French fleet could not continue their current course, Darren sensed that soon the Royal Navy would have an advantage. The so' east wind will force the French to wear their ships to the west or tack to the east and present their vulnerable sterns to the British.

"Deck there. The flagship is turning to starboard!"

Through his spyglass, Darren could see the sides of two groups of ships. One under Rear Admiral Hood turned toward the east to cut through the French line. Vice Admiral Rodney and *Formidable* led his ships through the French. Darren didn't count the ships, but thought that between the two columns, at least 20 Royal Navy ships were slicing through the French line.

"Sir, there's a signal from the flagship."

Midshipman Culver was up on the masthead and didn't have his signal book with him, and he didn't need it. "Deck, flagship is signaling general action."

Darren didn't hesitate. "Mr. Poteet, bring in the boats, get the watch aloft, and loose the topsails. Then get the topgallants out."

While the men clambered up the rigging, Darren yelled for his officers to come to the main deck, just forward of the quarterdeck. Second Lieutenant Shamus O'Steen and Third Lieutenant Judah Burton emerged from the gun deck bare-chested. The sleeves of their linen shirts were tied around their waists, and each had two pistols in their sword belts. First Lieutenant Chris Abbott stood next to his captain.

"Gentlemen, we are going to sail nor' nor' east to get to the windward of our French friends. Then we will support any of our bigger ships in trouble as we hunt for a ship we can take. Do not load or run out until we have a target. Mr. Palin, I want your Marines on the main deck to help with the sails until we get ready to close with the enemy. Once we are engaged, your men have the swivel guns on the mast tops and on the main deck. Good luck, gentlemen, let's get to work."

"Captain, we're steady up on nor' nor' east. Speed is increasing. With this wind, I fancy we're making six knots."

Now clear of the line, Darren studied the action unfolding in front of him, first with the naked eye and then with the spyglass. He suspected that his move may surprise the French, even Rodney.

Behind him, *H.M.S. Magnificent*, 74 guns, and *H.M.S. Agamemnon*, 64 guns, followed. Darren was sure their captains wanted to close with the French second and third raters to take as prizes.

Ahead, ships were side by side, trading broadsides that thundered across the water. As *Pompeii* sailed closer, the bellowing of the cannon became louder and louder.

"Mr. Spivey, fall off to nor' east by north. Mr. Poteet, trim the sails and yards accordingly."

With the steady wind coming over *Pompeii's* port quarter, the ship plowed easily through the green-blue water. The 4,747-foot peak of Mt. Diablotins on Dominica was visible off to the starboard. Curious, Darren studied the lush green mountain through his spyglass before returning to the French ships. None had turned toward *Pompeii*.

"Deck there, no signals from the flagship!"

To Darren, that meant either they hadn't noticed his move, or were too busy, or worse, thought *Pompeii* was running from the fight. Ahead, he could see the fleet action had dissolved into a series of ship-on-ship duels. Some were two-on-one, and others one versus one. Staying east of the fight gave him a view of the French rear.

Waterspouts popped up west of *Pompeii* caused by large cannonballs that missed a bulwark, mast, or yardarm. The balls' last splashes were a quarter mile from the frigate and were reminders of the furious battle taking place west of *Pompeii*.

"Deck, French frigate is tacking to the east. Now two points off port bow, four miles."

"Captain, aye."

The geometry of how he would take on this French frigate began to form in Darren's mind. Slugfests between ships trading broadsides were not the way he wanted to fight. French ships had large contingents of infantry or Marines on board, and his crew could be overwhelmed in a boarding fight. Darren wanted to force the French captain to maneuver his ship and fight simultaneously.

"Mr. Spivey, maintain course of nor' nor' east. My guess this Frenchman will try to cross *Pompeii's* bow at two to three hundred yards. We're not going to give him that chance."

When the French frigate started to tack to starboard, Darren waited until the enemy ship was committed to the maneuver. "Now, Mr. Spivey, fall off to nor' east by east. Mr. Poteet, let's get the sails around smartly."

Seeing that *Pompeii* had kept the wind gauge and was now threatening to rake his ship from the bow or stern, the French captain was forced to make a speed-sapping, tack to port. Darren could see the French frigate was also towing its boats, a sure sign its captain wanted a side-by-side shootout.

Not a chance, Mr. French captain. I learned a lot from my friend Jaco Jacinto and you, sir, are about to get a taste of his tactics which I think are brilliant.

Darren went to the forward railing of the quarterdeck. "Mr. O'Steen, you may load ball and run out. I want to give this Frenchman a good pasting as we pass him by! Range will be four hundred yards!"

For the fourteen 18-pounders on *Pompeii's* port side, the separation between the two ships was well within their lethal range. The question was how much of a pounding would *Pompeii* take from the French frigate's guns which were either 12- or 18-pounders?

O'Steen's gunners got off the first balls. The French frigate was probably still getting its braces and sheets tied down when *Pompeii's* guns fired. Wood flew from the hits in the French frigate's bulwarks. Its return fire was ragged, not a full broadside.

The heart rendering sound of wood being torn apart by cannon balls could be heard on the quarterdeck telling Darren that some of the French frigate's balls were hitting *Pompeii*. Darren put the thought of the wounds flying splinters were causing on the gun deck.

All 14 of *Pompeii's* portside cannons fired a second broadside almost simultaneously, and Darren heard the wooden wheels of the gun trucks rolling over the deck as the heavy guns were pulled back into battery. His bare feet could also feel the trembling of the ship as the wheels under the 4,200-pound cast iron and heavy oak carriage rumbled over the wood deck.

Gun #1 on the port side fired again, followed in quick succession by numbers two, three, four, and five. There was a slight pause made more noticeable by the break in the gray-white gun smoke seemingly glued to *Pompeii's* port side. Then, in quick order, the next five fired, another pause before the remaining four belched fire as they spit out their 18-pound balls of cast iron.

From where he stood, *Pompeii's* quarterdeck was now even with the French ship's main mast. More French balls screeched overhead while others thumped into *Pompeii's* hull. Up forward, between the beak and the foremast, a section of bulwark disappeared in a shower of splinters. Several hissed by those on the quarterdeck, but luckily no one was stabbed. Stays and halyards started flapping in the wind. Bosun Poteet was directing men to retie them in place when Darren heard glass breaking. The sound could mean only one thing, a ball ripped through his cabin.

Darren searched for a man who looked like a captain. The men on the French ship's quarterdeck were all either bare-chested or wearing white shirts. One man grasped the railing and then looked at *Pompeii* through a spyglass. Darren and the French captain stared at each other through their spyglasses for a few seconds.

If I were you, Mr. French Frigate Captain, and I had the slower ship, I'd be giving commands to wear 180^0 as soon as Pompeii passed. You know, as I do, that if we keep on the same courses, I will turn to port to try to rake your ship from the stern.

There was much arm waving, and the French frigate began to turn downwind. Seeing the turn start, Darren smiled as he spoke to his quartermaster and bosun. "Mr. Spivey, Mr. Poteet, it is time to show the French Navy how a frigate is properly handled. We are about to wear to port and cross the Frenchman's stern as close as we can. New course, so' west by so'. Standby to wear ship to port."

"Captain, if you pull this off, they won't believe it in your report. This is brilliant." The speaker was his first lieutenant, Chris Abbott.

Seeing the men needed to handle the sheets and braces were in position, Darren ordered, "Wear ship to port now, smartly gentlemen."

With the turn underway, Darren leaned over the forward railing of the quarterdeck and cupped his hands. "Mr. O'Steen!!!"

The red-headed lieutenant appeared with a bloody bandage around his waist. "Don't worry, sir, it's a splinter wound that ripped open my side. I'm fine, sir."

"Tell your gunners to double-shot, I want chain and ball in each gun. I will get *Pompeii* as close as I can to the stern of the Frenchman. Once you have done that, go to the surgeon and have him stitch you up. That is an order. I don't want you bleeding to death. Mr. Burton can handle the gun deck."

O'Steen responded. "Aye, aye, sir." and then disappeared.

When Darren turned his attention back to the relative position of the two ships, he could see men scurrying around the deck. He noticed that *Pompeii* was angling toward the French frigate whose name – *Décision* – he could now read. "Well done, Mr. Spivey, well done!"

"Thank you, sir."

The French captain came to the rear starboard quarter of his quarterdeck railing. As Darren looked at him through the clear lenses of his Dollond spyglass, he could see the concern on the man's face because his ship was about to be pummeled from the stern. Leaning over the quarterdeck railing, *Pompeii*'s captain yelled, "Mr. Burton, fire as your guns bear. Make every shot count, we don't want the efforts of Mr. Poteet and Spivey to go to waste."

The starboard #1 18-pounder belched fire and smoke. Wood flew from *Décision's* stern. The chain shot from *Pompeii's* starboard #2 cannon cut the starboard ratlines to *Décision's* mizzen mast. Men tumbled to the deck from the loose rigging.

Cannonballs from *Pompeii's* guns slammed into *Décision*, and the chain shot cut up its rigging. No masts fell, but from the loose stays, ratlines, and halyards, Darren could see the French frigate's rigging was badly cut up.

"Mr. Spivey, Mr. Poteet, stand by to wear ship to starboard, new heading, nor' nor' east so we can fall off to the east and again cross *Décision's* stern or bow. Eventually, she will haul down her flag."

With the Royal Navy frigate now on the same course as the French ship and offset by about a hundred yards, Darren was waiting for his frigate to gather some speed before he crossed *Decision's* stern again.

The distinctive crack was heard on *Pompeii*. The sound of splitting wood was followed by pops of stays and halyards being ripped from their tie-downs as the sounds of *Décision's* mizzenmast's top section crashed down to the deck, stripping the mast of its spars.

Sails, broken spars, and rigging now covered *Décision's* deck. The gold fleurs-de-lis was lowered and replaced by a white flag.

CHAPTER 14

– MUTINY BY ANOTHER NAVY

OFF DOMINICA, THIRD WEEK OF APRIL 1782

Its sails flapped loosely in the light breeze while *Pompeii* wallowed in the long, three-foot swells of the Guadeloupe Channel. Off its starboard bow, 300 feet in front, the crew of *Décision* cleared the mess made from the rigging, spars, sails, and the section of the mast that collapsed on its main deck.

With his ship's lookouts reporting there were no French ships within several miles, Darren Smythe decided to board his prize and formally accept the French captain's surrender.

Neither Darren nor the six Royal Marines who accompanied him in the longboat climbed on board *Décision* knew what to expect. Not hearing gunfire or fighting, Darren was the first to climb up the portside ladder to the French ship's main deck. He stood for a moment, surveying the scene around him.

French sailors, some bloodied and bandaged, stood sullenly in small groups. Lines and lengths of broken spars hung down from the netting rigged to keep the debris off the main deck. Up forward, what looked like a 6-pounder lay on its side with part of the carriage missing.

A man wearing a dark blue coat stepped forward, using both hands to hold his sword horizontally. He bowed his head and said, in accented English, "I am Jean Chouvette, Capitaine of His Majesty Louis XVI *Frégate Décision*. Please accept my sword as a symbol of my ship's surrender."

Darren took the proffered weapon, held it for a few seconds as he read the inscription on the blade that said it had been presented to another Chouvette for capturing a Royal Navy ship in 1760. "Thank you, Captain. I will hold this sword until we reach St. Lucia, when I will return this family heirloom."

Chouvette bowed slightly at the waist. "The sword was given to my father, and I carry it in his honor."

"Casualties?"

"Twenty-six dead, forty-one wounded, some will not survive the night. My second lieutenant is one of the fallen. That leaves two hundred and forty-three."

"I will not be putting a prize crew on board your ship. We will sail south to Barbados. Please signal when you need to heave to bury your dead. I need your word that you will not try to escape."

"*D'accord*. I give you my word that will not happen."

"Splendid!!! Signal when you are ready to sail."

By late afternoon, Captain Chouvette and his crew buried 31 men, and the two ships started south. With a top and main sail on her foremast and a jury-rigged mainsail on the mainmast, *Décision* made four knots. Barbados and an Admiralty Court were 170 nautical miles and 42 hours away.

While they were waiting for *Décision* to make repairs, *Pompeii* buried six of its own. Five others were still on the orlop deck and Lieutenant O'Steen was resting in his compartment and should survive.

With *Pompeii* sailing off *Décision's* starboard quarter, the ships headed towards Barbados, no one on *Pompeii* heard the argument between Chouvette and Lieutenant Claude de Tonnier. The French lieutenant told Chouvette that he had dishonored his king by surrendering his ship before it was a floating wreck. Chouvette disagreed. As captain, it was his duty to protect the lives of his men, and once the frigate lost a mast, the fight, in his mind, was over.

At the forward end of the berthing deck, 20 men gathered quietly in the darkness. They checked the pistols they kept from the action with *Pompeii*. Some had swords not returned to the armory. Others carried belaying pins as they crept through the hammocks.

Two men crept up the aft companionway behind de Tonnier, who drew his hand across his throat. One of his followers slit the throat of the Marine sentry. His musket and bayonet were added to their arsenal as they rushed up the aft companionway to take over the quarterdeck.

The attackers killed any man who resisted, including Capitaine Chouvette who ordered them to stop before he was run through by de Tonnier's sword and fell mortally wounded. Hearing the pistol shots, Lieutenant Jean-Henri Fagnant rushed to the armory and handed weapons to men he trusted.

Fagnant led his men onto the main deck from the forward companionway. In a volley of musket fire, they killed several mutineers. Others ran below to the berthing deck, where those not wanting to take sides stood by the cook's stove.

After 15 minutes of fighting, Fagnant and the men who followed him had de Tonnier and his surviving supporters lined up against the port bulwark. Fagnant had two sailors, each with a loaded musket and mounted bayonet pointed at each mutineer.

The ragged musket and pistol shots, even though they were muted by distance and the walls of two ships were enough to wake Darren. He rushed to the quarterdeck.

His second lieutenant, Juda Burton was studying the French frigate with a spyglass and was asked by his captain. "What happened?"

"Sir, I don't know."

Darren studied the French ship. "Mr. Poteet, put all our boats in the water." Seeing his senior Marine officer, Darren ordered, "Mr. Palin, I want all your Marines in the boats, armed and ready. Then, fill up the rest of the boats with armed sailors. We may have some ugly work to do."

Pompeii slid into position 200 feet from *Décision's* leeward side with its cannons run out as both ships hove to under flapping sails. The British boats approached the French frigate from the stern, and Captain Palin led his Royal Marines up both sides.

Darren was in the first group of sailors to board and came on deck just in time to see two French sailors gently lay Captain Chouvette's corpse by the mainmast. Another eight French sailors were put in the row, so there were nine whose blood flowed toward the scuppers.

Most of the French crew was massed on the main deck crowded into vee shaped area at the bow of the ship. Darren could sense the tension between the two groups and the larger group's simmering anger. The question in his mind was, who were they mad at?

Half of the Royal Marines had their weapons pointed at the French sailors who were guarding 12 other men lined up against the bulwark.

The other half of Palin's Marines, now reinforced by another dozen men in red coats with dark blue facings, had their muskets pointed at the men gathered in the bow.

Darren spoke in French at the man standing in front of the larger group in the bow. In French, he asked, "*Que s'est-il passé?*" What happened?

A man stepped forward that Chouvette had introduced as his third lieutenant. "Capitaine Smythe, if you remember, I am Lieutenant Jena-Henri Fagnant." He pointed to the dozen men standing at the wrong end of 12 Royal Marine muskets and spoke in flawless English. On Fagant's command, the French sailors under Fagant had de-cocked their muskets and pistols and laid them, along with their swords, on the deck.

Pointing at the men under guard, Fagnant, said, "Sir, those sailors under the Lieutenant Claude de Tonnier, comte de Caen, and *noblesse ancienne* tried to take the ship." His hand then pointed at the bodies on the deck. "These men died protecting their capitaine. Eight other mutineers are still lying on the gun deck."

"So, you killed eight of the men who wanted to take over the ship?"

"*Oui*, Capitaine Smythe."

"I see you are wounded, what happened."

"One of the men threw a knife at me."

"Which one?"

"He's down on the gun deck. I shot him with my pistol."

Darren looked at the rest of the French sailors. In French, he asked the group behind. "Is that what happened?

Two sailors stepped forward and added details of de Tonnier's charge to gain control of the quarterdeck and the ship. As he listened, Darren became convinced that this was a mutiny, pure and simple.

Again, he addressed de Tonnier in French. "Did you lead this attempt to take back *Décision?*"

Darren used the word insurrection to describe what he was told happened. Lieutenant De Tonnier standing in front of the men being held at gunpoint, acted surprised. "Insurrection? This is a French Navy ship that the coward Chouvette surrendered. As *noblesse ancienne*, it is my sworn duty to take back what is rightfully owned by my king."

Again, Darren asked pointedly in French. He was losing patience. "Who led this attack?"

De Tonnier replied in English, "I did. Your accent is terrible, and I have heard pigs speak French better than you."

Darren ignored the insult. "Who killed Capitaine Chouvette?"

"I did." Several of the other French mutineers shouted, "Moi!" Me.

Darren was boiling inside. "De Tonnier, Capitaine Chouvette gave me his word that no one on his crew would attempt to retake *Décision*."

The French officer collected saliva in his mouth and spit on the deck. "I spit on the word of Captain Chouvette. This is King Louis XVI's ship, not Chouvette's. As French sailors, we are honor bound to keep it from anyone, particularly you English."

From school and courses on history at the Royal Naval Academy, Darren had learned that since 1066, the French and the English had been at each other's throats in war after war. He was taught about French knights, and probably one of de Tonnier's male ancestors earned his title as a knight in a battle during the Hundred Years War that began in 1337 and ended in 1553.

For 116 years, the French and British kings fought to preserve their thrones, free from the influence of the other. In the end, the French won, and the Plantagenets found themselves fighting with those who favored the House of Lancaster over those who sat on the British throne. The Hundred Years War, just as what followed in the War of the Roses was, Darren learned, about raw naked power.

The wars continued off and on and the last one was the Seven Years' War. In most of them, the French and their allies lost.

None of this history mattered on the deck of *Décision*. De Tonnier had just killed his captain. "Lieutenant de Tonnier, you realize your actions are considered mutinous in your Navy and mine. I am within my rights to charge you under four Articles of War, which clearly suggest what punishment I can order."

Royal Navy regulations required Darren to read some or all the articles once a month to his crew, and he knew them by heart. Article 18 covered mutiny. Article 21 forbids striking an officer. Article 22 covered fighting, and Article 27 dealt with murder. Each gave him the authority to execute anyone found guilty of charges brought under these articles. Back at the Royal Naval Academy, one of his classes covered the French version of the Articles of War. The rules were much the same, but that didn't matter because *Décision* was a Royal Navy prize, and Royal Navy rules applied.

De Tonnier glared at Darren, his eyes burned with hatred. No words were spoken by either man for a few seconds, then de Tonnier noisily gathered more saliva and spat at Darren.

"I spit on your Navy and everything that it stands for. I spit on you."

The wind, thankfully, carried the saliva away. Darren had had enough, and anger got the better of him. He fired his pistol into de Tonnier's face, and the Frenchman's body crumpled to the deck, blood draining from the hole between his eyes. He pointed to two of the mutineers. "Throw him over the side so he can be with the sharks. Do the same with the mutineers that are below."

Once de Tonnier's body, the last of nine, splashed into the water, Darren turned to Captain Palin and Lieutenant Abbott. "Hang those men for mutiny and then toss them over the side to feed the fish. Once they are in the water, allow the rest of the crew to give the others who died defending Capitaine Chouvette a proper burial at sea."

He then faced the French sailors and spoke in slow but precise French and then English as he explained what he just ordered. At the end of his speech, he said Lieutenant Fagnant is now the Captain of *Décision*.

Nine of the 11 mutineers took the news of their impending death stoically, then shouted, "*Vive le roi Louis XVI.*" Long live King Louis XVI. Two begged for mercy, but Darren was not interested. He wanted to send a message.

Still seething inside at what he thought was a senseless act by de Tonnier, Darren stood at the forward rail of *Décision's* quarterdeck as he watched as the mutineers were hung, two at a time, from the mainmast's mainsail yardarm. As a sign of respect, he stood next to Fagnant when he conducted the burial service for the men who died defending Capitaine Chouvette. While standing there, he debated whether to return Chouvette's sword to his family after the war or keep it.

PHILADELPHIA, FOURTH WEEK OF APRIL 1782

How and where the information was gathered by the *Philadelphia Evening Post* and its competitor, *The Philadelphia Journal*, no one was sure. In the past, what was printed turned out to be true.

Copies of both papers were brought on board *Zephyr* for the crew to read. For those who couldn't read, others read the articles aloud that described the battle in which the French had lost four ships of the line and approximately 8,000 men were either killed or captured, including Admiral deGrasse, the same admiral that stopped the British fleet from rescuing Cornwallis. Editorials in both papers speculated what the defeat meant for France's continued aid to the rebellion.

Right after *Zephyr* docked in Philadelphia, his father gave Jaco several back issues of *The South Carolina Gazette*. One covered the British Army's withdrawal from Forts Granby and Motte, and an editorial speculating that the British Army withdrew unmolested under an unofficial truce between the sides.

In another issue of the *South Carolina Gazette*, a writer detailed the British deployments around Charleston, while in another section of the paper, a columnist speculated that with Cornwallis' defeat and the British Army's retreat into Charleston, it was only a matter of time before the British Army left the South Carolina city.

This was all good news to Jaco and the crew because they could sense victory was in the air. More good news came from Micah Chaffetz from the *Boston Gazette*, who was back in Philadelphia. Before another interview with Jaco began, Chaffetz gave Jaco four articles that covered *Scorpion's* construction but did not mention the layered hull or the testing of the long 12-pounders that devastated Royal Navy ships.

The reporter had done his homework and read Jaco's correspondence with his father and letters and records from the Marine Committee. In them, Chaffetz had read a letter from Stephen Hopkins to Malcom Radcliffe, Edmund's father, saying that he would find Edmund a captaincy on a new frigate being built in Kittery. These and other letters provided a rich tapestry of information on how Radcliffe arrived on *Scorpion's* deck as its second lieutenant.

Four hours after Jaco began answering Chaffetz's queries, Chaffetz called a halt. He was out of ink and paper for taking notes, and questions.

For Jaco, it was time to return to *Zephyr* and wait for his sailing orders which he was sure would send the fast, three-masted schooner back to Brest. He was not wrong. A courier from the Continental Congress followed him up the gangway with a thick bundle of documents. Jaco signed for them, and before he locked them in the dispatch box, he told Morton Geiger to get ready to sail immediately, confident that his officers and crew were back on board and that the ship's hold had a full load of provisions.

But before he did, Jaco dashed off a quick letter to Reyna telling her that peace was in the air, and he would see her soon.

CHAPTER 15

– BEGINNING OF ONE AND THE END OF TWO MARRIAGES

700 MILES NOR' EAST OF BARBADOS, FIRST WEEK OF MAY 1782

The only things Darren could see from *Pompeii's* quarterdeck were the blue-gray waters of the Atlantic, the sails of the six merchant ships, the flagship, *Stirling Cross*, and the two other frigates, *Jason*, and *Temptress*. The convoy was slowly beating against an east nor' east wind as it plowed through the waves, angling through the Horse Latitudes. Near 35^0 north, newly promoted Rear Admiral Harley Effingham hoped the ships would pick up the westerlies and turn nor' east toward England.

Darren was not surprised when the surveyor for the Admiralty Court in Barbados said that the Royal Navy decided that *Décision*, launched in 1761, was too old for service in the Royal Navy. Converting it to a merchant ship was risky; therefore, *Décision* was worth more broken up.

The court officer explained that his choice was to take the flat fee of £2,000 for the ship or risk getting less at the prize money auction, where sharp-eyed bidders will try to buy the frigate for as little as possible. Darren took the flat fee and signed the necessary documents so the crew would get their share of the prize money when they reached the end of their enlistment.

What was really gnawing on him was how Melody was bearing up. Emily could be quite assertive at times. His sister, he believed, kept it bottled up because customs and traditions dictated that she be a mother first. When his mother, Olivia, decides to retire or passes on, Emily will become Smythe & Sons' accountant, a job she was more than capable of filling. If his mother was willing, Emily and she could train one of his brother's wives to handle the firm's finances.

Already, he'd seen the results of the investments Emily recommended their father make with the sizeable fortune that the Smythe's had acquired over two centuries. The family was wealthy by any English standards but never showed it. Some of their wealth was in gold coins locked in a vault in the family factory, while the majority was in an account at the Bank of England.

His parents lived in the same house that generations had occupied. When his parents passed on, either Bradley or Gerald Smythe would move in with their families. Or, as was suggested by Emily, they turn the house into the Smythe & Sons offices.

All this paled in comparison to his worries about Melody. While he was there, Emily said she'd already written to their mother saying Melody was a perfect fit for him.

Nonetheless, his lack of time, distance, and his insecurities played on his mind. He hoped Melody would write to him via the Royal Navy's offices in Portsmouth. Theoretically, the Royal Navy would know where *Pompeii* was posted, something his parents wouldn't know. Either way, he assumed there would be long delays between when Melody posted the letters and when he received them.

These melancholy thoughts weighed on Darren as he stood on the quarterdeck. For the first time, the sense of purpose and joy he felt commanding a ship at sea was now second to his desire to be with Melody, not on a Royal Navy frigate in the middle of the ocean, thousands of miles away from Charleston and not knowing when he would see her again.

50°N, 0°E, THIRD WEEK OF MAY 1782

Right after *Zephyr* arrived in Brest, Samuel Gardner boarded the ship and took the dispatches. He also said Jaco needed to take some documents and two passengers to Amsterdam. By the time he returned and re-provisioned, he was sure more documents would be ready to be taken to

Philadelphia. All Gardner knew was that a new government was formed under Lord Rockingham and that Richard Oswald and David Hartley were negotiating a peace treaty with Henry Laurens, John Jay, John Adams, and Benjamin Franklin.

The night *Zephyr* left Amsterdam, the ship was lashed by heavy rain and strong winds. Jaco estimated they were plowing through 10-foot seas under less than half sail. He flew just enough sail to maintain steerageway and keep control of the schooner. The working jib split in the middle of the night, and they had to drop the mizzenmast's mainsail when a gust of wind ripped the canvass from top to bottom.

The working jib was replaced by the flying jib, and the gaff for the mizzen mainsail was dropped to the boom and lashed. Once the weather improved, his crew would attempt to patch the sail.

Cato Cooper came up to relieve Abner Jeffords in the middle of the night. Morton Geiger and Hedley Garrison tried to convince Jaco to leave the quarterdeck, but he refused. Dawn revealed gray, cloudy skies overhead and clearing to the so' west.

He sensed the ship was well off his intended course that would take the schooner through the center of the English Channel. He assumed the wind blew *Zephyr* closer to the French coast than he would have liked.

Gaskins reported no leaks or water in the bilge and started working on a canvas patch for the mizzen mainsail. Confident *Zephyr* had weathered the storm, and her hull was sound, Jaco ordered the main and foremast mainsails raised to their full height along with the topsails. Later, if they had enough spare canvas, Gaskins would cut a new working jib.

Jaco wanted to reach Brest as soon as possible. Hedley Garrison's sighting put their position directly south of London at 0^0 longitude and 50^0 north latitude translated to about 20 miles off the French coast. Their current course aimed the ship at the Cotentin Peninsula, which had many shoals according to their *Dépôt des Cartes et Plans de la Marin* chart. Jaco ordered a course change to nor' west by north to clear the tip of land and stay well clear of any place where they could run aground.

Finished with his repairs, Gaskins approached the quarterdeck, "Captain, th' ssssail isss fixed best I can. Sssshe'll hold in any breeze except what we had lassst night, but when we get to Brest, we ssssshould have a proper sssssailmaker cut ussss a new ssssail."

"Aye, thank you Gaskins. Go get some sleep."

The hissing when Gaskins spoke became more pronounced when the 50-year-old man was tired. "Ssssir, I will when you do!"

Jaco pointed to the companionway and was laughing. "Go! I will leave the quarterdeck in a few minutes."

Zephyr's captain was talking briefly with his two officers and quartermasters about the course he wanted before he went to his cabin when Landry called out. "Deck, I see a small sloop, two points off the bow at about two miles. Looks as if it lost most of its mast."

After last night's storm, any ship could have been crippled, and as the captain of *Zephyr,* Jaco was obligated to help. At a mile, he could see the mess of ropes and sheets on the deck through his spyglass. No one was at the wheel or waving at them to catch their attention, nor was a flag flying from a stern jackstaff.

Suspicious, he ordered Bosun Preston to break out the muskets, pistols, and cutlasses and get a boat ready to be lowered over the side. *Zephyr's* sails were luffed as the schooner slid to a stop less than 100 feet from the sloop.

The vessel's name was *Gazelle.* In these waters, the boat could have been either English or French. A dozen men on *Zephyr* crouched below the bulwarks, ready to rise and fire their muskets.

Jaco cupped his hands, wishing he had a speaking trumpet. "Ahoy *Gazelle,* do you need assistance?"

No response. Jaco tried again. Again, no response. Wind pushed the drifting hulk toward *Zephyr.* Jaco yelled out, again and again, no response was heard. The ships were now 25 feet apart.

"Mr. Preston, can you throw a grapnel onto *Gazelle?*"

"Aye, but as heavy with water as that sloop is, we need men ready to cut the lines if she starts to go down."

Jaco nodded and debated whether he should put a boat in the water or pull the sloop alongside. By now, the ships were less than 20 feet apart. "Mr. Preston, throw the grapnel and haul us alongside. Belay putting a boat in the water."

The four-pronged grapnel arced over the water and landed with a loud clunk just forward of the stump of a mast. Bosun Preston yanked the line, causing at least one of the steel barbs to dig into *Gazelle's* bulwark. Ten men pulled on the line, and the ships converged.

Other men on the crew had pikes with cast iron tips and hooks and kept the two ships from slamming into each other. Jaco had a pistol in each hand when he jumped from the top of *Zephyr's* bulwarks onto *Gazelle.* Bosun Preston followed with five other men.

Now that he was on board, he realized the ship's mizzen mast had broken at the deck, so this wasn't a sloop; it was a ketch since the small wheel was aft of the mizzen mast.

Seeing a small companionway that led forward, Jaco yelled, asking if anyone was on board. He heard a painful groan that only a badly injured man could make. Peering down companionway, he saw a man sprawled on the deck, blood seeping from his body.

Jaco stuffed his pistols into his belt. "Let me help you out of here."

"Can't move. Back's broken."

"Who are you?"

"Commander Sutcliffe, Royal Navy." The man gasped, struggling to breathe. "Who are you?"

"Captain Jaco Jacinto, Continental Navy."

"Damn, a rebel."

Jaco nodded his head. "Aye, where's your crew?"

"Don't know. Gone, probably over the side in last night's gale. There were only five of us."

Sutcliffe struggled to speak. "Bad storm last night. Was a damn fool to keep my sails up."

"Sir, let us take you to a doctor."

"No doctor, I'm done for. Let me die on my ship." Sutcliffe's chest heaved.

"Where were you headed?"

"London, Whitehall." Sutcliffe's eyes rolled into his head, and his chest sagged as the air went out of his lungs.

Jaco closed Sutcliffe's eyelids and didn't move for a few seconds. When he stood up, he ordered the seaman standing behind him, "Tell Mr. Preston to search this ship thoroughly. Look at everything, into everything. Leave nothing unturned."

He then went into the tiny cabin wondering why a Royal Navy Commander was the captain of a small vessel about a third the size of *Zephyr*. The only reason was that the ship carried important documents, and the most likely place was in Sutcliffe's cabin.

The dispatch box was bolted to the floor and forward bulkhead of the tiny space just wide enough for a small desk on the starboard side and a bunk on the port bulwark. The cabin windows were shattered, and the floor was covered with an inch of seawater.

Jaco went back to Sutcliffe's body and, for reasons he couldn't explain, said, "Excuse me, Commander, but I must search you." He patted down the coat, hoping the key was in one of the pockets. It wasn't, so he untied the strings at the top of Sutcliffe's linen shirt which revealed a leather thong. When he pulled it out, it had a small silver locket and a large cast iron key. Gently, he lifted the thong off Sutcliffe and went back into the cabin to unlock the box.

The lock opened with a clunk, and inside, Jaco found two bundles wrapped in oilskin. He searched the box for any other material before he went through all the drawers of the cabin. Finding nothing else, he ordered his men to chop holes in *Gazelle's* hull to sink the small sloop before returning to *Zephyr*.

One of *Zephyr's* seamen worked the grapnel out of the wood and Abner Jeffords steered the schooner as it fell away from *Gazelle*. Within minutes of *Zephyr* getting underway again, the men began guessing what their captain handed to his first lieutenant to ensure he didn't drop them when he jumped back on board.

"Mr. Jeffords, you have the quarterdeck. Make all sail and best speed on course nor' west until the Afternoon Watch takes over. After a noon sighting, we will adjust our course if necessary."

Morton Geiger placed the two bundles of oilskin, neither of which were very large, on the table in the captain's cabin. With his two officers present, Jaco untied the first bundle. Inside, were letters with Royal Mail stamps. The top one was addressed to Oswald House in London, and based on the addresses of the others, for the moment, he assumed the rest were personal letters from the British delegation in France to their family members. Those were set aside, untouched, at least for the moment.

Unwrapping bundle two revealed a British Foreign Office seal on each document. All three Continental Navy officers were grinning broadly like a basket of chips had just been served as they sensed they had stumbled on vital intelligence. Jaco stared at the top letter addressed to Lord Shelburne. "I think, gentlemen, this is cause for some jollification. Mr. Garrison, break out some fine wine, if you will."

Jaco drew the hunting knife he kept in his boot. The blade was made from German steel and handed down from his grandfather to his father and now to him. The wax seal popped off, and Jaco gently unfolded the letter and placed it flat on the table. The handwriting was not that of a professional secretary, but whoever wrote it, had a find hand.

LAST BATTLES

May 8th, 1782,

Lord Shelburne,

The news of our victory off The Saintes has caused much consternation here in Paris. The French now believe their efforts to continue taking our possessions in the Caribbean have reached their zenith. We have learned from contacts at Barings Bank and Bank of Scotland that have relationships here in Paris that France has run out of credit!

Yesterday afternoon, an emissary from Foreign Minister Talleyrand approached me asking if England would be interested in separate peace talks from the Americans, as they prefer to be called. Our immediate response was yes.

Accompanying this letter are two separate documents. One details our negotiations with the Americans, and the other summarizes the conversation with Talleyrand.

We await your guidance on how best to proceed.

Richard Oswald
David Hartley

The words "Those bloody French bastards…" came out of all three men's mouths almost simultaneously. Jaco picked up the second letter and read its contents aloud.

May 8th, 1782

Lord Shelburne

The French are interested in negotiating a peace with England that would end hostilities between the two countries. Foreign Minister Talleyrand said that France would give up its designs on retaining territory in North America and discuss returning our islands in the Caribbean that have been taken since the 1778 declaration of war.

Talleyrand has asked that we keep his discussions with England secret for as long as possible. He knows, as we do, that once the Americans *know the French are discussing peace without them at the table, their alliance with France will be over. It is, therefore, in England's best interest that these discussions continue even though the French are in no position to impose peace on the Americans.*

Monsieur Talleyrand alluded to his Spanish problem. Apparently, France has a secret treaty with Spain that we can only assume may be tied to their on-going efforts to retake Gibraltar, Minorca, and Spain's continued insistence that the area called Louisiana is theirs, not France's.

If these discussions fail to deliver a treaty with France, we still must come to terms with the Americans. Therefore, we recommend that the British government continue to pursue discussions with the Americans and the French separately and in secret. Later, England can choose which is the better agreement.

David Hartley
Richard Oswald

Before he opened the third, Hedley Garrison examined the seal. "Captain, you should be a thief. You managed to open the letter and not damage the paper. We can, if needed, reheat the bottom of the wax and re-attach the seals to the letters."

Now that the others had a chance to read the second letter, he opened the third. The wax seal plopped down on the table and started to roll off before it was stopped by Morton Geiger. With the letter open, Jaco again began reading aloud.

May 9th, 1782

Lord Shelburne

Per your instructions, we have had several productive discussions with the Americans. Mr. Henry Laurens, Mr. Adams, and Mr. Jay were present at every session, while Mr. Franklin was not. We know on one occasion Franklin was meeting with one of Monsieur Talleyrand's deputies when we were meeting at the Hôtel d' York.

We had agreed to full independence of the Thirteen Colonies because, as I informed you when I was meeting with Henry Laurens while he was incarcerated at the Tower, unless we agreed to this condition, there was no point in attempting to negotiate an end to this war.

Per your instructions, we originally agreed to give them all English territory from the Atlantic to the Mississippi. We clarified this to not to include Canada and Newfoundland. However, our one concession was that the Americans would still have fishing rights to the waters off Eastern Canada and Newfoundland.

One major item left to solve is protecting those Loyalists in North America who desire to remain behind. England must be prepared to evacuate those who wish to leave. Note, there are not hundreds but thousands who wish to leave. We will leave the resettlement question of where and how up to Parliament.

Regarding territory captured by England that will be within the new boundaries of the country the rebels are calling the United States of America, we have agreed to evacuate all our troops once the treaty terms are finalized. The Americans will not interfere with the evacuations, which will proceed once we have come to terms and not wait until the treaties are signed.

The Americans have agreed to provide free access to the Mississippi River even though they only control the east bank. The Americans will have to negotiate this with the French later since the French control New Orleans and the mouth of the river.

We believe three major issues are left to negotiate before a formal treaty can be signed. They are:

1. Exchange of prisoners of war.
2. Agreement on some formula to compensate Loyalists for their property seized by the Americans. By the same token, the Americans want restitution for property destroyed by the British Army and/or Loyalists.

> 3. Payment of any debts owed by businesses or individuals to English citizens and companies and vice versa.
>
> We are confident that a peace treaty that is reasonable and ultimately favorable to England and one that Parliament will approve is within reach. The negotiations are down to money.
>
> Like you, we believe it is in England's best short and long-term economic and foreign policy interests to agree to terms favorable to the Americans. If, in the future, the French decide to make mischief, it will be easier to gain American support if we treat them fairly. Therefore, we recommend concluding a treaty with the Americans first and as soon as possible should be the priority of His Majesty's government.
>
> Then we can settle with the French, followed by the Dutch, and lastly, the Spanish. The Spanish may be reluctant to have meaningful discussions with us until the issue of Gibraltar is resolved.
>
> If you have any instructions, please pass them on via the usual method.
>
> Richard Oswald
> David Hartley

Morton Geiger picked up one of the seals and examined the bottom. "You know, sir, if we were sneaky bastards, we could copy and carefully reseal the letters. I am sure Mr. Gardner could find a way to send them on their way to England."

Jaco smiled. "That, sir, is a brilliant idea we should discuss with Mr. Gardner."

Hedley Garrison held the last two letters, one in each hand. "Sir, do you think this is some sort of tomfoolery by the British."

Jaco took a deep breath. "Mr. Garrison, that is a fascinating thought. To carry this hoax off, they would have to have known our exact route, placed the letters on *Gazelle*, planned for a storm that wrecks the ketch, and thrown Sutcliffe down the companionway, causing a mortal injury. So no, I think these are genuine."

With the letters carefully folded, Jaco studied the chart where Hedley Garrison had fixed their position. He walked off the distance with a pair of dividers. "We're about two hundred and eighty miles from Brest. Let us take the most direct route as fast as *Zephyr* can sail. At twelve knots, we're less than twenty-four hours from the French port."

Morton Geiger asked, "What do we tell the crew?"

"The truth. They must know why we are about to charge through the night with all sails set."

CHARLESTON, THIRD WEEK OF MAY 1782

Right after breakfast, Francis Burdette kissed Emily on the cheek and disappeared out the front door with Lieutenant Colonel Muir. She saw both men mount horses and canter off. Muir was taking her husband on a tour of the British Army fortifications around Charleston and would be, he said, back for lunch.

After returning to her room, Emily dressed and left the Dockside Inn. Her destination – the law offices of Burrows & Soriano.

To Shoshana, the business concepts of the agreement between Reyna and Emily were clear. Ownership of American Medical and Industrial Products, she referred to by its initials AMIP was to be shared between Reyna, Smythe & Sons, and Miriam. Once the initial loan was paid off, Reyna would own 50% of the business, Smythe & Sons, 40%, the employees 4%, and Miriam, the Laredos and Jacinto families each, 2%.

A separate royalty agreement committed both Smythe & Sons and AMIP to pay a 25% royalty to Reyna on any instrument or medicine of her design sold by Smythe & Sons and a 15% royalty if sold by AMIP. Smythe & Sons would file patents in England and as appropriate in European countries if they didn't recognize an English patent. In the new United States of America, AMIP would file patents if the new country created a patent office.

Even though Francis Burdette didn't like the idea that his client had allowed the employees to have a minority stake in AMIP, Shoshana thought the agreement was fair. To Francis, giving the employees a share of the profits was a concept he had difficulty grasping. When Emily insisted saying she would try to talk her father into the same concept for the business in England, Francis became more adamant in his opposition but eventually caved. He figured he could convince Lester Smythe that giving employees a share in a business was a bad idea.

Shoshana was surprised when one of the law clerks stood in the doorway of her office saying Mrs. Burdette would like to see her. Shoshana pushed the papers she was reading into a pile after she ushered Emily into her small office. Emily looked nervous. "Emily, this is a surprise. Do you want to make a change to the agreement?"

"Oh no. They are well done. I am here on a very sensitive, personal matter. Before I explain, I need your assurance that what I say to you will remain confidential."

"Mrs. Burdette, I will consider anything you say confidential and privileged as long as it does not require me to hide a crime."

"Thank you. When I return to Gosport, I am confident I can convince my father to allow me to return to Charleston to be the Smythe & Sons board member. I can pay my way by being the firm's accountant."

Shoshana sat with her hands clasped, resting on her desk, listening intently, not knowing where Emily was headed.

"If my father agrees, I am sure Francis will not want to leave Portsmouth. That means we will have to have some type of separation agreement."

Emily's eyes flashed with what Shoshana thought was joy, and Shoshana was careful to respond in an even tone. "You mean you will want a divorce?"

Emily's voice was flat and unemotional. It was the first time she answered the question with the word "Yes."

"And you want to know how it is different here in South Carolina than in England where the man owns everything, including any inheritance, assets like houses and horses, shares in a stock corporation, and even the children. And, in England, a divorce must be approved by Parliament, making it public and embarrassing."

"So, you know English law?"

"Know is a bit strong. I always do research." Shoshana paused for a few seconds. "Mrs. Burdette, I cannot give you legal advice that would affect the relationship between AMIP and Smythe & Sons. That would be a conflict of interest."

Shoshana saw Emily's expression change from hope to despair. "However, I can speak hypothetically."

Emily brightened and smiled. "Please do."

"Mrs. Burdette, I see two scenarios."

Before Shoshana could continue, Emily interrupted. "Please call me Emily.... It is just the two of us speaking."

"Thank you, but in South Carolina, as a matter of courtesy, one uses Miss or Mrs. or Mr. or Doctor as being polite and as a sign of respect. And,

Mrs. Burdette, you may be a client, so I apologize if I do not address you as Emily."

"Fair enough, but when the two of us are alone, Emily is preferred, even if we are having a business conversation."

Shoshana cleared her throat. "Emily." She paused at how awkward and uncomfortable it felt but continued. "One, all your father has to do is assign you as an employee of AMIP and send you to South Carolina. Then, either I or this firm can advise you. Once here, we can file for divorce. In South Carolina, a woman must have two reasons, a man only one. Acceptable reasons are adultery, beating or maltreatment, not providing sufficient funds to support the household when it can be proven they exist and that they are being willfully held back. There are other reasons, but those are the most common. Custody of the children will be an issue. They must come with you and be willing to tell a South Carolina judge that they do not want to live with their father."

Emily nodded. "Francis only spends time with our three children at dinner and then when he must. The rest of the time, he is either working in his study and not to be interrupted or meeting with existing or potential clients. He hardly knows them."

"Good. Scenario two. You file in England. We have a relationship with a large, well-known law firm called Scoons and Partners that we have maintained through this war. From what I know from the papers on their experience they have shared with us, divorce is one of their specialties. I fear that if done in England, a divorce may take longer, be an ugly fight and might cost you a small fortune."

"Of that, I am well aware."

"May I ask two questions?"

"Please do, Shoshana." Emily was grinning broadly when she spoke the young woman's first name.

"One, does Francis suspect you are considering moving to Charleston and taking your three children with you?"

"No. Francis sees me as the dutiful wife who will remain so until death do us part."

"Two, if you leave, how does that affect his professional relationship with Smythe & Sons?"

"Do you mean will he lose them as a client?"

"Yes, and how much of his billings come from your family's firm?"

"The answer to the first part of your question is likely. My father doesn't suffer fools very well. Several times, Francis provided poor legal advice that has cost our firm thousands of pounds. But because he is my husband and my parents encouraged me to marry him, having Smythe & Sons as a client has helped Francis become successful. I can't say for sure, but I believe seventy percent of his billings comes from Smythe & Sons. Why do you ask?"

"Emily, losing you may destroy his professional life. He can find other clients if he is a decent solicitor or barrister. Until Francis does, he will make far less than he does now. What I mean to suggest is that money will be the key to any kind of divorce settlement. So, a quiet conversation with Francis by an intermediary will make things easier. To ensure you win, your father, mother, and brothers must all be on your side."

"When do I tell Francis?"

"Emily, I can't tell you that. You need to decide when and I would do so only after I consulted an attorney in England. If you need a letter of introduction to Scoons, who has an office in Portsmouth, my firm will happily provide one."

"Please do that. Have it delivered personally to me when Francis is not around."

"Excellent. Francis and I have a meeting this afternoon to review the final drafts. Your introductory letter to Scoons will be delivered to the Dockside Inn while Francis is here."

Emily was happier than she'd ever been in her life when she left the law offices of Burrows & Soriano. For the first time, she saw freedom on the horizon. It was like a bright, golden road, rich with choices and opportunities. She now had to figure out how to go down it. The key was AMIP and her being its chief accountant.

CHAPTER 16

- RUM IS THE WEAPON OF CHOICE

ONE MILE NORTH OF CHARLESTON, MAY 1782

Outside the British Army defenses of Charleston that were initially built under General Moultrie in 1778, Captain Pruett and his 25 men settled in for the night. They watched British Army sentries walk the parapets through their spyglasses from their hide. The British were now using the positions Moultrie's men built to control who entered and left Charleston. Pruett's orders were to watch and report but not to engage the British Army unless attacked.

EASTERN ATLANTIC, FOURTH WEEK OF MAY 1782

At dinner the night before, *Queen Boleyn*'s captain informed his six passengers that the convoy was, given favorable winds, within five days of Southampton. Once there, Francis planned to hire a carriage to take them to Gosport and a wagon for their baggage.

When Emily left England in January, both believed they would spend a month en route to Charleston, a month there, and a month on the return trip. Instead of the end of March, she noted in her diary that they would land in England around the first of June.

Twice on the trip east to England, squall lines battered the large East Indiamen with heavy rain and gusty winds. Other than the need to stay below decks during the storms that brought back Francis' sea sickness, Emily noted in her diary that the weather was glorious.

When seasick, Francis spent most of his time in his bunk miserable, subsisting on a diet of hardtack softened by rum and lime juice. The passenger compartments on *Queen Boleyn* were along the aft end of the berthing deck of the ship, forward of the officer's compartments. They were much smaller than those on *Star of India* and had room for only one person. In her small compartment that was, at best, 10 feet long and six wide, Emily had a small plank bed on which she placed the two blankets given to her by the crew. The bunk's railing kept her from falling out in heavy seas. At night, she used a wool shawl she'd bought from England as a cover but never needed in Charleston.

Her cabin had a small table at the far end next to where a crewmember lashed a chest with her clothes to the deck. And, unlike *Star of India*, her compartment was windowless, so even during the day, Emily needed a lantern to write in her diary.

Emily's diary was a log of what she did and a compendium of her thoughts and emotions. On the way back to England, she annotated the pages with thoughts that she had never written before.

Several times, Emily took Shoshana's letter to Scoons & Partners from its hiding place in her trunk and laid it on the small desk. Although Shoshana told her what the letter said, and each time she looked at the unopened letter, it was an inspiration to help her stay focused on what she believed would be a war.

Emily was convinced the trip was a complete success. The business rationale for sailing to Charleston was negotiating a royalty agreement with Reyna Laredo. That was accomplished with an agreement for a factory and sales offices in the new country. All of which will be good for the family business.

Meeting Melody provided the excuse to see part of the world that was not London or Gosport. In the process, they became very good friends.

Moving to Charleston was Emily's opportunity to have a professional career at AMIP and raise her children, just as her mother did at Smythe & Sons. Now, all she had to do was convince her father.

Darren, who also had shares in Smythe & Sons, had a say in if she would be allowed to accept a position at AMIP. What if he wanted to be the family board member? Would Reyna allow two Smythe family members to work at AMIP? The answers, she rationalized, would come in a few short months. Patience, she kept telling herself, is a virtue. With so much at stake, it was hard.

Now over his seasickness, Francis was frustrated he was not at his desk at Helmsley & Cole. He viewed the trip as productive, and undoubtedly there was more billable work to be done on the agreement, given the list of changes he'd like to see made. Some he discussed with Emily, others he would get Lester Smythe's approval and then force them down that Jewess solicitor who, he had to admit, knew her way around the law.

He would warn his client that he did not trust the rebellious colonials. Francis was sure Reyna would find a way to avoid paying royalties and renege on key parts of the agreement just as they refused to pay taxes and duties before the rebellion began.

Ever since that first meeting at Burrows & Soriano, he noticed Emily had become more assertive and wanted to step out of her role as her mother's assistant into a management position. While she made excellent suggestions, Francis was determined Emily should resume her primary role as the mother to his children so he could focus on his legal career.

When Francis left Charleston, he had a list of potential clients to approach now that he had what his firm referred to as "international contract experience." This would be good for Helmsley & Cole and for him as a partner.

GOSPORT, FIRST WEEK OF JUNE 1782

No sooner had *Pompeii* anchored and finished furling her sails, the signal flags started going up on the flagpole on the roof of the base's headquarters building. Midshipman Culver rattled them off because he knew the standard signals by heart.

"Sir, your presence is requested immediately at fleet headquarters."

"Thank you, Mr. Culver." Darren looked down the deck where two longboats were already being hoisted over the side. "Mr. Abbott…"

Christopher Abbott was leaning over the quarterdeck railing watching the two, 21-foot-long boats splash gently into the water. He could see the six sets of oars laid lengthwise, resting on the thwarts that also served as seats for the oarsmen. "Yes, sir. I heard. I'll have the longboats manned in a jiffy. Do you mind if Mr. Burton and Mr. O'Steen ride with you? They'll have our victualling order, and Mr. O'Steen wants to see whom we can take from the barracks ships."

"Splendid idea, Mr. Abbott. Good thinking."

"Are you coming back tonight?"

"Good question, Mr. Abbott. Let us see what the elves at base headquarters have in store for *Pompeii*. Somehow, I think it is more than welcome home. Plan on me coming back to the ship and then, hopefully, going ashore for the evening."

Darren went to his cabin to gather the packet of documents sitting on his desk. In one, he recommended that Christopher Abbott be promoted to commander or be given a command. Another had his recommendations that his lieutenants should move up, and the third said Midshipman Culver is highly qualified to sit for the lieutenant's exam.

When Darren walked into the headquarters building, Admiral Arthur's secretary stated the admiral wanted to speak to him immediately. Darren was ushered into the admiral's third-floor office where windows opposite his desk let him see all the ships anchored in Portsmouth. The heavy-set but not overweight admiral came around his desk and shook Darren's hand. "Welcome back, Darren. I heard about *Décision*. Damned good work, I say."

"Thank you, sir." Darren held out the bundle. "My full report and recommendations to promote my officers are in here."

Arthur took the packet. "I will pass them on to the personnel chaps who make those decisions. All hell broke loose around here. Every ship in the harbor must put to sea immediately. How soon can *Pompeii* be ready?"

"Two or three days. It depends on how fast we get our supplies. We're almost out of everything. What have the French done now?"

Arthur picked up a letter from his desk and handed it to Darren to read. "It is not the French. It is the Admiralty. This just arrived this morning from the First Sea Lord."

> *His Majesty the King has approved Parliament's recommendation that Savannah be evacuated as soon as possible. All British Army units in Savannah and Georgia along with those Georgians loyal to the King will be taken to either Halifax or British-controlled islands in the Caribbean for resettlement. All available ships —*

warships and cargo vessels - are to be dispatched forthwith to rendezvous with Vice Admiral Graves, commander of the North American Station in or near Savannah.

Darren's facial expression must have given him away.

"I know Captain Smythe that this is a kick in the shorts, but I have two ships that will be leaving in two days, and I expect you should be ready in at most three."

"Aye sir, we'll leave once we are re-provisioned."

So much for a few days to visit with his parents. He wondered if Emily had returned and what she had to say about Melody. Tonight, he'd find out.

Several hard knocks on the door of his parent's house in Gosport were needed before his mother came to the front door. Olivia Smythe had been in the back, putting a meat pie into the oven and was delighted to see her youngest son.

After hugging Darren, she held him at arm's length to examine his face as only a mother can. "I see you are surviving on that horrible Royal Navy fare. I can do better. How long are you here in Portsmouth?"

"I'm afraid for only a few days. Have you heard from Emily?"

Olivia Smythe grinned. "I have. The ship she was on, *Queen Boleyn* should have docked this morning in Southampton, and she and Francis should be home today."

"Mother, you know what I am asking?"

Olivia tenderly touched her son's cheek and smiled broadly as she looked into her son's eyes. "Oh, her!!! I should have known better and trusted your judgment. I owe you an apology. Emily wrote that Melody is wonderful, and they've become terrific friends. She refers to Melody as the sister she never had but always wanted."

"No apology needed, mother. I understood your concern, but you didn't have to send Emily to Charleston just to meet Melody."

"Aye, that was your father's doings. He'll be back shortly, and the news from Charleston is all good. Apparently, Emily helped Francis and the Laredos put together a very interesting new business called American Medical and Industrial Products. We'll own a portion and have a factory and sales offices in the colonies up and down the coast. Your father is very excited about this prospect."

"Splendid, mother. I've met Miss Laredo and her friends. I gather Emily got on with them quite well."

"Based on her letters, I would use the word famously and suspect, knowing my daughter, Emily had more to do about the new venture than Francis. Supper won't be for another two hours or so. How about some bread and cheese while we wait for your father?"

Darren expected to be mobbed by Emily's three boys, the oldest of whom was seven, and yet none had appeared. "Where are Emily's children?"

"Jonah is upstairs taking his afternoon nap. Jeffrey is in the kitchen stuffing his face with some biscuits I just made, and Jeremiah is still in school."

Several generations earlier, the Smythes, along with several other families, started a school to ensure that their children were taught to read, write, and do math, and learn history and French. The six founding families initially paid for everything - the building, teacher salaries, books, etc. Now, the school, known as Gosport Academy, charges tuition to cover expenses and is open to anyone who can afford to pay. The school's generous endowment from families in Gosport ensured the school would survive and could offer scholarships to deserving families.

The school was unique in several respects. Girls were allowed to attend, and it was non-denominational. This caused problems with the Anglican Church leaders in Gosport who wanted religion taught in the school. The school's founders insisted that its charter stated that no religion will be taught or practiced at Gosport Academy. If one wanted a religious education, the founders' believed parents were free to teach it at home or send their children to a church-run school.

To Darren, his mother looked tired. He thought she had aged since the last time he saw her. Maybe it was caused by taking care of three boys - Jonah, age 3; Jeffrey age 5; and Jeremiah age 11.

They were about to head into the kitchen when the door behind Darren opened. In rushed Jonah yelling at the top of his lungs, "Mum is home, Mum is home!!!"

Emily entered the house and nodded in the direction of Olivia, "Good afternoon, Mother!" Then to Darren, "Welcome home! This is a pleasant surprise!"

Hugs followed, and a beaming Olivia said, "I want to hear all about Charleston, Melody, and your impressions of Ms., I'm sorry, Doctor Laredo! We'll save the business until your father comes home."

"Aye, there is much of that to talk about."

Olivia looked behind her daughter, "Where's Francis?"

"At his office. The carriage dropped me off at the school, and he went with it to our home. Francis said he would supervise the unloading of our chests before going to Helmsley & Cole. He said he'd come here for supper. Knowing him, he'll arrive as we are starting dessert."

The adults went into the sitting room, and three-year-old Jonah plunked himself on his mother's lap. Jeffrey perched himself on her knee, and Jeremiah satisfied that his mother had returned safely, sat on Darren's lap. The family joke was that Jeffrey was really Darren's son. The five-year-old constantly expounded on what he would do as a captain in the Royal Navy.

Darren looked at his sister and opened his hands as if to say, "Well, what did you think of Melody?"

"I don't know how you did it, Darren, but you found a wonderful woman. If you don't treat her right, I will skewer you with one of the family instruments. She will make a wonderful addition to our family. And you sir, are one very lucky sailor."

Relieved, Darren felt the tension leave his body, instantly replaced by joy.

"However, my brother, you have some decisions to make, so I hope you are staying for supper."

True to form, Francis Burdette, knocked on the door as the family finished supper. The three boys face deep in a blackberry pie, hardly acknowledged their father. Their hugs were as cursory as their feigned affection.

Once the adults moved into the parlor for what Darren thought would be the "business" part of the evening, Emily went upstairs to organize the children. She came down with Jonah clinging to her dress and said, "Jeffrey is asleep and Jeremiah will be shortly, so I'll collect all their things tomorrow."

Lester Smythe took four glasses from the top of a table along with a decanter full of an amber-colored liquid. "I think we need to have a taste of what our kilted friends up north brew to celebrate."

He did the "honors" of pouring each person at least two fingers' worth of the liquid. Holding up the bottle, Lester said, "This is from Graybeard, one of the few highland distilleries that paid its taxes, which make it twice as expensive as it should have been. But then again, the King has to pay for his wars." Lester held up his glass, saying, "To the king, may he find a way to bring and keep the peace."

All acknowledged his toast, then Lester said, "To my son, the Royal Navy captain, may fair winds and following seas always bring him home safely."

To which Darren said, "Amen to that." Another sip by all in the room. "And last, to my daughter Emily and my son-in-law, who had a successful trip to Charleston and returned safely to Gosport."

Darren enjoyed the taste of the liquid that smelled of smoked peat and malt as it warmed its way down to his stomach. He drained the glass, and his father offered more, but Darren declined because he didn't want to risk appearing drunk when he returned to *Pompeii*.

Ever the master of ceremonies and aware of customs and protocol, Lester turned to his son-in-law, "Tell me about the arrangements you completed in Charleston."

Francis Burdette provided a precise, accurate summary of the two contracts but finished saying that before Lester signed them, he wanted to make some changes to reduce the chances of fraud. He also had concerns about the ability of the South Carolinians to produce the same high-quality steel made by Smythe & Sons.

Having heard these two arguments from her husband several times before, Emily thought they had been put to bed. The issue had to be settled now. She knew Francis was smarting from being outlawyered by Shoshana. Emily controlled her anger when she corrected him when he referred to her as 'that Jewess solicitor.' "Francis, first, let me remind you that Mrs. Bildesheim owns a gun shop that produces rifled muskets and pistols along with knives and swords. While I am not an expert on these weapons, from what I heard, the steel in them is equal to anything used by the British Army or that Smythe & Sons produces."

Francis' tone was curt and annoyed that his reasoning was being challenged by his wife, who should be quiet now that they are back in England. "Who told you this?"

Emily was ready. "Several British Army officers who examined captured rifled muskets and watched their fellow officers fall at ranges that far exceed that of the muskets used by British soldiers. I was also shown several knives and swords whose workmanship was superb. So, I am not worried, and if needed, I believe we can teach the Americans how to make our steel, just as we have taught our own workers."

Emily continued, "Dr. Laredo suggested that each surgical tool be marked with the Smythe & Son crest, three-part number with the model number and letters, the month and year it was made, followed by a serial number. This way, we can match the part numbers to our books which is something we should start right away."

Lester nodded. "I like that. We should have been doing this all along."

Emily continued, "Medicines would be given a number, and we would record and number the vials made. Their financial records will record these details, so we know what sells well and what doesn't and the profitability of each product."

Francis Burdette cleared his throat, "Yes, well it is still subject to fraud which means Smythe & Sons will not get its proper revenue."

Lester quickly asked, "Francis, why are you afraid of this arrangement?"

"Because I don't trust colonials. Worse, they are rebels who do not want to be English citizens."

"Francis, did they give you any indication whether or not this agreement would be terminated if the rebels won?"

The lawyer shook his head. "No, but they do not want it to take effect until a peace agreement has been reached."

"So, we have some time. There must be another reason that you oppose this deal. Emily seems to think Smythe & Sons will profit handsomely from this venture. What say you?"

Put on the spot, Francis looked around the room and drained his second glass of Scotch. "Because the Laredos, the Jacintos, and the Bildesheims – the whole lot of them are Jews. Worse, the Laredos and Jacintos are descendants of Spanish Jews. England doesn't trust Spain, and we shouldn't trust Spaniards. Trust me, they will find a way to cheat Smythe & Sons."

Lester Smythe took a deep breath and slowly put the glass of whiskey on the table next to his chair. Darren, who knew his father was slow to anger, but had seen explosions before and now saw one coming. His father believed every man was equal and those with ability will rise above the rest. None of the workers in his factory had ever worked with steel or made medicines until they were taught. Now they are well compensated for their skill.

"Francis, I will not tolerate that kind of talk in my house. Might I remind you that many of the doctors who buy Smythe & Sons instruments are Jews. Our distributor in the Netherlands is Jewish, and so is Rehuel Lobatto, our family doctor. I will hear no more of this talk."

"Sir, the church teaches that it was the Jews who killed our lord and savior, Jesus Christ. Therefore, they are Christ killers and should not be trusted."

Lester Smythe's hand banged down on the table next to him, causing his glass to jump and shatter into thousands of pieces when it hit the wood floor. He pointed his finger at his daughter's husband, "Damn you, Francis. That is enough! You shall never make that statement or any statement like that about Catholics or Jews or Anglicans or Lutherans or any man or woman's religion in the presence of anyone in this family."

No one in the room moved. Lester looked at Francis and Emily. "I will read the contracts tomorrow, and if they are as represented, I will sign them. Now, Francis, you may leave my house, now! Emily, please stay the night."

The implied words, "we have much to discuss," were left unstated.

BREST, SECOND WEEK OF JUNE 1782

When Jaco told Samuel Gardner what was in the documents, the businessman wrote out a second set. The originals were sent to Benjamin Franklin to alert his negotiating team that the French were dealing behind their backs.

Experience said the courier would reach Paris in five days. Gardner estimated that Franklin, Jay, Adams, and Laurens would need two or three days to craft a response that would sit in the courier's saddlebags for the five-day ride back to Brest.

Gardner said, "Captain, I have this dispatch that the Portuguese ambassador to France gave to Dr. Franklin. Originally, we were going to ask you to deliver these letters to the Governor General of the Azores on your way back to Philadelphia, but we have time to deliver them now. Portugal is planning to join the League of Armed Neutrality."

"Sir, what is that?"

"Ahhhhh, I'm sorry. Allow me to explain. Sweden, Denmark, Prussia, Norway, and Russia have filed vigorous protests in London against the Royal Navy's arrogant habit of stopping neutral ships they think may be carrying contraband. Often, these ships are taken and sold in Admiralty Courts. These countries informed the British that if this practice does not stop, they would start seizing English merchant ships, which could lead to more countries joining this war. So, this League of Armed Neutrality is good for us."

"Thank you. I didn't know this league existed. Apparently, we are not the only ones who do not like the arrogant practices of the Royal Navy."

Morton Geiger had already headed toward the shops where they bought supplies before. "Sir, we may be able to leave tomorrow. The Azores are about five days at 12 knots away so with luck, *Zephyr* should be back in twelve to thirteen days."

"Excellent. I shall get cracking on getting these copies off to Paris. Stop by my office just before you put to sea."

THE AZORES, SIX DAYS LATER

Gray clouds looked as if they were speared by the tops of the mountains surrounding Ponta Delgada on the island of São Miguel in the Azores chain. To reach Ponta Delgada, 1,282 nautical miles away, *Zephyr* had averaged 12 knots with strong wings from the nor' west in the Horse Latitudes that came over its starboard side. Staying on a beam reach with the daggerboards down all the way meant the schooner didn't have to tack back and forth as it sailed so' so' west. The ship would enjoy the same favorable winds on the way back to Brest.

Jaco had three documents to personally deliver to the Portuguese Royal Governor in the locked dispatch box in his cabin. One was a letter from Benjamin Franklin confirming the recognition by the United States of America that Portugal and its colonies were neutral.

Letter two was from the Portuguese Ambassador to France confirming his discussions with Franklin and the Americans. Letter three was signed by Portuguese Queen Dona Maria I. It stated Portugal's country's neutral position in the conflict between the United States and England and said Portugal was planning on joining the League of Armed Neutrality.

Nearby in the sheltered anchorage, the Royal Navy frigate *Successor*, 32 guns, swung from its two anchors. From what Jaco could see from the schooner, *Successor's* crew was repairing its broken foremast.

Since they were in a neutral port, Jaco ordered a small Continental Navy flag flown from the schooner's jackstaff. It met the requirement that the nationality of any ship anchored in a neutral harbor identify itself. *Zephyr's* flag was tiny compared to the Union Jack flown from *Successor's* halyard.

While Jaco went to the governor general's office, Morton Geiger went ashore with the ship's cook and Abner Jeffords to buy what they needed to replace the food and drink consumed during the trip to the Azores. They found a shop with a stock of Verdelho wines and were marking casks they wanted to buy when the captain of *Successor* and one of his lieutenants entered the store.

The pair stood amongst the racks of barrels listening to the two Royal Navy officers discuss whether they should take the rebel schooner as a prize even though it was anchored in a neutral port or should they wait for it to depart. The lieutenant reasoned aloud, asking, "Who could stop us?" The captain agreed, saying a ship like this schooner would fetch a premium in an Admiralty court in England.

Neither Royal Navy officer knew that Geiger and Jeffords had heard every word. They weren't wearing uniforms as they helped the winery's staff load three dozen casks, 12 on each wagon, that would be ferried out to *Zephyr*.

The 36 casks of the white wine known for its hints of lemon and citrus fruits was far more than the crew could consume on the way to Brest where they would replenish their stores. Verdelho was prized in Charleston and Philadelphia. Jaco hoped to sell at least a dozen or more of the casks in Philadelphia and split the profits amongst the crewmembers.

With their business in Punta Delgada done, Morton Geiger voiced at dinner a plan he and Abner Jeffords had discussed after overhearing the Royal Navy officers. Once Jaco heard Geiger's proposal, he said, "Go find Jeffords and meet me by the foremast."

There, Jaco, along with Hedley Garrison, studied the Royal Navy frigate. "Mr. Geiger and Mr. Jeffords, are you sure you can carry this out?"

Abner Jeffords nodded vigorously. "Aye, cap'n, I'm sure. If the weather is misty like last night, the British will never see us coming. Right after I return, we weigh anchor and sail away!"

"Who do you want to take with you?"

"Landry and Grantham. They're good lads with cool heads. Both can swim back to *Zephyr* if I have a problem."

Jaco looked at the 32-gun frigate again, and the more he thought about it, the more he liked their plan. "Mr. Jeffords, I expect you to come back on the boat you set out on, so I don't have to send another out to muck around in the fog collecting the three of you. At four bells on the Middle Watch, you pull away from *Zephyr*. That should give you plenty of time. We'll weigh anchor when we have a breath of wind."

Jeffords nodded his head, smiling. "Cap'n, this will be almost a party."

The last of the four tones of *Zephyr's* bell died away signifying it was halfway through the First Watch, i.e., 10 p.m. when the three sailors climbed into the boat. The oars were laying lengthwise with sections of cloth wrapped around the shafts where they would be placed in the oarlocks so they wouldn't creak or groan as the boat was rowed.

When the 14-foot boat, the smallest *Zephyr* carried, pushed off, a thick mist swirled around the schooner's deck just as Jeffords had predicted. They only had a few hours to carry out the attack. When the rising sun started heating the air, the mist would dissipate. What was left would be blown away by the wind.

From the schooner's deck, the dim glow of the lantern on *Successor's* stern was filtered by the mist and barely visible. On the schooner, the light from the lantern hung on *Zephyr's* stern could scarcely be seen from the forecastle.

With nothing to do but wait, *Zephyr's* crew sat on the main deck. Some shivered from the cool, damp mist.

After a series of strong pulls, Landry and Grantham shipped their oars and let the boat coast toward *Successor's* transom. Above, they could hear the clump of the boots of the two Royal Marines marching back and forth on the frigate's quarterdeck. When Abner Jeffords grabbed the rudder's safety chains, he pulled the long boat into a shadowed area where the dim light of the lantern hanging from a jackstaff was blocked by the overhang of the frigate's stern.

The rudder's painted wood felt slimy as Jeffords guided the boat under one of the two hatches in the stern that were tied open to vent the aft hold.

Gingerly, Jeffords pulled himself into a kneeling position on the top of *Successor's* rudder, where it was almost a foot thick. Slowly, he worked his way to where the tiller bar that moved the rudder came out from the ship's hull. Along the way, he had to keep from slipping as he ducked under the two safety chains that kept the ship from losing its rudder should the rudder post or tiller bar snap.

Jeffords carefully reached out for the edge of the open hatch. He did not want to fall into the water because the splash would give away their presence. Abner got one hand on the corner of the opening and then the other before he let his body swing out beneath him. Using one foot, he snagged the rudder safety chain and tested the links to see if they would hold his weight. They did.

He pulled himself up through the hatch and into the pitch-black compartment. Standing on a cross member and sure of his footing, Jeffords stuck his upper body out of the hatch so only his hips and legs were inside the Royal Navy frigate and reached down. Gingerly, Colin Landry handed him a candle, a bottle of rum, a bundle of rags soaked in pitch, a flintlock pistol that had been primed, and a small flask of gunpowder.

Now that he was inside the ship, Jeffords' first task was to light the candle. Jeffords sprinkled some powder on the cross member and cocked the pistol. Holding it upside down so that the sparks would fly down and ignite the powder, he pulled the trigger. He got sparks, but the powder didn't ignite.

He made the pile bigger and tried again. The powder flared and burned long enough for him to light the handle.

The light from the candle let Abner survey the compartment that contained the ropes and pulleys that enabled the helmsman on the quarterdeck to turn the rudder. Two rats, startled by the light, scampered away. Thankfully, the hatch that allowed access to the interior of *Successor* was closed. Jeffords dripped a globule of wax onto the rudder bar and pressed the bottom of the candle onto the wax and went to work.

First, he took the 12-inch hunting knife from the sheath on his belt and sawed partway through the rope on one side that came down from the ship's wheel to the rudder. Then, he cut into the three-inch thick hemp that looped through pulleys to pull the rudder bar left and right.

Satisfied that soon after *Successor* was underway, water resistance would snap one or more of the ropes he sabotaged, Jeffords opened the second hatch before he went about his second task. He placed the pitch-soaked rags on a plank in the center of the compartment before pouring all the rum over the rags. Jeffords counted to three to give the rum time to pool in the cloth and give off some vapors before he put the candle's flame near the fabric.

He was satisfied when it flared with a soft whoosh and yellow arrowhead-shaped flame with blue at the bottom. More rats ran around the now well-lit compartment, startled by the new danger.

Jeffords worked his way out of the hatch, so he was bent at the waist but had enough of his butt on the wood to keep from falling into the water. Already, he could feel the heat on his back from the burning wood and rope. Rather than retracing his steps, Jeffords lowered himself to stand on the rudder chain and maintain his balance by holding onto the rudder. Landry eased the boat under him, and Grantham helped him down into the boat.

Pulling away, one of the oars slipped out of the oarlock with a loud clunk. A Royal Marines sentry on the quarterdeck heard the sound and leaned over the railing, peering into the mist, unaware of the conflagration building under his feet.

"Who goes there?"

The men in the boat laughed like drunken sailors. A second voice yelled in a more authoritarian tone. "Who in the bloody hell are you?"

When the Royal Marine got no answer, he shouldered his musket and fired at the dim shapes in the rowboat. The ball zinged by and splashed into the water a few feet from the bow. A second ball smacked into the wood, just inches from Grantham, the aftmost man in the boat. Rowing hard back toward *Zephyr*, all three could see the roaring fire in *Successor's* rudder compartment through the two open hatches.

Landry began chanting a sea shanty at precisely six bells on the Morning Watch. Men manning the capstan bars could feel the freshening wind that filled *Zephyr's* sails and blew away the mist.

In the growing light as *Zephyr* left the anchorage, everyone on board could see smoke billowing out from *Successor's* rudder compartment and now its gunports. The schooner was well out of Ponta Delgada's harbor just as the men on Forenoon Watch were beginning their duties when a dull boom rumbled over the water. The sound told *Zephyr's* crew all they needed to know – the fire had reached the *Successor's* magazine. To celebrate, Jaco ordered Bosun Preston to issue a double ration of rum to the entire crew.

CHAPTER 17

– TIGHTENING THE NOOSE

GOSPORT, SECOND WEEK OF JUNE 1782

With the unchanged AMIP contract and royalty agreements signed, Francis Burdette dutifully applied the necessary wax seals on the signature pages. He then had a courier deliver them to the Portsmouth naval base to be put on a ship headed back to Charleston.

He was convinced that he'd offered the best possible legal advice on the risks of this deal. If his client wasn't willing to heed his suggestions, if problems arose, he – Francis Burdette – would prosper from more fees. With that project and the trip to Charleston now in a compartment in the back of his mind, Francis started approaching possible new clients for Helmsley & Cole.

In the Smythe family house's kitchen, Olivia gave the youngest boys sweet biscuits when they returned from school and sent them off to play. Sensing this was the moment, Olivia said to her daughter, "You're miserable, aren't you?"

"Yes, Mother, I am."

"Is Francis having an affair?"

"Lord, no. It is not that."

"Then what?"

"I respect him, but I do not love him."

"Is he a bad father?"

"He's an absent father. He pays about as much attention to the boys as one would to a rabid dog. That's cruel, but Francis is so absorbed in his work he doesn't take an interest in his sons or me."

"What do you want to do?"

"Is Darren coming to supper tonight?"

"Yes. It is his last night in port. *Pompeii* is leaving tomorrow. Why?"

"I want Darren's opinion."

"Why?"

"Because what I want to do involves both of us."

Olivia said nothing as she poured a cup of tea for her daughter. "You know divorces must be approved by Parliament, which means they are public. This could end Francis' career at Helmsley & Cole."

"Mother, of that I am well aware."

"Have you seen a barrister?"

"I have a meeting with one at Scoons later this week."

"How did you accomplish that?"

"I had an introductory letter from Shoshana Jacinto, whose firm has a relationship with Scoons. They handle Scoons' business in North and South Carolina and Georgia, and Scoons helps them with matters in England. And they are the firm that handles Darren's legal affairs."

"Scoons is a very well-regarded firm. Your father would like to use them but has been loyal to Francis and Helmsley & Cole because he is your husband. Henry York, one of their partners, handles Darren's affairs. Do you know the man you will be meeting with?"

"Aye, his name is Brian Holcomb. He specializes in divorces for peers of the realm and well-to-do clients."

Olivia was never interested in the comings and goings of London or even Gosport society. Still, she did talk to her friends at the school and those who were customers. "You could spend a fortune in legal fees."

"Maybe, maybe not. In her letter, Shoshana laid out a possible strategy that may work. I want to avoid a brawl."

"So, just separate and avoid this legal trouble?"

"Then what? I am still married to him, meaning he still owns my inheritance, possessions, and children. No, I want to be free of Francis so we can lead separate lives."

"Do you want to be the Smythe & Sons family member on the board of American Medical and Industrial Products?"

"I do and be its accountant."

"Has Dr. Laredo agreed to this?"

"Reyna said if I want the position, it is mine."

Olivia slapped her hands on both thighs. "This is a fine kettle of fish. Your marriage has gone rotten, and I am to blame." She was the one who encouraged Emily to marry Francis, and now, if Emily moves to Charleston, she may never see her grandchildren again.

"No, Mother, you are not. You were then, and still are, worried about your children's happiness. If anyone is to blame, it is me. I am the one who wants to have a professional career and be a mother. It is just not possible to stay married to Francis. He will fight me every step of the way."

"What do you intend to do?"

"Buy him out. That is why I need to speak to father."

"Do you know what Francis will accept?"

"My God, no! Francis knows I am unhappy but probably thinks that it will pass. Trust me, it won't. Every day, my desire to leave him gets stronger."

"Do you know what you want to offer?"

"I do. From our books, I know what Helmsley & Cole is paid and what his percentage of the billings is. In a bank account at Barings, we have a little over £12,000. The money came from my salary from Smythe & Sons and his bonuses from Helmsley & Cole. We have been living quite comfortably on his monthly pay. So, I intend to offer him three years' fees plus half of what we have at Barings. We will sell the house, and he can have half of it or pay me half the value and keep it. There is little I want in the house besides my books and some other items."

Emily almost said I don't want to pay to ship the furniture to South Carolina, but she didn't. Instead, she searched her mother's face for a sign of what she was thinking.

What seemed to be an eternity passed. Then Olivia spoke. "Convince your father of the wisdom of what you want to do, and the money will be available. I can teach my other daughters-in-law how to be accountants."

Emily crossed the room and knelt in front of her mother. "Thank you, Mother, thank you." Then she put her head on her mother's lap and sobbed. Olivia stroked the back of Emily's head as if she was still a little girl, assuring her without words that everything would be alright.

Darren couldn't stay for supper because *Pompeii* was leaving at first light. In the few minutes they had to speak, Emily asked if Darren wanted the position at AMIP. Without hesitating, Darren shook his head, saying that he didn't need the money. Until he was cashiered, invalided, or put on half-pay, he was a Royal Navy officer.

As he left, Darren hugged his sister and whispered into her ear, saying that it will be nice to have his sister as a neighbor after the war. He was in a hurry because his sailing orders directed him to take dispatches from the Foreign Office and Parliament to Governor Wright in Savannah and a second set to General Alexander Leslie in Charleston. According to Rear Admiral Arthur, the papers give General Leslie specific directions on who was eligible for evacuation and where they were to be taken if the decision was made to evacuate the British Army from Charleston.

On the boat out to *Pompeii*, Darren wondered if his answer to Emily was too hasty but then rationalized that he was a seaman at heart. Working at Smythe & Sons or AMIP wasn't in the cards. He didn't need the salary and will deal with his post-Royal Navy career when the time comes.

CHARLESTON, THIRD WEEK OF JUNE 1782

Before he left the shelter of the portico at the Dockside Inn, Rafer Muir thought the heavy rain accompanied by the blasts of thunder meant fewer people would be on Charleston's streets. In his mind, the fewer, the better, which reduced the risk of being seen where he was going.

Muir suspected if his fellow officers knew with whom he was about to have dinner, they would call him a traitor. Even Lord Islay might look askance at having dinner with a group of rebels. But it was a risk he had to take.

He held his oilskin cape above him, but by the time Muir knocked on the door of the house on Friends Street, the cape was heavy with water. He was, except for his legs and the outside of his arms, dry.

In a second behind-closed-door conversation with Greg Struthers, Rafer wanted specifics on who he should approach about employment should he return to Charleston once the war ended. Muir had seen the directive to evacuate Savannah and was told privately by Lord Islay that Charleston was next but did not know when.

The order from Parliament forwarded from General Clinton instructed General Leslie not to engage in any offensive operations. It was, Muir believed, a prelude to evacuating the British Army from Charleston. More instructions were coming, but for now, General Leslie wanted to ensure that the British Army in Charleston avoided combat.

Muir also didn't wish to risk combat either. The news was a Godsend, and he began to plan for the next phase of his life.

Each Loyalist who arrived in Charleston was interviewed to see what they knew about the Continental Army's disposition. The picture gained from the interviews was that the rebel army was bivouacked at Fort Watson. Muir assumed that the 4th Carolina was quietly watching who came and went from Charleston and believed that if a British Army unit ventured from Charleston, the 4th Carolina would make its presence known.

Muir's go-between to set up this meeting was Greg Struthers, the former Continental Navy officer and president of the Bank of South Carolina. Several years ago, Greg married the daughter of a rebel plantation owner, Phoebe MacManus whose father emigrated from Aberdeen.

It was, Muir believed, time to retire from British Army. Of all the places the army sent him, he liked Charleston the best. Struthers, always looking for new clients for the bank, invited Muir to a dinner where he could meet privately with Charlestonians whom he said, "Will be here after the war and in a position to offer you meaningful work."

Who they were, Muir did not know. Other than his boots, his clothes gave no signs he was a British Army officer. Not seeing anyone around him, Rafer rapped on the door twice. Phoebe Struthers, visibly pregnant with their first child, opened the door.

Greg waved him over to a table and held up an empty glass.

Muir's almost instant reply was, "Absolutely."

"Rafer, this is locally made whiskey from corn. Tastes different than what is distilled in Scotland."

"I'll have some anyway. Good whiskey is good whiskey."

Rafer held up the glass with the coffee-colored beverage. "To peace, prosperity, and long life."

"Amen to all that."

Seeing the table was set for six, Rafer wondered who was coming. All Greg would promise was that these individuals would have openings when the war ended, and how fast he could get back was up to him.

Another knock on the door again sent Phoebe to the front of the house.

Dr. Reyna Laredo, one of two women who entered, held out her hand, "It is nice to see you colonel socially instead of professionally." Reyna turned to the tall, elderly woman standing beside her, "I don't know if you two have met, but this is my grandmother, Miriam Bildesheim. She owns the largest general store in Charleston, the Dockside Inn, Shayna Enterprises and is a shareholder of the Bank of South Carolina."

Rafer bowed each time he took a woman's hand. "Mrs. Bildesheim, it is a pleasure to finally meet you. As you can imagine, I have heard much about you."

Miriam laughed, "I suspect zee British generals do not applaud ven my name ist mentioned."

Rafer laughed heartily. "Ma'am, I believe you are correct."

Dinner was venison Rafer suspected was killed, cleaned, and aged not far from where they were sitting. Rice with small noodles was served.

No one mentioned the current war during the entire meal. Instead, Muir was peppered about his childhood in Scotland and where he served during the Seven Years' War. With each person served a portion of peach pie and a glass of port, Miriam tapped the side of her glass as if to say the business part of the meeting was about to begin.

"Zo, Herr Leutnant Colonel Muir," Miriam used the German pronunciation of lieutenant, "you vould not be zitting here vit us unless two people close to me whose judgment I trust said you vere a gut man. Zay ist my granddaughter, Fraulein Doctor Laredo, und my grandson, Herr Major Amos Laredo. For obvious reasons, he cannot be here tonight vit us. To help you understand vat zee surveyors tell me ist zee lay of zee land, I vill tell you vat three families zat I can speak for represent."

Miriam explained Shayna Enterprises and the kollectiv, mentioning only that the farms grew food and raised animals for meat. Then she said she was part owner of the Bank of South Carolina, and her partners were the Jacintos and the Laredos. The Laredos owned ships registered in Sweden and South Carolina, and the Jacintos owned land farmed by Shayna Enterprises and an import and export business with offices shared with Laredo Shipping in several European cities and the rebelling Thirteen Colonies.

When she finished, Reyna asked, "Lieutenant Colonel Muir, do you know anything about metalworking?"

He laughed. "Doctor, the muscles in the arm you saved were built working in my father's blacksmith shop. We made metal fittings, swords, and knives for the local clans. Why?"

"I cannot give you any details at this time, but I may be involved in a business that requires metalworking skills."

Muir nodded. He never considered himself a blacksmith, but he was all ears if it meant making a living in Charleston. Miriam also outlined where she thought the businesses in which she invested or owned would need educated men who could help make them grow and be more profitable. When she finished, no one said anything, so she asked, "Herr Leutnant Colonel, vun last question. Vould you verk for my grandson Amos?"

"Yes, absolutely. Major Laredo and I have met several times on the battlefield and found him to be a man of his word."

"Gut…"

"Zo, Herr Colonel, ven do you zink zee British Army vill leave Charleston?"

Muir laughed. "I wish I knew. All I can tell you is based on this conversation tonight, not soon enough."

GOSPORT, FOURTH WEEK OF JUNE 1782

With Jeremiah in school, Emily, Jeffrey, and Jonah walked to the Smythe & Sons factory, where she shared an office with her mother. The first part of the building was built in the 1670s, expanded in 1701, and then again in 1750, and it now had three sections. The front faced the street was once, Emily believed, a small home that was now the Smythe & Sons company offices.

An earlier generation added a large-enclosed barnlike building on the land out back that was their factory. Four forges were in a covered area. Off to one side, iron rods and bags of coal were stacked in neat piles. Rust wasn't a concern because accumulated rust was long gone once the rods were heated, pounded, and shaped into steel.

The front office with its lath and plaster walls painted a light brown was convenient for two reasons. One, if visitors arrived, Emily and Olivia were there to greet them. The second was that they were far from the noisy hammering and grinding that went on in the factory. It also provided a place for Emily's children to play until they were old enough to attend school.

Francis Burdette knew his wife's routine as well as his own. This knowledge was, he believed, part of his duty as her husband. Emily's and his children's safety were his responsibility. According to English law, Emily and his children were also his property, meaning he owned any asset in their name, be it an inheritance, stock in a company, or title to land.

When studying to become a lawyer, he thought these provisions were medieval. While the 18th Century was far from the Middle Ages, these laws were enacted to protect the Lords from having their property taken by irate wives. In the Middle Ages, women were second-class citizens whose primary purposes were to cement alliances by marriage and produce male heirs.

Now 36 and far wiser than when he was studying to become a barrister, Francis could see the wisdom of these laws. They protected men who did the work that made England the wealthiest country in the world.

With Emily at work and their two youngest children with her, he used the excuse he wanted to personally deliver a document to a client so he could walk to his house. In their bedroom, he searched for Emily's diary or love letters from an admirer. He rationalized the invasion of his wife's privacy as something he could legally do as her "owner."

Not finding the diary or letters in her dressing room, he searched the kitchen, thinking he would find them there. Nothing. He stood with his hands on his hips and went around the house again. Still, he could not find her diary that she made entries in after he went to sleep.

Frustrated, Francis returned to his office, wondering what had caused the change in her attitude. Before they left for South Carolina, she was the typical, dutiful English wife.

While in North America, something happened. He blamed the change on the Jewesses Reyna Laredo and Shoshana Jacinto, who filled her head with nonsense. Jews, he believed, were the root of evil in the world because they killed Christ. King Edward II was correct to rid England of them, and he never understood why Cromwell let them back in in the 1650s.

In the evenings, with the children in bed and her nightly chores done, Emily sat in a chair with a lantern by her side, engrossed in a book. Usually, it was a romance novel, but sometimes history.

With the children in bed and a glass of scotch whiskey in hand, Francis stood facing Emily. "Emily, what has come over you since we went to Charleston?"

Emily looked up, hiding her annoyance at his presence, and the question, "Nothing, why?"

"What changed your attitude towards me?"

Emily understood his loaded question, which was a repeat, phrased differently from the first. It was Solicitor Burdette at work. She slid a bookmark into place and closed the book. Emily forced herself to look directly at her husband, not wanting to reveal her true intentions. "My feelings haven't changed."

"Yes, they have. You appeared to be annoyed whenever I'm around you."

"Sorry."

"Are you having an affair?"

"NO!!!! How dare you accuse me of infidelity!" Emily stood up. "This is not a conversation I wish to entertain. I'm tired and am going to bed."

Francis stood with his hands at his side. As Emily passed, he said, "And dream about your lover!"

Emily stopped, turned slowly, and glared at her husband as she faced him, her anger boiling. "I will forget that you said something as stupid as that."

"Is it Rafer Muir? I saw how he looked at you."

Emily wheeled and slapped her husband on the cheek, leaving marks where her fingers smacked his cheek. "Don't you ever again accuse me of not being faithful to you."

As she left the parlor, Francis bleated, "When did you stop loving me?"

Emily stopped and just looked at him. She wanted to say, "I never did," but she didn't. Instead, she said nothing as she glared at him and went upstairs to their bedroom, more determined than ever to get out of this marriage.

WESTERN ATLANTIC, FOURTH WEEK OF JUNE 1782

In the locked box in Darren's cabin, the two bundles of documents – one for Admiral Graves and one for General Leslie – sat under his sailing orders. He pulled his orders out for the umpteenth time and stared at the writing.

Captain Smythe,

You are to sail Pompeii as fast as possible to North America and deliver the documents given to you to Admiral Graves and General Leslie. Enroute, you are not to hunt for prizes or engage in any action unless an enemy ship is attempting to stop you from delivering the documents.

Once you have delivered the letters to their intended recipients, Pompeii is assigned to the North American Station whose warships' primary mission is escorting transports evacuating the British Army and English citizens from Savannah to their assigned destinations.

Augustus Keppel
1ˢᵗ Viscount Keppel
First Sea Lord

His take was that his orders gave him latitude on where he took *Pompeii* first. As his frigate plowed through the waters under full sail - mains, top, top gallants, and royals - he realized he would soon have to decide to angle nor' west towards New York or directly to Charleston and nearby Savannah which were only a few days away.

Looking at the calendar on his desk, Darren decided that he would go to Charleston first, convinced that Graves would be closer to South Carolina and Georgia than New York if the evacuation of Savannah had begun.

His real hurry was to tell Melody that the war would soon be over, and they could marry.

GOSPORT, FIRST WEEK OF JULY 1782

Francis Burdette "made" partner at Helmsley & Cole in 1776, but as the most junior member voted to be a firm member, he still had the smallest office. It was tucked down the hall on the second floor of the three-story building occupied by Helmsley & Cole. The only benefit to his office was that he had a window overlooking the street and was next to the firm's law library. Next to the law library was the records room that contained documents and files going back to when the firm was founded in 1676.

The two founders and the more senior partners had offices on the third floor, with the first floor reserved for the law interns and two conference rooms. One of the perks of being a partner, albeit a junior one, was that Francis now had a dedicated law clerk who doubled as a secretary to write contracts and other documents in what the firm called 'a fine hand.'

Burdette was sipping a cup of tea when his law clerk knocked on the door. "Sir, I have the Portsmouth Foundry contracts back from Scoons with the changes they would like made. Do you want to review them?"

"I do. Please put the contracts on my desk. I will get to them presently."

LAST BATTLES

The young man, whose first name was Neville Sampson, hesitated. He was working at Helmsley & Cole while he waited for his application to Grays or one of the other Inns to be ruled upon. If accepted, he would move to London for the time it took to graduate. If not, he would remain a law clerk and try again in a year.

Curious about why Neville was still in his doorway, Francis did his best to hide his irritation. "What is it, Mr. Sampson?"

The 18-year-old, whose face was pockmarked with acne scars, blurted out. "Sir, I saw Mrs. Burdette leave a room where Scoons meets with clients."

Francis Burdette stopped sipping his tea mid-sip. He slowly put the cup back down on the saucer giving him time to contemplate what he was just told.

"Did you recognize the barrister?"

"No, sir."

Trying to control his emotions, Burdette said, "Thank you, Mr. Sampson, that will be all."

Three scenarios raced through his mine. One, she was there on her brother's behalf. Darren was, after all, a Scoons' client and was recently in Portsmouth. All he could get out of Emily was that some Royal Navy captain left Darren a pile of money, and Scoons was helping him make it, along with the prize money he earned, grow.

Two, Emily was there on Smythe & Sons business. He remembered from his discussions with Shoshana, the Jewess mentioned Burrows & Soriano had a relationship with Scoons. So, Emily could be there for something related to the family business, which was outside the scope of the matters handled by Helmsley & Cole. He doubted that they were searching for another law firm because if they were, either Lester or one or both of his two sons, Bradley, or Gerard, would have been there.

Or three, Emily was there to ask for legal advice for herself. To him, that meant only one thing, divorce!!! In the legal profession, Scoons was known to have connections to the King and wasn't hesitant to use them. He was aware of a recent case in which the wealthy son of a London merchant who had a taste for the ladies was fleeced by his estranged wife. Scoons managed to get the divorce through Parliament without a mention in the society pages of the London newspapers.

Burdette took a sheaf of papers he had put in a drawer the day after Emily slapped him. With several blank sheets of paper with the Helmsley & Cole logo in hand, he went into the law library. He wanted to do more research before he acted. Francis Burdette was determined not to let his wife ruin him.

PHILADELPHIA, FIRST WEEK OF JULY 1782

While Javier Jacinto was not a member of the Foreign Affairs Committee, he knew its members quite well. The committee had just recently learned through the letters captured by Jaco and a spy that the French had approached the British to begin negotiations without the Americans after their defeat in the Battle of the Saintes.

Anger at France's duplicity was the prevalent emotion amongst the committee members. If the French wanted to negotiate a separate deal with Britain, that was acceptable to the Congress but would not change the Thirteen Colonies' key demands.

Jaco sat in the gallery as Congress debated what actions it would take against the French. The sense of the Congress was that excluding the French and their Spanish allies from the negotiations could minimize any influence either country had on the outcome of the peace talks.

He left knowing *Zephyr* would soon be en route to Brest. Morton Geiger had made sure the schooner had a hold full of food and then organized a small party for the crew. After the party, Jaco went to his cabin and began to write:

My dear and lovely Reyna,

As I write this letter, we are in Philadelphia — again! — and about to leave for Brest, again!!! I hope all is well with you. Congratulations on the contract with Smythe & Sons. I am sure that they will sign it.

Zephyr has proven to be a fine ship well suited to sailing back and forth to Brest quickly. We are making the 3,300 nautical mile trip in an astonishing two weeks or less.

On my last trip, we were sent to Amsterdam, and I spent a few hours with Eric. He is well and, as you know, enamored with a lovely Dutch woman Sera Winjschenk. Her ancestors came from Portugal, so she, like us, is Sephardic, but Sera looks more like a Viking than a Spaniard.

There is, from what I understand, progress in the peace talks despite the French stabbing us in the back. Without telling Mr. Franklin, they began negotiations with the British without our participation. You can imagine the reaction here in Philadelphia.

The English have agreed to grant us complete independence. However, there are still some sticking points, mostly over how we will treat the Loyalists who decide to remain in our new country.

Many in Congress want their pound of flesh because these men and women didn't join our cause, but I think that is wrong. As far as I am concerned, if they swear allegiance to the United States and are not spies, they are welcome to stay.

By now, you may know that the British evacuated Savannah. Charleston should be next, but no one here knows if or when.

I always think of you and cannot wait to be together as husband and wife. The time is coming soon! Unfortunately, I cannot define soon!

Be well, my love, and I will see you soon.

Your fiancée.

Jaco

GOSPORT, FIRST WEEK OF JULY 1782

When Emily walked into their house in Gosport, she found her husband sitting on a chair with a glass of whiskey in his hand and a partially finished bottle on the table next to him. Experience suggested Francis was an obnoxious drunk who could become bellicose. Sensing danger, Emily tried to shoo her three boys off to their rooms upstairs. Before they could leave, Francis Burdette stood up and confronted Emily.

Belligerently, he demanded, "What are you planning, woman?"

"My first name is Emily. Should you want to talk to me, you should address me by my first name and in a civil tone. If not, I shall go see to something to eat for my children."

Burdette sneered, his tone nasty, "Your children, they're mine. I sired them."

"Aye, you did that. Then I carried each one for nine months, nursed them when they were borne, cared for them when they were sick, and now, I, not you, take care of their daily needs."

Emily turned to go upstairs with the three boys to get away from her husband, who reeked from scotch. The thought of an unhappy, belligerent Francis made her shiver with fear. She fought the urge to run.

On board *Queen Boleyn,* he created a nasty scene in which three sailors had to manhandle a hostile Francis to his room, put him in his bunk, and bar the door from the outside. Emily was one of three targets of Francis' vitriol.

Francis called Emily a showy harlot who used her good looks to snare him. A few minutes later, he called her draggle tail which was slang for a nasty, dirty slut who does anything for money. Emily tried to get Francis to stop, but he was on a roll when he called her a pintle merchant, another slang term for a whore.

When the other three men at the table confronted Francis for his insults, he went on a tirade berating the two men, the months spent on what he believed was an unnecessary trip to South Carolina and the Jews with whom he was forced to negotiate.

Before fleeing to her cabin, Emily did her best to apologize to the other passengers and crew for Francis' rude behavior. Alone, as a catharsis and a refuge, Emily wrote as much detail as she could in her diary. Then, in the wee hours of the morning, she went up on deck to watch the sun rise before returning to her cabin to sleep for a few hours.

When Francis awoke the following day, he pounded on the door because he had to go to the bathroom. His hair was disheveled, and his clothes were soiled. At dinner, the atmosphere around the table was tense despite his attempts to apologize for his boorish behavior, but the damage was done.

Francis pointed to the floor in front of him as he spat out the words, "Come back here, wife."

Emily froze, as did her boys, despite her urging them to go upstairs. Slowly, she turned around. "My name is Emily, and while I may be married to you, which makes me your wife, do not speak to me as if I am a piece of property."

Burdette sneered. "Emily, my wife, you, and these boys are my property and everything you own. The law says so."

Emily glared back at him. Brian Holcomb had shown her how the interpretation of the law had changed. Initially, it was written to protect titles and peerages and the land that went with them. Parents arranged marriages to build alliances, and the daughter was treated as a negotiable piece of property. Since then, England and its interpretation of the divorce laws have come a long way.

Holcomb had shown her the formula he was sure a court would approve in a settlement to buy Francis out of their marriage if it got that far. He would solicit statements from the other passengers on *Queen Boleyn* to qualify for one of the conditions a woman needed to meet for a divorce. If she could prove physical abuse or infidelity, then any defense Burdette would try to argue would fail in court.

Emily steeled herself for what she was sure to come. The words came out of her mouth slowly and distinctly. "I… am… not… your… property…" She started to add, "I am free to make my own choices." The words never exited her mouth since Burdette's fist slammed into her jaw. Staggered, Emily went down in a heap. Blood oozed from her split lip.

Jeremiah and Jeffrey threw themselves at their father, pummeling them with their fists as Francis kicked Emily in the side. The burly Burdette grabbed his two boys by the neck and threw them to the side like rag dolls. Both came back at him, screaming, crying, and flailing.

Jonah, who was only three, understood only one thing, his mother was hurt. He wailed and flailed until his father kicked him. The blow sent him head-first into a banister post. Jonah slid to the floor unconscious.

Emily crawled to where her inert son lay and looked at Francis, who glared at her. "You bloody bastard. How could you do this to one of your sons?"

"Get out and take your mongrel children out of MY house." The words were followed by another blow to the face that sent Emily reeling and bloodied her nose. She put a hand on the wall to steady herself and wiped the blood flowing from her nose and down her face. "Gladly."

The walk to her parent's house took twice as long as the 10 minutes it usually took. For the first part, she cradled the unconscious Jonah in her arms as they plodded along. Along the way, he stirred, and by the time they reached her parent's house, the toddler was awake but couldn't stand.

Seeing her battered daughter and grandchildren, Olivia first ensured that only Jonah needed a doctor. She ran to the Smythe & Sons factory and brought back Lester and Bradley. Gerard went to fetch Dr. Rehuel Labatto.

After listening to his daughter, Lester Smythe went up two flights of stairs to his study used by several generations as an office where medical instruments were designed. He took a sword from the rack on the wall Joakim Schmeitz made when he first arrived in England 170-odd years ago. The sword he brought with him was in Darren's cabin on board *Pompeii*. One of the family traditions was that both men and women were taught at an early age to be expert swordsmen.

The other item he took from his study was the case with two pistols that were a gift from the Royal Navy. He started to load them when Emily put her hand on his. "Father don't. Francis is not worth you being hung for murder. I have a plan that will ruin him."

"Pray tell, what is it? A father cannot allow a man to beat his daughter for no reason."

Emily pointed to the chairs in the dining room where they took their weekly family meals. "Mother knows some of my plans. Brian Holcomb at Scoons has told me what to do. This beating just reduced the amount I will offer as a settlement. Before Dr. Labatto leaves, please ask him to write a statement and then send Bradley to fetch the magistrate who will, I hope, swear out a warrant for Francis' arrest."

Dr. Labatto arrived before Emily finished describing Holcomb's plan. After examining Jeremiah, he smiled when he said, "I do not think his skull was fractured, but he will have headaches and be dizzy off and on for the next few weeks. Now my dear Emily, let me have a look at you."

His gentle fingers turned Emily's head from side to side so he could see the bruising. Already one eye was swollen shut, and he wanted to make sure that her neck and spine weren't affected.

"Emily, who did this?"

"Francis."

"Bloody bastard. I never liked him. I thought he was a cad when he was more interested in his contracts than being at the house when Jeffrey was born. Any man who does this to a woman should be in jail."

With Dr. Labatto's written statement attested by members of the Smythe family in hand, Emily told her parents and brothers about the incident on *Queen Boleyn* and what was going to happen next.

CHAPTER 18

- NEW PERCEPTIONS

CHARLESTON, SECOND WEEK OF JULY 1782

When *Pompeii* glided to a stop in Charleston's outer harbor, its anchor splashed into the water just west of what was labeled "Middle Ground." Darren's Admiralty Chart noted his ship was in 33 feet of water at low tide. One hundred yards from where he stood, Darren could see by the changes in how the water flowed where, according to his chart, the bottom was only 15 feet from the surface. Fully loaded, *Pompeii* drew at least 16 feet, and Darren preferred 20 or more feet below his frigate's keel.

With both anchors on the bottom and sure the frigate would not drift, Darren ordered only one boat lowered into the water since Graves flagship, *H.M.S. Bedford,* 74 guns, was not in Charleston. Therefore, he decided the boat would take both Second Lieutenant Shamus O'Steen with their victualling order and him ashore. While delivering the dispatches to General Leslie, he would inquire where Admiral Graves may be.

"Captain, do you mind if we sail? We're well over a mile from the landing."

"Splendid! You can demonstrate your small boat handling skills."

O'Steen grinned. "Actually, sir, one of the quartermaster mates will be at the tiller. Like you, I will sit by the mast, clutching an oil skin full of paper to keep the victualling officer happy. While ashore, I will find the dried smoked meat the rebels call jerky. Our crew seems to like it, and it's a change in the usual Royal Navy fare."

"Splendid! If you need money, I can take some from the ship's purse."

"Thank you, sir, but the King's credit should still be good here in Charleston. The last time, the merchants were eager to bill the port captain."

Darren turned to Chris Abbott, "Mr. Abbott, I shall be going ashore to deliver the documents we have rushed across the Atlantic to deliver. Have the officer of the watch keep an eye out for signals. And do me a favor, try not to let *Pompeii* drift and run aground. I'd rather not have to explain why *Pompeii* needs to be pulled off a sandbar."

"Aye, sir. I'll do my best not to create an ugly entry into the ship's log."

"Splendid." Darren saw a bosun mate standing beside Lieutenant O'Steen, ready to sail ashore." Shall we?"

It was a Friday, and Melody should be in school here in Charleston.

Darren walked briskly and was sweating in his uniform when he entered General Leslie's headquarters. His feet, despite the stockings, chafed against the constraint of his leather shoes, and the wooden heels felt odd as they clumped on the cobblestones. On board ship this time of year, he was barefoot and wore only a linen shirt and breeches.

At the entrance, the sentries snapped to attention when they saw a Royal Navy captain. Inside, a British Army lieutenant asked politely. "Sir, may I ask what your business is here at General Leslie's headquarters."

Darren held out the bundle. "My ship just carried these from London, and my orders are to personally deliver them to General Leslie. So, please lead me to his office."

He wouldn't allow a mere lieutenant to delay him from doing his duty. With luck, he will be standing in the street when Melody leaves her school.

The lieutenant told the sergeant of the guard where he was going, and Darren followed him up two flights of stairs. At the top of the landing, the lieutenant rapped on the first office in the hallway. "Lieutenant Colonel Muir, I have a Royal Navy Captain who says he has dispatches and letters for General Leslie."

Muir looked up and seeing Darren, broke into a wide smile. "Captain Smythe, it is good to see you. Please, come in. I need to sign these orders, and then we shall pay General Leslie a visit."

The Scotsman scribbled his name on three documents and used a crescent-shaped blotter to dry his signature. While pulling on his uniform coat, he asked, "Good trip over?"

"Yes, we made Charleston twenty-two days after leaving Portsmouth." According to his log, *Pompeii* covered 4,327 nautical miles at an average of 8.2 knots.

"Excellent." Muir finished buttoning his red coat and pointed with the palm of his right hand. "Shall we?"

Muir's knock on the door frame to General Leslie's office was followed by an irritated, "Come in." The Scottish Highlander stuck his head in the door. "Sir, Captain Darren Smythe of His Majesty's Frigate *Pompeii* just arrived with dispatches he needs to personally deliver to you. They are marked most urgent."

The General's tone of voice changed from annoyed to pleasant. "Please come in."

Muir nodded in Smythe's direction. "May I introduce General Alexander Leslie, Captain Darren Smythe, Royal Navy."

The British Army lieutenant colonel pointed with the palm of his hand as he introduced the other men in the room, "James Wright, the Royal Governor of Georgia and Lord Islay."

Darren shook hands with each man before he placed the bundle, still wrapped in the string in which it was given to him in Portsmouth, on the table in front of General Leslie. The General used a knife he took from a sheath on his desk and cut the string. "So, Captain, do you know what is in these letters?"

"No, sir. All I was told was to deliver them to you. I have a second bundle for Admiral Graves once I find his flagship." The fact that Wright was in Charleston suggested that the evacuation of Savannah was complete.

"Last I heard, Graves was off New York someplace. The last British troops left Fort Provost outside of Savannah on July 11th. Graves' frigates are escorting transports to New York, Halifax, and ports all over the Caribbean."

Darren nodded to suggest he understood.

"How soon can your ship go back to sea?"

"Normally, we need three or four days to load provisions. We can do it faster if we are tied to a pier."

Leslie turned to face Rafer Muir. "Lieutenant Colonel Muir, see if you can get the good captain's ship alongside a pier as fast as possible. I have letters and reports I'd like brought to General Clinton." Turning back to the Royal Navy officer, Leslie said, "Captain, I'll have them delivered to your ship once you report to Lieutenant Colonel Muir that your ship is ready to leave."

Back in Muir's office, the Scotsman closed the door and spoke softly as if he was conspiring to commit a crime. "General Leslie's orders are to sit and wait for the order to evacuate. We know it is coming, just not the timing."

Darren let Muir continue. "I need a day or two to convince the port captain to make space on a pier for *Pompeii*. Then we will need to get the supplies together, so I expect you will be here for five or six days. So, go enjoy yourself."

En route to Melody's school, Darren felt like he was walking on air. He was early, so he went to her classroom, and the students started laughing when they saw him in the doorway before Melody did. She stopped mid-sentence.

Ever the professional, she invited Darren into the classroom. "Students, this is a good friend of mine, Captain Darren Smythe of the Royal Navy and commander of the frigate *Pompeii*."

There were more laughs from the students who had seen Darren before. "I'll come back. I need to send a signal to my ship."

"How long will you be in Charleston?"

"Five days, I hope."

"Wonderful. We have much to talk about. Did you see Emily?"

"I did, and yes, we do."

Darren said goodbye to the class and left. He was in the process of dictating a signal to *Pompeii* when he heard footsteps behind him. It was Lieutenant O'Steen. "Sir, no need. We were at the victualling office when the port captain came in with an order from General Leslie that we are to be berthed to a pier as fast as he can find us one. He thinks we should be pier side in two days."

Darren nodded, thinking Leslie must be in a big hurry to get him back to sea.

O'Steen continued. "Sir, may we have an open house and a party? The lads will like that."

"Let us talk about it once we are back onboard *Pompeii*."

GOSPORT, SECOND WEEK OF JULY 1782

While the magistrate took Emily's statement, he was reluctant to swear out an arrest warrant because he knew Francis well and the implications of what was being asked. Disappointed, Emily and her father put a copy of the document in a file the family was now keeping on Francis.

The next phase in the plan was to clean out the house of things that Emily felt were valuable to her. While Francis was at work, Emily, and the children, who were now living with her parents, went to the house each day and brought more and more items they wanted to keep to the Smythe's home. Today, they would bring her collection of books and the Delft China bowls, plates, and vases she had been collecting. These were carefully packed in boxes filled with sawdust and loaded onto a wagon parked in the back of the house.

Out front, two factory workers stood guard in the street. Emily expected that Francis would eventually figure out that the house was being emptied of everything except the furniture and his personal belongings. Her books were being loaded onto the wagon when Francis strode up.

When the factory workers blocked his entrance to the house, Francis demanded to know what was going on. Not wanting a confrontation, Emily asked the men to step aside and retreated into the parlor.

"What are you doing in my house?"

"Taking my belongings and those of your children?"

Burdette angrily demanded. "You will do no such thing! They are my property. You must return everything at once!"

"Really? Legally, this is not your house. It is my father's. If you remember, my father gave us the money to buy the house. We have not paid off the loan, so my father owns the house."

Emily placed the original loan on the table and slid the paper out an arm's length so Francis could see the document but not close enough so he could touch it. She pulled it back when he reached for the paper, afraid he would rip it up.

"My father never asked us for a shilling, so my father still owns the house and has the deed. So, Francis, I'm willing to discuss rent should you want to continue living here. If not, you have five days to move out, or I will evict you. You can take whatever furniture you wish as a gift from me."

Emily slid a different piece of paper across the table. "This is the day, time, and location of a meeting with Mr. Brian Holcomb, a partner of Scoons at their Portsmouth office. I suggest you be there to hear my offer of a settlement that will buy me out of our marriage. Should you not attend this crucial meeting, we have other surprises for you."

Francis came around the end of the table, his face contorted and red with anger. "You…. You…."

"Say it, Francis, say what you are thinking if it makes you feel better."

Frustrated, Francis got to the end of the table where Emily calmly stood. Her face was still black and blue, but the swelling had receded. He raised his hand with his fist clenched, when he felt a sharp object pressing into his side.

"Francis Burdette, if you ever touch my daughter again, I will slowly slice you into pieces that a minnow can swallow."

Feeling the steel through his coat, he slowly lowered his hands and turned. Lester Smythe's 30-inch sword glistened in the sunlight streaming into the parlor. "Slicing you into pieces would be my pleasure. If you know what is good for you, leave now and return when we are gone. And, as Emily suggested, it would behoove you to be at the meeting with Mr. Holcomb."

Francis Burdette pursed his lips and scooped up the invitation. He glared at Emily and then Lester and started to say something but then thought the better of it and left.

PORTSMOUTH, TWO DAYS LATER

Lester Smythe escorted his daughter to Scoons' office on Alfred Street, a short walk from the harbor where the boat from Gosport dropped them off. They arrived at the Scoons' office half an hour before the appointed time of 10. Lester Smythe was there for a separate meeting and would, of course, be available if needed. Brian Holcomb was confident that Francis would agree to the offered terms if he was as greedy as Emily, and he believed he was.

The conference room was pleasantly furnished, with wood paneling and comfortable chairs around a highly polished table. Emily steeled herself to be cold and unfeeling but civil as she waited for the man who would soon be her ex-husband to arrive.

A clerk leaned into the room. "Mr. Holcomb, your guest has arrived."

"Please show him in." Only three chairs were in the room, and two were occupied, which made it obvious where Francis was to sit. Francis put his briefcase on the floor, adjusted his coat as he sat, and rested his forearms on the table's edge with his hands clasped. The gesture screamed the words, "Well, start talking."

Emily wanted to present the offer. While she had not rehearsed what to say, Holcomb wanted her to be very precise in her language. In a civil but emotionless voice, Emily began speaking. "Francis, thank you for coming. Do you want us to have a secretary to record the conversation?"

"No." He didn't want to say that the fewer people who knew the details of this conversation, the better, but he didn't.

Emily continued. "The purpose of this meeting is to present an offer that will provide you with a substantial sum in return for ending our marriage. I know this is hard for you, but if you accept my offer, we can go our separate ways and enjoy the rest of our lives."

She forced herself to breathe. If Francis had touched her hands, he would have learned they were wet with moisture. "If you agree, Mr. Holcomb will move a private bill through parliament at no cost to you because we both know we meet the two requirements for divorce. One was your attack on me, and the second was your boorish behavior on *Queen Boleyn*. We're basing our offer on how much you made from the Smythe & Sons account for the past three years. Smythe & Sons is your largest single account which pays Helmsley & Cole an annual retainer of £300. Over the past three years, on average, you have billed an additional £2,293. We rounded up to £2,300 in our calculations. Your employment agreement with Helmsley & Cole entitles you to twenty percent of the retainer, forty percent of your billed hours, and twenty percent of hours billed by law clerks or other firm members."

Emily slid a sheet of paper across the table. "This is a summary of our income based on the money Smythe & Sons paid Helmsley & Cole. It shows that you made just over £1,500 from my family's firm and another £500 from your other clients every year."

Francis Burdette ran the tip of his finger up and the columns. Emily assumed he was checking the math. Satisfied or not, he pushed the paper aside and glared at Emily.

"So, this is the offer. My father sells the house on which there is no mortgage. The house is worth at least £2,600 and we give you fifty percent of the sale price. That's £1,300. The divorce agreement gives me custody and financial responsibility for the children. For that concession, I will give you a Bank of England draft of £1,500 plus £6,200 which is half of what is in our Barings Bank account on which I will no longer be a signatory. In other words, you will have at least £9,000 in cash once the house is sold. If you do not agree to the settlement, you will have five days from today to vacate the house and can have none of the furniture."

"May I see the settlement agreement?"

Emily nodded. Brian Holcomb slid the two sheets of paper across the table. No one said a word while Francis read. "What if I want to visit my children?"

"Sorry, Francis, that will not be allowed. They saw what you did to Jonah and me and do not want to see you again." She did not want to tell him that as soon as the settlement was signed and the bill approved by Parliament, Holcomb would notify the town's clerk that the marriage had been dissolved and change the last names of her boys to Smythe.

Francis rubbed his forehead with the thumb and forefinger of his left hand as he perused the document. "What if I do not agree?"

Emily turned to Brian, who spoke as if on cue, "One, the divorce will be messy and more public than you would care it to be, but it will happen. Two, by the time we win, you will be destitute and unemployed with no prospects. I can assure you Scoons will use its contacts to ensure that no law firm in England or any of its colonies would hire you. And, I might add, what is being offered is roughly twice what I suggested. So, I strongly recommend you take the money."

"Should I assume that Smythe & Sons will terminate Helmsley & Cole?"

Emily's voice had cold steel in her tone. "Yes. If you do not agree to this agreement, the termination notice will be delivered today. If you sign, my father will wait until we settle, and I give you the drafts before he sends the termination letter."

"How much time do I have to decide?"

"Francis, I want our marriage to end now. The papers before you are ready to sign and guarantee you at least £9,000 in cash. If the house sells for more than £2,600, you will get half of the overage."

Burdette looked at his soon-to-be ex-wife. "You're quite a hussy and should have been an abbess. You know, the law allows me to have you auctioned off and then the children one by one."

Emily smiled as she stood up. "Francis, you and I know that won't happen. And, if you continue to insult me by calling me a whore and a madame, I will rescind the offer. So, I suggest you focus on what is in front of you. If you prefer, Mr. Holcomb and I will leave you alone with all the papers. You must decide before you leave this office. If you say no, Scoons and I will take the steps necessary to ensure the divorce happens, and you will get nothing. Your arrogance will be to blame for walking away from £9,000."

Burdette winced when he heard Emily's words. She left the room, and Brian Holcomb placed all the papers in front of Francis that he would need to sign. As he left, the Scoons lawyer said that when Francis decided what he would do, tell the law clerk outside the door. Brian will have their signatures authenticated and the necessary seals applied if he signs them.

Lester Smythe was sitting in another room with Henry York when Emily and Brian Holcomb entered. Both stood, and Holcomb spoke first after he held out the chair for Emily and she sat down. "He'll sign because his other choices are rather unpleasant. If you'll excuse me, I have another matter to attend to, so Emily, if you need me, I'll be down the hall."

Emily had met York, Darren's attorney, during an earlier visit to Scoons with her father. "Emily, I'll have some fresh tea brought in."

When he sat back down, York spoke. "Your father gave me a copy of the agreement that forms American Medical and Industrial Products. You are to be congratulated for an excellent piece of work. The idea to base salesmen at the Laredo Shipping and South Carolina Exports offices in other North American cities was yours. It is a positively brilliant idea."

Henry York was almost finished telling Lester and Emily about the accounting apprenticeship program they have for young men and women when Holcomb entered carrying a sheaf of papers after a soft knock on the door. "Burdette's gone, but he signed every one of the agreements."

"What about the money?"

"He left this note."

Holcomb,

I expect Emily to bring the drafts at 7 in the evening three days hence where this all began.

Francis Burdette
Partner
Helmsley & Cole

Emily stared at the words, racking her brain as to where Francis was referring. She ran through the four possibilities – they were formally introduced at a Christmas Reception held by the Navy in Portsmouth. That was unlikely because she would need access to the naval base. Francis courted her at her parent's house and eliminated this location since it would be a hostile place.

Their house was out since her father didn't buy it for them until after Jeremiah was born. So, neither it nor his office made sense.

Something flashed through her mind. Francis proposed on a rampart of Southsea Castle near a stand where the garrison sold cakes and ale.

The old castle was initially built in 1544 by Henry VIII. In 1759, the fort was damaged by an explosion in the powder magazine that killed 17. The fort was never repaired and was now manned by a small garrison that allowed visitors.

Emily spoke precisely. "He wants to meet me on battlement at Southsea Castle where he proposed." Scenarios ran through her mind. "Seven is just before sunset when the guards lock the gates. So, if he decides to create some mischief, it won't be discovered until the next day."

Lester Smythe tapped the table. "You are not going there alone. Your brothers and I will accompany you to ensure my grandchildren do not become orphans."

"Father, I have thought of that. Francis can be vindictive at times, but he is not stupid. Murdering me will have him dangling in the Gosport's sheriff's picture frame in short order, so I know not what he plans. I will bring the drafts, give them to Francis, and be done with him. If I see him ever again, it will, I can assure you, be by accident."

SOUTHSEA CASTLE, PORTSMOUTH, THREE DAYS LATER

In July, the weather in Portsmouth ranged from blue skies and puffy clouds to overcast and rainy. The conditions could change very quickly. Through the window in the carriage taking Emily to Southsea Castle, she could see the dark clouds rolling in from the west. She hoped the rain would hold off long enough to give Francis the two drafts in her purse.

Once the exchange was completed, Emily didn't care how wet she became. A good soaking would help wash away her memories of her marriage to Francis. Across from her, Lester Smythe had a grim expression on his face, as did her oldest brother, Bradley, four years her senior.

Lester's pocket watch said it was 6:46 in the evening when they arrived at Southsea Castle's gate. The soldier waved them through with a warning that they had no more cakes or ale and would close the gates once the rain began.

LAST BATTLES

Emily strode confidently toward the battlement where the cannon pointed south. Emily spotted Francis's broad shoulders and stopped 20 feet from where her soon-to-be ex-husband stood looking out over Portsmouth harbor.

After taking deep breath, she forced herself to speak forcefully without emotion. "Francis?"

Slowly, the man turned around and smiled. "So, you figured it out."

"Aye."

"This is where it all started."

Emily didn't say anything since she wanted this last meeting with the man she'd come to dislike, even despise, to be over as quickly as possible.

"What are you going to tell the children?"

She wanted to say, "Do you care?" but rejected that. Emily did not want to provoke Francis. "That their father is gone. Later, when they are older, I will tell them the truth, which is the marriage did not work out, and we divorced."

Francis nodded slightly. His expression softened. "For what it is worth, I have been a bit of a cad. For that, I am sorry."

Emily thought cad was the wrong word. Francis, you are a bully and a mean-spirited, self-centered boor. She said nothing as she kept looking at him.

"Did you bring the draft and the papers?"

"I did."

"Give them to me."

Emily looked around. She would not let Francis get close enough to grab her. A painted cannon was off to her left. She put the oilskin pouch with the two documents on the touch hole. "I've withdrawn my half of the money in the Barings account and removed myself as an authorized signatory. The money left in the account is yours. The papers from the bank and your copy of the settlement are in the pouch with the draft for £1,500."

"Wait."

Francis Burdette walked over to the cannon and picked up the pouch. He took out the letter from the bank, nodded, looked at the draft and smiled. He slid them back into the pouch and walked toward Emily, who retreated several steps.

"Francis, do not come near me."

"Why not?" His mouth now had a lecherous grin as he continued toward his retreating ex-wife.

Emily held out her hand. "Francis, stop! I don't want you near me."

"After all those flings in bed that led to three children. Tell me you didn't enjoy it because I know you did. In the first few years, you wanted all the sex you could get."

Her eyes started to water from anger. She pulled a small pistol from a pouch in her dress and pulled the hammer back to full lock. "Francis, do NOT take another step toward me or trust me, I will shoot."

Another voice, "And I will do the same. You will not survive three lead balls in your body."

Francis turned to see Lester Smythe holding a brace of pistols aimed at him. The lawyer stopped and sneered, "Be off with you! I pity the man who falls for your good looks. You're a pintle merchant, nothing more."

Burdette put the pouch in his coat and strode arrogantly between Emily and her father. With Francis gone, Emily ran to her father, who wrapped his arms around his sobbing daughter. "Now father, you know what I have been living with all these years."

"Aye, I wish you had told me sooner. I am so sorry. Your mother and I are to blame. But now the bastard is gone from our lives."

With each step Emily took arm-in-arm with her father toward the entrance to Southsea Castle, she felt better and better. The old castle's gate was the entrance to a new life, one she was confident would bring her happiness.

CHAPTER 19

- PEACE IN THEIR TIME

NEW YORK, THIRD WEEK OF JULY 1782

The humidity and temperature in the low 90s made the air feel steamy as *Pompeii* eased through the narrow area between New Jersey and the western end of Long Island. Just standing in the sun on the quarterdeck, Darren felt droplets of sweat stream drip down the small of his back.

Pompeii crept along under partially reefed mainsails as the incoming tide carried the frigate toward the southern tip of Manhattan Island. The frigate's top and topgallants were already furled tight against their spars. The only other sail being flown was the jib.

Ahead of *Pompeii*, the ships of the North American Station were anchored on both sides of the harbor, and one, a large three-decker, flew an admiral's pennant from the top of its mizzenmast. The second-rater was streaming with the tide, and its bow was pointed toward the harbor's entrance.

In the middle of this naval splendor, a small sailboat sailing close hauled, headed toward *Pompeii*. Through his Dollond spyglass, Darren saw a man wearing a navy-blue coat without an epaulet indicating he was a lieutenant. A midshipman held the tiller, and two seamen were in the bow to handle the jib sheets and help with the mainsail. From the halyard, the boat flew the flag with white and red bars that British harbor pilots were beginning to use.

Deftly, the midshipman, tacked so that sailboat came alongside and luffed the sail to match *Pompeii's* speed. A seaman in the bow grabbed the railing alongside the steps bolted to *Pompeii's* hull. The Lieutenant clambered up *Pompeii's* side, and the sailboat fell off.

Once the officer was on the main deck, *Pompeii's* second lieutenant, Shamus O'Steen, led the Lieutenant to the companionway at the forward end of the quarterdeck. "Captain, permission to bring Lieutenant Gurnsey onto the quarterdeck. He's here to guide *Pompeii* to where we are to anchor."

"Permission granted."

Gurnsey pointed to an area west of Governor's Island. "Sir, there's a sand bank with about five fathoms of water. The sand will give a good purchase to your anchors. The admiral requires you to use both anchors and ensure you have enough room to swing."

Darren looked at the Lieutenant, trying not to be sarcastic. The added instruction about a second anchor and room to swing was a practice all Royal Navy captains should know. "Thank you, Mr. Gurnsey. I've been here before, and the tides here can be quite formidable. We'll set a watch to monitor bearings, so we'll know straightaway if *Pompeii* starts to drift."

"Sir, I'll let the port captain know. Are you carrying dispatches for the Admiral?"

"Aye, I am and was asked by General Leslie to personally deliver them to Admiral Graves and General Clinton."

"Sir, Admiral Graves has returned to England and replaced by Rear Admiral Digby on *H.M.S. Prince George*, 90 guns. Since I will be ashore first, I will send a messenger to General Clinton. When you are ready to leave, signal the flagship so they know you are coming."

"Splendid." Information passed. Darren ordered Quartermaster Spivey to fall off two points to starboard. Seeing that *Pompeii* was headed toward its anchorage, Gurnsey's task was completed. He left the quarterdeck and went down to the sailboat that had come alongside again.

The decks of *H.M.S. Prince George* loomed over Darren as the longboat coasted to a stop below the hatch on the lower gun deck. The gunports on its three gundecks were all run out to allow the breeze to flow through the ship.

Darren recognized the 12-pounders on the main deck, the 18-pounders on the middle gun deck, and the huge 32-pounders on the lower gun deck. As he studied Admiral Digby's flagship, Darren wondered what the flagship's tonnage might be and the size of its crew. His guessed 900 men lived on this 2,000-ton ship.

Even with the gun ports open and light flowing through the gratings, the lower gun deck was dark. The contrast from the bright sun and glare off the water to the partially lit lower gun deck stopped Darren in his tracks. He blinked several times as his eyes adjusted to the darkness.

"Captain, may I have the pleasure of your name and ship?"

Standing in front of Darren was a midshipman. "Darren Smythe, captain of His Majesty's Ship *Pompeii*, 38 guns."

"Thank you, captain. Please follow me to Admiral Digby's cabin."

The young man Darren was following took the steps of the companionway to the main gun deck two at a time. The midshipman's long strides covered the ground on the middle gun deck to the entrance of the admiral's cabin which was, on the three-decker, one deck below the captain's cabin on the main deck.

At the door, the Marine sentry came to attention and port arms as a salute. The midshipman knocked sharply on the door and received a "Please come in."

Darren wasn't surprised when the midshipman entered and said, "Admiral, Captain Darren Smythe of His Majesty's Ship *Pompeii*, 38 guns." What did surprise Darren was that the midshipman stayed in the great cabin.

Admiral Digby came forward, "Captain, where did you come from?"

"Charleston, sir." Darren glanced toward the midshipman, expecting him to be asked to leave.

Sensing his unease that a junior officer was about to hear a sensitive discussion, Digby smiled as he nodded toward the young man. "Captain, may I present His Royal Highness, Midshipman and Prince William Henry."

Momentarily surprised to be in the presence of the third son of King George III, Darren turned to square himself in front of the midshipman and bowed at the waist. "Your Highness, it is a pleasure to meet you."

Prince William Henry laughed softly. "Sir, I am on board to learn about the Royal Navy, and you, Captain Smythe, outrank me in matters of running a ship, experience, seamanship, and tactics. It is only by an accident of birth that I am in line to be the king of our country. Rear Admiral Digby does me the honor of allowing me to participate in important matters to help further my education."

Darren nodded his understanding and held out the pouch he was carrying. Digby began untying the eighth-inch thick cord that bound the two layers of oilskin that were weighted by a two-pound bar of cast iron.

"So Smythe, how are things in Charleston? Tell me the truth. Don't sugar coat it."

"Sir, I am not an Army officer, but my sense is that the Army has pulled in its horns, so to speak. The rebels have them bottled up but are not strong enough or more likely, don't want to risk destroying the town in an attack, and General Leslie is not strong enough to defeat them in the field. Supplies, at least when *Pompeii* left, were plentiful but would run short if the rebels decided to cut off food supplies to the town. I believe that General Leslie is preparing to be evacuated."

"Captain Smythe, your assessment is quite accurate. We're waiting for more transports. My orders are to evacuate the British Army and any of our supporters who may want to leave North America. Supposedly, in these letters are estimates of the number of Loyalists who want to leave."

Darren didn't say anything.

"Smythe, what are your orders once you deliver these letters and the ones to General Clinton."

"Return to Charleston, immediately, sir." And Melody.

"Then what?"

"Wait to escort convoys back to England."

"Under Hood or Rodney?"

"No sir, Rear Admiral Effingham on board *Stirling Cross*."

"That seems awfully boring. So, as commander of the North American Station, I will amend your orders slightly. We have two transports loading with Loyalists from New York who have agreed to go to Halifax. They leave in two days, and I want *Pompeii* to escort them. Then, you are to return to Charleston, and if no convoy is present, patrol southeast to watch for the French fleet. General Clinton does not think General Washington will try to take New York. That leaves Charleston as the next target, and General Clinton fears the French will assist in an attack on Charleston. That means the French Navy will make an appearance to land troops. You will have your new sailing orders tomorrow."

"Aye, aye, sir."

In a battle between the French and British armies, Melody could be killed, and Charleston could be destroyed. It was bad enough that he was in the line of fire but Melody being in danger was unacceptable. *This damned war must end!*

CHARLESTON, FOURTH WEEK OF JULY 1782

Rafer Muir liked being a major. Being a lieutenant colonel brought more responsibility and more opportunities. He's been responsible for logistics and operational planning on a general's staff. Each promotion took him farther from what he called the useful end of a musket and reduced the chance that he would be killed or wounded.

Now, he was assigned as General Leslie's chief of staff, Rafer Muir was sitting at the table listening to each regimental commander give the status of his unit - number of "effectives" – healthy soldiers, number on the sick list, ammunition on hand and readiness to deploy or march. At the end of each verbal description, General Leslie nodded, and the next commander reported. Rarely did he make a comment.

A major named Prior from the 65th Regiment of Foot stumbled through his answers. Out of the corner of his eye, Muir could see General Leslie controlling his anger, not wanting to lambaste the man in public for his inadequate preparation. To be fair, the 65th had been one of the regiments hardest hit by the 4th Carolina in two forays into the interior. The unit had been reinforced by men from Fort Motte to bring it back up to its full strength of 600 men.

From his inspections, Muir believed the 65th suffered from poor leadership. Its commander, the oldest son from a peerage, returned home to assume the responsibilities of his family when his father died.

When Prior was dismissed along with the other officers, Leslie turned to his chief of staff.

"Lieutenant Colonel Muir, I need you to assume command of the 65th and sort it out as soon as possible. Both Lord Islay and I believe that you should be a full colonel, so since it is in my power to promote deserving officers, as of this moment, you are a full colonel. My adjutant will prepare the necessary papers documenting your promotion and new command. Good luck. I'll miss you around here but turn the 65th around and do it quickly. We may need them before we leave this god-forsaken country."

Muir had no choice but to say aye, aye, sir. Retiring as a full colonel meant a larger pension, but turning around a regiment in short order would be no easy task. However, with a bit of luck, the British Army will be out of North America before the year is out. Which meant he will be out of the British Army shortly thereafter.

BREST, FOURTH WEEK OF JULY 1782

All day long, Jaco watched the thunderstorms build. By late afternoon, day had turned into dusk by dark gray clouds bellowing thunder. The darker it became, the more the lightning was visible. The gusty winds became stronger, and he worried that *Zephyr* might drag her anchors.

Jaco's shifted his study of the oncoming storms to wondering if the ship's boat would chance sailing across the bay with a load of provisions. As his eyes went back and forth between the approaching storm and the dock, Jaco debated if *Zephyr* should weigh anchor and weather the storms sailing in the bay or remain at anchor. The ship's boat which should have headed back by now, hadn't left the pier.

While he trusted Hedley Garrison and the four men who went ashore implicitly, this was, after all Brest. And, in France, anything was possible. Usually, a merchant increased his prices at the last minute – he always wanted more - or an attempt to pass off poor quality as being the best, or, or, or…. The list went on. Then there were the thieves who might target Garrison, suspecting he may have a purse of gold.

Now that he was commuting to Brest, Jaco had noticed subtle changes in the city. The two that concerned him the most were the rise in crime and the new, surly attitude of the merchants, and he wondered why. Samuel Gardner warned him two trips ago to arm all *Zephyr's* working parties. To Jaco, that meant two pistols per man plus a sword.

To give the men in the crew a break, one officer and eight members of the crew alternated going ashore to pick up food – fresh and smoked meats, milk, chocolate, wine, bread, vegetables, etc. - for the next 24 hours. With a hold full of casks of beer, rum, and meat, along with crates of oats, beans, and peas, *Zephyr* was kept ready for an immediate departure.

A strong gust of wind pushed Jaco back, forcing him to grab the railing to keep from falling as large raindrops of cold water pelted him. *Zephyr's* two anchor hawsers groaned as the hemp fibers stretched while the bollards to which they were looped around moaned in sympathy.

Jaco turned to Cato Cooper, a quartermaster but was filling in as the ship's bosun since Bosun Preston was ashore with Headley Garrison. "Mr. Cooper, go below and get everyone up, and I fear we may need all hands on deck shortly."

The tall, broad-shouldered former slave put the back of his hand to his head and disappeared down the companionway to the berthing deck as the wind whistled through the schooner's rigging. The waves were now three and four feet high, and salty spray mixed with the heavy rain.

The sound of a log snapping followed by planks splintering brought men out of the fore and aft companionways like ants attacking an intruder. Jaco raced forward to where the port anchor hawser had ripped out the bollard and lodged across the hawsepipe through which the three-inch thick rope passed.

Zephyr drunkenly slewed around, and the hawser to the starboard anchor tightened around the bollard. There was no chance of being able to loosen the hawser from the bollard and then re-loop it around the capstan. Even if they could, the men manning the capstan would have to pull the 150-ton schooner against the waves and wind.

The schooner had already lost one anchor that ripped a hole in the bulwark and planking from of the deck. To Jaco, it looked repairable, and none of the supports for the foremast appeared to be loose. With Haskins with the shore party, an accurate damage assessment would come later. In his mind, if the masts and hull were intact, they had a chance.

His other choice was to cut the existing cable, raise the sails and attempt to keep the schooner off the rocks. Waiting or sailing? Jaco hesitated, not liking either choice.

Just as suddenly as the winds picked up, they slackened as the heavy rain slickened the deck. "Man the capstan."

The bars were taken from a nearby rack and shoved into place. Colin Landry yelled, "Lads, there's no shanty for this, just put your backs into it. On my count, push!!!"

Instead of two men per bar, there were now four with shoulders rubbing shoulders. "Lads, one…. Two… Three, push!!!"

"Again, one…. Two… Three, push!!!"

Feet slipped on the wet deck. Two men fell, one smashing his nose. Blood streamed down his face as he picked himself up and retook his position.

"Lads, one… Two… Three, push!!!"

Slowly the capstan bars moved. Each push generated more movement.

Jaco yelled, "Mr. Geiger, once the anchor is free, get the jib up and send me three men to raise the mizzen mainsail. Mr. Cooper, you have the wheel."

The wind slackened noticeably, but not the rain. More men fell, creating bumps and bruises along with a gashed forehead.

"Anchor is aweigh."

Jaco could feel *Zephyr* start to drift with the current and the wind. The jib went up quickly. As he helped raise up the mizzen mainsail, Cato Cooper called out. "Captain, we have way. I have rudder control."

"Aye, Mr. Cooper."

Jaco looked around. The schooner was headed toward the west end of the bay where it shoaled, but for the next mile or so, they had deep water under the keel. He yelled out. "Mr. Geiger, as soon as you get the anchor stowed, raise the mainmast's and foremast's mainsails halfway."

His next moves were going to be critical. Hollow thumping against the hull told him the starboard anchor was being secured.

"Anchor secure. Foremast main sail going up."

With the wind coming over the stern quarter, *Zephyr* leapt ahead as if it was excited to be free of the device that tethered it to the harbor bottom. "Mr. Geiger, Mr. Cooper, stand by to wear ship to starboard. Once we come around, lower all the daggerboards.

Jaco estimated they had about a mile to the southern shore of the bay and plenty of room to turn 180^0 back to the west and the harbor mouth. His gut said turn now!

Once his first lieutenant had the men in position on all three masts, Jaco ordered. "Mr. Geiger, Mr. Cooper, wear ship to starboard. Mr. Cooper, get us around quickly. New course due west."

"Aye, captain. Helm a lee." Cooper turned the wheel, and *Zephyr's* bow came around like an obedient racehorse.

Once the bow was through the wind, the jib was sheeted home. Lieutenant Geiger watched carefully as the booms for the masts swung across the centerline of the ship. Once in position, he ordered them boom secured and the daggerboards lowered.

With the added push, *Zephyr* accelerated. Jaco felt that the schooner wanted to escape the confines of the harbor and the thunderstorms pelting its decks with rain. Now, with the narrow harbor entrance several miles ahead, Jaco left the quarterdeck to inspect the damage to his ship from the berthing deck. The danger now was from rainwater and spray entering the ship and ending up in the bilges.

Without prompting, Lieutenant Geiger disappeared down the companionway into the hold to see how much water had accumulated and if any of their provisions were in danger of spoiling.

Jaco pushed and pulled on the ribs and cross members on the berthing deck. Above, on the main deck, there was a three-foot gap in the deck where the anchor ripped the bollard from the planking and the cross-members.

As he looked for signs that the ship's frame was seriously damaged, Jaco brain flashed back to the damage a rock did to *Scorpion*. What felt like a glancing blow, broke the back of the ship. Within hours, it was clear that the frigate was in danger of breaking up. Right now, the good news was only rainwater was coming into *Zephyr* through the hole in the main deck.

The wind abated as the gust front passed, leaving the schooner sailing in a steady rain. Approaching *Pointe des Espagnois* near the entrance of *Rade de Brest*, Jaco ordered the crew to tack *Zephyr* back to the west. This time, he wanted to sail the schooner close enough to see the docks where, once the storm passed, *Zephyr* could tie up to make repairs. The extra fees be damned.

The storm started at four bells into the Forenoon Watch, and two bells had just rung of the First Dog Watch when *Zephyr* glided to a stop on the long side L-shaped wharf that jutted out into the bay. Located on the west side of the river that divided the city of Brest, the quay provided easy access to the walled town through the Porte du Brest. The afternoon summer sun, now peeking through puffy clouds, warmed the crew as they tied *Zephyr* to the pier.

The calm water by the pier let Jaco closely examine the damage now that the pumps had rid the bilges of the rainwater. His inspection convinced him that it had to be fixed before they could return to Philadelphia.

With the gangway down, Jaco stuffed two pistols in his belt along with his tomahawk. On the main deck, he handed two more pistols along with a cutlass to Colin Landry before turning to his first lieutenant.

"Mr. Geiger, I will find Mr. Gardner to get the money to buy the material to fix *Zephyr*. If Mr. Garrison and the rest of the shore party arrive, get Mr. Gaskins going on cutting away what he must to effect repairs."

Samuel Gardner was a member of a Boston merchant family who was born and raised in Boston. Originally, his parents sent him to Brest as their agent. When the war broke out, Gardner set-up the courier service the Continental Congress used to send correspondence between Brest and Paris.

Happy to see Jaco, the Bostonian slid several English newspapers across the table. Jaco's eyes widened as he read one and then the other.

The headline of the British paper screamed "Lord Rockingham Dead." The paper was dated July 2nd. Another paper printed on July 4th shouted, "Lord Shelburne New Prime Minister." A third said on the second page, "Peace Talks with Colonials and French."

Jaco read the latter story and then asked. "So, do you have dispatches for me to take to Philadelphia?"

"I do, but I am expecting another courier in three days, can you wait?"

Jaco, whose clothes were still soaking wet, said, "I have no choice. The storm damaged my ship. I think it is repairable but may take a few days."

"Do you need a shipwright? I know several who are reliable, good, and reasonable."

"Not yet. My carpenter is looking at the damage now."

"What happened?"

Jaco gave him a precis of what the storm did to *Zephyr*. After listening to his description, Gardner said, "I have twelve and twenty-four gold livres which should speak quite loudly."

"Thank you, but I am more worried about getting suitable planks. I fear shipbuilders making ships for the French Navy have gobbled up all the good wood."

"Au contraire, Captain Jacinto. This is France. The best wood is kept for the merchant ships and the houses of the nobility. The wood you and I would never approve for a ship goes into French ships-of-the-line and frigates. Again, find out what you need, then I will take you to a sawmill where I am sure your carpenter will find the necessary wood that can be cut to his specifications."

When Jaco returned, he found Gaskins waiting for him. He didn't have to ask. "Sssssir, the hull is sssstill ssssound but the ssssome of the ribsssss were loosened above the waterline. I can fix everything, but do you want another bollard?"

"Yes, why are you asking?"

"Because, I will have to add ssssome cross-members to ssssstiffen the ssssupports. I can sssssplice the cross-memberssss."

"How much time do you need?"

"A week, maybe more."

"How about three days?"

Gaskins whistled. "I'll do my best, but I won't compromise on the work. When are we getting the wood and where?"

"Funny you should ask. I will be taking you and a working party to a sawmill. There you will get what you need. We leave as soon as possible."

Gaskins put the back of his hand to his forehead, "Aye, ssssir. I'm ready now."

Brest is divided in two by a river known as the Port Militaire. It has a narrow entrance called the le Fer a Cheval, that loosely translates to 'iron shoe' in English. Once past the two large forts on either side of the river, Port Militaire provided a secure anchorage.

Ferries provided transport between the two halves of Brest which was surrounded by large walls designed to keep out invaders. Farther out from the city, the French had built a ring of large forts to keep attackers from bombarding the fort from the land.

Immediately to the west of the pier where *Zephyr* was tied-up, there was a large French fort guarding the east side of the entrance to le Fer a Cheval. On the west side of the channel, an even bigger fort known as the Batterie Royale guarded the entrance.

The road into the Porte du Brest that crossed the moat was built by convicts in the 1640s. The convicts piled the dirt inside the moat to form a parapet from which musketeers and archers could fire on anyone trying to cross the 12-foot deep and 50-foot-wide moat.

The moat went from the bay around to the north side of the city, where it emptied into the Port Militaire was now as much a canal for traffic as it was a defensive barrier. The moat on the east side was matched by a similar man-made waterway on the city's west side.

Tying up at the wharf made walking to Samuel Gardner's office on the east side of the Port Militaire easier. The agent had three wagons ferried across the river to the west side. Gardner led them past the large St. Sauven's church and monastery and through the *Porte de la Recouvrance* (door of recovery) to a small village called Cinretiere.

This was not the first foray by members of *Zephyr*'s crew into the French countryside. Gardner frequently took them to local wineries, farms, and cheese makers to avoid mark-ups from local merchants. Unlike Brest whose narrow streets reeked from centuries of sewage, animal feces, and garbage, the countryside smelled fresh and clean.

Past Cinretiere, at the western edge of Guilers, the convoy stopped outside a sawmill. Oak logs lay neatly stacked in the walled courtyard. Inside a shed, the owner had planks of different lengths on racks. Jaco listened quietly as Hugo Lagadec, the owner, explained to Gardner that the wood was for an order from a shipbuilder in Brest.

When Lagadec finished speaking, Gardner placed a gold Louis d'Or 24-livre coin on the workbench between the two men. Lagadec eyes focused on the coin, and then Gardner, who said. "We need some of that wood."

"How much?"

Gardner pointed to Gaskins. "He knows. We'll load the wagons and then pay you for what we take. You can keep the Louis D'Or as a token of my country's gratitude."

Given his discussion with Gardner on the way to Guilers, Jaco suspected the 24-livre coin was probably double the cost of the wood. Lagadec reached for the coin, but Gardner gently put his hand on the Frenchman's. "Not until we have our wood loaded on the wagons."

The Frenchman nodded, and Gardner turned to Leo Gaskins. "Mr. Gaskins, go pick your wood."

Jacinto was sure Gaskins selected one and a half times the amount of planking he needed, along with four short logs. The planking and logs filled two of the three wagons. The carpenter came over to where Gardner and his captain were standing. "Sir, I need more boltsssss and nailsssss. Issss there a blacksmith we can visit on the way back?"

"Aye, Mr. Gaskins, there is in the port on the way back. He sells them either individually or by the barrel."

Gardner returned to the Frenchman and handed him a demi-Louis d'or worth 12 livres. "This is for the wood."

As Jaco and Samuel walked back to their horses, Gardner spoke softly. "Like our Continental dollars, the French paper notes are not worth their face value. Gold talks. When we return to my office, I presume you will sign a letter documenting that we paid 36 livres for wood to repair *Zephyr*. A receipt would complicate matters for Monsieur Lagadec should the shipyard come out to his mill to enquire as to why their wood delivery was delayed or incomplete."

"Aye, that I will. Thank you."

With more iron bolts and nails than he needed, Gaskins and *Zephyr*'s crew set about repairing the schooner. The sawing and banging went from before dawn to just after dark. At night, the sawing of wood needed early in the next day was done on deck under the light of lanterns.

The men turned in around midnight after a double ration of rum, only to begin again at dawn. Gaskins fabricated a third rib to sit under the port and starboard bollards to provide more strength. The ribs were braced and re-bolted to the hull's planking, then re-caulked. New overhead beams were cut and put in place.

The two whittlers on the crew were given a short segment of a log, hammers, and chisels and asked to fabricate another bollard. The last item to be built was a second anchor. The flukes were bought from the Brest ironsmith and hauled by wagon to the pier. The new anchor did not match its mate on the starboard side, but no one cared.

On the afternoon of day four, the repairs were almost complete. Gaskins was directing the fitting of the last decking planks when Samuel Gardner appeared at the edge of the gangway. "Captain Jacinto, how soon can you leave?"

"As fast as we can raise the gangway and the sails. We just finished loading some extra stores. We can paint the new planks at sea."

"Excellent." He handed a pouch full of letters to Jaco. "Take these to Philadelphia as fast as you can."

Jaco put the tips of the fingers of his right hand to his forehead. "We will be underway before you get back to your office."

Jaco started giving orders as soon as Gardner left. "Prepare to get underway immediately. Raise the gangplank. I want to be sailing into the Atlantic by dark."

Work on fitting the planking stopped, and Gaskins came running aft. "Captain, ssssir, we have two more plankssss to get into posssssition, then we have to paint them and finish the anchorsssss."

"Can you assemble the anchors on the way home?"

"Aye, ssssir if the water issss not too rough."

"Good. You can also paint the deck while we are at sea, Mr. Gaskins. We're leaving as soon as we can cast off."

By the time the wind pushed *Zephyr* away from the wharf, Jaco had a thick stack of English newspapers to share with his father and other members of the Continental Congress. The newest was printed a week before the schooner left Brest. The oldest, three months. By the time *Zephyr* arrived in Philadelphia, they would all be almost three weeks older.

LONDON, SECOND WEEK OF AUGUST 1782

One of the pleasures of Rear Admiral of the White Stacey Davidson's days at the Admiralty was reading the copy of the *London Gazette* delivered to his office daily. He worked for the Second Naval Lord and was responsible for recruiting sailors and Royal Marines and manning ships.

The Royal Navy's hierarchy has three levels of admiral - Rear, Vice, and Admiral, each with its own sub-ranks. At the rear and vice admiral level, the most junior admiral's flag was red, next higher was white, and the most senior rear admiral rank flew a blue flag. For full admirals, the red and blue colors denoting rank were reversed, so Admiral of the Blue was junior to an Admiral of the White who was junior to the Admiral of the Red.

When he was promoted from Rear Admiral of the Red to Rear Admiral of the White, Davidson was given one of the most powerful positions in the Royal Navy. He was now responsible for all officer assignments. What man went to which ship was decided by his small team - four captains, two commanders, and six lieutenants. Once Davidson signed off on the assignment, he sent it to the Second Naval Lord for final approval before the orders were issued.

Ship commanding officer billets were the most contentious because admirals commanding squadrons at sea made their input. Some of Davidson's decisions were unpopular because he valued performance and combat experience over seniority and titles.

The *London Gazette* was the official newspaper of His Majesty's government. First printed in 1665, the paper had governmental announcements, court rulings, laws passed by Parliament, and transcriptions of the debate on the floor from the previous day along with items of interest. To Davidson, the *London Gazette* gave him the pulse of the government, which helped him plan future assignments.

The gazette had another function unique to His Majesty's Navy. When an officer was assigned to a ship as its commanding officer, his new command was posted in the *London Gazette*, hence the term post-captain. The postings enabled the country and those in the Royal Navy to know who was being promoted and given command of important national assets - the ships in the Royal Navy.

His work interfered with his desire to watch the debate in Parliament on the peace negotiations with the new United States of America. He scanned the section on the status of the negotiations with the Spanish, Dutch, and

France. He noted France's willingness to relinquish the Caribbean islands it took from the British in exchange for colonies in Africa.

When Davidson joined the Royal Navy in 1758 as a 13-year-old midshipman, England was in the middle of the Anglo-French Carnatic Wars being fought in India between 1744 and 1763. Davidson could not visualize a world without a war with France either about to start, being fought, or being close to a treaty to end the hostilities, albeit temporarily.

He read Lord Shelburne's words that informed the Parliament for the first time that his position was to grant the Americans full independence without any requirement to remain part of the British Empire. Davidson read it a second time to make sure he saw what was on the page.

Up until this point, most in Parliament and the halls of the Admiralty assumed independence would be granted to a country that would remain under the watchful eye of England. Shelburne chose his words carefully, saying the new United States would be a free, fully independent country with no legal or military ties to Britain.

Peace with an independent United States would have a huge impact on the Royal Navy, which was still fighting the French and Spanish in North American, Caribbean, European, and Mediterranean waters and off the coast of India. An end to the war in North America would enable the Royal Navy to concentrate on the French. Or, if England and France signed a peace treaty, Parliament would immediately cut the Royal Navy's budget.

New ship construction would stop, and those ships in the best condition after being surveyed would continue to be active. The rest would be broken up or put in ordinary, i.e., storage.

Davidson's head hurt thinking about how many captains and officers would be put on half-pay. Unless another war broke out soon, many would never return to the Royal Navy, and their valuable experience would be lost forever.

If there was a reduction in the size of the Royal Navy, his staff would recommend to the Second Naval Lord who should stay and who should be put on half pay. Many officers, particularly those who made a small fortune through prize money, would say thank you and retire. But then there would be those who want to stay and will pull whatever political strings they can to guarantee them a place.

In Rear Admiral of the White Stacey Davidson's mind, the Royal Navy should retain the best captains based on their performance, not their political connections. Younger men should be kept over those in their 50s. And so on.

Davidson folded the newspaper, pulled a sheet of paper with the Second Lord of the Admiralty logo at the top from a desk drawer, and began to outline how he would recommend the navy decide which officers should be retained and which should go on half pay. Once he had an outline, he would wait a day, dictate a policy recommendation, and bring it to the Second Naval Lord.

CHARLESTON, SECOND WEEK OF SEPTEMBER 1782

Every year, rain or shine, Adah and Max Laredo had a celebratory dinner for what Adah Laredo referred to as the Bildesheim clan. Those living in the country came in for at least 10 days. Ever since the British occupied the town, rather than stay at their inns, the families from the farms up north stayed at the homes of Rivkah and Yael. This year, the only two missing members were Eric Laredo, who was in Amsterdam, and Amos Laredo, who was with the 4th Carolina, outside town, watching the British Army.

Rosh Hashanah, the Jewish New Year, was the reason for the celebration. Ten days later, after Yom Kippur, the clan would go home. But, for the moment, Miriam's extended family, or at least most of it, was in Charleston, which meant the nest was full. Life, she believed, had treated her well.

Unfortunately, the cloud over the holiday was the continued British occupation of the town, now in its 29th month. Some Loyalists living in Charleston were preparing to evacuate. Others were trying to figure out how to survive if they stay after the rebels won.

It was an open secret that the British Army was planning to leave. The unanswered questions were when and would the British take all the Loyalists who wanted to leave with them?

The uncertainty affected prices for those Loyalists wanting to sell their property. The British promise was that the Loyalists would be transported to a British colony where they would be offered jobs.

After dinner, there was a knock at the door. Adah Laredo, who was in the parlor, opened the door and found a British officer saying it was important to speak to her mother, Miriam Bildesheim.

The septuagenarian was speaking to her granddaughter when Adah approached her.

"Excuse me, *mein engel*." Suddenly serious and hiding her annoyance that the British wanted to speak with her on a holiday, "Let us go find out vat zee damned British vant."

On the porch, a major stood waiting patiently attired in the red coat of the British Army and a red, white, and black kilt of the Stewart tartan. Seeing the tall 76-year-old Miriam open the door, the man bowed in respect. "My apologies, Mrs. Bildesheim, I'm Major Fairbairn, General Leslie's adjutant. The general would like to meet with you this evening if possible. If not, at your convenience."

"And vat is the subject of zee meeting?"

Major Fairbairn didn't hesitate. "Food."

"Ist zee British Army running out?"

"Mrs. Bildesheim, I think it best you speak directly with General Leslie. May I tell him when you can visit his headquarters?"

Miriam took a deep breath and looked at her daughter. "Tomorrow morning. 10 o'clock."

The major bowed his head slightly. "I shall so inform the general. Again, my apologies for interrupting your holiday celebration."

Mission accomplished; Fairbairn walked down the steps. As Miriam re-entered the house, she asked Adah to ask her daughters Chaya and Leah along with their husbands, to join her in the parlor along with Reyna. She also asked if someone would ask Shoshana to come for a few minutes, saying, "Tell Shoshana it ist about business mit zee British."

The next morning, a British soldier held open the carriage door. Emory Fonseca was the first to step out and hold out his hand for Miriam and then Shoshana. Shoshana marveled at Miriam's ability to stride up the stairs as if she was in her 30s to where Major Fairbairn stood waiting. He bowed and said, "Mrs. Bildesheim, thank you for coming."

The major's eyes took in the tall and lovely Shoshana. "Miss, I apologize, but I do not believe we have met because I would not forget someone as beautiful as you."

"Thank you, major. You are most gallant. I am Shoshana Jacinto." She decided not to say that she was Shayna Enterprises' attorney.

Fairbairn turned to the male. "And you sir, may I have your name."

"Emory Fonseca, I run one of Mrs. Bildesheim's larger farms." *I am married to one of her daughters. And, given the chance, I would kill every British soldier I could find for what they did to my son Michael.*

"Excellent!" Major Fairbairn pointed with the palm of his hands to the great room of the Royal Governor's mansion where General Leslie, like General Rawdon and Lord Cornwallis before him, held court.

A soldier opened the door to let Major Fairbairn step inside the room and announce the guests. Miriam saw only three British officers in the room, Major Fairbairn, General Leslie, and another senior officer standing off to the side she recognized as Lord Islay.

Leslie came around the table to stand before the three South Carolinians. "Mrs. Bildesheim, Miss Jacinto, and Mr. Fonseca, thank you for coming. As I am sure you know, the British Army has decided to stay in garrison here in Charleston. I am also sure you are aware that the British government intends to evacuate any Loyalist who decides to leave South Carolina as we did at Savannah."

He started to say, which should make you happy, but the words would not come out of his mouth. Leslie needed their help.

"We have seen a large influx of Loyalist families coming to Charleston. The British garrison is duty-bound to protect, feed and house these Loyalists until they can be evacuated. We do not know how many more will accept our invitation, and again, as I am sure you are aware, we are housing them wherever we can. Our agreement with General Greene is that if we stay in Charleston, we can avoid any more bloodshed. Our biggest problem is food. We're running out of rations for my troops and the Loyalists."

Leslie stopped let his audience digest what he said. He was sure they knew what he was about to ask.

Miriam didn't wait for the question. "Zo, Herr General, you vant Shayna to deliver more food to Charleston." It was spoken as a statement, not a question.

Leslie's head bobbed up and down. "Exactly."

"Venn ist zee British Army und zee Loyalists leaving?"

Leslie took a deep breath. "Mrs. Bildesheim, I wish I could give you a specific date. My orders say by the end of the year."

"How much extra food do you require?"

"Again, I wish I could give you an accurate answer. Right now, we have two thousand Loyalists under our care. I expect the number to triple. My staff has prepared a list of what we need based on an estimate of Loyalists we are caring for. Major…"

Fairbairn picked up a sheet from the desk and handed it to Miriam, who held it so that Emory could read it as well. It allowed Fairbairn to look over the tall woman standing quietly off to one side. It was clear, even though Ms. Jacinto had not said a word, her eyes were taking in everything going on in the room. He flushed the passing thought about asking if he could court her because he knew the answer before the words would come out of his mouth.

"Herr general, I vish I could help you, but vee cannot deliver all zat you require. Zee Loyalists have left zer farms zo zay have no crops. If zer vas something to harvest, vee could. I can speak mit other farmers to zee vat zay can zell, but I vould be surprised if vee could produce all of vat you need."

"We will pay handsomely if you can meet our demands."

"Herr general, zis is not about money, it is about crop yields. Vat vee haff ist not enough, even if vee killed all our chickens, goats, sheep, und cows. Vat I am zaying is zat all zee extra food you need doesn't exist. And, if you send hunters into zee forests to kill our deer and turkeys, you still von't find enough. I vill repeat myself. Vee can deliver some of vat you want, but not all. Zo, I suggest you haff Major Fairbairn deliver zis list to my store. Zen, I vill tell you vat vee can provide und at vat price."

Leslie's expression hardened. "Then, as we run short, we will have to sally out of Charleston and take what we need."

"Or Herr general, you could have supplies brought in by zee Royal Navy."

"I have asked for that, but so far, what we have received is a fraction of our needs."

"Zen, herr general, leave zooner zan zee end of zee year." Miriam smiled as she looked at General Leslie. "Zat vill make everyvun happy. Zee British boys go home to their mothers. Fewer of our brothers, sons, und fathers vill die. And, best of all, vee vill be free."

General Leslie's eyes flashed, and his face reddened as he controlled his anger. He asked the question, and the woman who could help said no. The date of departure was not something he could control or even influence. He didn't think she was lying or reluctant to help. Leslie believed that she, as one with rebel sympathies, would extract her pound of flesh, so to speak, from his country. The British Army was trapped in Charleston, and as its commander, he had no choice but to deal with this proud woman he and his predecessors' thought was an arrogant Prussian.

When supplies ran low, Leslie would send out foraging parties in violation of the truce. The rebels would attack them, and the bloodshed will resume. It couldn't be helped.

"Mrs. Bildesheim, Ms. Jacinto, Mr. Fonseca, thank you for coming. Our business today is finished, and I thought you could help us."

Miriam couldn't resist. She took two steps forward to look directly into General Leslie's eyes. "Herr general, in zis room two years ago I told Herr General Cornwallis that zee British vill lose zis var because zey made var on vomen und children. Take my advice, going into the countryside vill not verk because you cannot take vat ist not zere. Vat vill happen is zat zere vill be more British boys buried in zee British cemetery in Dorchester zat has over four hundred graves. It ist on land zat I donated und I do not vant to give more. If you wish, I can arrange a visit before you leave for England."

Leslie's eyes widened. He was not used to being challenged by anyone, much less a woman and a rebel. His jaw tightened as he glared at the woman almost a head taller but said nothing.

The three South Carolinians left. Within an hour, a family member was riding to Dorchester to let Amos Laredo and the Continental Army soldiers know the British Army's intent. Within 24 hours, chickens were caged and moved with livestock from farms within 10 miles of Charleston to farms where they could be kept safe. The distance would force the British Army to extend itself into the South Carolina countryside, where the 4th Carolina could cut the foraging parties to pieces.

CHAPTER 20

– PLANNING FOR THE END

CHARLESTON, THIRD WEEK OF SEPTEMBER 1782

The sugary, cinnamon smell from freshly baked rolls and milk heated with cinnamon and chocolate greeted each person who entered the parlor. Next to the plates next to each chair, there was a small dish with freshly made peach preserves and cups for the hot chocolate.

With everyone - Miriam Bildesheim, Greg Struthers, Shoshana Jacinto, Reyna's father - Max Laredo - and Javier's oldest son, Isaac, seated at the table made from polished willow oak, Gento Jacinto unfolded a letter he'd recently received from his older brother, Javier.

Greg Struthers had been invited because he ran the Bank of Carolina that held loans from Loyalists whose property was used as collateral. The Jacintos, Laredos, and Miriam Bildesheim owned the bank. "What about legal debts such as mortgages?"

"Ahhhhh, Greg, it is good that you ask. In my brother's last letter, he said the treaty will require citizens, governments, and companies to honor all legal debts. Owners of abandoned properties must be compensated fairly. So, my fear, as I am sure is the same as yours, is how does the bank collect on a loan when the person is in some far away British territory? Enforcing the treaty terms via a court on a Caribbean island will be expensive and time-consuming."

Gento, whose black hair was streaked with gray, smiled as he looked at the others at the table. All had many investments in which they were all shareholders. "So, we now get to the reason we are here today. While Greg cannot divulge the terms of each loan, those of us on the bank's board must be informed as to which loans are at risk. The board will require the bank to enquire if the Loyalist wants to sell his property at a price greater than the loan balance. How much greater will be determined by the buyer and seller."

He slid Javier's letter to Miriam Bildesheim, who was to his left. "Gut. Ven can vee make offers?"

Shoshana leaned forward so that others around the table could see her face. "Now. Assuming my father is right about the treaty terms, if we make formal offers that are fair, we should not have any problems with our Loyalist neighbors and their solicitors. And, if there is a loan and the bank has filed a lien, when the property is sold the bank is paid first after any taxes due are paid. The important word, however, is fair. Before anyone in this room makes an offer, either the bank or my office can check the tax rolls."

"Shoshana, vould you define fair?"

The attorney finished chewing on a bite of one of the cinnamon rolls and licked the sugar off her fingers. She giggled like a little girl as she enjoyed the treat and then smiled guiltily. "Start at ten percent over the loan value and taxes. You can always go up."

Miriam put down her cup gently on the porcelain saucer whose reflection could be seen in the polished wood that had a reddish hue. "Gut. For zee property of zee Loyalists who are leaving, vee buy zere property und zey are gone. But zere vill be many Loyalists who vill stay. Vee must treat zem fairly if zay swear allegiance to our new country. Und, I vant everyvun to agree zat if vee buy property and it koms mit slaves, vee free zee slaves. No von should own another man or voman!"

When she finished, she was looking at Max Laredo who was married to Miriam's daughter Adah. While the Laredo's didn't "own" slaves, they had "servants" to whom they paid living wages. This arrangement was something Miriam tolerated but did not approve.

VICINITY OF 40°N, 27°W, FOURTH WEEK OF SEPTEMBER 1782

Just after four bells rang on the First Watch, Jaco emerged from his cabin to, as he did every night, speak with the watch officer. On the main deck, he paused for a few seconds to study the cloudless sky lit only by the twinkling of the stars. It was the new moon when the earth and sun were on opposite sides of the moon, making the planet nearly invisible.

He leaned over the railing and listened. The hissing as *Zephyr* cut through the two-foot seas was occasionally drowned out by the slapping of waves on her hull. It was, Jaco thought, a wonderful night at sea.

Zephyr was sailing under reduced sails, i.e., rather than not fly the top gaff sails, the booms for all three masts were let out to reduce the pressure and stress on the rigging. Still, as Morton Geiger noted as Jaco came onto the quarterdeck, "We're making an easy ten knots, captain."

Jaco nodded and looked at the bubble on the inclinometer. *Zephyr* was heeled over only five degrees as it ran on a beam reach with the wind coming over the port side.

"Mr. Geiger, in your turnover to the Morning Watch, have them pull the sails in at first light to increase our speed, assuming the winds are about the same."

"Aye, Captain."

Before first light, Brandon Grantham, who was the lookout on duty, came down the ratlines from his perch, where the gaff for the mainmast's top sail joined the mast and ran to the quarterdeck. He'd just come on watch, and the Morning Watch's first bell had not yet rung. "Mr. Garrison, suggest we get the captain up. There are sails all around us. Me thinks, sir, we have overtaken a British convoy during the night."

Garrison looked around him, and behind *Zephyr* to the east, the first hint of sunrise was beginning to light the sky. "Good work, Grantham. Knock on the captain's door and tell him what you told me. Then, wake Mr. Preston and get the rest of the crew up. No yelling or shouting. Mr. Cooper, do not ring the ship's bell."

The faint sound of three different bells wafted over the water as Jaco came on deck, still lacing up his breeches. Grantham, who had resumed his position as the lookout, came down again.

"Captain, I can make out a two-decker three points to our starboard bow and a three-decker, a point off our port bow. There's a smaller ship directly ahead and what looks like a frigate a point on our starboard quarter."

"Mr. Preston, hoist the flying jib and haul in all the booms until we are heeled twelve degrees to port."

The sound of drums could be heard clearly on *Zephyr* telling everyone who could hear them that at least one of the Royal Navy ships had spotted the schooner and was clearing for action. In the growing light, they could see flags being run up the halyards of the Royal Navy ships. A red rocket arced up from the frigate to their starboard side, alerting the other Royal Navy ships that an intruder was in their midst.

From the quarterdeck, Jaco didn't need a spyglass to see sails dropping from the topgallant yards of the two- and three-deckers. The frigate was letting loose its royals as well. As dawn broke, Jaco could see the sails of the other ships of the convoy. They had stumbled into the rear guard and were lucky they weren't closer.

All the Royal Navy ships were within three miles of *Zephyr*, and inside of a mile, they would be well within the lethal range of the large guns on the two- and three-deckers. Jaco assumed they were carrying a mix of 18-, 24- and maybe even 32-pounders while the frigate probably had 12- and maybe 18-pounders.

While he studied the ships around *Zephyr*, trying to plot a way out, the small ship ahead of the schooner began to tack to port. Its profile suggested that it was a sloop-of-war, probably armed with 6-pounders.

The three-decker began to slowly turn to starboard. Jaco was certain that its captain was ensuring that his ship would be upwind of *Zephyr* and retain the weather gauge. The frigate hadn't changed course, only added sail, suggesting its captain wanted to block any attempt by *Zephyr* to sail away toward the nor' east. This meant that the frigate captain had the option of turning to port and running downwind or turning to starboard and letting loose a broadside at *Zephyr* if it tried to run past.

Cannons now poked out from the sides of all four Royal Navy ships. In Jaco's mind, any cannonball that hit *Zephyr* could be fatal to either his ship or the crew. Slowly, a plan began to form in Jaco's mind. Choice one would be to fall off and run with the wind, but in his mind, that would enable the frigate to starboard to fall off the wind and cut *Zephyr* off.

"Mr. Preston, get the lads on all the sheets. We're about to show our Royal Navy friends the Continental Navy's tactical and sailing skills."

Beneath his feet, he could feel the three-masted schooner. It felt alive and eager to go faster. Jaco looked at where the booms were sheeted home. "Mr. Preston, pull the booms in at least another foot."

The bosun looked at his captain for a few seconds. The hesitation made Jaco say, "Mr. Preston, just do it. *Zephyr* is going to fly."

LAST BATTLES

With the sails set and the booms sheeted home, the schooner's crew stood on the starboard rail, looking at the other Royal Navy ships whose sides were dotted with the black snouts of cannon run out and ready to fire.

Ahead, on the port side, there was now enough light to read the name of the two-decker – *H.M.S. Edgar*. The third-rated ship of the line had turned about 45^0 from its original heading of due west when its captain gave the order to fire. Smoke billowed along the side as its starboard battery – thirteen 32-pounders and fourteen 24-pounders – let fly.

Either their aim was off, or the gunners misjudged *Zephyr's* speed. Most of the balls fell way short and behind the schooner. However, at least three skipped several times before sinking to the bottom, 200 yards or more from the schooner.

The broadside caught Jaco a bit by surprise. He thought the British captain would wait until he got closer.

"Mr. Preston, get ready to wear ship to port on my command. New course, so' by so' west. Mr. Jeffords, we want to pass no less than 800 yards behind *H.M.S. Edgar*."

The clock in Jaco's brain counted down as he studied the side of the two-decker. When he saw the second gun on the upper gun deck pulled back into battery, he yelled out, "Wear ship now!!! Do it smartly lads. We don't want to have to patch a hole made by a lucky hit by a 32-pounder. New course, so by so' west!"

Zephyr's bow came around and was about 30^0 into the turn when the cannons on *H.M.S. Edgar* began to fire. *Zephyr* was closer to the two-decker this time, and the aim and judgment of distance of its gunners were better. Several balls screeched overhead, but most landed where the schooner would have been had Jaco waited.

"Deck, frigate behind us is wearing around. It is three miles astern, aft on the port quarter."

"Captain, aye." *He'll never catch us unless a lucky hit takes down a mast.*

Zephyr was now approaching the rear quarter of *H.M.S. Edgar,* which Jaco thought would limit it to firing only its 12-pounder stern chasers at the fast-moving schooner.

"Deck, new frigate, four miles, broad on the starboard beam."

Damn, I was focused on the two-decker.

Once *Zephyr* was past *H.M.S. Edgar* and Jaco could see the Royal Navy frigate on a course to intercept. If *Zephyr* turned to the west or back to the north, the frigate could cut him off and fire a full broadside at a close range.

And, if this new frigate didn't disable *Zephyr*, they would again be in range of *H.M.S. Edgar's* 18- and 32-pounders. If he turned more to the south, the frigate might be able to close and fire a broadside at long range.

Turning back to the west would enable the first frigate, now in pursuit, to box *Zephyr* in. Jaco was debating options when he saw the flash of one of *H.M.S. Edgar's* stern chasers. Before he heard the boom, there was a loud crash just forward of the main mast.

There was now a gap in both bulwarks. The hole on the port side was wider than the one on the starboard side. "Get Mr. Gaskins to check the damage." *Zephyr* didn't seem affected by the hit, and Jaco turned his attention back to the on-rushing Royal Navy frigate.

He sensed that the eyes of those on the quarterdeck and the main deck were on him. It was obvious to everyone on the crew that the two Royal Navy frigates were trying to put *Zephyr* in a vise.

"Mr. Preston. Break out the staysails and the booms. We're going to run with the wind and with luck, show our Royal Navy friends a clean pair of heels."

Jaco waited until the sails were on deck. "Stand by to wear ship. New course east by so' east. Signal when you are ready, Mr. Preston, time's a-wasting!"

Seeing the staysails were hooked to their halyards, Jaco ordered, "Mr. Jeffords, Mr. Preston, wear ship to port. New course, east by so' east. Mainsail, staysails, and jib on the port side, mizzen mainsail, foremast mainsail and flying jibs to starboard."

Seeing the carpenter standing by the railing, Jaco nodded toward him and held up his hand. Once the sails were in position, he leaned over the quarterdeck railing.

Gaskins didn't wait to be asked. "Ball hit right above the deck on the sssstarboard sssside and carried away the top of the rib and sssome planking. *Zephyr* has sturdy sssskantlings. Once we clear thessse Royal Navy sssships, we can sssstart fixing her. I have enough wood to fix the deck and the ribsssss, but the bulwark above the deck will be a mix of wood and netting."

"Aye, Mr. Gaskins. Thank you."

Jaco turned to look at the frigate that had been closing in. Now, the bow of the frigate was angled more to starboard as its captain tried to get parallel. "Look out, ranges to the frigate to our starboard and astern."

"Nine hundred yards to the one starboard. More than a mile to the one behind us with the gap increasing."

Zephyr is still within range of his 12- or 18-pounders on his gun deck. The frigate captain has turned parallel to our course because he's figured out, he can't catch us. "Mr. Preston, we're going to wear ship about two points to port, now. Mr. Jeffords, new course east by south."

As soon as the bosun responded, Jaco ordered the change in course. Seconds after he did, *Zephyr* turned, and the frigate fired. Two balls whined overhead, popping through the mainmast's mainsail and the mizzenmasts topsail. Jaco thought they were out of danger when he felt and heard a loud crash beneath his feet.

A sailor stood in front of the quarterdeck after opening the door to the captain's cabin. "Sir, a cannonball went into your cabin. It is in shambles."

Jaco waved his hand to let the sailor know he'd been heard and turned his attention to the frigate. He looked up at the mainmast. "Lookout, distance to the frigate?"

"Mile and a half, sir. He's now bow onto us."

Jaco's answer was drowned out by the boom of the frigate's 9-pounder bow chasers. Neither ball came close to the schooner. "Lookouts, any other ships in front of us?"

"No, sir!"

"Mr. Preston, Mr. Jeffords, we will continue on this course until the British sails are below the horizon. Then, we shall have a meal and double rations of rum all around while we thank God that British gunnery is not very good and *Zephyr* is as fast as the wind."

Later that evening, Jaco cleaned up his cabin which now had a large hole on the starboard side. His bunk was destroyed, but now he could enjoy the refreshing breeze coming through the holes made by the 12-pounder ball. Before dark, Gaskins screwed four pad eyes into the overhead beams of his cabin so he could sling a hammock.

CHARLESTON, SECOND WEEK OF OCTOBER 1782

Immediately after the meeting at the Jacinto's house, Miriam made her first moves. First, she wanted to expand both the Dockside and the Charleston

Inns. Both had houses on either side owned by Loyalists whom she did not know if they were planning to leave.

She had a messenger deliver a proposal Shoshana wrote that suggested that if they were interested in selling, meet her in the Dockside Inn's Great Room at a specific time. Miriam allocated two hours for each meeting, with sessions scheduled at 9 a.m., 1 p.m., 3 p.m. and 5 p.m.

Two years before, she offered to buy the four homes. At the time, all four owners were confident the British would win and turned her down. Her letter said she would pay in pound notes at closing and would take possession when the owners left or on January 1st, 1783, whichever came first.

Yael brought a tray with freshly baked biscuits and peach jam to accompany pitchers of hot water for tea and her mother's favorite, hot chocolate. The first session went, as Yael thought, according to her mother's plan. The owner of a three-story 12-room house to the west of the Dockside, asked what Miriam planned to do with the land, barn, and the house that had been in their family since 1740.

She told them that she planned to connect the Dockside with the house to increase the number of rooms in the inn. Their barn would be joined to the Inn's and turned into a carriage house. The extra land would become a garden. Satisfied with the price, the owner asked when she could close. Miriam responded with tomorrow and asked for and received a guarantee that the owner would not damage the house before leaving.

After lunch, Gregory Driscoll stood over the table and tossed Miriam's written offer on the table. In a belligerent, aggressive voice, he glared at Miriam as he spoke. "This offer is an insult. Others have offered twice what is in your proposal."

Miriam said pleasantly. "Then, Herr Driscoll, vy did you kom? Zis ist zee middle of October. Gott only knows vat zee others vill offer in November or December." She pushed the paper towards Driscoll. "I think zis vill be zee best offer."

Driscoll was visibly angry and slammed his fist on the table hard enough for the saucers to jump. "This is highway robbery."

Miriam was smiling, almost enjoying Driscoll's anger. "Zen vy are you standing here?"

Driscoll didn't say anything. Miriam waited for what she thought was enough time. "Vell, do you vant to sell Herr Driscoll?"

"Are you willing to come up in price?"

"No."

"Does the price include the furniture?"

"Do you vish to take some vith you?"

"Yes, a few pieces."

"Zenn, please do. Zee price does not change."

"And you are paying in pounds?"

Miriam nodded emphatically. "Zats vat zee offer says. You get zee Kings money at closing."

"And I can stay in the house until I leave?"

Another nod. "If you do, I vill hold back twenty percent to cover any damage to zee house. I vill pay you zis balance venn you valk out zee door to zee ship."

Driscoll's jaw worked. He clearly was not happy. Whatever he thought he could get for the house that his grandfather built was now a pipe dream. Miriam was offering about 70 percent of what he thought the house was worth. Others had offered him much less.

"When can you close?"

"Venn ever you vant?" Miriam slid the copy of the offer back across the table and then a bottle of ink and a quill pen. Driscoll took the hint and signed.

By the end of the day, Miriam had contracts on three of the four houses. She figured that the remaining owner would either walk away or come begging later.

The next day, Miriam was in her store in Charleston that sold dried meats, bacon, dried foods such as beans, corn, rice, dry goods, and hardware. Known as the Charleston General Store, or in the local vernacular, "the Store," it was the largest of its kind in Charleston and was run by her daughter Devorah who had three children before her husband Abraham Nuñez died from smallpox in 1765. Devorah's daughter Sara died in 1769, and Moses, her 29 year-son was serving in the Continental Army with Washington. Albert, 27, helped run the store.

"The Store" was the front half of a large warehouse located at the end of Union Street and rented from the Jacintos. "The Store" was next to another large warehouse owned by South Carolina Imports and Exports. Both buildings ended at the two piers the Jacintos owned.

Miriam was reviewing the ledger with each day's sales summed up along with the profit. Each week, the numbers were totaled and recorded in a separate journal. The numbers told her that while the store was doing well, Devorah had done what she asked - make sure their neighbors had what they needed. How and when the Charleston General Store would be paid back would be discussed later.

Being repaid by those who supported the revolution was not what worried her. A dozen Loyalists had run rung up debts, and she and Devorah were discussing what to do. If the Loyalist was staying, no action was necessary. If the individual was planning to leave, then she wanted the store paid in full.

"Where is she?" The booming voice came from the counter where customers paid for their purchases at the front of the store. Abigail, a teenage girl who worked at the store, simply pointed to the back of the store. The "she" was Miriam Bildesheim.

Clyde Dundee was a large man and the owner of Dundee's Emporium. He strode through the displays as if he was on a mission. Miriam pretended to read the ledger in front of her.

"So, you are buying houses now."

Miriam looked up and smiled. "Good afternoon, Herr Dundee."

Dundee put both his hands on the counter and leaned over with fiery intensity in his eyes. "First, you buy plantations to control the food. Now you are buying houses! Next you will want to buy my store."

Still smiling, Miriam's eyes sparkled. "Herr Dundee, zer ist nothing in Dundee's Emporium I vish to buy. Everything you haff, vee haff here and much more. So, please tell me vy you are interrupting my verk."

"Do you want to buy my store?"

"Ist zee store for sale?"

"Hell no, particularly not to you."

"Gut. Zat means vee vill always haff a competitor."

"Clyde Driscoll says you bought his house. Is that true?"

Miriam didn't answer.

"I've wanted that house for a long time."

"Zo, you should haff offered him a higher price."

Dundee snorted and leaned forward until his face was less than a foot from Miriam's. His voice was a hostile hiss. "Damn your eyes. You're no better than the Jewish moneylenders in Scotland. Between you, the Laredos, and the Jacintos, you own half of ruddy Charleston. What you don't own, you control. I hear that you won't bring more food into the city even though your neighbors may go hungry."

Miriam's face hardened. Dundee was just like the damned Prussians. Everything they didn't like was the Jews fault even though their stupid laws caused the problems and forced the Jews to be bankers, lawyers, and doctors.

"Zee British have asked me for help but I cannot provide vat I don't have. Zee British have created zis problem by inviting their Loyalist friends to come to Charleston by promising zat zey will evacuate zem. Zee patriots who support our cause won't starve. Maybe zee British and zer Loyalist friends vill all leave sooner if zey are hungry."

She wasn't finished. Her cold blue eyes bored into Dundee's. "Herr Dundee, if you haff come to buy something from my store, then please do zo. Zee Charleston Store has much to zell. If you have come to insult me, zen you have failed, zo please leave, now!"

Dundee stood up and took a step back. "This is not over. If anyone starves to death, Mrs. Bildesheim, I will hang their deaths around your neck."

Now angry, Miriam took a small ledger out from under the counter and slammed it on the countertop. The smack caused Devorah's head to spin around from where she stood a few feet away folding some cloth. "Herr Dundee, zis ist a ledger containing the list of all zee people in Charleston who vee haff given free food because zey haff no money. Vee may never be paid back but I vould not let any of my neighbors starve. Does Dundee's Emporium have such a book?"

Clyde Dundee stood still, speechless. It was well known that Dundee's rarely offered credit, and when it did, the rates were usurious.

"I didn't zink zo." Miriam voice was as cold as Baltic ice in February. "Now, Herr Dundee, get out of zee Charleston Store. Do not come back until your manners improve."

When Dundee left, Miriam asked her daughter what they could do to cause Dundee's Emporium financial pain. Devorah smiled and said, that was easy. She was friends with the owners of the warehouse where his goods were stored who thought Dundee was a bully. She would suggest that they raise his rent substantially.

BREST, SECOND WEEK OF OCTOBER 1782

Zephyr had been hurriedly repaired in Philadelphia before it left, and Gaskins was still working on the captain's cabin when it sailed down the Delaware River. While Gaskins was satisfied with the work done by the shipyard workers, he still complained that he was being rushed. The new wood didn't match the aged wood on either side of the repaired gaps and were a stark reminder of what could happen if *Zephyr* was again hit by a cannonball.

With the schooner anchored in the *Rade de Brest* after a fast, 11-day crossing, the sound of cannon fire brought Jaco running from his cabin to *Zephyr's* main deck. Every man in the crew had the same reaction. More cannons boomed and clouds of white smoke rose from Batterie Royal. In the early morning sun, those on board the schooner saw six French Navy ships – two, two-deckers, a three-decker, and three frigates in a line about a mile apart steering toward the *Le Fer a Cheval*.

Although he didn't need a spyglass to see that the ships had been in a battle, Jaco went below to get his Dollond spyglass. Examination of the French ship's hulls showed where repairs were made and, he wondered where the fight occurred.

"Mr. Geiger, I am going to pay a visit to Mr. Gardner today while the victualling party is ashore. I'd like to leave at four bells into the Forenoon Watch."

When Jaco stepped onto the pier, the fall sun was high in the sky. He could see clouds off to the west and wondered if they would bring more rain. Colin Landry, Cato Cooper, and their captain walked side by side as they entered through the Porte de Brest. Outside the city walls, the air was full of pleasant countryside and sea smells. Inside the walled city, the stench of animal and human feces mixed with centuries worth of rotting garbage smacked the three men in the face.

The men, each armed with a sword and two pistols wound their way to Samuel Gardner's house, which also served as his office. An attached building was a warehouse with goods waiting to be shipped to North America, usually wine. Earlier in the war, the building was filled with gunpowder that, had it exploded, would have leveled his building and those on either side.

Gardner was glad to see the three men. He offered bread and cheese and plopped two newspapers, *Le Journal de Paris,* and *The London Gazette* on the table in front of Jaco. "Read these."

Jaco slid *The London Gazette* so that Landry and Cooper could read it while he stood over the table, reading the front page of the French newspaper. He waited until Landry and Cooper were finished with *The London Gazette's* three-paragraph story was much shorter than the ones that started on the first page in *Le Journal de Paris.*

The first time Jaco and Samuel Gardner met after Edmund Radcliffe asked Gardner to put letters to the Continental Congress that were detrimental to Jaco, Gardner pulled him aside and apologized. He claimed he had no idea what was in the letters and thought he was helping a family friend out when Radcliffe had told him that Jaco wanted the letters sent.

Since then, Gardner had gone out of his way to be helpful. One trip, he confessed that his family members living in Boston thought Radcliffe was a cad and had sent him copies of the articles written by both Radcliffe and Micah Chaffetz. The ones he received had notes from his family about how Chaffetz was referencing interviews and documents such as Radcliffe's journal and Jaco's reports while Radcliffe quoted nothing other than "a reliable source in the crew."

Jaco re-read the *Le Journal de Paris* as he cross-checked the terse words in *The London Gazette*. A slight nod of the head was his only reaction.

Gardner asked, "So captain, way say you?"

"I think the French and Spanish suffered a major defeat that ended their dream of retaking Gibraltar. Their defeat may embolden the British who may further harden their stance toward us and offer us less favorable terms."

"Aye, I agree. The French and Spanish have been having at Gibraltar since June 1779 and it is now October 1782, three years, four months later, and they still haven't taken the fortress. Methinks they won't."

"When do you think the next courier from Paris will arrive?"

"Any day."

"We'll be ready to sail."

"I'm counting on that."

CHAPTER 21
- FAMILY FEUD

CHARLESTON, THIRD WEEK OF OCTOBER 1782

As the afternoon wore on, the clouds rolled in, darkening the sky, and telling all the residents that rain, probably heavy at times, was coming. The gloom outside matched the atmosphere at the Winters' dinner table.

Halfway through dinner, Theodore Winters looked at his daughter, who was her cheerful self as she replayed a recent conversation with Shoshana. A letter from Javier to his family was full of optimism that peace was coming soon. With the war ending, she speculated that Darren would be put on half pay, freeing him to come to Charleston so they could marry.

Her father, a staunch Loyalist, was visibly unhappy. Peace talks meant that the British Army would be leaving Charleston. He'd just been assured by General Leslie that his family would have a place on a ship that would take them to either Barbados or Jamaica.

Leaving Charleston also meant Theodore Winters, who preferred to be addressed as Theodore, not Ted, would have to abandon his cabinetmaking business. He was known throughout South Carolina and parts of Georgia for quality furniture and had orders that would take a year or more to fill. Repair work on other makers' furniture added to the backlog.

Winters' three apprentices said that they were not leaving. None had ever voiced support for the rebels or the British, and Theodore suspected they were waiting for him to leave so they could take over his business.

He rationalized that the business that built their house in Charleston and made him comfortable financially would eventually be sold to them because neither his sons, Asa nor Ezekiel, showed any interest in becoming cabinet makers.

The issue was not if, but when the Winters were leaving and who would go with him, simmered beneath the surface. It raised its ugly head when Melody happily said, "Mr. Edward Rutledge came to the school today to tell me that if the British leave by Christmas, he plans to re-open the College of Charleston by the end of January. And when it does open, I will be one of the language professors. Isn't that exciting?"

Melody's announcement was greeted with a frown from her father. "Pray tell, my daughter, who says the British will be gone by then? They may drag out their departure for months."

"Father, the British already have left Savannah. Charleston, Javier believes, is next."

Theodore Winters glared at his daughter. "I presume you are not going to leave with your mother, brother, and father."

"Father, I am not leaving Charleston. This is where my friends are. This is where I can have a career, and Charleston is where I will marry and raise my children.

The head of the Winters household looked at his wife. "Olivia, talk some sense into your daughter."

Olivia looked at her husband at the opposite end of the table. "Why? I agree with her. Melody makes perfect sense …"

Theodore Winters slammed his hand down on the oak table he'd built decades ago, and the plates jumped. He scrambled to grab a glass of wine before it fell over. "Damnation, woman. Has the devil taken control of both of your minds? Once the British leave, chaos will take over. The economy will collapse. No one will have money for furniture. Then what?"

He glared at his wife and then at his daughter. His 16-year-old son sat quietly opposite his sister, glued to his chair, and desperately not wanting to get involved. What Ezekiel really wanted to do was leave the table and let the adults argue.

The cabinetmaker turned to Melody, "And you, my beautiful daughter will waste away, pining for a Royal Navy captain who probably has a woman in Portsmouth, or maybe London or God knows where. His life is dedicated to the service of his king, as it should be. If he does ever return, he will demand that you, as his wife, follow him to England where you know no one. Then what? At least where we go, you will have family, and the Royal Navy has bases!"

Melody glanced at her mother before she spoke. She forced herself to be unemotional. "Father, Darren is coming back. He is a man of his word. He will go on half-pay once the peace treaty is signed because England will not be at war. We have a plan. I will spend some time in England, but Darren likes Charleston better than Gosport."

"So, says he."

Melody's eyes narrowed. "Father, I tire of this conversation. Go if you want to take Mother and Ezekiel to Barbados or Jamaica. For the last time, I AM staying here. I have a stipend from the Catholic school where I teach and will get another from the College of Charleston. It will be enough, so I will not need charity."

"Where will you live?"

"Here in this house unless you sell it. If you do, I will find a place to rent." *Because many Loyalists will have left, there will be many houses to buy or rent that will be affordable.*

"It is preposterous that you are even considering living alone…"

"Father, I am twenty years old. When the war is over, Asa will return to Charleston so he and I can live together until Darren and I marry."

"Damn your eyes for mentioning his name. I told you I never want to hear Asa's name again, ever."

"Father, Asa is your son. While you may not like his siding with those of us who want independence, he is still your son. He did go to Yale for three years…"

Theodore Winters interrupted, "Where they filled his head with nonsense about not needing kings and republican ideas about individual freedoms and self-governance. He is NOT my son. When he went off to join the rebels and fight against his king, he became a traitor. Members of the Winters family are not traitors!"

Melody put her fork down on the table gently. "I will not hear you blaspheme my brother's good name. He is not a traitor. Asa is fighting for a good cause and one that will carry the day. Better you make your peace with him…"

"Damn your eyes, Melody, I will NOT!!!"

"Father, I have had enough." Melody tossed her napkin on the table and stood up suddenly. Her chair clattered as it fell over. "Mother, Ezekiel…"

With that, she stormed from the dining room, hoping her tears were not showing.

CHARLESTON, FOURTH WEEK OF OCTOBER 1782

On the large oak table in the front of the room that General Alexander Leslie used as his "command center," there was a map of Charleston, the town, and its defenses. Leslie, just as his predecessors, used the Royal Governor's mansion as one part living quarters and one part headquarters for his staff.

Also, on the table was another map, the one Robert Sayer and John Bennett printed in 1775 in London based on surveys by Henry Mouzos. This one had small squares of blue paper with the names of Continental Army units deployed north of the city.

General Leslie had just listened to each of his unit commanding officers report on their food and munitions needs and the physical health of their regiments. The British Army in Charleston had plenty of ammunition. What it needed was more food. Based on the current consumption, he would order rations to be cut.

His most recent letter from General Clinton stated that Royal Navy and British West India ships would begin evacuating Loyalists in mid-November. He'd already sent a dispatch to Clinton saying that he thought 12,000 civilians would need to be taken out along with his 5,000-man army.

To avoid a significant cutback on the food being issued to his army, the British Army needed more. So far, the Continental Army had not stopped food deliveries. Now, Leslie was in the uncomfortable position of telling the townspeople that unless more food came into the city, rationing would begin. If needed, he would seize food from the residents of Charleston to keep the British Army fed.

Doing this, he believed, could turn a volatile situation into open resistance. Major General Leslie looked over his audience, none of whom knew how critical the food situation was. They knew they would be leaving soon and were to defend themselves only if attacked. Other than that, they were to stay in their encampments and wait.

"Gentlemen, thank you for coming. I do not have a good answer to our dwindling food supplies. I am working on a solution. I hope to have a better answer in a week or so other than what I am to tell you, that fourteen days from now, you will reduce what you are feeding your men by twenty-five percent."

He waited until the murmurs died down, and before any regimental commander could speak, General Leslie said, "Thank you for your reports. That will be all."

He waited until the officers began to file out of the great room in the Royal Governor's mansion. Seeing Colonel Muir talking with Lord Islay, he spoke. "Colonel Muir, a minute, sir."

Colonel Rafer Muir knew a command when he heard one. He'd been promoted far higher than he thought he ever would be when he joined the British Army.

Muir came to attention in front of General Leslie. "Sir." Better say nothing and wait to hear what is on the general's mind.

"Colonel, you know these rebels and how they think better than any member of my staff. I need you to take your regiment out with no more than a week's rations and find the rebel commander. If not, the people of Charleston will starve because I will not let my army go hungry. Tell him that if our food needs are not met, when I leave, I will burn Charleston to the ground."

The Scotsman's eyes opened wide. "Aye, sir, I am sure I can find the rebels because they will know the moment when we march out of Charleston. Would the general be so kind as to put his direction to me in writing so I may pass it on to the Continental Army. A note from you, sir, would carry much more weight than mere words from me."

"What do you know of this General Greene?"

"Other than he is wily and will never let his army onto the field with the British Army unless he can control the terrain and the engagement. Lord Cornwallis chased him all over North and South Carolina, only to use up his supplies and run to Wilmington."

"And this Major Laredo, I understand you know him well."

"I do, at least as one can know his enemy." Muir didn't want to admit that he knew the Laredos and the Jacintos well. The admission would raise more questions that he would like to answer.

"What say you on how he might respond?"

"They will welcome any reasonable solution that ends in a prompt British Army departure."

"Aye. I will give you a letter for General Greene. Do what you can to minimize the butcher's bill. Send word back as to when you can march."

Muir nodded. "Aye, sir. I will."

EIGHT MILES NORTH OF CHARLESTON, TWO DAYS LATER

The 65th Regiment of Foot marched out of Charleston with Colonel Muir riding head of the column. Right behind him were men carrying the Union Jack, the unit's regimental colors, and the drummers.

Muir missed the sound of bagpipes and drums that accompanied a Scottish unit on the march. Bagpipers stirred his soul right down to his bones. Today, there were only drums, which, to Muir, sounded almost effeminate.

A half a mile from the northernmost British Army outpost of the Charleston garrison, Muir sensed he was being watched. Twice, he saw the reflection from what he was sure was a spyglass.

Muir turned to his executive officer, Magnus Shaw, the 4th Earl of Shropshire. "Major Shaw, keep the men marching. Do not deploy unless the rebels start a fight."

When he assumed command, the 4th Earl of Shropshire was one of the few officers Muir kept in their original billets. He decided that demoting Shaw would have caused more political problems than it was worth. However, he made a point of never addressing him by his title, only by his rank.

When newly promoted Colonel Muir took command, the 65th Regiment of Foot consisted of a grenadier company, a light infantry company, and eight "regular" infantry companies, each commanded by a captain. During the first week of his tenure as the commanding officer, Muir put the regiment through drill after drill. He started with exercising individual companies and then in groups until he was convinced the regiment was ready to fight.

Very quickly, Muir's experienced eye saw which officers knew what they were doing and had the respect of their subordinates and those who didn't. Muir was not here to go to parties and strut around Charleston. They were here to fight the rebels; if they did, he would make sure the 65th would fight to the best of its ability. If the regiment could not perform up to British Army standards, they would put themselves at risk along with Muir's and soldiers of other regiments who depended on their skill.

For two weeks, the regiment drilled, often firing volleys at targets set up 50 yards away. Only five of the captains survived his evaluation and the rest were reassigned elsewhere.

Muir wheeled his horse and rode so he was next to the man carrying the regimental colors. He leaned back, pulled a large white cloth from his saddlebag, and tied it to the flagstaff. Then, he took the flagstaff and rested it on his stirrup.

Pointing to his adjutant, Captain Belleview, who was in the leading group of officers on horseback, Muir said, "You come with me." To Shaw, he said, "Keep the march going. If you see us with some rebels, come no closer than five hundred yards. Do not deploy into the fields because the rebels will take that as a signal that the 65th is preparing for battle. Meanwhile, I will attempt to keep us all alive so we can all go home in December."

Muir spurred his horse forward, followed by the adjutant who said nothing for the first 100 yards, then he said, "Colonel, sir, are we surrendering the regiment?"

"No, Captain Belleview, we are not. Hopefully, we are about to have a parlay with the rebels that will bring our garrison more food. I don't want the marker on my grave to say, 'Here lies the man who allowed Charleston to be burned to the ground.'"

"Sir, you do not think that the rebels will pick us off?"

"The 4th Carolina is not trigger-happy. They are honorable men and will see the white flag as a signal we want to have a chat. But make no mistake, when we do talk, we will be in several of their sharpshooters' sights."

Muir didn't want to say that as close to the woods as they were, if the rebels wanted to pick us off, they could do it any time.

The two men rode at a fast canter. Muir wanted to put himself at least a half mile ahead of his regiment, if not more, when he met the rebels. He saw the dust from the road before he saw the men on horseback. Muir yelled out. "Captain, let us stop here and wait."

Both horses shifted nervously as the four riders approached. The size of one of the horses suggested that Amos Laredo was among the officers. He guessed Laredo's Percheron was several hundred pounds heavier than his mount and at least six hands taller.

Amos Laredo stopped his horse 20 yards from the British officers and then, seeing who was in front of him, eased his gray and white horse forward. Seeing that Muir wearing the insignia of a colonel, he saluted. "Congratulations, sir, I see you have been promoted. I assume it was well deserved."

Rafer Muir smiled. "Thank you, Major Laredo. You taught me many lessons, so now I have the honor of commanding the 65th Regiment of Foot. Highlanders they are not, but they are good soldiers. Allow me to introduce my adjutant, Captain Belleview. Captain Belleview, meet Major Amos Laredo and Captain Giffords of the 4th Carolina Dragoons."

Belleview and Laredo waved at each other to acknowledge the introductions. Then, Muir nodded in the direction of Amos' left arm, hanging loosely on his right side. "How is your arm?"

"It has been better."

"What Captain Vickers did was dishonorable besides being stupid."

"Colonel, we are at war, and we have seen things that make us both sick. So, what brings you out of Charleston?"

"Food, Major, food. Or to be more precise, the lack of it."

Amos looked around. "Colonel, I am not a farmer. I am a poor cavalryman. Just like the British Army, I must find food for my men and horses. The 4th Carolina doesn't have any extra to give. Is the British Army going hungry? If it is, shouldn't the Royal Navy bring your rations."

Muir smiled believing the rebel officer was enjoying the repartee. He, no both, must be careful not to reveal the extent of his conversations with the Laredos. Muir knew he was more at risk than his rebel counterpart. "Major, let us not fence, so please allow me to be blunt. General Leslie wants Mrs. Bildesheim to send more food to Charleston. If not, he will seize whatever food coming into the city, and your fellow Charlestonians will go hungry, and …"

Muir let his voice tail off.

"And what, Colonel?"

"General Leslie will send troops into the field to take whatever the British Army can by force."

"That would be very bloody for the British Army. And you won't find much."

"Why is that?"

"Look around, Colonel. The fields are all harvested. We've moved all the farm animals farther north.

"Sir, General Leslie says if we cannot get more food, he will burn Charleston to the ground when we leave."

"And pray tell, when is that?"

"Soon."

"Colonel, give me a date. General Greene will want one."

"End of December."

"How about December 15th. This way, my fellow South Carolinians can celebrate Christmas and Hannukah as free men and women."

"I don't know if that is possible."

LAST BATTLES

"Well, then, Colonel Muir, I strongly suggest you make it so."

"Major, if I may…" Muir opened the map case on his saddle bag and took out the note from General Leslie before urging his horse forward. He held his hand with the letter out. His horse's chest was about three-quarters the size of Laredo's Percheron, and he sat at least a foot lower.

Amos took the note and handed it to Lieutenant Giffords next to him. Muir noted that Amos made no attempt to use his left arm. Giffords opened the note, read it, and returned it to his commanding officer. Amos read the note before folding it along the creases and sliding it into his map case.

"Colonel Muir, I can make no commitments for General Greene who, as you and I, would like to see the bloodshed end. However, you need to tell General Leslie that if he orders any building in Charleston to be burned, I will hunt him to the end of the earth to make him pay with his life. Again, tell General Leslie we'll find more food in exchange for fully evacuating Charleston by December 15th."

Muir didn't say anything.

"Colonel Muir, I will get this to General Greene, but it may take three days to get there and for me to receive an answer. If General Greene agrees, food wagons will appear by magic at the British Army's northernmost outpost on the road into Charleston. If they don't arrive, you have your answer, we have no more to spare. In the meantime, I suggest you take your regiment back to Charleston. The longer it stays in the field, the more food it consumes, some of which may consist of lead balls."

"I take your point. More food for a commitment to being out of Charleston by December 15th."

"Colonel, that is the proposed arrangement. I do not mean to be rude or impertinent, but the sooner the British Army leaves Charleston, the better for all of us."

"No, Major, you were not rude, just a soldier being blunt. No offense taken."

With that, Colonel Muir saluted and wheeled his horse around. "Captain Belleview, we need to get back to our regiment. With luck, we will be back in our beds by midnight with our mission accomplished."

Captain Giffords waited until Muir and Belleview were out of earshot. "Captain, send this note to General Greene telling him that I will ensure more food is delivered now that the British have committed to being out of Charleston by December 15th. Selling them more food for leaving two weeks before they planned is an excellent bargain made better because no one was wounded or died."

Captain Belleview waited until Muir finished watching the columns make a U around in an empty indigo field. As they rode back to the head of the column, he asked, "Sir, I presume you know this Major Laredo well. How did that come about?"

"The battlefield. Major Laredo gave the British Army a bloody nose every time we fought. Never were we able to defeat him. He, and his fellow South Carolinians and others like him, are the reason we lost this stupid war. Each time he beat us, he treated our dead and wounded with honor."

"Sir, is he to be trusted?"

"Aye, captain, Major Laredo is a man of his word, and I trust him more than many of our fellow officers." Muir just realized what he said. "If you repeat that, I will deny I said it and demote you to private!"

Still dusty from the march, Muir walked into General Leslie's headquarters just after 11 p.m. When he met the general, Leslie wore only his breeches, boots, and a linen shirt.

"You're back early, Colonel. Did you meet with General Greene?"

"No, sir, I did not. I met with Major Amos Laredo, commander of the 4th Carolina and the grandson of Miriam Bildesheim. If anyone can find the food, she can."

"When will we know, and what will the food cost us besides money?"

"Sir, we'll know in three days. The price is we – the British Army and our supporters – must be out of Charleston by December 15th of this year."

"Colonel Muir, are you telling me that a mere rebel major demanded that we leave by that date?"

"Aye, General, I am." Muir paused before he spoke again choosing his words carefully. "I would submit, sir, that Major Laredo has the ear of General Greene and would not have made such a statement unless he was pretty sure that General Greene would support him."

"And, if we are not out of Charleston by December 15th, then what?"

"Then, sir, I fear all hell will break loose."

"Did you tell them what I plan to do?"

"I did, sir."

"And what was Major Laredo's reaction?"

"I do not think the general wants to know."

"Tell me, Colonel. If I must, I will make it an order."

Muir complied, and General Leslie laughed. "He can't be serious."

"Sir, if I were you, I would take him at his word."

"He wouldn't dare kill a British Army general."

"Sir, if you were on the battlefield, you would be his first target, along with every other officer."

General Leslie's face turned red as he put his hands on his hips. "How dare he!!!"

"Sir, if you looked at the casualty lists of when we have encountered the 4th Carolina, you'd find the names of many officers."

"We should have put this 4th Carolina out of business when we had the chance."

This was one of the few times Muir wished he'd not spoken what was on his mind. "Sir, we tried several times, and there is a large cemetery in Dorchester filled with British and Scottish boys."

Leslie started yelling, his eyes bulging. "Damn your eyes. I could cashier you right now for your impertinence. Colonel Muir, if the food doesn't arrive in three days, I will have you brought up on charges. I sent you into the countryside to bring back food, and you didn't. In three days, either the food arrives, or on the fourth, you will be brought in front of a court martial for disobeying my orders!"

Muir watched the general throw his tantrum, thinking that if the food didn't arrive, he'd simply take off his uniform and leave his quarters. He was determined not to be the scapegoat for a situation he didn't create.

NORTH OF CHARLESTON, FIRST WEEK OF NOVEMBER 1782

Within 36 hours of Rafer Muir's meeting with General Leslie, a wagon stopped the British Army checkpoint a half mile north of the parapet that guarded the city. A dozen British Army soldiers were packed in the bed with their hands and feet tied and gags in their mouths. Pinned to the uniform coat of the senior officer, a lieutenant, was a note addressed to General Alexander Leslie.

The sentries could see other wagons stopped on the road, a quarter of a mile away. Once the soldiers were unloaded, the wagon turned around and headed north. The sergeant in charge of the guard post gave the lieutenant a horse and sent him galloping toward town.

The column of wagons then started south toward Charleston. After each one was inspected, several continued toward town to deliver their cargo of food to the British Army. Most peeled off to the Shayna Enterprises' and South Carolina Imports and Exports warehouses.

Lieutenant Liam O'Keefe of the 60th Royal Americans, whose clothes were muddy, was ushered into the great room where General Leslie waited. At the time, the general was not aware that food was being delivered and that 12 British Army soldiers who had gone missing the day before had been returned unharmed.

"Who are you?"

"Lieutenant Liam O'Keefe, sir. 60th Royal Americans." The lieutenant held out the letter that had been pinned to his chest.

"You look like you have been mucking about with pigs."

"Sir, we were captured and held in a barn overnight."

Leslie wrinkled his nose. "Well, that accounts for the smell!" He held up the piece of paper. "What is this?"

"A letter, sir, from a rebel officer named Major Amos Laredo."

Leslie grunted as he popped off the wax seal. He looked at the penmanship and thought the man had a fine hand.

> General Leslie,
>
> The Continental Army agreed to allow food to be delivered to Charleston. We did not agree to allow British soldiers poach deer, turkey, and other game on our lands.
>
> These men were lucky in that we captured them without a fight. The next time, we will not be so kind because poachers, like horse and cattle thieves, are allowed by law to be hung in South Carolina.
>
> The Continental Army has kept its word to deliver food. We expect you to do the same.
>
> I hope your evacuation plans are well underway because the clock is ticking. December 15th is coming faster than you think.
>
> We are watching!
> Amos Laredo,
> Major and Commander
> 4th Carolina Dragoons

General Leslie threw the letter onto his desk. "What a cheeky, insolent bastard!!!"

Then, realizing that both his adjutant and aide, along with Lieutenant O'Keefe, were still standing in his office, he asked O'Keefe to tell him what happened.

When he was finished telling how the members of his Loyalist unit from north of New York who were accomplished game hunters were on the trail of a small herd of deer when they were taken. The rebels, O'Keefe said, were more interested in taking their powder and shot. After capture, they were tied to railings in a barn and fed smoked meat and beer.

General Leslie nodded and dismissed the young lieutenant. He assumed that Colonel Muir already knew the food was coming into town, and if he didn't, he would find out in due course. The general's next order was to ask his adjutant to find the Royal Navy Port Captain and ask him to come to the Royal Governor's mansion.

CHARLESTON, SECOND WEEK OF NOVEMBER 1782

The first transport and cargo ships began arriving during the first week of November. Most were chartered from the British East and West India companies. Others were Royal Navy ships pressed into service for the evacuation of Charleston.

Each time the ships came in, Melody studied those that arrived in the harbor looking for *H.M.S. Pompeii*. Each group of transports that left was escorted by frigates and two-deckers, but none were *Pompeii*.

Despondent, Melody sat in her room, wondering where Darren was. She would not believe that he had decided to walk away and convinced herself that Darren was dead, either felled by a rebel or French ball or some tropical disease for which no one knew how to cure.

Melody sat staring out the window in a melancholy mood and did not hear her mother Amelia when she called her name the first time. Melody wiped the tears from her eyes and opened the door to her room. "Mother, what is it?"

"Dear, you have a letter from Darren. It was just delivered by Commander Rathbun from *H.M.S. Liber*. He suggested that you arrange to have a letter taken to *Liber*, which will be escorting ships to England.

Commander Rathburn said when he gets to England, he will personally deliver it to Darren's parents."

Melody couldn't get down the stairs fast enough. With one hand, she held the folds of her dress and the other, the railing of the stairs, not wanting to fall.

Amelia held out the letter. "I do hope it is good news."

The young woman was walking on air as she found her way to the parlor and a chair. The wax seal popped off easily. Melody recognized Darren's precise penmanship.

> *Melody, the love of my life,*
>
> *Alas, the North American Station Commander wants Pompeii to escort the seven transports carrying some 1,200 men, women, and children loyal to King George. I am to be the commodore of the squadron – Pompeii plus two 32-gun frigates and a sloop – carrying Loyalists to Port Royal, Barbados, and Trinidad which will then sail to England.*
>
> *So, this is a roundabout way of telling you that Pompeii will not be supporting the evacuation of Charleston, which should, by the time you get this letter, be well underway.*
>
> *From New York, it is 1,600 nautical miles or 13 – 14 days, given decent winds and a speed of five knots, to Port Royal in Jamaica. Then, we will sail to Barbados, 1,250 miles, and 10 – 11 days to the so' so' east. From there, Trinidad, is a day and a half and a mere 250 miles to the so' so' west.*
>
> *We will spend a few days taking on supplies in Trinidad before sailing nor' nor' east for 45 days to cover the 5,350 miles to Portsmouth. I suspect we, i.e., my squadron, will be escorting transports of some kind, so the pace will, again, be slow.*
>
> *However, do not lose faith. By the time I return to Portsmouth, the war may be over. If history is any indicator, the elves in the Admiralty have begun making plans to scale back the fleet. Ships like Pompeii will be put in ordinary, and many of us shall be placed on half pay, something I will volunteer to do, if not asked.*
>
> *So, my love, I shall endeavor to return to Charleston as fast as possible. If the French decide to attack again, it will be someone else's problem. Once I return to Charleston, I will not leave your arms again. Already, we have missed too much time together.*
>
> *All my love,*
> *Darren*

Melody read the words a second and then a third time, admiring the precision and clarity with which the love of her life wrote. She added the sailing days, assumed four days in each of the three ports, and came up with 84 days. So, by the end of February or mid-March 1783, Darren would be in England. Then, he might be leaving England for Charleston two more months after that, which would put him in her arms in June or maybe July.

It was then she noticed her mother standing in the doorway to the parlor. She held out the letter. "Mother, it is all good news. Darren should be here in Charleston in June or thereabouts, which means we can have a summer or a fall wedding!!!"

"You may have plans for a summer wedding, but neither your mother, brother Ezekiel nor I will be there." Melody recognized her father's gruff voice. "I was just notified that we will be on a ship leaving Charleston on December 7th. We are each allowed three large chests to take to Barbados where I have been offered a position as a sugar plantation manager. There, we will live comfortably."

"Father, I am not going to Barbados."

"Neither am I!" Ezekiel stood behind his mother and older sister.

"Ezekiel, you have no choice. Amelia, what say you?"

"As your wife, I have no choice. I am too old to learn a skill to support myself and have no inheritance. But, Theodore, I must tell you again that I am going very, very reluctantly."

"Noted. I will tell the Royal Navy that it will be three of us and nine chests, all of which are in my workshop."

Theodore Winters took a few steps toward his daughter and took both her hands in his. At first, she tried to withdraw, but his grip was too strong, and she relented. "Melody, you are beautiful, smart, and will make Darren a wonderful wife if he ever comes back. If he doesn't, then what?"

Melody half laughed. "Darren is coming. And if he doesn't, I will be a professor of languages and will find a husband. After the war, there will be plenty of eligible men in Charleston."

"I wish you the best. This saves me from selling the house at a discount to some rebel who wants a bargain. Instead, I will leave you £500 in cash and sign over the deed to you. This way, you can do with the house and everything in it as you wish."

"Thank you, Father."

The two hugged before Theodore Winters recovered from his moment of sentimentality. "Then, it is settled. I have sold the workshop, so I am a free man, so to speak. Amelia, Ezekiel, we have some packing to do."

Melody went back up the stairs. She had two letters to write. One to Emily Smythe Burdette and one to Darren.

CHAPTER 22

– FREEDOM, AT LAST

BREST, THIRD WEEK OF NOVEMBER 1782

Zephyr rode easily at anchor, about a quarter mile from the landing that the schooner's boats used. The gray overcast that had hung over the port for two days and brought strong winds and intermittent rain was gone. Overhead, Cato Cooper noted that raw weather was replaced by a bright early winter sun, puffy white clouds, and a steady breeze strong enough to create white caps on the bay. He noted on his slate that the temperature was 45^0F at two bells on the Forenoon Watch. Later, the temperature and wind he wrote in chalk would be recorded in the ship's log.

Even wrapped in a wool cloak, the breeze and the temperature were enough to make the son of a former slave shiver. The tones of the bell telling him that he'd been on watch for 60 minutes were dying away as he studied *Zephyr's* long boat coming out from the pier.

Each day in port, the daily routine was that at four bells on the Morning Watch, Mr. Geiger and four members of the crew who were coming on watch later during the day sailed the long boat to the pier to buy food and would return during the early part of the Forenoon Watch.

Zephyr had two 18-foot-long longboats and two smaller, 14-foot-long cutters slung over the side when the three-masted schooner was in port for more than two days. They were tied to booms extended over the side and could quickly be brought alongside the schooner when needed.

Seeing the baskets of food covered with canvas to protect them from the spray, Cato leaned over the railing. "Mr. Preston, please pass to our new cook, Mr. Giradeau, that breakfast will arrive shortly."

The ship's bosun, who had seen the longboat, waved his acknowledgment. On the way over to France, *Zephyr's* cook, who also stood watch, was found dead in his hammock halfway to Brest. There were no signs of foul play, and the man, who was in his sixties, was well-liked. Jaco wrote in his log that the man expired from old age in his sleep and was buried with honors at sea.

When they arrived in the French port, Samuel Gardner found a Frenchman who wanted to come to America and, as it turned out, was a chef for a local French nobleman. Guillaume Giradeau was unhappy with his employer, who had not paid him in over two years. Giradeau met with Jaco, and a deal was struck. Giradeau would sail on *Zephyr* as its cook until the war was over. Then, he would be paid off with the rest of the crew and free to find work in the new United States of America.

The nobleman, now with one less mouth to feed and pay, did nothing. *Zephyr* now had a man who could turn out, with the pots and utensils they bought for Giradeau, much better meals than his predecessor.

A net was lowered to bring the food on board from another boom rigged supported by a bipod and, whose base was lashed to the mizzenmast. While the baskets were being hoisted on board, Morton Geiger climbed up the side and knocked on the door to the captain's cabin.

"Come in."

"Good morning, sir. Mr. Gardner wants you to come to his office as soon as possible. He said it is of the greatest importance, and we shall have a passenger on the way back to Philadelphia."

"So then, I gather we are leaving soon?"

"Aye, sir, with your permission, I will take the long boat back into town with four crew members to pick up some additional cheeses, smoked meats, and salamis while you meet Mr. Gardner."

"Well then, I should make myself presentable. While I am doing so, please tell Mr. Giradeau that he will have to feed those of us who go ashore when we return."

The red ball that was the sun was now starting its journey down in the western sky when 12 crew members took positions, two to a bar on the capstan. Colin Landry waited until the quartermaster on watch, Abner Jeffords rang *Zephyr's* bell two times, telling everyone that the First Dog Watch was half over, then began the shanty known as Amsterdam.

Landry

In Amsterdam there lived a maid.
Mark well now what I say!
In Amsterdam there lived a maid,
And she was mistress of her trade.
I'll go no more a-ro-o-vin'
With you, fair maid.

Men at the capstan

A-rovin', a-rovin'. Since roving's been my ru-i-in.
I'll go no more a-ro-o-vin' with you, fair maid.

Landry

I met her walkin' on th' Strand
Mark well now what I say!
I met her walkin' on th' Strand
An' said "Good day" an' took her hand.
But I'll go no more a-ro-o-vin'
With you, fair maid.

Men at the capstan

A-rovin', a-rovin'. Since roving's been my ru-i-in.
I'll go no more a-ro-o-vin' with you, fair maid

Landry

She said, "Young man, you're rather free."
Mark well now what I say!
She said, "Young man, you're rather free."
Then turned around and walked with me.
And I'll go no more a-ro-o-vin'
With you, fair maid.

Men at the capstan

A-rovin', a-rovin'. Since roving's been my ru-i-in.
I'll go no more a-ro-o-vin' with you, fair maid.

Amsterdam was one of the seemingly limitless repertoire of shanties Landry would sing depending on the task. Some, like Amsterdam, were for heavy hauling, such as raising an anchor. He had others for pumping the bilges and hauling lines.

While the men hauled up the port anchor, another group raised the working jib and foremast's mainsail. They flapped noisily in the wind as a reminder that they needed to be sheeted home.

With the port anchor weighed and stowed, the 12 men on the capstan were replaced with the same number to bring up the starboard anchor. With the wind from the nor' west, the schooner was straining against the anchor hawser as the wind tried to push the ship back into the harbor.

Another team of men hauled up the mainsail on the main mast, and with the starboard anchor off the bottom, the three-masted schooner fell off to the south. Jaco ordered the men to pull in the sheets to the jib and the boom on the foremast to take advantage of the wind. As they were being pulled in to accelerate the schooner, the same was done with the mainmast's mainsail.

The mizzen mainsail was quickly raised and sheeted home before the drop keels were lowered. *Zephyr* picked up speed as it sailed so' west toward the *Pointe des Espagnois*. Under full sail, Jaco estimated that it would take about 30 minutes to cover the five miles to where he would order the ship tacked to sail north toward the *Pointe du Portzic*. By nightfall, *Zephyr* would be out into the Atlantic.

With the sails were trimmed, Jaco turned to his passenger, who stayed on the quarterdeck, carefully moving to keep out of the way. "Mr. Varley, I apologize that we did not have much time to welcome you aboard *Zephyr*. With fair winds and weather, we should have you in Philadelphia in less than three weeks. With what is in my strong box, maybe God will help us out."

In his office, Samuel Gardner introduced Jethro Varley to Jaco, saying that he was one of the two secretaries for the negotiating team of Benjamin Franklin, John Jay, and Henry Laurens. Varley, who was in his late 40s and was a thin, short man, smiled. "He should. We are carrying a draft of the treaty that will, when it is signed, change the world. Some things are still to be negotiated, but Dr. Franklin and Mr. Adams believe much of the hard work has been done. Not since the Romans and the Greeks, will we have a country free of kings, queens, and princes. We will all be equal with one man who has one vote. We, Captain Jacinto, are about to make history!"

"Do you think the Continental Congress will approve the draft?"

"I do. It has more than we asked for. We will have all the English land from Canada to the Gulf of Mexico, except Florida, and west from the Atlantic to the Mississippi River. That land alone makes our country bigger than France and Spain combined."

"And the fighting, do you think it will stop?"

"Aye, I do. Clinton has been ordered to cease all offensive operations. As far as the rest of the world, I do not know."

"That, sir, is what troubles me."

Jaco turned away because it was time to tack *Zephyr* to starboard. Soon, the schooner will be in the Atlantic, and if the treaty has been blessed by the Shelburne government, the war will soon be over, and he can spend the rest of his life in the arms of Reyna.

CHARLESTON, FIRST WEEK OF DECEMBER 1782

Melody referred to this day in her diary as "departure day," i.e., the day her mother, brother, and father would board a British ship and sail to Barbados. She couldn't answer whether she would ever see any of them again. Once she married Darren, she would ask him if he could find a way to bring her mother back to Charleston.

The nine chests, stacked in three rows of three at the entrance to their house, were a stark reminder that "departure day" had finally come. She'd already deposited £750, £250 more than her father originally promised her, in an account at the Bank of South Carolina.

Melody fought back the tears as she hugged her mother and Ezekiel who had suddenly grown over the past month or two. Now, he was 5'11" and 180 pounds.

After a perfunctory hug, her father held both her hands in his. "Melody, I understand why you are not coming with us, and I wish you the best of luck. You know where we'll be if your Captain Smythe does not return. Barbados can't be that big of an island."

Melody smiled as she nodded. "Thank you, Father. Mother and I will correspond."

"Excellent." Theodore Winters took one last look around the house that had been in the family for three generations. He could see the man with the wagon waiting in the street. "Well, then, we need to be off. Do you want to see us off at the docks?"

Melody shook her head. "No, Father, I have classes to teach." Melody didn't want to prolong the goodbye. Somehow, in her heart of hearts, she knew she would see them again. How and when, she did not know but felt it in her bones, which made the parting easier. Melody was sure the separation was temporary. What did bother her was the question of time. Would it be months or years? Only the future will tell.

CHARLESTON, SUNDAY, DECEMBER 15TH, 1782

The sun was out, and many Charlestonians were gathered on the parapets at the city's southern tip. There, amongst the spiked guns left by the British, they could see the Ashley and Cooper Rivers along with the roadstead. Only a few British ships were left, taking on the remnants of the British garrison.

John Wells, the owner and publisher of the *South Carolina Gazette* stood with a table piled high with copies of his paper. During the occupation by the British, he changed the name to *The Royal Gazette*. Now that the British were gone, the paper's front-page headline screamed, "They're Gone." In the story, reporters documented that 130 ships were needed to evacuate 14,000 souls – 4,800 British soldiers, 4,200 Loyalists with their 5,000 slaves.

The day was a cause for celebration because the people of Charleston now had their city back. That was Tuesday.

Today, on Thursday, the 4th Carolina entered the city. Many of the residents stopped to wave as the men passed by. Amos Laredo stopped at the Wilkins Battery at the southern tip of Charleston and ordered the men to dismount.

He remained on his Percheron so that he could see over the men gathered around him. "Gentlemen, it has been my honor and pleasure to serve with you and lead you. We have accomplished many great things. Now, with luck and God's help, we can continue with our lives. However, the war is not over. The peace treaty has not been signed. So, keep your powder dry, and your rifled muskets close. Godspeed to you all."

After the cheers died down, Amos wearily climbed from his horse. The first person he hugged was his mother, then his father. Reyna waited off to the side because she was the only member of his family he saw during the British occupation.

Waiting patiently was his grandmother. The two embraced. Then, Miriam pushed him back gently to arms-length. "Zo, every von in Shayna vants you to be Shayna's new prezident. Ven can you start verking?"

Amos laughed at his Baba. She does not miss a trick, nor does any moss grow under her feet. He suspected she'd been planning this for years.

PHILADELPHIA, THIRD WEEK OF DECEMBER 1782

The weather was fair, but the winds from the so' west in the Horse Latitudes forced Jaco to sail *Zephyr* so' west by south until the schooner was west of the Canary Islands. There, the winds shifted to more to the north and nor' west, allowing the schooner to take a more westerly course across the Atlantic. Near the halfway point, Jaco had *Zephyr* on a beam reach with the wind coming over the starboard side.

Once Bermuda was 100 or so miles to the north, Jaco ordered a course directly toward the entrance to Delaware Bay. For most of the trip, the schooner averaged 12 knots through the water, but the less-than-direct route cost time. Cold wind and a chance for snow greeted *Zephyr* as the schooner coasted to a stop at a pier in Philadelphia 24 days after leaving Brest.

With the pouch in hand, Varley ran down the gangway to the waiting carriage that took him to the Pennsylvania State House. With *Zephyr* securely tied to the pier, Jaco ordered Morton Geiger to get the ship provisioned as quickly as possible and Bosun Preston to ensure that work on needed repairs began right now. He concluded by warning, "I don't think we will be in Philadelphia for more than two or three days."

Javier Jacinto hurried down to *Zephyr* to see his son as soon as Varley's dispatches were read to the Continental Congress. Once the officer of the watch rendered the proper honors by piping him aboard and announcing, "Member of Congress, arriving," Javier couldn't wait to get to his son's cabin to tell him the good news. "Jaco, the British have left Charleston. Everyone is safe. Soon, we are going to be our own country."

Father and son shared a drink of whiskey. "Please ask your officers to join me for dinner tonight. I have two letters from Reyna waiting for you."

Later that night, and back on *Zephyr*, the lantern bathed the revamped captain's cabin in a soft yellow light. On the port side, a bunk with a railing ran the length of the space. Under it were three new drawers that held his clothing. To create more space, the forward bulkhead had a polished plank that became a desk when pulled down and the legs extended. Along the starboard wall were racks containing rolled charts attached to a small table on which the officer of the watch plotted *Zephyr's* position.

Jaco lit a second candle and placed it on the corner of the desk as he gently opened the most recent letter from Reyna. He'd already read and re-read the first one, but this one was dated December 19th, 1782.

My Dearest Jaco,

Charleston is again free!!! Shoshana, Melody, and our friends watched the last British ships load and leave Charleston. It was a wonderful sight as they sailed down the river to the sea, never to return.

The gloom that hung over us while the British were here has now lifted. We are all more optimistic about the future.

Your mother told me we are still far from a peace treaty with the British. But I am confident that Mr. Franklin and company will conclude a peace fair to us all.

The good news is that Amos came home the day after the British left. He is well, but he has very limited use of his left arm. The 4th Carolina Dragoons are no more unless the British return or some stupid die-hard Loyalists create trouble.

Daba has told everyone that Amos will eventually take over Shayna Enterprises whenever she decides to retire. Knowing my grandmother, she will outlive us all.

There are many hard feelings against the Loyalists who have remained behind. I, for one, bear them no ill will.

Melody received a letter from Darren and hopes he will arrive in Charleston sometime after June of next year. That will be the second wedding we will have to attend. The first will be ours, of course.

Shoshana, as you can imagine, is setting the world on fire as an attorney and will be a force to be reckoned with in South Carolina. We need to find her a man.

We just heard from Eric and his wife Sera. They are both well and by the time you read this, he will be a father. When you return, we will do our best to catch up! Be safe, my love. Everyone here sends their love.

Reyna

It took the Continental Congress only two days of debate before sending Varley back to France with a demand for reparations for the damage the British Army and their Loyalist allies did to property in the Colonies. Given the time of year, *Zephyr's* course back to Brest was already plotted.

CHAPTER 23

- COMING TO AMERICA

BOSTON, SECOND WEEK OF JANUARY 1783

Outside, the air was bitter cold. Inside, the fire in the far side of the room kept where Uriah Trent worked warm enough so that he didn't need a woolen cloak. The primary beneficiary of the roaring fire was the area where two printing presses churned out the weekly issues of the *Continental Journal*. The heat kept the precious ink from freezing and the paper warm.

Usually, Trent could see the Boston Common across the street through the window, but today, frost made the window opaque. He could not see how much new snow had fallen.

He was in the process of writing a mea culpa piece when a familiar face opened the door letting in a blast of air that chilled the room. The cold set the stage for the meeting he was about to have.

The visitor was Edmund Radcliffe bringing his weekly article on the Continental Navy and its failings. The primary target of his ire was Jaco Jacinto. At first, Trent thought the highly critical articles were "fact-based," but as of late, he had changed his mind.

Letters from readers and from *Scorpion's* crew that enumerated the inaccuracies and biases of Radcliffe's stories were difficult to dismiss. His rival paper, the *Boston Gazette* printed a series written by Micah Chaffetz citing sources such as the captain's log, journals kept by officers not named Radcliffe and were bolstered by quotes attributed to crew members by name. Chaffetz's articles put his *Continental Journal* in a difficult position since Radcliffe's articles only quoted "sources among the crew."

The only conclusion that Trent could reach was that Radcliffe's stories were horribly biased. Yesterday afternoon, a courier delivered the letter yesterday afternoon informing him that he and the *Continental Gazette* were being sued for libel. This represented a significant potential liability that could force him to shutter his paper.

Edmund Radcliffe closed the door behind him and stamped his feet before he shrugged off his woolen coat. He used his one hand to brush off the snow before draping the dark blue garment over a waist-high banister that separated the print shop from the newspaper's office.

Trent did not rise from his chair as Radcliffe approached holding a folded document. He was still unsure what he would say, much less do. The thin, almost scrawny Bostonian put his latest creation on Trent's desk.

The publisher looked up quizzically, "What is this?"

Radcliffe answered confidently. "Another excellent article on the failings of Captain Jacinto."

Trent left the handwritten story on the front of his desk. Now, anything written by Edmund Radcliffe would be treated as if it was poison. "I can neither accept nor print it."

"Why not?"

"Have you not been reading Micah Chaffetz's articles in the *Boston Gazette*?"

"Yes, they are garbage. No one reads them. Why?"

"My newspaper's readers do." Trent turned to the table behind him and placed a stack of letters on the desk. "These are just those we received last week. Most come from concerned subscribers and readers who know excellent, well-sourced journalism from what comes out of the arse of a horse."

"That, sir, is a matter of opinion. I stand behind what I have written."

"Well, Mr. Radcliffe, you may be the only one." Radcliffe's arrogance was angering Uriah Trent, whose very livelihood and the reputation of the *Continental Gazette* were put at risk by Radcliffe's writing. He held up two letters he had received with his ink-stained fingers. "Do you know what these are?"

"No. Should I care?"

Trent forced himself to be calm. "If I were you, I would. One is the notification that the *Continental Gazette* is being sued for libel. The other informs me that I, as the publisher and editor, am also being sued for libel by Captain Jacinto and a long list of his crew members. I suspect you, too, will receive these as well."

"They don't have a case."

"I think they have a very good one. Earlier this morning, Micah Chaffetz stopped by to interview me for an article on the lawsuit. After he finished asking me questions, we had a lengthy discussion about the papers made available to him and the interviews he conducted. I'm no lawyer, but I suspect Captain Jacinto and his fellow crew members will win if this goes to court."

Radcliffe just stared at Trent. His mouth worked, but no words came out.

"So, Mr. Radcliffe, I will keep the few pounds I owe you to help defray my legal costs. You made a mockery of good journalistic work by quoting yourself as your source. You are an excellent writer, but your articles are so far from the truth they are almost fantasy. Had you put them in a novel, you might have had something. As a news story and an exposé, they are unsupported drivel. Now, leave my office, and do not darken my doorway again. I have an editorial to write in which I must apologize to my readers."

Radcliffe turned on his heel, slung on his cloak, and slammed the door as he left, leaving his latest work on the desk. Trent thought the cold blast of air was refreshing and cleared his mind so he could write. Before he did, he read the latest from Radcliffe and had to admit, the man could write.

By firing Radcliffe and refuting the two dozen articles, he believed he was on his way to settling the lawsuit before it bankrupted him or forced the *Continental Gazette* out of business. Credibility and honesty with his readers were, in his mind, paramount.

LIVERPOOL, THIRD WEEK OF JANUARY 1783

The troop transport *Jane Seymour* with Colonel Rafer Muir and 250 members of the 65th Regiment of Foot docked in Liverpool 35 days after it set sail from Charleston. The other half of the regiment was on the transport *Queen Catherine*, which was tied up at another nearby pier.

The British Army logisticians had wagons ready to haul the regiment's kit to its barracks. There, the regiment turned in its muskets. The officers kept their swords and pistols, assuming they were theirs when they entered the Army or were taken from the rebels.

After two days in Liverpool, those in the regiment who wanted to stay in the British Army were assigned to a separate, three-story barracks. The 208 men who wanted to leave the British Army were ordered to march to Shropshire where they were enlisted. The town was three days and 71 miles away. Wagons would carry their food. Muir was given a map showing where the men would camp each night. Once at the Shropshire's army depot, Colonel Rafer Muir was ordered to help the local officers officially muster the soldiers out and pay them off.

The last man on the paid-off list was Colonel Rafer Muir, who had officially notified the War Office of his planned retirement. Once his official duties were over, he intended to ride to London, collect his money from the Bank of England, and find his way to the new United States. His first choice of destination was Charleston. Muir's second was any other city in the former British Colony.

CELTIC SEA, FOURTH WEEK OF JANUARY 1783

The thermometer on the binnacle said the air temperature was 30^0 Fahrenheit. *Zephyr* had been sailing in the cold air all night, and the railing around the quarterdeck was cold to the touch. Low clouds brought a mist that frosted any exposed surface. When Jaco came on deck at first light, the mist had turned to drizzle and then a light rain.

Jaco estimated that the long North Atlantic swells were only about two feet, top to bottom. *Zephyr* was cutting through them nicely with a steady, up-and-down motion that he absorbed easily with his legs.

He shivered as he looked at the tops of the bulwarks and railings, which were now thinly coated with ice, along with the masts and booms. While what was on the ship might make a nice painting, the ice shrieked danger. Ice made the schooner top heavy, and a strong gust of wind coming over its port beam could cause *Zephyr* to capsize even with its daggerboards out.

Fighting panic because he was sailing in a weather condition he'd never seen before, his mind raced with ideas. First, he ordered Bosun Preston to ensure that the three dagger boards, one under each mast, were fully down. The resistance to sideways movement caused by the square footage of the daggerboards would help keep the schooner from capsizing.

Next, he called the watch on deck. Miserable as the conditions were, they had to keep the ice from coating the masts and sails.

Sheets were loosened and shaken, sending small tube-shaped chunks of ice flying. One at a time, halyards were released and shaken. Gravity pulled the gaff booms down, flexing the canvas sails and breaking the ice coated sails, which had been let out to reduce the heel.

Still not satisfied his crew was staying ahead of the ice, Jaco had sailors bang on each boom with belaying pins to knock off any accumulated ice. The top of the bulwarks received the same hammering.

For a few moments, he debated changing course to get out from the freezing drizzle. But which way? He could not see more than a quarter mile.

Jaco had no choice but to continue to sail toward Brest, less than a day away. He had the crew working in two shifts, one below warming up and enjoying a ration of rum while the other half cleared the ice. Weight above the waterline was the enemy, and according to the inclinometer, *Zephyr* was heeled nine degrees to port, one more than normal for this sail trim and tack.

The freezing rain became worse. When the halyards were released to be freed of ice, the jib, now heavy with ice, came crashing down. Small, jagged sheets of frozen water ¼" thick flew around. Thankfully, none of his sailors were hurt.

The mainmast's main sail wouldn't come down. Neither would the mizzen mainsail. The ice had stiffened them into a large, curved boards. The weight of the gaff boom didn't cause either sail to bend.

Sailors scampered up the ratlines and banged on the sail. Nothing worked.

Even Abner Jeffords, who was taking his turn at the wheel, looked worried. Having grown up in New England on fishing boats that went out all year long, *Zephyr's* senior quartermaster had never seen this type of ice before. "Cap'n, if we tack to reverse our course, we let the booms and sails swing freely before stopping them suddenly. The stop may be enough to break loose the ice. Once the ice falls off, we tack back to our course to Brest."

"Good idea, Mr. Jeffords, let's try it!" Jaco yelled for his bosun and explained the plan to him.

The booms for the fore and mizzen masts came around. As they did, the ice fell off in thin sheets, covering the deck with shards. Now, *Zephyr* had its main sails on its fore and mizzen masts set on a starboard tack and one – the mainsail on the mainmast – positioned if the ship was on a port tack.

Zephyr slowed abruptly, its booms banging freely, broadside to the waves. The ship rolled once and then a second time much farther than the first. Jeffords calmly called out as if it happened every day in just loud enough so that only Jaco could hear, "Cap'n, we heeled fourteen degrees."

Both men knew that if the schooner passed 20^0, *Zephyr* would be in danger of capsizing. If the ship rolled onto its side, they would be swimming in the cold, 45^0 Fahrenheit water.

Ropes were slid between the bottom of the sail and the mainmasts boom. Everyone on board was assigned a position on a line. It took several coordinated yanks before the boom came free, sending more sheets of ice flying through the air. Some flipped slowly in the wind before they shattered on the deck or fell into the gray-blue sea.

The freezing rain continued. Jaco joined the crew banging on the bulwarks with belaying pins until he felt it was time to tack again. This time, all the sails behaved, and again, showered the deck with thin pieces of ice that, due to the temperature, would not melt soon.

To keep the freezing rain from freezing the ice to the deck, Bosun Preston had the crew use planks as brooms to push the ice to the edge of the deck next to the bulwarks. Jaco waited for the hourglass to be turned, and the bell rung before ordering *Zephyr* to tack back to its base course. The loose ice slid across the deck as the schooner heeled.

The crew was so busy trying to keep their ship from capsizing that no one paid much attention to the ship's bells. The fight against the ice marched through the last hour of the Morning Watch, through the Forenoon Watch, and then into the Afternoon Watch.

Suddenly, even maybe miraculously, the freezing rain ended just as Cato Cooper, who took over from Jeffords, rang two bells. Jaco looked at the thermometer, and the liquid showed that it was now 25^0 Fahrenheit, five degrees cooler than when the freezing rain started. He looked at the gray sky and wondered if, instead of freezing rain, would *Zephyr* soon be covered in snow?

With the ship back on course toward Brest, Jaco wasn't sure which was worse - summer thunderstorms and their gusty winds or freezing rain. "God," he thought as he looked to the sky, "I think I hate sailing in the winter more!"

GOSPORT, FIRST WEEK OF FEBRUARY 1783

Emily heard the sharp knock at the door to Smythe & Son's office and when she looked up, she could see the Royal Mail letter carrier through the window. Emily Smythe, now officially divorced and having legally resumed using her maiden name, blotted the ink on the ledger where she was making an entry and called out. "Coming."

She took a shilling coin from her purse and gave it to the carrier, who handed her three letters. Olivia Smythe came around to the front room, which was more of an entry hall than a room. "Who are the letters from?"

Emily held out one of the three letters. "This is for Darren." Then she held up a second. "This is to me from Melody Winters."

Olivia knew that Emily and Melody had been corresponding regularly ever since Emily returned from Charleston. "And this one is from Reyna Laredo. It is also addressed to me, but Father should probably read it too."

"Well, then. Let us see what the young Doctor Laredo has to say."

Emily,

I am sure that you know that the British Army has left Charleston and that peace negotiations between our two countries have been underway for some time. According to my future father-in-law, the most difficult issues have been resolved. Now, it is only a matter of working out the details so that both Parliament and the Continental Congress can authorize them to be signed. Once that is done, this damnable war will be officially over.

Therefore, I believe it is time to start AMJP. My correspondence with the three medical schools has been promising. All are amenable to offering students a discounted set of Smythe & Son's Instruments to each graduating student and introductions to Smythe & Son's medicines whose use is taught at the schools. American Medical will have to pay the schools a fee for this license but I see that as a cost of doing business that will be recouped through more sales. The schools will provide a list of graduates to whom we can make entreaties to buy our existing and any new products we may create.

My father and I have given some thought as to where the factory could be located. It should be near or close to a source of coal and quality iron ore. There are many options here in the new United States, some better than others. Again, where is a subject better discussed in person than via letter.

My question to you is, when do you think you and the boys will be coming to Charleston? We have two grandmothers-to-be who would be delighted to help you raise Jeremy, Jeremiah and Jonah.

Please let me know what you are planning.

Your friend and excited and soon partner-to-be,

Reyna

Olivia stood by quietly, waiting for her daughter to finish reading. Emily handed the letter to her mother. She started to smile and then realized the seriousness of what she was about to say. "Mother, I think I need to make travel arrangements."

AMSTERDAM, SECOND WEEK OF FEBRUARY 1783

As soon as he rode out of the British Army depot, Muir had a plan. Get to Amsterdam, find the Laredo Shipping and South Carolina Import and Export offices, and book passage to Charleston.

Conceptually, this was simple, but execution was far more difficult than he originally imagined. First, he had to ride to London and visit the War Office. Because he was a senior officer and didn't enter from the Shropshire Army Depot, the commanding officer wouldn't allow him to retire from the Shropshire facility. Muir was told that he could only retire from where he enlisted in Scotland or the War Office in London.

London was 135 miles away to the southeast and the preferred choice. Six days after leaving Shropshire, with five years' back pay in a money belt and his campaign chest strapped to the back of a pack horse, Muir dismounted at a British Army barracks near the Tower of London.

After a hot bath and a chance to wash his red uniform coat, Colonel Rafer Muir presented himself with his papers at the War Office early the next morning. He refused to be put off by two days of toing and froing as one clerk passed him to another until, Muir demanded to see a senior officer who could approve his retirement. Irritated by the lack of progress, Muir was about to start threatening the clerks with bodily harm when he was ushered into a brigadier's office. The general handed him his retirement certificate and asked where his pension should be deposited. Oddly, the general did not wish him well and for a few seconds, he wondered why before he pushed the thought out of his mind. *He was now OUT of the British Army.*

According to the clock on the Tower Bridge, Muir walked out of the War office at precisely two in the afternoon. By three, he was standing in a tailor shop having some, as he said, decent clothes made. He defrayed some of the cost by trading his uniforms, made from top-quality Scottish wool for his new civilian clothes.

The next day, he walked the docks, inquiring about ships going to Amsterdam. Finding one leaving in two days, he booked passage.

Once in the Dutch city, Muir rented one of the many wheelbarrows parked in a row to carry his chest and other belongings. When asked where Laredo Shipping was located, the owner of the wheelbarrow rental business pointed to a building less than 200 yards away. The Continental and Swedish flags made it easy to identify.

Two brass plaques were at eye level on the right side of the door. One said South Carolina Imports and Exports, the other Laredo Shipping.

I am in the right place. Step 1, retire, and Step 2, get to Amsterdam are now complete. Step 3, get to Charleston is next.

No one answered his knocks, so Rafer cracked open the heavy oak door. Inside, he could hear a baby crying. The retired Army colonel called out, "Allo, anyone here."

A woman with blond hair entered the room holding a baby she was clearly nursing. *"Wie ben je?"* Who are you in Dutch.

"My name is Rafer Muir, and I want to book passage to Charleston, South Carolina."

The woman took a deep breath and said in English, "Wait, please." Then she called out in Dutch, *"Eric, er is een mann vor je."* Eric there is a man for you. Then turning to Rafer, she said in English. "Sorry, my English is still not good."

A tallish man with light brown hair entered the entranceway, wiping his hands. What Rafer did not know is that this was a typical Dutch business building. On the ground floor, South Carolina Imports and Exports and Laredo Shipping had a large warehouse that could store enough cargo to fill the holds of six ships. To reach the warehouse from the front, one went through the office. In the back, there was a dock on a canal onto which cargo could be loaded onto smaller boats to take out to ships in the harbor. Laredo Shipping used the building as an office and when needed, rented "floorspace" from South Carolina Imports and Exports.

"Good morning, I am Eric Laredo, manager of Laredo Shipping's business here in The Netherlands and Sweden. What can I do for you?"

"I am Rafer Muir, and I'd like to book passage on the next ship you have going to Charleston." As much as he tried to hide it, his Scottish brogue and accent was noticeable.

"You're Scottish?"

"Aye, that I am."

Eric wondered if he was a British agent, and then his mind went back to the topic at hand. *Business is business, and passage is money.* "Our ship *Malmo* is scheduled to leave Amsterdam in a month. It will stop in Southampton to pick up cargo and passengers before going to Charleston. I can offer you passage in a single compartment for £25 that includes food and drink. Do you have a place to stay while you wait?"

"No, I just arrived a few hours ago."

Eric looked at the broad-shouldered man. "I need help in the warehouse, and I am willing to pay you five shillings a day for a ten-hour day. There is a room with several beds in the warehouse where you can sleep and several taverns where you can eat. Are you interested?"

Muir held up both his hands. "I accept your offer. I am not afraid to get my hands dirty."

"Good. We can start straight away." Eric pronounced the first word as if he was speaking Dutch. Then he said, "Oh, excuse me, this is my wife, Sera, and our son, Solomon."

Sera nodded and left. "Mr. Muir, may I ask how you found Laredo Shipping and why you want to go to Charleston?"

"You may. And the story best be told over a glass of whiskey or beer."

"Really, is it that interesting?"

"Aye, lad, it 'tis. It seems I know your brother Amos and sister Reyna quite well. And I am sure your grandmother Miriam, Shoshana Jacinto, and other friends and family will also vouch for me. When I arrive in Charleston, they said they would put me to work."

"When was the last time you saw them?"

"December of '82."

"Pray tell, sir, what were you doing in Charleston?"

"I was a colonel in the British Army. I retired as soon as I returned to England. After twenty years, I was tired of being sent from pillar to post and dodging musket balls and want to emigrate to the new country called the United States."

"I agree that is an interesting story. A drink is in order." Eric spoke loudly in Dutch. Rafer could hear Sera respond. A few minutes later, Sera, now without the baby, appeared with two glasses and a bottle of Scotch whiskey.

Rafer recognized the brand as Glenturret, which officially began distilling Scotch in 1775. Before then, the owners unofficially distilled whiskey and spent as much time dodging the English tax man as they did managing the fermentation process.

GOSPORT, THIRD WEEK OF FEBRUARY 1783

Now that her father had booked passage for her, Emily sat at her writing desk to compose two letters. The first part of the letter told Reyna that she would arrive on the Laredo-owned and Swedish-registered *Malmo* sometime in May.

The second topic covered was that a Smythe & Sons employee – Evyn Griffiths – would accompany her. He had come from an orphanage and joined Smythe & Sons as an apprentice. When Emily first entered the boy's name in the company's books, she wanted to use an 'i' or an 'a' as the second vowel, but Olivia said that the boy preferred the 'y'.

The 29-year-old Griffiths started working for Smythe & Sons at 12 as an apprentice. Along the way, he learned to be a draftsman and how to turn iron ore into high-quality steel. Once he mastered the forge, he learned to shape and grind pieces to match drawings.

Griffiths had married at 20, but his wife and child died three years ago. When he overheard Emily discussing collecting a set of drawings to take to Charleston, he asked if he could move to the new country. On the voyage, Evyn would serve as Emily's "escort."

The letter to Melody was much harder to write. She struggled for words to express her excitement about leaving England for the New World. She felt she could share her innermost thoughts with Melody and to some degree Reyna who would now be a business partner as well as a friend.

Melody,

I find it difficult to express my excitement about my new adventure. I can't wait to see you again.

If you have yet to hear, Pompeii is on its way to Portsmouth. What will happen when the ship arrives is anybody's guess. The British Parliament has already announced that the Royal Navy's budget will be significantly reduced with peace coming in North America. How that will affect Darren is anybody's guess. He did say that he would volunteer to leave the Navy and find his way to Charleston as fast as he could. I think the only thing that would stop this is if the French did something stupid as they are wont to do.

Evyn Griffiths, a Smythe's & Co. employee, the children, and I are booked on Laredo Shipping's Malmo, which should arrive in Charleston sometime in mid-May.

It is hard for my family in England to understand, but I can't wait to leave. Charleston will be a new beginning where I will be known as Emily Smythe, not by my married name. Like a bird leaving the nest for the first time, I will have a chance to spread my wings.

While I am sure there may be difficult, even hard times ahead, I am confident I can weather any storm.

To be frank, there is nothing left here for me in England. Remarrying? Hah!!! Any man who may be interested in me will want me to be a traditional wife and lift my skirts anytime they need pleasure.

That is simply not my lot. While I thoroughly enjoy the challenges of being a mother, I believe, as you do, there are other things us members of the fairer sex can aspire, no CAN do. If Reyna, with my help, can make AMTP successful, we will take one small step to be seen as equal to men.

See you soon.

Emily

BREST, THIRD WEEK OF FEBRUARY 1783

For Jaco, life was a shuttle between Brest and Philadelphia. Two to three weeks at sea, a few days, maybe a week in port, and then back to sea

In Brest, he'd learn the latest news from London from week-old copies of English newspapers Gardner acquired. The Bostonian would also have news from the ongoing negotiations in Paris.

In Philadelphia, if Jaco had time, he attended the sessions in the Continental Congress when the topic of peace negotiations was debated. Then he waited for new dispatches to be written before *Zephyr* set sail for Brest. His sailing orders were always the same - get to Brest as fast as possible, avoid capture, and do the same on the return trip.

As important as this mission was, Jaco was bored and impatient. No matter how often or well his father or his friends explained the issues, he found it hard to understand why the process of finalizing the treaty took so long. He believed the British were dragging their feet.

LONDON, FIRST WEEK OF MARCH 1783

Recently promoted to Rear Admiral of the Blue, Stacey Davidson, was surprised when a senior captain appeared in the doorway to his office. The captain apologized for the intrusion and asked if Admiral Davidson would come to the office of the Second Naval Lord, the second most senior officer in the Royal Navy.

The captain knew better than to address Rear Admiral Davidson by his title, the Duke of Somerset. Davidson believed he earned his rank, and his title was inherited because he was lucky enough to be born into England's nobility. And, while his title was important, he was proud to have worked his way up the officer ranks from midshipman to Rear Admiral of the Blue. Before being assigned to the Admiralty in the middle of 1782, he'd commanded a squadron that blockaded Marseille and Toulon. In several actions, his ships captured two French frigates and one two-decker as prizes without a loss.

Davidson reported to the man responsible for all personnel matters, which in 1783 included recruiting seamen, midshipmen, selection men for promotion above lieutenant, pay, and discipline. The Duke of Somerset handled all officer assignments for the Navy.

The Second Naval Lord waved toward a chair in front of his desk as if to say, please sit there. "Thank you for coming, Admiral…" The Second Naval Lord slid a sheet of paper in front of him and looked at Davidson, who had just turned 38. Davidson's sandy brown hair had started to gray noticeably.

"Apparently, Lord Shelburne's government believes peace is about to break out. The Admiralty has been notified that its budget will be cut severely once the terms of the treaties with the rebels, the French, and their Spanish and Dutch friends are worked out."

Davidson forced himself not to react. He'd experienced cuts in fleet size at the end of the Seven Year's War. Parliament was always in a hurry to reduce expenditures, and the British Army and Royal Navy were at the top of the list.

"Our sources tell us the sense in Parliament is to cut the Navy's budget by fifty percent. I am sure your brother, a member of the House of Lords, has told you the same thing. Half the bloody fleet will wind up in ordinary or sent to the breaker's yard if this comes to pass. Therefore, the First Naval Lord wants to stop all promotions above lieutenant and prepare a list of those captains to be retained and another with those to be put on half-pay or pensioned off."

Davidson anticipated this would happen. "Sir, I suspected this was coming our way and have prepared a list of captains who should be retained based on their ability as well as those, due to their length of service, should be asked to retire."

The Second Naval Lord narrowed his gaze. "I agree that anyone who has been in the service for more than 25 years should be forced to retire. That should be done immediately. After that, I suggest we prune the tree, so to speak, from the bottom. We can't ask those who have been in the service most of their lives to suddenly be beached."

"Sir, I disagree. It is to our benefit to keep those who have done well and demonstrated their leadership, courage, and tactical skills, regardless of their time in service. Those that rank lower are the ones put on half-pay or retired."

"I, and the First Naval Lord, wish to reward length of service. However, for those top performers whom you think the Navy should retain, offer a reduction in rank – captains to commanders, commanders to lieutenants. That should placate them."

"Again, sir, I must respectfully disagree. It is hard to accept a demotion for no reason other than budget cuts and be forced to re-climb the ladder. I fear we will lose many, if not most, of these men who will be sorely needed if we have to do battle again with our friends on the other side of the English Channel."

"Admiral, I take your point. Start with the older chaps first. Then, make the list as directed, and let us see how big a butcher's bill Parliament will create. That will tell us how many young men we can keep in the service."

Davidson nodded and left the office, believing many fine officers would see the demotions as an insult and leave the service. He was sure another war with France would come, just not when.

CHAPTER 24

- A NEW MAN IN HER LIFE

SOUTHAMPTON, SECOND WEEK OF MARCH 1783

The gray skies and rain that made Gosport a dismal place to live gave way to blue skies and puffy clouds as the coach traveled farther north toward Southampton. Emily's youngest son Jonah, lay across her lap, fast asleep and tired from the excitement and sadness that hung over their departure from Gosport earlier in the morning.

Rather than have his daughter and grandchildren ride in an open wagon, Lester Smythe hired the coachman and his carriage drawn by two horses to take them to Southampton. Inside the coach, the padded seats were covered with worn leather that was polished and smooth. Each side had a door that latched as well as window frames. If it was raining, canvas shades would be pulled down to keep most of the water out.

Olivia Smythe fought back the tears as she hugged her three grandsons and daughter for what she hoped was not the last time. Lester Smythe held Emily at arms-length, looked at her, and said, "Emily, I am confident you will do well and make us all proud."

In the front seat, Jeffrey, age five, initially sat with his arms crossed and pouting. His sullen disposition caused by the realization that he would not see his playmates in Gosport again had changed as the green English countryside rolled by. Now, he was looking out the window, taking in the scenes he'd never seen before, and was excited he was going to spend a month on a ship.

Jeremiah, the oldest at age 11, did little to contain his excitement about leaving England and going to this new place called America. He adored his uncle Darren and whenever they were together, Jeremiah peppered Darren with questions whenever he could about where he'd been and what he'd seen. He wanted to be an explorer, and the United States of America, with its vast, yet to be explored land would be, he hoped, his future playground.

Behind the carriage, Evyn Griffiths sat next to the driver of the wagon carrying all their baggage. Emily had two chests with her clothes and one each for the children that would go in the hold. There were also chests with her book collection and another with the Delft China and a few other items she did not want to leave behind.

Each Smythe had a separate chest that would be placed in their cabin. Besides clothes, Emily's had a few books to read and her diary.

Also on the wagon, driven by one of Smythe & Sons employees, carried a chest containing drawings and molds and a book with the formulas the firm used to create the medicines it marketed. Evyn Griffiths' two wooden boxes of his belongings was also on the wagon. When he was told that Smythe & Sons would honor his request to go to America, he allowed himself to say, "Adzooks!!!"

From that moment, Griffiths was more ebullient than usual, and yesterday, he asked to see Lester Smythe privately. Evyn Griffiths was a 10-year-old and an only child when cholera claimed both his parents.

Evyn had a knack for drawing which led to him being trained as a draftsman and then, later as craftsman that turned ideas into working instruments. He saw going to America as a chance for promotion and opportunity.

Rather than recount the conversation, Lester Smythe told his daughter that Evyn is the perfect man to help AMIP. He gave the young man a draft for £250 as a bonus to deposit in the Bank of South Carolina.

When the carriage pulled onto the dock after taking the better part of a day to reach Southampton, *Malmo* was already at the quay. Its crew was loading bolts of cloth into the forward hold. Seeing the carriage and wagon from the *Malmo's* quarterdeck, Pierce Simmes, captain of the merchant ship, walked down the gangway to greet his passengers. The 39-year-old Simmes was a stocky man, about 5' 10" tall who walked with confidence.

When *Malmo* arrived in Southampton, he was informed by the Laredo Shipping agent that Ms. Emily Smythe, her three children, and a man named Evyn Griffiths would ride the ship to Charleston as his new passengers.

After the coachman and his assistant helped Evyn stack the chests on the pier, Emily handed the coachman two gold Guineas (worth £1 and

1 shilling) after thanking him for the smooth, pleasant, and fast ride to Southampton. Even though this was only her third voyage on a ship, Emily felt like an old hand as she looked at *Malmo*.

Simmes bowed slightly with his hands clasped behind his back. "I am Captain Pierce Simmes of the merchant ship *Malmo*. I presume you are Miss Emily Smythe, along with Masters Jeremiah, Jeffrey, and Jonah. Nodding toward Evyn Griffiths, who was standing slightly behind Emily. "And you are Mr. Evyn Griffiths."

Emily nodded. "Aye, that we are."

"Excellent." Seeing the chests neatly stacked on the pier, Simmes addressed the two adults. "If you will show me which ones go to which cabin, I will have them delivered as required. The rest will go in the hold."

Before Emily could answer, Simmes yelled out four names, and the seamen ran down the gangway. She pointed out which chests would go into her cabin she would share with her boys. Griffiths did the same, and Simmes pointed to the gangway. "Please, we have almost finished loading and will leave on the outgoing tide at first light tomorrow morning."

On the main deck, Simmes stopped. "Miss Smythe, is this your first sea voyage?"

Emily shook her head. "No. I went to Charleston and back last year. But for the others, this is their first."

"May I enquire as to which ship you sailed?"

"*Star of India* to Charleston and *Queen Boleyn* on the return."

"Ahhhhh, I am familiar with *Star of India*." Simmes paused and then continued. "*Malmo* is bigger than *Star of India* and I presume, *Queen Boleyn*. Fully laden, she'll weigh about eighteen hundred tons. The main deck of the ship is just under two hundred feet long, and fifty feet wide. We draw about eighteen feet."

He didn't tell his new passengers that *Malmo* had the structure to be converted easily into a large frigate carrying forty-four 12-pounders or thirty-six 18-pounders. Nor did he say that the ship carried no armament to maximize the cargo it carried.

Simmes waved his hand. "*Malmo* was built in Charleston, and we escaped a week before the British occupied the city. *Malmo* makes between seven and eight knots; two to three faster than the typical Indiaman."

The proud captain of *Malmo* explained that his ship would make the 4,325-mile journey in 26 days versus the usual 36 needed by slower East Indiamen. The difference in time wasn't lost on Emily.

"Please, enough of my prattling on about my ship, allow me to show you to your cabin and where you will dine."

Malmo's captain said that the ship had eight compartments, which he called staterooms. Passengers had their own lounge, which during mealtimes, doubled as a dining room. The ship's officers ate with the crew in the berthing area. Simmes mentioned that all but one of the eight staterooms were occupied and that most of *Malmo's* passengers had gone ashore but would be back before dark.

Once Simmes excused himself, Emily and her children waited patiently in their stateroom, which had a bed where she would sleep and a bunk bed. Jeremiah, being the oldest, would have the top bunk, and Jonah and Jeffrey would share the bottom.

With their chests unpacked and lashed down, Emily led the boys down the passageway and up the companionway to the main deck. Both Jeremiah and Jonah were fascinated as they watched the crew load heavy barrels in nets off the pier, lift them up over the side, and then lower them down into the hold. Jeremiah led Jonah by the hand as they ventured to the edge of the forward hold where he pointed out to his younger brother where their chests were stacked.

Rotting seaweed and the smell of garbage in the water mingled with seawater made Emily think of Gosport and Portsmouth. She wondered for a few moments what her mother was doing.

Jeremiah ran back to the cabin to get his journal to sketch what he saw. Proudly, he showed his drawing, which to Emily was not the work of a young boy, but of someone who may have talent.

"Well done, my son." Jeremiah smiled at the compliment from his mother. He hurried to the top step of the companionway from the main deck to the quarterdeck, where he could sketch the forward half of the ship.

With her two youngest boys on each side, she walked them around the entrance to the hold, pointing out the things she remembered from her two previous trips. They ended up at the aft companionway, and she was looking at Jeremiah's latest drawing when her oldest son bobbed his head as if to say, "Mother, turn around. Someone is looking at you."

Emily hoped her sons didn't see her reaction when she saw Rafer Muir with half a dozen books cradled in his arms. "Mrs. Burdette, this is a most pleasant surprise. What are you doing on *Malmo*?"

Emily flushed noticeably and felt a stirring in her loins she'd not felt since the last conversation she had with Lieutenant Colonel Muir. She took a deep breath to get hold of herself. "I could ask you the same thing, Lieutenant Colonel Muir."

"Aye, 'tis a fair question. I retired from the British Army as a full colonel and am headed to Charleston to, hopefully, find honest work?" The "and you?" was implied.

"Congratulations, Colonel Muir, I am no longer Mrs. Burdette. The boys and I go by Smythe which is my maiden name."

Muir smiled at the attractive woman standing in front of him. "I see. That is a good thing, I hope."

"Aye, that it is."

Muir nodded his head. "Well then, we shall see enough of each other over the next few weeks, so I shall deposit these books in my stateroom and see you at dinner."

Emily's head followed the ruggedly good-looking Scotsman as he disappeared down the companionway. Her reaction did not go unnoticed by her two oldest children. Jeremiah blurted, "Who is Colonel Muir?"

Emily again blushed and stammered for a few seconds before saying without thinking, "Colonel Muir is a fine man." Realizing that may not be enough, she said she met the good Colonel in Charleston last year.

"Do you like him?"

The words came out of her mouth before her brain could stop them. "I do."

"Mummy, is he going to be our new father?"

Emily tried not react as she realized her mouth had opened wide. Were my feelings for Colonel Muir that obvious to my son? Would adults see it the same way. No words came out. Emily didn't want to say anything that would cause her son to ask more questions, none of which she could answer. However, seeing Colonel Muir meant going to America was off to a good start.

PORTSMOUTH, THIRD WEEK OF MARCH 1783

When his small convoy of ships came around the Isle of Wight, Darren could see the gray-white stones of the ramparts of Southsea Castle in the early morning light. The steady westerly wind made it easy for the merchant ships escorted by his small squadron - *Pompeii, Wilder, Ashley,* and *Madeira*

- were escorting to sail up The Solent to Southampton. He ordered that the Union Jack be dipped as a salute to the seven merchantmen.

Now free of his escort duties, Darren examined the entrance to Portsmouth Harbor. From a mile outside, it looked like a forest of barren trees. He didn't try to count the number of ships anchored in the bay, but guessed it had to be more than 20. Space to anchor would be at a premium.

With so many ships already at anchor, he suspected what was afoot. Were they going to sally out en masse against the French or Spanish navies? Or were all these ships being surveyed so a decision could be made to break them up or 'store' them for use in the future.

The docked ships suggested that the Royal Navy would decide whether he would be put on half-pay. Senior captains were kept in the past, and junior ones like him, along with those with less than 20 years' service, were sent out to pasture. Years could pass before they were recalled.

A small sailboat came through the narrow entrance and headed toward *Pompeii*. Through his Dollond spyglass, Darren saw an officer in the stern, two sailors in the bow, and a lieutenant sitting amidships. They were, he presumed, en route to his squadron to guide them to where the port admiral wanted them anchored.

The sailboat led the frigate past the two and three-deckers to the end of the row of frigates. The lieutenant used a trumpet when he pointed where he wanted *Pompeii* to anchor in the bay's north end. Darren's chart indicated there was only about 20 feet of water under his frigate's keel at low tide.

Darren was watching the men stow the sails in what was known as a harbor furl when *Pompeii's* Third Lieutenant, Judah Burton called out. "Captain, signal from the base commander asking you to repair to the port headquarters, forthwith."

"Thank you, Mr. Burton. Once the sails are all furled and the boats in the water, I shall go ashore and see what our Naval Lordships have in store for us."

He didn't want to add that it probably wasn't good news. He assumed that whatever his orders were, they would interfere with his hopes to go to Charleston as soon as possible.

Darren glanced overhead, and the puffy clouds that greeted their entrance to Portsmouth had darkened noticeably. Maybe, he thought, they shared his mood.

Pompeii was anchored a half mile from the base landing, so one of the longboats, ably sailed by *Pompeii's* quartermaster – Hiram Spivey - and two seamen took him ashore. Before he left, Shamus O'Steen, *Pompeii's* Second Lieutenant, handed him the list of supplies the frigate needed to return to sea.

On the way to the base's headquarters, Darren stopped at the victualling office on the way to the base's headquarters. An officious commander looked at the list of supplies needed and then at Darren, saying, "Captain, we'll get to this when we can. In case you haven't noticed, we have a fleet of ships in the harbor. So, unless you can show me sailing orders sending you to sea in the next fortnight, *Pompeii's* request will be filled in good time. Right now, we are filling only provisioning orders signed by Admiral Arthur."

The officer's comment meant *Pompeii* would be anchored for some time. Darren walked into the three-story brick naval base's headquarters building with mixed emotions.

Inside, Darren told the lieutenant on watch that he was ordered to report to the headquarters building. The lieutenant nodded, checked a list, and handed him a letter before he asked him to wait until he was called. The Duke of Somerset's logo was pressed into the wax seal.

Darren was about to pop open the letter when Admiral Arthur's aide came to attention in front of where he was sitting. "Captain Smythe, Admiral Arthur will see you now."

The bulky admiral who was in his fifties, pointed to a chair and then held up a decanter of port, "A taste?"

The young captain, who would turn 25, in July, nodded.

The admiral poured two glasses and held his glass, "Welcome home, Captain Smythe."

"Thank you. Home, it 'tis."

Arthur decided to get right to the point after taking a long sip of the tawny dark red wine and enjoying its sweet taste. "Captain Smythe, Rear Admiral Davidson asked me to speak to you directly. Parliament had decided to slice the Royal Navy's budget by forty-six percent. As a result, many admirals, captains, and commanders are being beached. Most captains are ordered to come into this building. When they arrive, they are ushered into the office of my captain in charge of personnel where they are given their pay and told they are leaving the navy, forthwith. Admiral Davidson tried to save a cadre of young, capable officers like yourself, but was soundly rebuffed. After an acrimonious argument with the First Sea Lord, he was lucky to keep his flag."

Darren didn't respond and suspected, as in the past, that older captains would be rewarded for their tenure. Those who were young, and the future of the navy would be pushed aside. In the next conflict, a new generation of officers and sailors would pay with their lives as they fought with outmoded tactics and made mistakes that could have been prevented had the Royal Navy kept the young tigers that consistently defeated England's enemies. The Continentals gave a good account of themselves but didn't have enough ships or crews to defeat the Royal Navy. Instead, they dealt the Royal Navy and the King's merchant marine a series of painful pinpricks that hampered its ability to support the British Army.

Admiral Arthur continued speaking, bringing Darren back to the room. "Unfortunately, as one of the more junior captains, you are on the wrong list. If it is any consolation, I am also a casualty and was told that I am retiring on June first."

"So, what about a billet in the Admiralty, or am I going straight to half pay?"

"Yes. You will be relieved of your command tomorrow or the next day, and your crew will be paid off. Do not go ashore to visit your parents or say anything to your crew or your officers. Only the lieutenants will be offered positions and sent to those ships the First Naval Lord wishes to keep. Those few positions for captains are going to those far more senior than you. And, if you wish to stay on active duty, you must accept an assignment as a lieutenant because you spent less than three years as one."

The Royal Navy made the decision for him. Going back to being a lieutenant was unacceptable.

Darren flushed with anger despite his effort to control himself. "Admiral, since our Parliament is so parsimonious, I will save them even more money. They can keep my pension."

"Captain, I will pretend I didn't hear that. Admiral Davidson wanted me to make sure you don't do something rash. As I understand it, he will be here in a day or two to interview those willing to accept a reduction in rank to make assignments. I know he will want to see you."

"As a civilian or as a Naval Officer?"

Admiral Arthur's expression changed from compassion to annoyance bordering on anger. "Captain Smythe, don't be a bloody fool. Admiral Davidson thinks the world of you and wants to help. I strongly suggest you hold your tongue."

"Aye, sir. I will. Admiral Davidson has been a great help to me, but I must say, this is a shock." *Only because the Royal Navy is making it easy for me to go to Charleston and marry Melody. I fully expected to be retained in active service.*

Admiral Arthur chuckled. "Aye, Captain. You should see it from my chair. It is bloody chaos. You would think that a service that has kicked Frenchie's arse more times than I can remember could get its sums to add up on reducing its force. But, Captain Smythe, that will be someone else's battle, not ours."

As he walked from the Royal Navy's Portsmouth base headquarters to the landing, he could see a sailboat pull away from the nest of boats tied up alongside *Pompeii*.

Part of him was sad because he would no longer be a Royal Navy captain within days, something he had dreamed of becoming since he was a little boy. Another part of his mind was happy because his orders, albeit generated by his brain, were now to find the fastest passage to Charleston. He thought if he could catch a transport headed toward New York, he could get there and take a packet down to Charleston. Possibilities and timelines ran through his mind as he waited for the long boat to come to the landing.

Once back aboard *Pompeii*, Darren was noncommittal as to what their next set of orders might entail. What saddened him was that the reverie and comradeship built on a combination of a sense of duty, a desire to fulfill their ship's orders, and a shared sense of adventure and danger was ending.

After the other officers retired for the night, Darren sat at his desk to read the letter from Admiral Davidson.

Captain Smythe,

I assume that by the time you read this letter, you will have talked to Admiral Arthur and been given the sad news. During the last few weeks, I have fought hard to prevent what I believe is a colossally stupid and idiotic decision by the First and Second Naval Lords. In the end, despite the facts I presented, the strength of my logic, and the passion in my entreaties to retain many young officers such as yourself, I was overruled.

So, as a good naval officer, I, too, must step back, say a cheery aye, aye, sir, and follow orders despite how despicable and short-sighted I find them.

I am surprised that they still want me around in my same billet. Maybe it is because no one wants this wretched job.

You and I have spent many an hour on the quarterdeck, both together, and believe our service should, no must, retain the best and brightest officers, even if it means asking others who have been in the service longer to step aside.

It pains me to write this letter because I saw a flag someday soon in your future. Already, twice you've demonstrated your abilities as a commodore. Alas, as you found out today, this is not to be.

If I were a betting man, within 10 years, we and the French will be at each other's throats again. When that happens, this country and the Royal Navy will need your skill and leadership.

So, I implore you to write a letter to tell this office and, by definition, the Admiralty where you will be hanging your hat. I suspect I know where, and if that is your choice, so be it. Nevertheless, I hope England can count on you if, and when that time comes .

Stacy Davidson
Rear Admiral of the Blue

Darren read the letter a second time. Knowing the Duke of Somerset, he could read the man's emotion into the letter. This letter came from a man who helped him in many ways and whom he respected a great deal. The two came from different worlds but found friendship and mutual respect on the quarterdeck.

It had been a long day. In the morning, he would write a response and post a letter to Melody.

PORTSMOUTH, FOURTH WEEK OF MARCH 1783

The few days that Admiral Arthur noted turned into five. Darren Smythe was tired of making excuses to his officers and crew as to why their victualling order was not being delivered or why they were riding at anchor. He was also tired of the delay which was keeping him from getting on with the next stage of his life.

Pompeii was shipshape, and Bosun Louttit was running out of "projects" to keep the crew busy. Idleness and a lack of purpose would soon send morale plummeting. Fights would begin, and he'd have discipline problems to deal with to go with the excuse-making.

Darren was spending his last days as a captain in the Royal Navy as a prisoner on his own ship and did not like it at all. He would have preferred to leave the Royal Navy at a time of his choosing, but that was not to be. The days let him focus on how he would travel to Charleston, South Carolina.

Breakfast was over, and his cabin was cleaned up. Since they were in port, the eight chairs arranged around the table that dominated the cabin's center were left in place. At sea, once a meal or a meeting was finished, they were stacked and lashed to the starboard bulkhead in two racks of four.

Two bells on the Forenoon Watch had just rung when there was a knock on his cabin door. Darren had just put on his uniform coat because he had informed Bosun Loutitt that he would inspect the berthing deck and gun deck at five bells of the Forenoon Watch. "Come in."

Seaman Antonio Drago opened the door and stood at attention. "Captain, the base just signaled *Pompeii* to expect visitors. A longboat is headed our way with a captain and a commander on board."

"Very well. Please prepare to receive them and rig the bosun's chair to have it ready, if needed. Muster the officers and the crew on the main deck. I will be there shortly."

Darren was prepared for this moment. He had been living out of his sea chest since he left Rear Admiral Arthur's office. He carefully folded the blankets he'd had since he'd been a student at the Royal Naval Academy and placed them along with the sheet on his bunk as the top layer inside his sea chest. The last item he put in the oak chest was the latest volume of the journal he'd kept since he was a midshipman. With it latched, he took one last look around the cabin. Before he came out on deck, he stacked the boxes with his Dollond Sextant and spyglass on top of the one with the brace of pistols. They rested on his sea chest against which he leaned his sword.

With packing finished, Darren went to the quarterdeck to watch the boat approach, knowing its arrival meant the end of his naval career.

"Captain, any idea why these officers want to come to our ship?" The speaker was Lieutenant Christopher Abbott, who, with his other officers, is about to discover what is next in their careers.

"Mr. Abbott, I suspect all our lives are about to change."

Darren didn't wait for an answer. The longboat with a hawk-faced captain who ran the base's personnel office had climbed up the side and stood in the hatch. Loutitt blew "all call" on his whistle, and then his assistant rang the ship's bell two times. When the tones died down, Loutitt spoke loudly; some might think it was a forced bellow, but the Scotsman had a naturally loud voice.

"Captain, Royal Navy, Arrrrrrrriving."

Compared to Darren, who was lean and 5'10", the post captain was scrawny, almost emaciated, and Darren suspected he was in his forties, but whose gray hair made him look much older.

"Captain Smythe, I am Captain Coslett, and this is Commander Zinke. Please ask your officers to join me on *Pompeii's* quarterdeck and have the crew muster aft of the mainmast.

Darren did so and followed the senior man up the companionway and stood next to him, facing forward while the crew moved aft. He looked up at the mizzen mast and the commodore's pennant for some reason. Today would be the last time that flag flew over his ship.

Coslett looked at the crew and whispered so none of the other officers arrayed behind them could hear. "Captain Smythe, I presume you know what is about to happen?"

"I do. However, I would like to keep my commodore's pennant after it is hauled down."

"I didn't know you were a commodore."

"Aye, twice. *Wilder, Ashley,* and *Madeira* are, or were, in my squadron. We've been escorting convoys from New York. Before I commanded the frigates *Gladius* with *Pilum* and *Hasta* on a hunting expedition."

Coslett nodded and spoke softly while facing forward. "I did not know. Absolutely, you may keep your commodore's flag. This evolution pains me. Each time, it becomes harder, and I must steel myself to be cold and ruthless."

Seeing the crew was mustered and settled down, Coslett began speaking in a loud voice that Darren didn't think would come from his emaciated frame. "Crew of *Pompeii*, it is my sad duty to relieve Commodore Darren Smythe of his duties as both a commodore and as captain of *Pompeii*. He is being relieved, not because of his performance which has, as I am told, been outstanding, but because our civilian masters in Parliament have decided that the Royal Navy should be reduced in size. As a result, *Pompeii* will be inspected and, if still seaworthy, put in ordinary. As members of its crew, you will be posted to barracks ships where those who wish to remain in the Navy, will be assigned to other ships. The rest will be paid off. All the officers will keep their commissions except Commodore Smythe, who will be placed on half-pay. Commander Zinke will be your new commanding officer whose sole purpose is to supervise the movement of the crew ashore and the subsequent survey of the frigate. Bosun, please pipe All Call before we haul down Commodore Smythe's flag."

Grimly, Darren watched the white flag with the red cross and red circle in the upper left corner slowly come down. Quartermaster Spivey carefully folded the flag and gave it to his now-former captain. "Sir, serving under you has been an honor and pleasure."

"Thank you, Mr. Spivey."

Coslett then gave his next order. "Commodore Smythe, please say your good-byes to the officers and join me in the long boat. Do you need to pack?"

"No, Captain, I do not. My belongings are in my cabin, ready to go."

"Excellent, Commander Zinke, please have Captain Smythe's effects transferred ashore in one of *Pompeii's* ship's boats forthwith."

A line of men wanted to shake Darren's hand as he walked to the hatch. Next to the end, Bosun Loutitt held both of Darren's hands in his massive paws. "Captain, I've not served with a finer officer than you. God bless you, sir, and may you enjoy fair winds and following seas for the rest of your life."

Chris Abbott, the last man on deck before the hatch, grinned as he spoke. "Sir, it has been an honor, and enjoy the lovely lass, Melody. She is quite a find."

As he turned to face the crew, someone yelled, "Three cheers for Captain Smythe." Darren hoped no one could see the tears in his eyes. Once in the long boat, he looked toward shore so neither of the seamen in the boat could see his face and the tears coming down his cheeks. It was only when Darren stepped onto the landing, that he turned to look at *Pompeii*.

He went with Captain Coslett into the base's headquarters and signed the form stating he was on half-pay. He initialed the line that said he was refusing the pay, which by the acceptance of the pension, required that he live in England. Darren scratched a note saying that if his services were needed again, the Royal Navy could reach him through Smythe & Sons, Gosport, England.

Rather than accept the wagon Coslett offered to take him and his cases around the bay, Darren chose a boat to take him to Gosport, where he would hire a wagon to take his boxes to his parent's home. Darren wondered what his parent's reaction would be when he said he would find the fastest boat to America. His new mission gave him a sense of joy and purpose.

CHARLESTON, THIRD WEEK OF APRIL 1783

After learning at dinner from Captain Simmes that *Malmo* would arrive off Charleston shortly after sunrise, Emily couldn't sleep. The boys fell asleep right away, and confident the three youngsters were fast asleep, Emily sat on the main deck in one of the chairs passengers used during the day. At night, they were lashed to rings bolted to the deck.

One sailor on watch saw her struggling with the knots and came over. As he started to untie the half-inch hemp rope, she heard a familiar accent. "Please, allow me."

Rafer Muir placed two chairs abeam the mainmast. "Miss Smythe, 'tis a lovely night."

Emily agreed. During the voyage, Muir was careful to spend time with the other passengers, hoping his interest in the single mother of three wasn't obvious. By the time they were halfway across the ocean, he knew he was in love with this very handsome woman.

He had never married and always wanted to be a father. Soldiering and campaigns all over the world made it nigh impossible. Muir didn't believe it was fair to a woman and children to leave on a campaign that could take months, if not years, and have a high probability of not returning.

He'd turned down two offers to join the Territorial Army in India, one before he was on half-pay and the other when he was at British Army headquarters, trying to retire. Those who went to India were paid better and lived in luxury with their wives. Those who returned came back as wealthy men. India, however, was not where Muir wanted to go.

The question Muir wrestled in his mind is where does he go from here? Early in the cruise, Emily made it clear that she was not interested in marrying again, but later changed the statement when asked by another passenger to "not anytime soon."

Without prompting, Emily said, "Tomorrow is a new beginning for me. This voyage across the Atlantic was the transition."

"Aye, 'Tis for me as well. I boarded this ship back in Amsterdam and know not what tomorrow brings. This will be an adventure. And,

Miss Smythe, I am excited. What will be will be, but I am free to do what I wish."

Emily touched Rafer's arm. "I, too, as I have said several times, feel a sense of freedom. Free from the constraints of English society's norms, free to do what I wish and prosper. Free to associate with whom I choose. The words that keep running through my mind are free at last."

"Miss Smythe, that is a lovely turn of phrase."

"Thank you." Emily was about to say something else when Jeremiah put his hand on her arm. "Mother, when will we see South Carolina?"

Emily put her arm around her son's waist. "Soon, my son, soon."

The trees of the shoreline emerged in the dawn. Captain Simmes barked out a series of orders, and *Malmo* altered course toward the gap in the trees. Jeremiah Smythe ran down the deck to the companionway to wake his brothers.

Sensing the moment was right, Rafer Muir, asked. "Miss Smythe, once we are settled ashore, I would be honored if you would allow me to court you."

Emily looked at the ruggedly handsome Scotsman. "Your offer, sir, is accepted with pleasure. Give me a few days to find more permanent lodging. Like you, I am staying at the Dockside Inn." Her loins were stirring in ways she had never felt, and her heart was pounding. Emily's head and heart asked an unsaid question, "Rafer, what took you so long?"

CHAPTER 25

– HELPING AN OLD FRIEND IN NEED

BREST, FIRST WEEK OF MAY 1783

Each time *Zephyr* arrived in Brest, Jaco went ashore with Hedley Garrison and four sailors. Garrison's job was to buy provisions, Jaco's mission was to deliver the pouch with the letters from the Continental Congress. While there, Gardner would tell him when *Zephyr* needed to get underway and sail back to Philadelphia.

The visit with the Continental Congress' agent also gave him time to learn what had happened with negotiations between the U.S. and Great Britain. When Jaco walked into Gardner's office near the Place d'Armes inside the city's walls, the Bostonian was arguing with a local French merchant from whom Jaco's crew bought smoked meats and salamis. There was much arm waving and shouting, but eventually, both men calmed down when Gardner handed the Frenchman two gold Louis d'or coins.

The Frenchman smiled as he said as he passed Jaco, "*Bonjour, Capitaine Jacinto. Bienvenue à Brest.*" Good morning, Captain Jacinto, welcome to Brest."

"Mr. Gardner, what was that all about?"

"Oh, the usual. Like a typical Frenchie, he agrees to one price on a contract and wants more when he delivers. Happens all the time. So, we agreed upon a bonus for good service. I suspect he will return in a month or two and want another bonus. One of the reasons we are popular is that we pay in gold and silver French coins and do so promptly."

Gardner abruptly switched subjects as he turned to a stack of newspapers. "I see you made very good time."

Jaco unslung the strap over his shoulder attached to the pouch. "Yes, sir, we did. Philadelphia is twelve days in our rear. By its weight, there are many documents for Doctor Franklin."

Gardner became solemn and handed Jaco a copy of the *London Gazette*. "I am afraid that everything may be for naught. Here read this."

One headline read, "Shelburne's Government Falls." Another column headline stated, "Lord North to Form a New Government."

Seeing Lord North's name as the possible head of a new British government caused Jaco's heart to sink. Lord North's majority in Parliament resisted any calls to let the Thirteen Colonies become independent. Cornwallis' surrender at Yorktown enabled Lord Shelburne and his supporters to carry a vote of no confidence and cause North's government to fall. Now that North was back in power, Jaco wondered if North had rethought his and his party's position.

"How many days of supplies do you still have on board?"

"A week, maybe two if we reduce rations. Why?"

"I need you to make a short trip to bring a man named Pfeiffer here to Brest. Once I know his arrival date, Mr. Jay or Mr. Laurens will want to talk to him to get a sense of the new British government's position on independence. Then, you can bring Mr. Pfeiffer back."

"Where do you want *Zephyr* to go?"

"Southampton. My agent and second son, Josiah Gardner, will accompany Mr. Pfeiffer back here. I will give you a letter to him as an introduction."

"Will Mr. Pfeiffer be there?"

"Assuming you leave tomorrow or the next day, he should be. When Parliament is in session, Mr. Pfeiffer is in London, Monday through Thursday. He rides back to Southampton for the weekend. My son will be looking for *Zephyr*."

"And, if Mr. Pfeiffer is not in Southampton?"

"Then, Captain Jacinto, you must use your initiative to help my son find Mr. Pfeiffer."

"Would it not be better if we picked him up at Mr. Oswald's house in Sheerness?"

"That would not be advisable. Mr. Pfeiffer is Robert Thistlethwayte's secretary who is the Parliament member representing the Hampshire Constituency. If found out, Mr. Pfeiffer's actions would be considered treasonous. No one, including Mr. Thistlethwayte or Mr. Oswald, knows of Mr. Pfeiffer's support of our cause."

Jaco's eyes widened. "And, after Pfeiffer meets with Mr. Jay or Mr. Laurens, then what?"

"You bring him back to Southampton. I have an Admiralty chart of the harbor and a Portuguese flag if they will help."

"How about bringing Mr. Jay or Mr. Laurens to Southampton to meet with Mr. Pfeiffer?"

"I asked that question and was told no."

"So, two trips to Southampton and back it will be. Today is Monday. *Zephyr* will be ready to sail on Wednesday afternoon."

"Mr. Jay will be here when you return."

Jaco knew the route that Garrison would take in his search for provisions. He needed to ensure they bought at least a week's worth, preferably two, on board.

When he found Garrison at the cheese monger's store, he asked him to step into the street and whispered that *Zephyr* had to be at sea in two days with as many supplies as possible. Garrison smiled and went back into the store and tripled the order.

Between the French and British charts, Jaco estimated that from where *Zephyr* was anchored to the entrance to Southampton's harbor was only 280 nautical miles. At 12 knots, the English seaport just to the west of the Royal Navy base at Portsmouth was only 23 hours away. So, if they left at dawn in two days, they would arrive after first light the next day.

SOUTHAMPTON, SECOND WEEK OF MAY 1783

The pick-up of Mr. Pfeiffer went smoothly. The schooner was in Southampton Harbor for less than three hours. Once out of the harbor, *Zephyr* was under full sail until it anchored a quarter mile from the long quay where its boats loaded and unloaded.

The captain's cabin on *Zephyr* was used for the meeting with John Jay and the mysterious Mr. Pfeiffer since neither Gardner nor Jay wanted the Englishman seen in Brest. Since Jay came alone, Jaco was pressed into service to take notes of the meeting Jay could use to brief the other

Americans negotiating with the British. Several times during the three-hour meeting, the two men paused to let Jaco catch up with his notetaking. When they did, the loudest sound in the small cabin was the scratching of his pen on paper.

After the meeting, Jaco was asked to make a second copy. It was cleaner than the original and became the "official" meeting notes.

Pfeiffer said Shelburne government fell for two reasons. First, he proposed free trade between England and the new nation called the United States. Second, the prime minister introduced a bill to reform the current civil service. To gain support, he proposed drastically increasing the salaries paid to government workers in return for the authority to punish those who were corrupt.

While there was broad support for the civil service reform measure, Pfeiffer said Shelburne's abrasive personality irritated many members within his ruling coalition who wanted him out of office.

The king asked Lord North to form a new government and told the new prime minister that concluding a peace treaty with the United States was his first and most important item on his agenda. After studying the treaty's terms, the North government agreed, and Pfeiffer said Lord North informed the British delegation in Paris.

As Sam Gardner left with John Jay, he handed Jaco two letters, saying, "Please deliver these personally to my son Josiah in Southampton. I realize it entails some risks to you, but they are important. His office is just off the waterfront on Millbank Street."

"Aye, I will take care of it. If peace is truly at hand, it should not be a problem."

"Thank you. 'Twere I you, I'd plan on sailing back to Philadelphia eight or nine days after you return from Southampton."

With the boat crew that brought Jay and Gardner back to the landing in Brest back on board, *Zephyr's* crew weighed anchor and sailed west into the setting sun. From the quarterdeck, Jaco could sense the boost in speed from the outgoing tide. The water's speed was always a concern because it could carry a ship and its unwary captain onto the rocks that bordered both sides of the entrance to the *Rade de Brest*.

Zephyr was not flying a flag of any kind, just as it did on the first trip. No one approached the ship while anchored in Southampton for the first time, and Jaco didn't expect trouble on this journey. They didn't have a cover story that would hold up under scrutiny, so the less time they spent in the port, the better.

LAST BATTLES

When the schooner entered The Solent, they found it lined with anchored transports and cargo ships. All had tightly bound sails, suggesting to Jaco they would be swinging at anchor for some time.

Pfeiffer guided Jaco and Zephyr to a place to anchor at the southern tip of Southampton where the Rivers Itchen and Test meet and become The Solent. The long boat went over the side once the schooner was anchored. The Englishmen offered to lead Jaco to Josiah Gardner's office, saying that he would have to find his way back to the landing.

At the corner of Millbank and Bond, Pfeiffer stopped. "Captain Jacinto, thank you for your service to the cause of peace, but here we must part ways. We are on Millbank Street, and Mr. Gardner's office is the third house past Bond Street. The sign on the door simply says Gardner and Sons, Shipping Agent."

With those words, Pfeiffer hurried off, leaving Jaco alone with the letters given to him by Gardner senior in his coat pocket. Without anyone around he knew, much less trusted, Jaco felt very lonely.

The only reassurance Jaco had was that Southampton smelled like every other port he'd visited. Only here, the smell of rotting vegetation was stronger. On the way in, Zephyr passed several shipyards with piles of dead and dying seaweed next to their ways taken from the bottom of ships being careened.

Taking a deep breath, Jaco headed down Millbank and saw a sign next to Gardner & Sons that stopped him in his tracks. The faded sign read Laredo Shipping. He peered into the window, and it appeared that the offices had not been occupied for some time.

The younger Gardner gave Jaco four letters and asked him to wait for a few minutes while he wrote another.

A door chimed, and Josiah Gardner stopped writing and stood up, "May I help you, sir?"

Jaco didn't move from his chair, but the man looked familiar.

"Aye, I was curious if you know when the Laredo Shipping office will be open."

"It is closed because their agent died recently, and I am handling their affairs until another agent is appointed. How may I help you?"

"I am looking to book passage to North America, particularly Charleston, South Carolina. Do you know of any ships that may be going there?"

"Aye, I just received word that one will be stopping here in Southampton in mid-June. I could inform the owners if you would like to book a cabin."

"Splendid."

"I would need some information to confirm your booking. The fare is …."

Jaco couldn't help himself any longer. The pieces – the face, and there couldn't be many Englishmen who wanted to go to Charleston. He knew of one. He'd been sitting quietly, almost in the shadows. "Darren?"

The Englishman with sandy brown hair and a lock falling onto his forehead turned around. When he saw the stocky American, Darren's eyes opened in surprise, and his jaw dropped. "Jaco!!!! Good God, man, what are you doing in Southampton? Don't you know that half the Royal Navy would like to toss you into jail and throw away the key."

"Aye, I suspected that."

Jaco stood up, and the two men stood awkwardly apart. Neither was in the uniform of their respective service. Then Jaco, put his hands on Darren's biceps. "Have you, my friend, left the Royal Navy?"

"I have. Much of our Navy is being put on half-pay or being paid off. Peace will soon be here, and we will no longer be enemies trying to kill each other."

"Peace between our countries will be good for everyone." Jaco took a deep breath. "Darren, it is good to see you are alive and well. However, I can't answer your question about why I am here. Still, I can offer transportation to Philadelphia, where you can take a packet to Charleston on one condition."

"And that is?"

"You don't marry Melody until I can be there!"

Darren laughed nervously. "How did you know?"

"You forget that Melody, my sister Shoshana, and my fiancée Reyna all grew up together. They tell each other everything and hold few secrets. So yes, I know you proposed, and she gave you the same answer Reyna gave me – marry after the war!"

Darren nodded understanding. "Aye, I am sure we can wait until we know this damned war is over."

"Perfecto!"

"Did I hear you say your ship will sail to Philadelphia in three weeks?"

"I did."

"How? No one makes the trip that fast."

"We do. Eastbound, this time of year, takes less than two weeks."

"What kind of wizardry do you use?"

"My secret. If you can be in Brest in less than less than eight days, you will get to see my magic. Mr. Gardner may be able to help in that endeavor."

Jaco turned to Josiah Gardner as if to say, "Can you?"

"It can be arranged."

"Perfecto! Darren, once we get to Philadelphia, you can book a berth on the packet that stops in Hampton, Virginia before arriving in Charleston. The voyage takes five days. So, if you will allow Mr. Gardner to finish his letter to his father, I will be off."

Jaco's mind raced as he made his way back to the landing. Seeing him on the pier, Morton Geiger sent the boat to bring *Zephyr's* captain back to the schooner. Noticing Jaco's buoyant mood, Morton Geiger looked at his captain. "Sir, you look as if someone handed you a small fortune. What are you so happy about?"

"Mr. Geiger, let us get *Zephyr* underway, and I will tell you. We may have a good friend grace us with his presence as a passenger on the way home."

CHARLESTON, SECOND WEEK OF MAY 1783

When Yael Bildesheim Baez saw Emily walk through the door to the Dockside Inn, she came around the counter and hugged the English woman. Then she knelt so her head was close to the height of the three boys who clung to their mother.

She held out three small dark brown squares. "Welcome to Charleston. You might like this candy. Your mother does."

Jeremiah, always interested in something new, tasted his piece of chocolate and said, "This is very good." Jeffrey, who was about to turn six, hesitated but hearing the approval of his older brother, took a piece and quickly downed it. Jonah buried his face in the folds of his mother's dress and refused to look at Yael.

The wagon driver who drove them from where *Malmo* docked to the Dockside, put their cases in a stack just inside the front door. Emily gave him a generous tip and then looked around and giggled.

Yael started to laugh. "Emily, what is so funny?"

"If you had asked me if, when I walked in here last year, I would be back as a single woman, ready to help run a business, I would have laughed in your face. Now, it is true."

"Well, when you left, I told my husband you would return soon. I didn't know when, but you would be back. So, when Reyna told me, I knew a dream was coming true. We've saved a suite of three connected rooms for you, so you will have your own room, the boys will have one of their own, and you'll have a sitting room. We'll put the chests you don't need in our storeroom."

"Thank you."

"Well, let me take you to the suite, and I'll have someone bring up the chests. Have your boys ever had a chocolate drink?"

Emily shook her head.

"I'll send Ester up with more bars and some warm chocolate milk straightaway."

"Thank you."

"Miss Smythe, Mr. Rafer Muir asked me to tell you that he moved to the Charleston Inn."

Emily tried not to react. "Yes, we were both on *Malmo* and we spent several wonderful evenings together." Her mind said thank you, Rafer, because if you were here, we both would be tempted to share a bed. *Focus, Emily, focus.*

"Now that you are here, the Laredos would love to have you and the boys dine with them tonight. I am sure Melody will come along with her older brother Asa."

"I don't want to impose."

"Miss Smythe, this is Charleston. If one of us makes an invitation, you are not imposing. Hosting you is our pleasure. You'll learn about southern hospitality because my mother Miriam, my sisters Adah and Perla Jacinto, and Melody want to quickly wash all that English stuffiness off your body."

Emily smiled broadly. "I can't wait. My first order of business is to find a place to live and get the boys in school."

"We know. Reyna has some places for you to consider, and Melody will bring them to the school where she teaches. Trust me, we will take good care of you!"

Emily had only been in Charleston for a few hours and already felt at home. Now, she had to get the boys to feel the same. She wasn't worried about Jeremiah or Jeffrey, who would follow the lead of his older brother. It was her youngest Jonah who concerned her the most.

IN THE ATLANTIC, THIRD WEEK OF MAY 1783

Zephyr's coming and going had become routine to the French port officials. They no longer came out to the schooner to inspect it for cargo for which they could collect import duties because it had none. The daily anchorage fee was paid by Samuel Gardner after each visit.

The ship's in-port daily routine was the same as it had been in every prior visit – daily trips to buy fresh food and visit Samuel Gardner's office. Every other day, Jaco watched from the quarterdeck as Bosun Preston supervised holystoning the main deck with small sandstone bricks. The eight-man task was rotated amongst the crew, and when it was performed, they were serenaded with a song or led in a shanty by Colin Landry.

The men moved the stones in unison as they sang. Holystoning was a "spectator" event on board *Zephyr*. Those not rubbing the stones on the deck joined in the music. They were good-natured critics and supervisors of their shipmates. The process took about two hours, and the deck was rinsed with seawater to remove the grit.

Today, Landry was leading the men in "So Handy," a song that could be used for holystoning or hauling a sheet, brace, or halyard.

> <u>Landry</u> – Now handy high and handy low
>
> <u>Crew</u> - Handy me boys, so handy
>
> <u>Landy</u> - Oh, it is handy high and away we go
>
> <u>Crew</u> - Handy me boys, so handy
>
> <u>Landry</u> - Hoist her up from down below
>
> <u>Crew</u> - Handy me boys, so handy
>
> <u>Landry</u> - We'll hoist her up through frost and snow
>
> <u>Crew</u> - Handy me boys, so handy

With holystoning done, Jaco went into the hold with Gaskins, the schooner's carpenter, and all-around Mr. Fix-it to make his daily inspection. He was almost finished when Brandon Grantham came down into the hold.

"Captain, Respects from Mr. Garrison. A boat is approaching with Mr. Gardner and another man along with some chests."

The crew expected a local sailmaker to deliver a new foremast main sail, not a passenger. On the trip back from Southampton, the tearing sound of the canvas got the attention of those who heard the sharp and distinctive ripping sound of canvas tearing. While Gaskins made a temporary patch, the canvas had aged noticeably, and Gaskins opined that it would tear again outside his patch, so a new one was ordered from a local sailmaker.

Zephyr's captain kept his face focused on the planking and rib in front of him. *Darren!!! Don't be too eager to rush up to greet a friend.*

On the quarterdeck, Hedley Garrison studied the sandy-haired man sitting in the middle of the boat. He handed the spyglass he was using to his captain and said, without turning his head to speak, "Is that your Royal Navy captain friend?"

"I believe it is. He will be our guest and passenger on the way to Philadelphia. Mr. Smythe is no longer in the Royal Navy. And may I remind you that the secrets of *Scorpion's* design and cannon are not to be revealed."

"Well, it will certainly provide for some interesting dinner conversations. We can relive battles from both sides. I'll have Bosun Preston ready the crew to hoist his chests aboard."

The second surprise came when Gardner met the afternoon shore party with a pouch full of documents. He handed Morton Geiger a note for Jaco and said that he hoped Zephyr was well on its way to Philadelphia when he awoke in the morning.

Captain Jacinto,

I am entrusting you with a copy of the first full draft of the completed treaty. It has been initialed by Benjamin Franklin, John Jay, and Henry Laurens for the United States of America and members of the English delegation. This document and all the supporting notes and letters are in the pouch. Should Congress approve, they must send word back so that both countries can formally sign the treaty.

How and what you tell Captain Smythe, formerly of the R.N., is up to you.

Godspeed and good luck. At last, peace and independence are in our hands!

Samuel Gardner

Just before *Zephyr* weighed anchor, Jaco mustered the crew on the main deck. Darren Smythe, late of the Royal Navy stood off to one side, away from the crew, "Men of *Zephyr*, we will be under full sail day and night until we reach Philadelphia with the first full draft of the treaty between our new country and England. It remains to be ratified and signed, but it means we have won our war for independence."

He held up his hand to stop the cheering because he wanted to get *Zephyr* underway. "As you know, we have a passenger, Mr. Darren Smythe, formerly a captain in the Royal Navy and our enemy. Some of you first met him when *Cutlass* captured *H.M.S. Sorcerer*. Mr. Smythe is going to our country to marry a woman in Charleston. He is to be treated as my friend because that is what he is. However, neither you nor I shall discuss any aspect of *Scorpion*'s construction, armament, or sailing qualities with Mr. Smythe. Let us get *Zephyr* underway and let her fly to Philadelphia. Dismissed."

After they relived the battles in which they participated on opposite sides, most of the evening discussions amongst the officers were about what they would do now that the war was over. Hedley Garrison was adamant that he would attend Harvard and pursue a career as a lawyer. Morton Geiger's original thinking was that he was going to work for his father.

Both Darren and Jaco were non-committal. Both wanted to marry and then figure out what they wanted to do. Jaco could join South Carolina Import and Export or work for the Laredo's as a merchant ship captain, but now, neither was attractive.

The noon sighting showed that *Zephyr* was $32°W$ $42°N$, roughly seven days from the entrance to the Delaware River and a week out of Brest. When Jaco showed Darren the plot, the Englishman said he was sure there wasn't a ship in the Royal Navy or Merchant Marine as fast as *Zephyr*.

CHAPTER 26

– WEDDING BELLS IN THE FUTURE

PHILADELPHIA, FOURTH WEEK OF MAY 1783

Zephyr arrived, as it normally did, with little fanfare. However, Jaco insisted on accompanying the courier to the Pennsylvania State House when he came on board to pick up the dispatch pouch. In the building where the Continental Congress met, *Zephyr's* captain ensured the courier interrupted a Foreign Affairs committee meeting.

With that done, Jaco sought out his father and told him what he just delivered. When he mentioned that Darren had been a passenger on *Zephyr*, his father insisted Darren be his guest until he could board *Alacrity* on its southbound trip when it arrived in three days.

Dinner at the Jacinto house in Philadelphia was a festive affair. Jack Shelton was delighted to meet Darren Smythe. He hadn't heard all the stories Darren shared onboard *Zephyr* about the Royal Navy's frustration in not bringing *Scorpion* to heel. Or, about the Royal Navy's disbelief in *Scorpion's* capabilities to defeat ships larger that had a heavier broadside.

With Jack and Darren involved in a discussion, Javier pointed to the kitchen. The smile from his face was gone, and his mood had turned somber. "Jaco, the Congress has decided to disband the Continental Navy now that peace is at hand. Tomorrow, you will be ordered to sail *Zephyr* to Boston and pay off the crew. The ship was built there, and the Congress hopes they'll find a buyer. You will board *Alacrity* or another packet and either come here or return to Charleston."

"What about the treaty? Who is going to take the dispatches to and from France?"

"The Congress is ordering Colonel David Franks from General Washington's staff to board the frigate *Alliance* captained by John Barry to go to France and bring back the signed treaty. That will be the frigate's last voyage in the Continental Navy."

Jaco felt as if he had been shot in the stomach. "Why *Alliance*? *Zephyr* had set records going to and from Brest. It was more than capable of performing this mission."

The elder Jacinto read his son's face. "Congress wants to send a proper warship. It is the only large frigate we have left that is seaworthy, and John Barry is a very capable captain."

"Aye, that he is." Jaco's head bobbed up and down. "I will do as ordered. Father, I am ready to go home. When are you coming back?"

"I don't know. However, your mother and Adah have agreed to delay the wedding until I return. Once the treaty is signed, I hope the Congress will recess. If not, I plan to come home in October for a month or so. We have a country to run. In the meantime, Reyna and you must spend some time together."

Jaco didn't say anything. His brain was still processing that his Navy career, just like Darren's, was over, and he had survived.

"Son, thanks to your prize money, you are a wealthy man. Your funds are in the Bank of South Carolina in English pounds. My suggestion is you start thinking about what you want to do with the rest of your life."

"Father, I have given it some thought and want to discuss my idea with you."

"Good. In time, we can. Let us not be rude and rejoin our guest."

CHARLESTON, FIRST WEEK OF JUNE 1783

When *Alacrity* tied up at the pier in Charleston on Saturday, Darren paced back and forth until the crew of the small schooner lifted his chests from the hold. As a former captain, he watched the unloading with a practiced eye and could not find fault with the crew's work. He had to control his impatience as the unloading process took longer than he wished.

Darren had a wagon waiting to take him to the Dockside Inn long before the net with his last chest touched the pier. He wanted a room to stay in before going to Melody's house. Her last letter was dated November 9th, 1782, and he believed other letters, addressed to him care of his parents, were still in transit. None of this mattered, he was in Charleston.

When alone in his cabin on *Zephyr* or *Alacrity*, he refused to believe Melody had decided to marry someone else. Or her father had forced her to follow him to Barbados. If she had left, he was sure the trail to finding her started in Charleston.

At the Dockside, Darren helped the wagon driver unload his two chests and four boxes. The chests contained clothes. One box had his pistols, another his sextant, and the third, his spyglass. The fourth and lightest, contained the paintings from Langdon Herring. He gave the man two silver crowns (10 shillings) and walked inside.

He gently pulled the toggle on a bell hanging by the deck that looked like a ship's bell. Yael Baez came in from the great room wiping her hands. Through the glass, he could see the pendulum swinging on the clock, which chimed as it showed the time to be noon.

The former Royal Navy captain cleared his throat, unsure what to do, having never spent a night in an inn before. "Good afternoon, do you have any rooms available?"

Yael Baez gave the young man the once over. "We do, sir. It's three shillings a night for a room by yourself. Breakfast and lunch are a shilling each, and dinner is two."

"Thank you. I'll take a room for myself."

Yael spun a book around. "Sir, please, write your name and where you are from on my ledger along with today's date, the fifteenth of May."

Darren dipped the quill pen in the ink well and scrawled his name, Gosport, and the date in the proper columns. As he turned the book around, he asked, "Do you know if my sister, Ms. Emily Smythe is still staying here?"

Yael glanced at the name on the ledger, "And you are ..."

"Her younger brother Darren."

Grinning, Yael pointed to the entrance of the Great Room. "Ms. Smythe is eating lunch, as we call it here in South Carolina, in there with some friends."

Going in the door, Darren saw a rectangular table in the back with four women. The two "mothers," Perla Jacinto and Adah Laredo, were sitting at the ends. Between them, Melody and Shoshana had their backs to him. Reyna and Emily faced the two young women.

Reyna was the first to spot Darren. She nudged Emily, who looked up, her jaw dropped and her eyes opened wide. Making eye contact with his sister, Darren shook his head, but Emily couldn't keep a straight face.

Melody turned around and shrieked, "Darren!!!!" Her chair clattered on its back as she ran toward him. The two held each other for a few seconds before Darren broke the silence. "Melody, you are as lovely as I remembered."

"And you, sir, are a handsome sea captain." Melody pushed back and looked at the group at the table. "I apologize. That was very unladylike."

Reyna laughed. "Just wait, soon my Jaco will be here, and he will be lucky if I don't maul him!"

After Darren finished eating, four women made their "excuses" and left. Emily and Melody remained and said, "Knock on my room door when you return. The boys will be delighted to see you; we have much to discuss." She kissed her brother on the cheek and left Darren and Melody alone.

Neither spoke for several minutes, just enjoying the serenity of being together. Darren spoke first, delivering what he believed to be the most important words. "I am no longer in the Royal Navy, so Charleston is now my home if that is where you want to live."

Melody's eyes opened wide with surprise, asking the obvious question, "What happened?" Darren responded with a short version of the story and then asked about her parents.

"They're in Barbados. I received a letter from my mother telling me that Ezekiel is now a midshipman on an East Indiaman. My father is managing a sugar plantation, and from her words, I don't think he is happy, nor is she."

Darren didn't know what to say, and his nod indicated his understanding. Melody placed her hand on top of his. "Go move your things into your room. Then, you, sir, can escort me to my house."

BARBADOS, FIRST WEEK OF JUNE 1783

The gentle morning breeze pressed Amelia Winters' dress against her legs. Underfoot, the silky white beach sand slid between her toes as she walked along the water's edge, letting the remains of the surf wash her feet.

They – her husband Theodore and her son Ezekiel – arrived in Bridgetown just after the first of the year. The voyage from Charleston to Barbados took 21 days because the convoy stopped in Nassau, Antigua, St. Kitts, and then Barbados before continuing to Trinidad. At each stop, Loyalists from Charleston and Savannah went ashore to begin their new lives.

Theodore's job was managing a sugar plantation for the Knotts family, who were absentee owners. They were given a small house on the 150-acre farm. The Knotts lived in London and expected Theodore to make a profit each year. The plantation was paid a fixed fee for each wagonload of cut sugar cane taken to a refinery where it was turned into raw sugar.

He did not anticipate that he was now the day-to-day manager of 75 slaves who worked the fields. Neither he nor Amelia approved of slavery, and Theodore's first instinct was to find a way to pay the slaves a living wage.

He also 'inherited' two foremen hired by the Knotts. Their management style appalled Theodore Winters, who suggested they make changes to improve production. Their response was even more appalling, and Winters retreated to ensure the books were accurate. His spare time was spent at the refinery, learning the process and with traders learning how the sugar market functioned.

By the end of January, Ezekiel had convinced the local office of the British West India Company to take him on as a midshipman. This achieved two goals for him. One, it got him off Barbados, and two, it enabled him to begin a career that would lead to becoming a merchant ship captain or even a commission in the Royal Navy.

Amelia was now an empty nester and very much alone. Barbados society was stratified. At the top, there were the English landowners, some lived on the island, most like the Knotts, were absentee owners. Those who lived on the island kept to themselves, and only a title or wealth earned in England facilitated entry.

Below the wealthy owners, the next level down was the civil servants who governed the island, those who ran businesses or managed plantations. Below them were the working poor who scratched out a living anywhere they could. And, well below the Europeans, there were the slaves.

Amelia had accompanied her husband to Barbados out of duty to him and their marriage. Melody's first letter said that Asa had returned to Charleston. Now, two of her children and future grandchildren were 1,566 nautical miles nor' west from where she was walking on the beach.

For some reason, Amelia stopped as she felt a wave of happiness wash over her. Given what she was living through, there could be only one source of this mysterious feeling – Darren had returned to Melody. Amelia looked up at the puffy clouds and vowed that she would return to Charleston before she died.

BOSTON, SECOND WEEK OF JUNE 1783

Once *Zephyr* was in Delaware Bay and heading toward the Atlantic, Jaco asked that the crew muster on the main deck. Sadly, he told them they were not returning to Brest but Boston. There they will be paid off, and *Zephyr* put up for sale. The Continental Navy, once the peace treaty was signed, would be disbanded. He thanked them for their service, saying serving with them was an honor and pleasure.

One would think that the mood would be upbeat since the war for independence was won, and every man on board was wealthier than when he signed his first enlistment in the Continental Navy. Yet the mood on *Zephyr* was somber, even melancholy.

At the pier in Boston, one by one, Jaco counted out each man's pay and then shook his hand. Abner Jeffords and Bradley Preston waited until the crew had left, leaving only Jaco, Morton Geiger, and Hedley Garrison on board.

"Cap'n, I believe I am speaking for every man who served with you. If you ever need a crew for a ship, you find the Bosun and me. We know where Landry and Cooper live, and we'll get you a crew."

"Thank you, Mr. Jeffords. We've done much sailing since our days on *Providence*. Good luck, and God Bless you."

With no one else on board, Morton asked, "I insist that you stay with us while you wait for *Doylestown*."

CHARLESTON, THIRD WEEK OF JUNE 1783

Jaco's arrival back in his hometown was a quiet one. A wagon brought him to the house where he grew up and, with the help of the wagon driver, piled his chests inside the door. After hugging the second oldest of her four children, Perla Jacinto said, "Reyna is in Dorchester and will be back late tonight."

He couldn't hide his disappointment. Jaco sat down to watch his mother work the dough he recognized as a mixture that, when pulled out of the oven, be a crusty, round Spanish *pan basico*.

After undergoing what he kiddingly called "the inquisition" by his mother, the subject turned to Reyna. "Have you and Reyna discussed a date yet?"

Jaco assumed the date was shorthand for the date of their wedding. "No, Mother. Father wants the wedding to be in October after the High Holidays and Sukkot."

This would be a wedding between two of the wealthiest families in Charleston. As such, it was going to be a significant social event. "Reyna, Adah, and I are thinking about Sunday, October 18th."

As in, Jaco what say you? "Then October 18th, it is."

"Good."

"You know, mother, there is another wedding which Reyna and I must attend."

"You mean Darren and Melody's?"

"Yes."

"Do not fret about it. We have a small committee of mothers helping her organize a very nice wedding on September 17th. Emily and Darren have sent a letter inviting her parents to come, which gives them time to make the passage."

Jaco felt out of sorts discussing his wedding. Others were in control, and he was no longer in command, making decisions. In some ways, he was relieved, but it also made him uncomfortable in that he was not consulted on a wedding date, not that any of them would have listened. "So, there is not much for me to do."

Perla shook her head. "No, my son. Planning weddings is women's work. You must be there, not get drunk and avoid making an ass of yourself!"

"I will make sure I do the first and promise not to look foolish." Jaco waited a few seconds before he changed the subject. "Where's Shoshana and Saul?"

Perla stopped kneading the dough for a few seconds and used her hands to shape the dough into its traditional round shape. Two strokes with a knife made an X in the top of the loaf. "At work and in school. Saul has an interview at Harvard in Boston at the end of July. Now that you are back and the war is over, he will ask you to accompany him."

"I would be happy to do that. Why wouldn't Harvard simply accept Saul as a student?"

Perla slid the loaf of bread into the oven and let the cast iron door slam shut as if she was venting her frustration. "If you ask me, the snobs at Boston don't think anyone from Charleston is smart enough to attend their school."

Jaco smiled. "Well, Saul will prove them wrong."

Perla Jacinto put her hands on her hips and nodded. "Aye, that he will."

Jaco left his family house with three stops in mind. One, to see his oldest brother Isaac whom he had not seen since the last time he was in Charleston. Then, he would visit Greg Struthers before stopping at the firm where his sister worked, now named Burrows, Soriano, Jacinto & Partners.

When he saw Jaco enter the Bank of South Carolina, Greg asked an assistant to bring Jaco's account book to his office. The two former officers in the Continental Navy shook hands, and Jaco congratulated Greg on the birth of his first son.

After relating his experiences since the last time he was in Charleston, Jaco took the draft that was his pay from his pocket. "Greg, please deposit this in my account."

The banker looked at the draft, then the account ledger, which told Greg that his friend and former shipmate was a wealthy young man. "Jaco, you've done quite well. I see that you earned £27,128 in prize money over the course of the war plus £813 in interest. The total is £29,741. Well done. You have a princely sum." (£29,741 is worth ~£5,619,605 or $7,136,898 in February 2024)

"Greg, several times, I told my father to use some of my prize money to pay the crew, buy supplies, or repair *Scorpion*. That number seems high to me. You must not have deducted the money from my account."

"I know you made that request, but your father told me not to take the money from your account."

"Where did it come from?"

"His funds and from others."

Jaco was surprised by this news. All this time, he thought he was helping pay for the war with his prize money.

"Don't be angry at your father. Those who helped him all know you, and they were not only eager to help fund the Continental Navy, but they could also easily afford the expense."

Nodding, Jaco decided to broach the other reason he came. "Do you know of any properties that might be for sale?"

"I do. I have a list. What are you looking for?"

"A house for Reyna and me."

"Some will be more attractively priced than others. Reyna has already expressed an interest in several but was waiting until you were back in Charleston before picking one."

"Perfecto." *At least there are some things in this world in which I have a say in the decision.*

Jaco's next stop was his sister's office. She was in court, so Jaco walked to the Dockside Inn to see if Darren was there. He was not.

Feeling a bit lost at sea, Jaco went to the Laredo's house, if for nothing else to say hello to his future mother-in-law. Adah opened the door and smiled when she saw her daughter's fiancée. "When did you arrive?"

"This morning."

"Reyna's in Dorchester and will be back this afternoon."

"I know, my mother told me."

"Well, I am glad you went to see your mother before you came here. Please, sit and tell me the latest news while I fix you lunch. Down here in South Carolina, we learn things in dribs and drabs."

Jaco knew not to argue with a Jewish mother who had decided to feed him. Adah, like his mother, was an excellent cook and always had something good to eat. She put some dried peaches he was sure came from one of the orchards in Shayna Enterprises along with a chunk of smoked chicken and a piece of bread on a plate.

"Chocolate or something stronger?"

"Chocolate."

Jaco finished giving Adah an update on what he learned about the progress toward a peace treaty about the same time he'd emptied the plate. He tore off a chunk of the freshly baked bread and was chewing it when both heard a commotion in the back made by someone opening the door and dropping saddlebags on the floor.

Reyna entered the kitchen saying, "Mother, I came…." She stopped dead in her tracks and looked at Jaco. "What are you doing here?" Her tone was almost accusatory.

She ran toward him saying, "I'm so sorry. That was rude." As they hugged and Reyna kissed Jaco passionately on the lips before she said, "I am so happy that you are back, safe and sound."

Reyna looked at her mother sheepishly, knowing that any sexual displays of affection before marriage were not permitted. "I'm sorry, *màma*."

"You're entitled to kiss your war hero fiancée." Then, Mother Laredo took over. "You look hungry, I'll get you something to eat."

"Yes, *màma*, I am famished."

Between bites, Reyna pummeled Jaco with questions on what he knew and if he thought the war was really over. When Adah sensed a break in the conversation, she sat down opposite Reyna and Jaco. "Now that you're back, we have some things to discuss."

Jaco looked at Reyna, who looked at her mother, "Like what, *màma*?"

"How about we set a wedding date? We need to start making plans now that Jaco is not about to sail off into the sunset."

The former Continental Navy captain smiled at Adah's reference to the sea. "My mother said you were thinking about October 18th. Do we want to wait that long?"

Adah gave Jaco the "you stupid man" look as if to say, we will not rush into this wedding. "I think that the weather will be cooler, and it is after the sickly season and the High Holidays."

Faced with that logic, Jaco said, "October 18th, it 'tis."

"Good, it is settled then, and I will let Perla know the date is now official."

Jaco picked up Reyna's hand. "I can't wait."

"Me neither. Let me change clothes, and we can sit outside and talk."

Jaco looked at his fiancée and asked, "Did I have a choice of any other date?"

Reyna shook her head and smiled. "No."

TO BE CONTINUED IN THE NEXT
JACO JACINTO AGE OF SAIL NOVEL,
FOR A FEW FRANCS.

ABOUT THE AUTHOR

MARC LIEBMAN, CITIZEN SAILOR, ENTREPRENEUR AND AUTHOR

Marc retired as a Captain after twenty-six years in the Navy and is a combat veteran of Vietnam, the Tanker Wars of the 1980s, and Desert Shield/Storm. He is a Naval Aviator with just under 6,000 hours of flight time in helicopters and fixed wing aircraft. Captain Liebman has worked with the armed forces of Australia, Canada, Japan, Thailand, Republic of Korea, the Philippines, and the U.K.

He has been a partner in two different consulting firms advising clients on business and operational strategy, business process re-engineering, sales, and marketing; the CEO of an aerospace and defense manufacturing company; an associate editor of a national magazine, and a copywriter for an advertising agency.

The Liebmans live near Aubrey, Texas. Marc is married to Betty, his lovely wife of 54+ years. They spend a lot of time visiting their seven grandchildren.

Made in the USA
Coppell, TX
03 June 2024

33077936R00215